The Dow Jones-Irwin Dictionary of Financial Planning

Robert William Richards

DOW JONES-IRWIN
Homewood, Illinois   60430

© DOW JONES-IRWIN, 1986

ISBN 0-87094-612-9
Library of Congress Catalog Card No. 85–073704

Printed in the United States of America

1 2 3 4 5 6 7 8 9 0 K 3 2 1 0 9 8 7 6

PREFACE

Because of the ever-changing climate and pervasive nature of personal financial planning, its abundant quantity of terminology encompasses many professional fields ranging from life insurance to investment strategies. Various levels of specialization have been attained within each profession resulting in a continual supply of new ideas and financial products. Such change increases the pool of esoteric language. In addition, accountants, lawyers, financial planners, insurance specialists, stockbrokers, bankers, and others may be quite familiar with terms common to their respective profession, but financial planning covers an incredible amount of information that is not used every day.

This reference is designed to be an important source of terms to help alleviate problems caused by the volatile and broad-range characteristics of financial planning. It contains over 3,000 entries and is intended to be used by professionals and lay persons alike. All users can benefit from the quick-referencing subject index as well as the comprehensive dictionary format.

I wish to thank the following people for their generous support in making this book possible: Milly Richards, G. C. Richards, RoseMary Richards, Ken McEver, Jim Musselwhite, Sherry Musselwhite, Lentis Lee, Tim Jenkins, Helen Lansing, Bob True, Ernie Larkins, Dan Legare, Dave Jones, Chet Richards, Ginger Richards, Wilmah Lansing, Fred Tillman, Ted Englebrecht, Al Roberts, Keith Walton, Mark Kurzawa, and Fred Akers.

Robert William Richards

A

Abandonment — The voluntary surrender of the rights of ownership, or other interest such as future ownership, in property without intending to transfer title. An abandonment may result in a tax loss, depending upon the circumstances (e.g., the basis of abandoned property less salvage must be considered).

Abatement[1] — (1) A reduction; (2) a decrease in value that usually applies to ad valorem taxes; (3) a diminution in testamentary gifts as a result of an insufficient amount of assets in a testator's estate.

Abeyance — In the administration of an estate, a condition not yet determined or settled as to the ownership of assets held by an estate. Unsettled estates are said to be held "in abeyance" until the assets are properly distributed.

Abode — A home; permanent residence.

Abridgment — A condensed version of another writing.

Abrogate — Generally, to nullify or repeal; to exchange an existing agreement with another one.

Absconding debtor — An absent debtor who intentionally hides from creditors.

Absolute estate — See "Fee simple estate."

Abstract of title — A summarized history of title to a parcel of land that contains all liens, prior conveyances and interests, and in some cases an opinion made by an attorney as to the condition of title.

Abusive tax shelter[1] — An investment formed primarily to provide investors with tax-avoidance items (depreciation expense, tax credits, etc.), but having virtually no economic substance. Many of these arrangements also use peculiar leveraging techniques designed to enlarge investors' taxable benefits, sometimes without a corresponding amount of assumed risk. The Internal Revenue Service has launched a vigorous campaign against these types of investments and their promoters.

Accelerated cost recovery system (ACRS)[1] — A statutory method of depreciation for tangible assets over a predetermined period, in accordance with the asset's class life.

Accelerated depreciation[1] — Any depreciation method that provides more depreciation expense in the early years of an asset's life than

---

[1]*The Financial Planner's Tax Almanac, 1984,* by Robert W. Richards, Robert J. Nagoda, and Patrick R. Smith (Homewood, Ill.: Dow Jones–Irwin, 1984).

straight-line depreciation. Examples include accelerated cost recovery system (ACRS), sum-of-the-years' digits method, double-declining balance method, and, in some cases, units-of-production method.

Acceleration clause — A clause found in an installment financing agreement which gives the lender the right to demand immediate payment for any unpaid balance of debt if a certain event occurs, such as when the borrower fails to make a timely installment payment. An option for the lender that is customary in most contracts is to allow for late payment accompanied with a penalty. Other such events commonly named in an acceleration clause include changes of ownership of encumbered property without the lender's consent, destruction of the encumbered property, or any disposition of collateral.

Acceptance — The voluntary consent to the terms and conditions of an offer, which if all other criteria are met will create a legally binding contract. The receipt of goods with an intent to keep them may constitute acceptance. An acceptance may also be a special type of negotiable instrument where one party (usually a bank) "accepts" the agreement by signing it and in so doing guarantees payment. Also see "Banker's acceptance." In insurance, acceptance is the agreement by an insurer to carry a certain risk and thereby issue a policy.

Access — In real estate, an owner's right to enter and exit an ajoining road from his or her property without hindrance.

Accession — (1) An increase or addition to something; (2) a right of ownership to all things that become a part of existing property.

Accessory contract — A contract made subsequent to and assuring the performance of a previous agreement.

Accident — An occurrence which is both unintentional and unforeseeable; a violent mishap derived from an unexpected cause. For tax purposes, a casualty loss may arise from an accident that is sudden, unexpected, and unusual in nature. Also see "Casualty loss."

Accident and health benefits — Fringe benefits commonly provided by an employer that covers a portion of or all payments for medical expenses.

Accidental bodily injury — A health insurance policy clause that specifies coverage for an accident resulting in an injury to the body.

Accidental death benefit — An option generally found in life insurance contracts that provides a certain sum of money to be paid to the beneficiaries, in addition to the regular death benefit, only if the insured dies in an accident not specifically excluded in the policy. The terms typically stated are that death must occur before a certain birthday or policy anniversary date, and death must not occur directly as a result of suicide, war, disease, or aviation mishap. Other types of insurance sometimes include an accidental death benefit as an added feature. Also see "Double indemnity."

Accidental means — A clause generally found in health, life, and disability insurance policies which states that the cause of the mishap must be unintentional, unforeseeable, and unexpected in order for coverage to apply.

Accident policy — An insurance policy only indemnifying an insured for losses as a direct result of bodily injury arising from a sudden and unexpected accident. A strict accident policy does not cover losses resulting from illness or disease.

Accommodation line — In the insurance business, a special acceptance of risk by an insurance company which would ordinarily be denied if the risk were only considered by its quality. Customarily, insurance companies will accept such risks only from preferred customers.

Accommodation party — A party who signs a promissory note or other obligation (without consideration) for the benefit of another. This is usually done to secure credit for another party, who is in need of financing. The accommodation party is liable for the debt in the capacity signed (e.g., as maker, indorser, acceptor, or co-maker).

Accord — An agreement where one party (usually a creditor) accepts a differing amount from what was originally owed. Ordinarily the acceptance is less than what was owed or is different from the specifications of the original contract.

Accord and satisfaction — The substitution of a new agreement for an old agreement (accord) and the completed performance thereof (satisfaction).

Account — A record-keeping device used to maintain a separate balance for money-related items in accounting for the financial activities of an entity. The left-hand side of an account is known as "debit" and the right-hand side is known as "credit." The categories of accounts are assets, liabilities, owner's equity, revenues, and expenses.

Accounting[1] — The recording, summarizing, and classifying of financial information of an economic entity into a prescribed format and interpreting the condensed information. Different areas of accounting (cost accounting, auditing, tax accounting, financial accounting, governmental accounting, etc.) prescribe different formats and interpretations.

Accounting control — A plan of organization, prescribed procedures, records, and actions taken by an entity to safeguard its assets, to ensure compliance of management's policies and public laws, to evaluate employee performance, and to ensure the reliability of financial records and statements.

Accounting methods[1] — Methods of determining revenue and expenses. The two major methods are the accrual method and the cash method. Under the accrual method of accounting, revenue is recorded when earned and an expense is recorded when incurred, regardless of the actual exchange of cash. Under the cash method, revenue is only recorded when cash is received, and expenses are only recorded when cash is paid. The accrual method, however, follows generally accepted accounting principles. Other accounting methods include hybrid methods, completed-contract method, income tax method, fair value method, price-level accounting, installment method, and accounting for nonprofit entities.

Accounting period[1] — A certain period of time, generally 12 months, used for financial and tax reporting purposes. A fiscal year is any 12 consecutive months; a calendar year is a regular year beginning on January 1 and ending December 31. An accounting period may also be one month, one quarter, etc.

Accounting Principles Board — A nongovernmental board that established generally accepted accounting principles from 1959 to 1973.

Account rendered — The presentation by a creditor to a debtor for an amount owed.

Account settled — An account of a previous debt no longer due; an account that has been paid or otherwise settled.

Accounts payable — Amounts owed to another entity, usually from the purchase of goods and services on account during the ordinary course of business. They are classified as a current liability if due within one year or within the operating cycle of the business.

Accounts receivable — Amounts to be collected by an entity, customarily arising from the sale or exchange of its goods or services on account. They are classified as a current asset if they will be converted into cash within one year or within the operating cycle of the business. Net accounts receivable is the ledger balance of accounts receivable reduced by the credit balance of allowance for doubtful accounts.

Account stated — An acceptance by a debtor of a total amount owed to a creditor.

Accretion — The growth of assets from external sources. In real estate, additional land created on the shore or bank of a body of water.

Accrual method of accounting — A method of accounting which recognizes revenues when earned and expenses when incurred, regardless of actual cash receipt or cash payment.

Accrued benefit — In a qualified retirement plan, an amount of retirement benefit attributable to an employee. If the employee follows the plan's requirements for retirement, then he or she will have full accrued benefit; if early retirement occurs, then the accrued benefit may be less. Also see "vesting." For a fully insured individual policy plan under an allocated funding instrument, the accrued benefit is generally equal to the cash surrender value of the insurance or annuity contract at retirement.

Accrued dividend — A dividend that has been declared by a corporation's board of directors, but not yet paid.

Accrued expense — An expense that has been incurred, but not yet paid (e.g., accrued property taxes payable and accrued salaries payable).

Accrued interest — In bond trading, an amount of accumulated interest that a buyer must pay (in addition to the purchase price) because the bond was purchased between interest payment dates.

Accrued revenue — Revenue that has been earned, but cash has not been received.

Accumulate — In commodity trading, the gradual buildup of a commodity position in a fluctuating market, instead of all at once.

Accumulated deficit — See "Deficit."

Accumulated depreciation — The total amount of depreciation expense previously taken on assets under the property, plant, and equipment classification of a balance sheet.

Accumulated-earnings tax[1] — A tax assessed only on corporations for "unreasonable" accumulation of earnings beyond the needs of the business. This tax is levied on corporations that do not declare and pay enough dividends.

Accumulated profits — See "Retained earnings."

Accumulation trust — A trust designed to retain all earnings over a certain period of time before distributions are made.

Accumulation units — See "Annuity accumulation unit."

Acid-test ratio — A measure of liquidity used in financial statement analysis that signifies an economic entity's financial ability to pay its short-term debts. Generally, short-term creditors are interested in this computation for credit rating purposes in that only cash, near-cash items, and current liabilities are used in the ratio:

$$\text{Acid-test ratio} = \frac{\text{Quick assets}}{\text{Current liabilities}}$$

"Quick assets" are cash and items that can be quickly turned into cash, such as net accounts receivable and marketable securities. The acid-test ratio is also known as the "quick ratio."

Acknowledgment — A written statement signed before a notary public (or other authorized person) declaring the certain identity of the person signing the statement.

Acquiescence[1] — For tax purposes, the agreement of Internal Revenue Service policy with the results reached by the U.S. Tax Court concerning a tax-related matter.

Acquired rights — Rights that are not naturally enjoyed by the masses, but are obtained through the ownership of property or from holding an important position.

Acquisition costs — Generally, amounts spent (or incurred) for acquiring an asset other than its purchase or invoice price. For example, when purchasing real estate, some of the following items are usually recorded as acquisition costs: attorney's fees, escrow fees, title insurance premiums, real estate commissions, back taxes, surveying costs, clearing costs, landscaping, local tax assessments, repairs to an existing building, and any other similar costs. Acquisition costs can also be found in the purchase of other assets, which include transporting the item, customs, duties, additions to an existing structure in preparing for the item (e.g., computer facilities), insurance-in-transit premiums, and any other costs incurred to ready the item for service. These costs are capitalized expenditures. If real property involves an existing building, then the acquisition costs are to be allocated between land and building unless the building is to be razed. In insurance, acquisition costs are the amounts spent by an insurance company for the purchase or renewal of an insurance contract. They include commissions, medical examinations, policy issue costs, fees paid to bureaus, and underwriting costs. Such expenses are usually directly borne by the insurance company (indirectly by the purchaser).

Acre — A measure of land consisting of 160 square rods, or 43,560 square feet.

Acreage allotment — The maximum portion of farmland that can be planted in crops without losing governmental benefits of financial assistance and price supports.

Acreage reserve — A governmental program that provides money to farmers for not planting certain crops on all or a portion of their acreage allotment.

Acting within scope of authority — As used in agency arrangements, the acts of an employee (agent) for his employer (principal) as authorized by the principal. The authority may be directly conferred by the principal (actual authority), or may be reasonably assumed by a third party that an agent has authority as determined from the principal's conduct (apparent authority or authority by estoppel). The principal may be liable for the negligent or wrongful acts of an agent if the acts were performed while on duty in connection with employment.

Action — In legal terminology, a dispute brought to court.

Act of God — An unpreventable event derived strictly from natural causes (usually associated with hurricanes, storms, earthquakes, etc.).

Actual balance method — A technique of recording interest on a savings account balance. Interest is earned on the balance of a savings account at the close of the business day on a daily basis. Generally, this technique provides the maximum amount of interest earnings on savings accounts. The actual balance method is also known as the "day-of-deposit-to-day-of-withdrawal method." Also see "Savings account."

Actual cash value — In property insurance, a value assigned to insured property. For inventory or other items traded in the ordinary course of business the "actual cash value" is their replacement cost. For assets in use (e.g., equipment, automobiles, buildings, furniture, and most consumer items), the actual cash value, generally, is the replacement cost less depreciation and any residual income value. Other considerations may include market value, utility value, and the location of the property.

Actual notice — An appropriate amount of knowledge given to and received by a certain party, directly and personally, for a prudent person to reasonably act under similar circumstances.

Actuals — A cash commodity, such as corn, wheat, sugar, or soybeans, as compared to a futures contract for a specific commodity.

Actual value — See "Fair market value."

Actuary — A professional employed by insurance and pension companies to determine such items as risks, rates, premiums, rating systems, reserves needed for future liabilities, and evaluations for experience systems.

Additional extended coverage — As used in fire insurance, supplemental coverage providing additional insurance for losses arising from such perils as windstorm, vandalism, riot, smoke, ice, hail, explosion, faulty plumbing, and several other risks. Additional extended coverage is an extension of the original fire insurance contract, not an increase in the policy's face amount.

Additional insured — Automobile insurance covering persons other than the named insured, as stated in a liability policy's omnibus clause, when the car is used by other persons with insured's permission. Also see "Omnibus clause."

Add-on clause — In financing arrangements, a clause in a security agreement that allows the lender to attach future-acquired assets as security (collateral) for an existing obligation without further action on the part of the lender. Words similar to "...now owned and hereafter obtained" are an example of a phrase used in an add-on clause. This usually applies to inventory purchases in the manner of a floating lien. It could also apply to consumer purchases, if additions are installed or improvements (accessions) are made to the encumbered property, or if other goods are obtained within 10 days after the lender gives value. The add-on clause is also known as an "after-acquired property clause" or a "future-acquired property clause."

Add-on installment loan — A type of consumer loan where the periodic installment payment is found by adding the total interest charges to the principal and then dividing this sum by the total number of payments to be made. Regardless of the rate of interest used to calculate interest charges, the add-on installment method does not yield a true annual percentage rate (APR), which must be accurately stated in a financing agreement as required under the Truth-in-Lending Act. Usually, the APR is much higher than the rate used in simple interest computations. Add-on installment loans have become fairly rare in consumer financing arrangements because the Truth-in-Lending Act requires the annual percentage rate to be stated within .125 of a percentage point in most all consumer loans. This loan is also known as an "add-on interest loan" and an "installment-interest loan." Also see "Truth-in-Lending Act."

Add-on interest loan — See "Add-on installment loan."

Ademption — The revocation, withholding, reduction, or extinction of a testamentary gift by some act of the testator. For example, Jones puts in his will that from his estate his brother is to receive a certain diamond ring. Before Jones's death, however, he gives the ring to his son. Jones is survived by both brother and son. The testamentary gift to his brother fails (i.e., it is "adeemed").

Adhesion contract — A contract generally written by a dominant party on a "take it or leave it" basis, allowing little or no opportunity for any significant bargaining. This ordinarily occurs when large institutions require their employees to use a standard contract without modifications and by individuals who are in a position to exploit an unfair advantage.

Adjudication[1] — A decision reached or a judgment given by a court.

Adjustable life insurance — A type of life insurance that provides an insured with certain options, such as switching the type of protection, increasing or decreasing the protection period, raising or lowering the premium payments, and increasing or decreasing the policy's face amount.

Adjustable mortgage loan (AML) — See "Adjustable rate mortgage."

Adjustable rate mortgage (ARM) — A type of loan generally associated with consumer home purchases, where the mortgage interest rate fluctuates (within limits) with money market rates. Although there are many different versions of ARM, most are tied to a published rate or price index promulgated by the government (e.g., Treasury bills). Usually the monthly installment payment is fixed over a certain period of time (from 6 months to 5 years, depending on the contract) before any adjustments are made to compensate for the change in interest rates. Most contracts call for the adjustment of an interest rate by using the prevailing market rate as of a certain date. With any adjustable rate mortgage, there are two important concepts to consider: the payment rate and the accrual rate. The payment rate (effective rate) is used to determine the monthly installment payments. The accrual rate (note or actual rate) determines the interest charged against the balance of principal. If the payment rate is less than the accrual rate, then the principal is enlarging every year rather than decreasing (negative amortization). If the payment rate equals (or is greater than) the accrual rate, then the balance of the principal is decreasing as in normal amortization. This type mortgage is also known as an "adjustable mortgage loan (AML)" or "variable rate mortgage (VRM)."

Adjusted balance method — A method of computing finance charges (i.e., interest) on consumer borrowings by a lender. Usually, the finance charge computed under the adjusted balance method is levied on an individual's charge account at a department or other retail store. Interest is calculated on any remaining account balance on the last day of the billing period:

Beginning balance	xxx
Less: payment	− xx
Plus: new charges	+ xx
Remaining balance	xxx

Also see "Finance charges (consumers)."

Adjusted basis[1] — For tax purposes, an adjusted basis is, generally, the cost (or other basis if acquired by gift or inheritance) of property with certain adjustments: The cost must be increased by capitalized expenditures and decreased by depreciation allowed (or allowable) and/or other basis reducing events. Most any disposition of a portion of the property resulting in the receipt of proceeds (e.g., sale, exchange, insured damages, and payments received for an easement) may also decrease the basis. The adjusted basis is used to determine gain or loss upon final disposition. Also see "Basis."

Adjusted gross estate — An amount previously used to determine the maximum marital deduction allowed (before 1982).

Adjusted gross income (AGI) — For income tax purposes, gross income reduced by allowable investment losses, business expenses, and "adjustments to income" (i.e., deductions for AGI). Adjusted gross income is used to determine tax deductible amounts of medical expenses, charitable contributions, optional sales tax, and casualty losses. It is also used to determine the alternative minimum taxable income (for the alternative minimum tax), the dependent-care expenses credit, earned income credit, etc.

Adjusted taxable gifts — For estate tax purposes, taxable gifts transferred after 1976, not included in a decedent's gross estate, that are net of the charitable deduction, marital deduction, and $10,000 annual exclusion. The adjusted taxable gifts are added to the taxable estate to figure the unified transfer tax. Also see "Estate tax."

Adjuster — A person sent by an insurance company to examine damaged property, to determine the cause of damage, to assess the amount of loss, and to determine the company's liability. The adjuster also attempts to reach an agreement as to the amount of loss. An adjuster may be an employee of the insurance company, self-employed, or an employee of an independent organization specializing in adjusting a particular type of loss.

Adjustment — In insurance, the procedures of an adjuster, especially in determining the amount of indemnity an insurance company is required to pay.

Adjustment bond — See "Income bond."

Adjustments to income — A section on the individual income tax return (Form 1040) showing certain deductions before adjusted gross income: moving expenses, employee business expenses, individual retirement arrangement contributions, Keogh contributions, penalty on early withdrawal of savings, alimony paid, and working married couple deduction.

Administration of an estate — The management and distribution of a decedent's estate: collecting and arranging the order of assets for distribution, paying the estate's expenses and debts, distributing the remaining assets to the beneficiaries, and closing out any other necessary business.

Administrator (executor) — For estate purposes, a person designated to manage the administration of a decedent's estate. If a person is named in the will, then he is an executor (if a woman, an executrix). If a person is appointed by a court, then he is an administrator (for a woman, an administratrix).

Administrator c.t.a. — An administration of an estate having a will, which either does not name an executor, or the named executor does not act or is unable to act. Also see "Administrator (executor)."

Ad valorem tax[1] — A tax assessed on items according to their value. These assessments are typically made by state and local governments on real and personal property.

Advance — Cash received before services are rendered or goods are delivered. Ordinarily, such advances are includable in gross income when received, but not deductible when paid, depending upon the circumstances. An advance may also mean to supply goods before any arrangement for repayment is made.

Advance decline (A-D) index[2] — Often used as a measurement of

[2]*Words of Wall Street: 2,000 Investment Terms Defined,* by Allan H. Pessin and Joseph A. Ross (Homewood, Ill.: Dow Jones–Irwin, 1983).

market sentiment (i.e., relative bullishness or bearishness of the stock market). One frequently used formula: divide number of advancing issues by number of declining issues on a market day. For example, if 900 issues advance and 450 decline on a market day, the A-D index is 2. Numbers greater than 1 are bullish, numbers less than 1 are bearish. Another formula: divide number of advances plus one half of stocks unchanged by number of issues traded. Numbers above 50 percent are bullish, numbers less than 50 percent are bearish.

Advancement — In estate planning, money or other property given to or expended for a prospective heir and a simultaneous equal reduction of eventual inheritance.

Advance premiums — In insurance, premiums paid before the premium due date (which sometimes qualify for a discount, depending upon the policy).

Adverse parties — Opposing sides in a proceeding, action, vote, settlement, etc. Adverse parties also may arise from similar interests that are adverse to each other, such as interests in the same property, person, etc.

Adverse possession — A manner of acquiring title to real property by actual possession over a continuous period of time (from 5 to 20 years, depending upon state statutes). The possession must also be notorious, exclusive, under a claim of right, and knowingly made against the owner's rights.

Adverse selection — In insurance, the tendency for persons, who are expecting a loss or are in poor health, to seek more insurance coverage than those persons without such expectations or conditions.

Adverse use — The improper use of a professional designation, land, position, or other item without permission or authority.

Advice — Generally, an informative memorandum concerning the shipment of goods or money (e.g., remittance advice).

Aesthetic value — A portion of the value of property (either real or personal) attributable to beauty. Either the property or its surroundings may have the quality of beauty characteristically associated with aesthetic value.

Affidavit — A voluntary statement of fact written, signed, and sworn or affirmed under oath before a notary public or other authorized person.

Affinity — (1) A relationship created by marriage between one spouse and the other spouse's blood relatives (i.e., in-laws); (2) personal attraction between individuals.

Affirmation — A formal confirmation that something is truthful and correct.

Affirmative warranty — Statements in an insurance policy disclosing certain conditions that existed on or before the time of writing such policy.

After-acquired property clause — See "Add-on clause."

After-market — A description of the market of a particular security after its original issuance through underwriters.

Age limits — A specified range of ages (minimum and maximum) that is used by a life insurance company as one criteria to accept or renew an insurance policy.

Agency — A fiduciary arrangement authorizing one party (agent) to act for and be subject to the control of another party (principal) in dealing with third parties. The relationship between an agent and principal includes employee-employer, servant-master, and independent contractor-customer. Both parties must consent to an agency arrangement.

Agency company — An insurance company operating under a marketing system of agents (either exclusive or independent) rather than from direct-selling methods. Also see "Agency system."

Agency coupled with an interest — A special agency arrangement whereby the agent has an interest in the subject matter of the agency agreement.

Agency reinsurance — A reinsurance arrangement where an agent of an insurer will cede (place with a reinsurer) a certain amount of business in order to reduce the exposure of the insurer to a desired level. Typically, the agent will issue only one policy to the insured (representing a large amount of risk) and acquire reinsurance from other companies.

Agency system — A type of marketing system for insurance companies where agents are authorized to write most of their business, as opposed to direct-selling methods where the insurer sells directly to prospective insureds. Customarily, life insurance companies use general agents to supervise sales in given territories (an exclusive arrangement); property and casualty companies use either an independent agent or an exclusive agent for their sales. Examples of direct-selling methods include direct-mail advertising and airport vending machines.

Agent — A party to an agency relationship who must act in a fiduciary capacity for and on behalf of another party (principal) with third parties. The specific (actual) authority of an agent is determined by the principal; generally, agents have the authority to contract with third parties for the principal only in the capacity of the agency agreement.

Age of majority — The age of an adult as specified in state statutes, commonly either 18 or 21.

Aggregate deductible — In health or property and casualty insurance policies, the amount of total losses applied to one deductible amount during a period of a year, rather than separate deductibles applying to each loss.

Aggregate indemnity — The maximum amount of money that can be received from an insurance policy. Generally, this refers to disability insurance. The aggregate indemnity may be stated as the maximum that can be collected during any one period of disability, for any disability, or under the contract as a whole.

Agreed amount clause — A stipulation in an insurance contract that the insured will carry a certain amount of insurance.

Agreement — A voluntary consent between two or more parties as to the acceptance of an opinion, a determination, or a business transaction. An agreement may not have all of the essential elements of a contract, although it is used synonymously with the term "contract." Also see "Contract."

Alienation clause — (1) A provision in a fire insurance contract that automatically voids the policy upon the sale, exchange, or gift of the insured property; (2) see "Due-on-sale clause."

Alimony[1] — Amounts paid by one spouse and received by the other spouse in accordance with a legal-separation or divorce agreement. Generally, alimony is deductible by the payer and includable in the gross income of the recipient. Payments must be pursuant to a legal agreement, be made in cash, and continue for six years. Payments made for child support do not constitute alimony.

All faults — See "As is."

Allied lines — A term describing a type of insurance covering certain perils, such as rain delays of baseball games, sprinkler leakage damage, earthquake damage, flood damage, and crop hail damage. Some of these perils are included in multi-peril contracts, some are endorsements on a fire insurance contract, while others are separately written policies.

All-lines insurance — A type of insurance company that writes business for a combination of perils: life, casualty, health, and fire.

Allocated benefits — Itemized benefits of a health insurance policy that are listed with the corresponding maximum indemnity for specified services.

All or none (AON)[2] — (1) Use of an underwritten offering: it is conditional to a total subscription of the shares offered. If every share is not subscribed, the issuer has the right to cancel the offering. For example, the Women's Bank offered shares on an all-or-none basis. If all shares are not subscribed, Women's Bank may cancel the offering; (2) Use of an order ticket by a buying or selling customer: buy or sell the entire amount on a single transaction. Order entry symbol: AON. All-or-none instructions that require immediate execution must be marked fill or kill (FOK). Thus, AON restricts the size but not necessarily the time of the transaction.

Allotment — As used in the sale of new securities, the apportioning of an initial offering to more than one underwriter.

Allowance — (1) Money earmarked for a specific activity, such as a travel allowance; (2) a provision for money or necessities to a dependent or other beneficiary, such as from the assets of an estate; (3) the satisfaction in whole or in part of an obligation; (4) a partial payment or discount, such as a trade-in allowance; (5) In the ordinary course of business between a buyer and a seller, the tolerance of slight defects as to quality or quantity which is customarily permitted within a particular industry (e.g., breakage and spoilage).

Allowance method — A method of estimating the bad debt expense that a business is expected to experience during the course of a year.

All-risks insurance policy — A property insurance policy written to provide broad automatic coverage of all perils that are not specified in the policy.

Alteration of trust — Any act by the grantor of a trust changing its terms.

Alternate valuation date — Property passing from a decedent's estate can be valued for estate tax purposes either on the date of death or the alternate valuation date, whichever is chosen by the administrator or executor. The alternate valuation date is either six months from the date of death or the date the property is disposed of (if less than six months from the date of death). It can only be elected if the total value of an estate can be reduced.

Alternative minimum tax (AMT)[1] — A tax imposed on individuals if it exceeds the regular tax due. The AMT is based on adjusted gross income, tax preference items, and allowable deductions. It is computed by adding to adjusted gross income certain tax preference items, then decreasing this sum by the amount of alternative-tax itemized deductions and an allowed exemption. The result of this computation is called the alternative minimum taxable income (AMTI), which is then multiplied by a 20 percent tax rate to yield the AMT.

Amalgamation — A combination of different or diverse elements, segments, unions, or corporations into a one entity.

Amenities — In real estate, qualities that enhance the desirability of property in a pleasurable or enjoyable manner rather than as an indispensable necessity. Examples include view, landscaping, location, and access to a body of water.

American Bar Association (ABA) — A national organization of attorneys whose fundamental purpose is to improve the quality of professional legal services and control the licensing of lawyers.

American College — A professional, educational institution which administers the Chartered Life Underwriter's (CLU) designation.

American Experience Table of Mortality — A table which deals with statistics of life expectancy, based upon the mortality experience of 15 large life insurance companies. It has been adopted by all states. Also known as "Commissioners Standard Ordinary Mortality Table (CSO Table)."

American Institute for Property and Liability Underwriters — A professional, educational institution which administers the Chartered Property and Casualty Underwriter (CPCU) designation.

American Institute of Certified Public Accountants (AICPA) — A national organization of CPAs whose primary purpose is to improve the quality of professional accounting services and aid in the control of licensing of certified public accountants.

American Municipal Bond Assurance Corporation (AMBAC) — An insurer of principal and interest payments on municipal bonds. Typically, the policy is purchased by an issuing municipality (or other issuing entity) in order to receive a higher bond rating.

American Stock Exchange (AMEX or ASE) — The second largest U.S. stock exchange. It began before the Civil War by conducting business in the open streets (hence, the name "curb exchange"). The AMEX is located in New York City.

Amorphous — Without definiteness; something lacking structure or organization, as an amorphous financial plan.

Amortization — (1) In taxation, an expense resulting from the ratable allocation of the cost of an intangible asset, such as patents, copyrights, and organization costs. The intangible asset must have a definite useful life (goodwill does not have a definite useful life and is, therefore, not amortized) and not be subject to the accelerated cost recovery system. (2) The reduction of debt resulting from any payment applied to the principal (e.g., a payment of interest and principal) as opposed to a payment consisting only of interest; (3) any gradual reduction over a certain period.

Amortization of bond discount — For the purchaser, an annual inclusion in gross income that is based upon the difference between the face amount and the purchase price of a taxable bond when purchased for a price that is less than its face amount (i.e., at a discount). Taxpayers, who purchased an original issuance in such manner, must include both interest receipts and amortized discount in gross income on all taxable bonds. The bond's basis is gradually increased by the amount of amortized discount. Such discount occurs because the coupon rate (stated rate or contract rate) of interest on the bond is less than the prevailing market rate as of the date of issuance; thus, the marketplace is only willing to pay an amount that is less than the bond's face value because of the differences in interest rates. There are two methods of computing discount amortization of bonds: straight-line and effective interest rate. Also see "Effective interest rate method" and "Straight-line method." The reasoning behind a bond-discount amortization is that the bond was purchased for a price that reflects the "true value" of a bond at the market as computed by present value and influenced by risk factors. Therefore, the discount is actually deferred interest being amortized over the life of the bond. Also see "Carrying value."

Amortization of bond premium — For the purchaser, an annual amortization of the difference between the purchase price and the face amount of a bond, when purchased for a price greater than its face amount (i.e., at a premium). The purchaser of taxable bonds has the option to elect to amortize the premium. The purchaser of nontaxable bonds does not have an election and must amortize the premium over the life of the bonds. The amortized portion of a premium has the effect of gradually reducing the bond's basis, which is generally its cost. Investors in taxable bonds are permitted to deduct, as interest expense, the amortization of a bond premium. Tax-exempt bonds do not afford this deduction. Generally, the amortization method for a premium is straight-line, although the effective interest rate method is sometimes used. Also see "Carrying value."

Amortization of debt (loan amortization) — The gradual process of reducing a debt through scheduled periodic payments. Typically, such payments are made over a specified period that is divided into equal lengths, the amount of each payment is equal for most all simple interest loans, and each payment consists of two elements: principal and interest. For each installment, the portion attributable to interest is greater in the early stages because the principal is larger in the beginning. As payments continue, the principal is gradually reduced. Because of principal reduction, the portion of each payment attributable to interest becomes smaller during the latter stages of the pay-off period. Generally, in income tax figuring, amounts paid for interest are an itemized deduction for personal-use loans; no deduction is allowed for principal reduction payments. Also see "Negative amortization" and "Adjustable rate mortgages".

Amount of coverage — As used in insurance, the amount of insurance protection that is provided by an insurer for a person or object.

Amount of loss — (1) As used in insurance, the portion of a total loss that is covered by insurance; (2) total losses caused by or resulting from damage, destruction, disease, loss in value, distress, etc., both direct and indirect, suffered by an individual or business.

Amount realized[1] — For income tax purposes, the amount received upon the sale or exchange of property. The amount realized is equal to the sum of cash and other property received (at fair market value) less selling expenses. The difference between the amount realized and the adjusted basis of property given is the gain or loss realized. Also see "Gain realized" and "Gain recognized."

Anatomical gift — A gift of a bodily organ, such as a kidney, while living or at death.

Ancestor — (1) Technically, a person from whom another directly descended, such as mother, father, grandmother, or grandfather; (2) a previous owner of land, who is deceased, from whom another has inherited the property.

Ancillary — Something (an action, proceeding, clause, etc.) that is subordinate to or aids another portion, which is considered the principal element.

Ancillary administration — A subordinate administration of an estate located in another jurisdiction (usually another state). An ancillary administration normally occurs when the decedent owned property in a state other than the one in which he was domiciled. Some state statutes require that a resident of the state, where other such property is owned, must act as an administrator to a certain extent (ancillary administrator).

Anniversary date — For insurance policies, an annual recurring date marking a policy's initial issuance.

Annual accounting period — For income tax purposes, any consecutive 12-month period consistently reported whereby taxes are determined. Also see "Accounting period," "Calendar-year taxpayer," and "Fiscal year."

Annual depreciation — A periodic expense derived from the ownership of fixed assets and used in a trade or business. The theory behind depreciation expense is that because of the normal wear and tear, obsolescence, or decay of an asset over its productive life, the cost of acquisition should be expensed during the period of use. Federal tax laws allow depreciation over a statutory class life period. Also see "Accelerated cost recovery system."

Annual exclusion — An amount ($10,000 per donee) a donor can gift during a period of one year which is excluded from gift tax computation. The donee must have an immediate right to ownership.

Annual percentage rate (APR) — The cost-of-borrowing rate that must be disclosed in a financing agreement according to the Truth-in-Lending Act. The APR yields a true rate of interest that can be used for comparison with other sources of credit.

Annual report — A financially related report made annually from the management of a company to the stockholders and other interested parties. Included in an annual report are an income statement, balance sheet, statement of changes in financial position, a retained earnings statement, footnotes to the financial statements, report of the independent auditors, and a report from management of the past year's activities and future expectations.

Annuitant — An individual who is entitled to receive annuity payments.

Annuity — An arrangement whereby an annuitant is guaranteed to receive periodic payments for a certain number of years (annuity certain) or for life (life annuity) or both. Usually a portion of each payment, based on an exclusion ratio (cost/expected total benefit), is excluded from gross income. An annuity may be classified by plan of distribution (straight life verses refund annuity), by type of purchase (single premium versus installment premium), by timing of receipts (deferred versus immediate), by parties in the contract (single life versus joint life versus survivorship versus joint life with survivorship), and by annuity payment (fixed versus variable). Also see "Annuity certain," "Cash refund annuity," "Contingent annuity option," "Deferred annuity," "Employee annuity," "Fixed annuity," "Group annuities," "Joint life and survivorship annuity," "Life annuity," "Private annuity," "Refund annuity," "Retirement annuity," and "Variable annuity."

Annuity accumulation period — An installment payment period during which the purchaser of an annuity makes deposits in accordance with the annuity agreement. It occurs before the start of annuity payments.

Annuity accumulation unit — An accounting device used to calculate the value of an annuity's accumulated balance prior to the start of annuity payments. Before the election of a payout method is made by the owner, the annuity accumulation units remain the property of the owner. When a payout method is chosen, however, the accumulation units will be converted into annuity units. It is at this latter stage when the annuitant surrenders the accumulation units in exchange for the right to be paid future receipts from the insurance company. Annuity accumulation units can be used for both variable and fixed annuities. For a variable annuity contract, the value is figured by multiplying the number of units attributable to an individual's accumulation account by the prevailing market price per unit. Also see "Fixed annuity" and "Variable annuity."

Annuity accumulation value — The total value of the annuity accumulation units of a variable annuity's account at a certain date.

Annuity certain — A type of guaranteed refund annuity where an insurance company guarantees annuity payments for a specified period of time. If an annuitant dies, payments continue to a designated beneficiary until such period expires. Under a life annuity plan, an annuitant will receive payments beyond the specified period until death. For example, Thomson has an annuity certain, which guarantees payment for the longer period of 25 years or life. If Thomson dies in 10 years, then a beneficiary will receive the balance of 15 years. If Thomson lives 44 more years, his annuity will continue until the time of death. Also see "Annuity."

Annuity contract — A contractual obligation providing an annuitant with certain periodic receipts (fixed annuity) or variable periodic receipts (variable annuity) over a stated period or for life. Also see "Annuity," "Fixed annuity," and "Variable annuity."

Annuity ratio — For income tax purposes, a ratio used to compute the tax-free portion of an annuity receipt. It is also known as an annuity exclusion ratio and is computed as follows:

$$\text{Annuity ratio} = \frac{\text{Amount contributed}}{\text{Estimated total receipts}} \times \text{Each receipt}$$

Annuity trust — A trust arrangement typically providing periodic fixed payments, regardless of the trust's income, to one or more beneficiaries.

Annulment — (1) A nullification; (2) the permanent abolishment of a marriage by determining that a marriage never existed.

Antedate — To place an earlier date on a document than the date which it was actually written. Insurance policies and negotiable instruments are sometimes antedated in order for them to take effect at an earlier time.

Antenuptial agreement — An agreement entered into before marriage usually to resolve certain issues that commonly arise (e.g., division of property and child support) in case of death, separation, or divorce.

Antichurning rules[1] — Special tax rules that prevent a taxpayer from converting certain nonrecovery property (placed in service prior to 1981) to qualify for the accelerated cost recovery system.

Antitrust legislation — State and federal legislation attempting to prevent the restraint of free trade and commerce. Unlawful price fixing, monopolies, price discrimination, tying sales or arrangements, etc., were specifically targeted. The major federal antitrust acts are the Sherman Act, Clayton Act, Federal Trade Commission Act, and the Robinson-Patman Act.

Apparent authority — For an agency arrangement, an assumed authority "given" to an agent by a principal, either knowingly or negligently, which permits the agent to do whatever is normally performed (as far as third parties are concerned), though the agent does not have the authority. It is sometimes viewed under the "prudent man rule" (how would a prudent man, using reasonable discretion, view this situation in regard to the actions of the principal?). Apparent authority typically surfaces when a third party detrimentally relies on the actions or statements of an agent because the principal, either intentionally or accidentally, causes the third party to believe that the agent possesses the authority to perform, which in reality he does not have.

Appellate court — A court having the authority to review and either uphold or overturn the findings of a lower court. The U.S. Court of Appeals and the U.S. Supreme Court are the two appellate courts in the federal judicial system. These courts only review cases and are not the courts of original jurisdiction.

Application for life insurance — A statement made by a prospective insured, who is applying for life insurance, declaring that the information supplied to a life insurance company is correct. The insurance company assesses the information to determine the acceptability of risk.

Apportioned tax — A tax collected by one political entity and subsequently shared with another (usually larger) political entity. For example, property taxes collected by one county or parish are shared with other counties and cities, and also with the state in which the county is located.

Apportionment — The allocation of expenses, costs, or revenues in terms of a specified ratio or procedure. Generally, the apportionment process is determined by rational, systematic, or equitable procedures designed to allocate items in proportion to a common factor (e.g., real estate taxes are allocated between two parties by the ratio of ownership during the year).

Apportionment clause — A clause found in insurance contracts stating that an insurance company is to indemnify the insured in a manner proportional to total coverage of all policies pertaining to the same property.

Appraisal — An estimate of value performed by an independent expert.

Appraisal clause — A clause in insurance contracts which gives the insurance company the right to an appraisal of loss or damages.

Appraisal remedy — For a dissenting shareholder, the privilege of selling shares back to the corporation at an amount valued immediately prior to approval of an issue to which the shareholder disagreed.

Appraised value — An estimate of the value of property at a specific point in time by an independent expert who considers all relevant facts and circumstances.

Appreciation[1] — The increase of a property's fair market value because of factors such as inflation or increase in demand (from expanded desirability, higher expectations, etc.). Appreciation is usually associated with increased equity or equity buildup. For tax purposes, a taxable transaction must occur before taxes are assessed, so mere appreciation is not taxable.

Apprendre — Generally, a fee, given or received, for professional services performed; also a right to share profits with the owner of land.

Appropriation — The setting aside of money and its authorization to be spent in a specified manner.

Approval — A ratification or confirmation by an individual possessing adequate knowledge.

Appurtenance — A subsidiary attachment, accessory, appendage, or something belonging without attachment. In real estate, an appurtenance is considered part of the property and is conveyed to all subsequent owners (e.g., easements, buildings, waterways, and gardens).

APR — See "Annual percentage rate."

Arbitrage[3] — Strictly defined, buying something where it is cheap and selling it where it is dear; e.g., a bank buys three-month CD money in the U.S. market and sells three-month money at a higher rate in the Eurodollar market. In the money market, it often refers: (1) to a situation in which a trader buys one security and sells a similar security with the expectation that the spread in yields between the two instruments will narrow or widen to his profit; (2) to a swap between two similar issues based on an anticipated change in yield spreads; and (3) to situations where a higher return (or a lower cost) can be achieved in the money market for one currency by utilizing another currency and swapping it on a fully hedged basis through the foreign exchange.

Arbitration — An arrangement for a disinterested, impartial, and knowledgeable third party to settle a dispute. The decision reached by the arbitrators is binding because both parties have agreed in advance to follow the outcome after both sides have been heard.

Arbitration clause — A clause found in contracts calling for mandatory arbitration in the case of disputes over values, rights, compensation, scope of authority, breach of contract, etc.

Arm's-length transaction[1] — A transaction which results in a fair price in accordance with the prevailing market influences. Viewed by the courts as an amount reached by a willing seller and a willing buyer, both having knowledge of all relevant facts and neither being unduly compelled to act.

Arrears — Anything overdue and not yet paid; dividends are said to be "in arrears" on cumulative preferred stock when amounts due to preferred shareholders have not yet been declared or are unpaid.

Arson — The malicious and willful burning of property with illegal intent.

---

[3]*Money Market,* by Marcia Stigum (Homewood, Ill.: Dow Jones–Irwin, 1984).

Arson clause — A clause in many property and casualty insurance policies which voids insurance coverage if a fire is set or directed to be set by the insured.

Articles of incorporation — An instrument filed with the state, usually the Secretary of State, containing proposed name, purpose, temporary directors, duration, amount and type of stock authorized, powers, original stock subscribers, principal place of business, home office, and authorized agent of the corporation.

Ascendant — One's relative in the ascending line, such as parents, grandparents, or great-grandparents. Compare "Ancestor."

Ascent — For estate planning purposes, the passage of an estate from a decedent to an ascendant (upward passage).

As is — A stipulation in a sales agreement that a buyer will assume all risks, in the absence of fraud by the seller, as to quality of merchandise and, therefore, must trust his own inspection before making a purchase. Warranties are normally excluded from such sale.

Ask price — An amount listed by a seller for property offered for sale. The final sales price may be lower after negotiating with a buyer. In securities trading, though, it is commonly the lowest offering price. See "Bid and ask."

Assessed value — A value placed on property for tax purposes by a taxing authority. The fair market value is usually not the same as the assessed value.

Assessment — (1) The process of evaluating and adjusting an amount to be contributed by persons with whom a common objective is sought (e.g., limited partnership assessments); (2) an estimation of the value of property for tax purposes; (3) the determination of tax due; (4) the levy of tax.

Assessment insurance — A type of mutual insurance arrangement, usually life insurance, that is typically purchased by groups with similar interests, but in some cases by the general public. If enough funds are not available to pay claims, assessments may be made against the members. Also see "Fraternal companies."

Assessment of tax — An additional amount of tax due as evaluated by the Internal Revenue Service.

Assets — All tangible and intangible property owned by an entity, such as money, securities, equipment, buildings, land, copyrights, and patents. Such items are generally available to pay the owner's debts.

Also see "Capital asset," "Current asset," "Fixed assets," "Frozen asset," "Intangible asset," "Liquid asset," "Quick assets," "Real asset," "Tangible assets," and "Wasting asset."

Assign — (1) To transfer ownership or other interest; (2) to designate for a certain purpose.

Assigned risk — An ordinarily unacceptable risk which must be insured because of state laws. The underwriting is handled through a pool of insurers on a rotating basis. Assigned risk generally deals with automobile and workers' compensation insurance.

Assignee — (1) A person or other entity who receives an assignment, such as a grantee; (2) a person appointed to act for another, such as an agent.

Assignment — (1) The transfer of any property; (2) the transfer of any right or any interest in property. It includes leases, mortgages, title, negotiable instruments, and deeds of trust; (3) the transfer or allocation of a task or duty.

Assignor — A transferor of assignment.

Association — For federal income tax purposes, an unincorporated organization that is taxed as a corporation.

Association group — A group made up of trade or professional society members for group insurance under a master health plan.

Assumable mortgage — According to the terms of contract, a mortgage that is available for assumption by a qualified buyer. Also see "Novation."

Assumption clause — A clause found in a mortgage stating that it can only be assumed with written consent of the mortgagee.

Assumption fee — Charges assessed by a bank or other lender for the expense of processing an existing loan for the borrower.

Assumption of debt — The transfer of a liability, which ultimately obligates one party to pay the debt of another. In a taxable transaction the relieved party is generally considered to have received cash.

Assumption of mortgage — An agreement whereby the buyer (or other party) assumes a liability secured by mortgage or deed of trust.

Assurance — (1) This has the same meaning as "insurance" in England and Canada; (2) to inspire confidence.

Assured — One who has been insured by a company or underwriter in accordance with the policy of insurance.

At arm's length — As it refers to financial transactions, beyond the control of all parties involved and no party is under the control of the other; a financial transaction resulting in a selling price at or near fair market value. Also see "Arm's length transaction."

At risk — For income tax purposes, an amount equal to an investment in a project, which is subject to loss: cash contributed plus adjusted basis of contributed property plus allocated gains plus recourse debt. Nonrecourse debt is generally not considered to be "at risk."

At-risk limitation — A stipulation limiting the amount of losses to be reported by an investor during a taxable year. Losses are deductible up to the amount "at risk." It usually does not apply to real estate deals. See "At risk."

Attachment — The process of seizing property (or persons) by court order and bringing them to court. Typically, it involves the seizure of a debtor's property to secure a creditor's claim in connection with a pending judgment and is commonly used against fraudulent or concealed debtors.

Attest — Affirm, certify, bear witness to, etc. An attested copy is one that has been examined and compared to the original and carries a mark of certification as to its genuineness.

Attestation clause — A clause in a document (e.g., will, deed, mortgage, contract, etc.) providing certification that the signing parties witnessed the document's proper execution.

At the market — The purchase or sale of securities by immediate execution, which results in the prevailing market price. Also see "Limit order" and "Market order."

Attorney-at-law — A person licensed by the state to practice law. He or she may act as counsel, advocate, or agent for a client in legal proceedings.

Attorney-in-fact — An attorney appointed to act as an agent for another party in accordance with a written power of attorney.

Auction — A public or private sale of property whereby the highest bidder becomes the buyer. An auctioneer is a person who conducts the auction process and is an agent of the seller until such property is sold, at which time he becomes an agent of the buyer. The customary falling of the hammer signifies the completion of sale. The seller may or may not sell to the highest bidder, unless the goods are explicitly put up "without reserve"—which means the highest bidder will automatically become the purchaser.

Audit — (1) For tax purposes, the process of examining, verifying, and locating financial data pertaining to taxes by an agent of a revenue authority; (2) for financial reporting purposes, the process of inspecting, accumulating, and evaluating evidence pertaining to the financial information of an entity for the purpose of attesting to the degree of conformity with established criteria.

Audit committee — A special committee made up of members of the board of directors, who are not part of management, to oversee and maintain certain relationships with the independent auditors (certified public accountants). The main purpose is to help keep such auditors independent of management.

Auditor — A person who engages in the audit process.

Auditor's report — An opinion given on financial statements at the end of the auditing process by independent certified public accountants as to the degree of conformity with established criteria. The opinions are classified as unqualified, qualified, adverse, or disclaimer. An unqualified opinion states that the entity is in conformity to the specified criteria. A qualified opinion states that the entity is in conformity to specified criteria "except for" or "subject to" a designated aspect. An adverse opinion states that the entity is not in conformity. A disclaimer of opinion means the auditor is not reporting an opinion.

Augmented estate — A decedent's probate estate reduced by funeral expenses and administrative expenses, homestead allowance, family allowances and exemptions, and enforceable claims, to which are added certain property transfers (made to anyone other than a bona fide purchaser by the decedent for the benefit of any person other than the surviving spouse), Uniform Probate Code Section 2-202. The general purpose is to protect against disinheritance of one's spouse.

Austerity program — An economic policy directed at preventing waste by encouraging strict frugality in order to attain certain objectives, such as a balance of payments, a balanced budget, or alleviating the national debt.

Authorized issue — The total number of shares of capital stock that a corporation can issue, as specified in the articles of incorporation or charter.

Automatic premium loan — An arrangement in life insurance whereby the company may draw on the accumulated cash value of a policy to pay the premium, when such premium is not paid by the end of the grace period. It is considered to be a loan, and the rate of interest charged is usually stated in the policy.

Automatic reinvestment plan — An arrangement generally pertaining to mutual funds and certain publicly held corporations where fund-holders or stockholders are provided the privilege of choosing be-tween cash distributions or additional shares as a dividend receipt; in either case the distribution is usually taxable.

Automatic withdrawal — A feature usually applying to mutual funds where fundholders are permitted to receive a specified amount each month, quarter, or year. The source of such payments arises from dividends, capital gains, and interest experienced by the fund, as well as share liquidations.

Automobile insurance — A broad term encompassing the coverage of different risks associated with owning and operating an automobile. The two basic coverages are casualty and physical damage. Casualty coverages include property damage liability, bodily injury liability, uninsured motorists, medical payments, and no-fault coverage. Physi-cal damage coverages include collision, theft, fire, and miscellaneous coverages, such as explosion, windstorm, vandalism, and riot dam-ages. Sometimes miscellaneous coverages are grouped with fire and theft into what is called "comprehensive physical damage" coverage. Maximum coverage of losses deriving from liability for damages as a result of an accident are usually stated on the face of the automobile's policy. Limits of property damage liability are initially provided in three figures, which are bodily injury for each person, bodily injury for each accident, and property damage for each accident. Also stated are limits for medical payments (for the insured, family, and other passengers), uninsured motor vehicle (in three categories as property damage), and no-fault coverage. Also see "Additional insured" and "Liability limits."

Automobile liability insurance — Protection against financial loss from a legal liability for personal injury or property damage caused by the insured's automobile. Also see "Automobile insurance."

Automobile physical damage insurance — Coverage for losses caused by damages to or theft of an insured's automobile. Also see "Automobile insurance."

Autonomous investment — A type of investing where generally an-ticipated market or economic conditions are not influential consider-ations. Development of new products or processes and investment in not-for-profit entities typically exemplify autonomous investment.

Avail — Generally, the residual amount after deducting expenses. Two common examples include the proceeds of a discounted note (after taking out interest) or the amount of an estate after all expenses and debts have been paid.

Averageable income — For income tax purposes, an amount used to determine eligibility for and tax liability under income averaging. See "Income averaging."

Average base period income — For income tax purposes, an amount used in the income averaging computation. See "Income averaging."

Average clause — In property insurance contracts, a clause providing coverage for similar items, either in one location or in several locations, in that each will be covered in accordance with the proportional value of all items.

Average daily balance method — In consumer financing, a method of figuring finance charges for purchases on credit. It applies a stated rate of interest to the average daily balance of an account. Such balance includes any previously unpaid balance, all purchases, all payments, and purchase returns made during the billing period. The primary difference between this method and all other financing computations is that the average daily balance method uses a weighted average of the account balance throughout the period, which is customarily one month. For example, Norris has a charge account with Simpson & Co. Department Store and had the following data for the month of January:

Balance	Jan. 1	$500
Purchase	Jan. 10	100
Payment	Jan. 12	(300)
Purchase	Jan. 25	200

Accordingly, the average daily balance is computed as follows:

Balance	Period	
$500	× 10 days =	$ 5,000
$600	× 2 days =	1,200
$300	× 13 days =	3,900
$500	× 6 days =	3,000
Total		$13,100

Average daily balance = $13,100/31 days = $422.58

All financial arrangements, however, must explain in detail how finance charges are assessed. Also see "Finance charges (consumers)."

Average earnings clause — A clause placed in disability insurance policies to prevent overinsurance. The amount disability benefit is reduced if the entire amount of disability benefits from all insurers is greater than a certain percentage (such as 80 percent) of the insured's gross income (usually per month) at the beginning of disability or the average earnings for the two-year period before the disability, whichever is greater.

Average indexed monthly earnings (AIME) — A complex method used to determine retirement and other Social Security benefits.

Averaging up (down) — Purchasing the same corporation's security at different price levels resulting in a change in average cost.

Aviation clause — A clause in life insurance policies limiting the liability of the insurance company where the insured is injured or dies in connection with a specified manner of aviation-related accident.

Aviation insurance — A specialized insurance business providing protection against losses arising from damages and liabilities because of aviation-related accidents.

Away-from-home expenses — Traveling expenses (including amounts spent for meals and lodging other than amounts which are lavish or extravagant under the circumstances) while away from home in the pursuit of a trade or business are deductible when ordinary, necessary, and reasonable business expenses are incurred or paid (IRC Section 162(a)(2)). Generally, "home" is considered to be the place where a taxpayer's business, trade, or profession is located.

Backdating — Predating; the writing of a date on a negotiable instrument or other document to a point in time before it was actually drawn. This does not affect negotiability of an instrument, according to the Uniform Commercial Code (Section 3-114). It is commonly done in life insurance contracts and mutual fund purchases in order for the agreement to take effect at an earlier date.

Back-end load — In mutual fund investing, fees charged in redeeming the fund's shares.

Back order — An unfilled customer's order ordinarily due to an inadequate supply of inventory.

Back title letter — In real estate, a letter provided by a title insurance company to an attorney for the purpose of advising the attorney on the condition of title as of a certain date. The attorney begins the examination of title as of that date.

Backup offer — In the complex process of purchasing certain large assets, such as real estate, a secondary offer submitted in case the primary offer fails (usually due to difficult stipulations or contingencies).

Bad debt[1] — An uncollectible debt. For income tax purposes, there are two types of deductible bad-debt expenses: business and non-business. Business bad-debt expense is deducted in the year in which the debt becomes worthless. An accrual basis taxpayer using the reserve method (an allowance for doubtful accounts) may reasonably estimate bad-debt expense incurred in the pursuit of a trade or business during the year. Non-business bad debts require substantiation and are treated as a short-term capital loss in the year the debt became worthless.

Badges of fraud — A legal phrase which generally means that facts were used to throw suspicion on a transaction and, in turn, call for an explanation. Such circumstances do not prove fraud, but warrant an inference of fraud and are usually done by a debtor to hinder, delay, or defraud creditors.

Bail bond — A written guarantee provided to a court of law that a defendant will show in court or the surety will pay. Also see "Surety bond."

Bailment — The delivery of personal property from one person (bailor) to another (bailee) for the purpose of holding the property until a certain event occurs or when the bailor returns to claim it. Bailment applies only to personal property, and the contract can be either express or implied. Parking a car in a parking lot operated by a bailee, renting equipment, leaving a coat in a checkroom of a nightclub are examples of bailment.

Balanced budget — Any budget where the sources of revenue equal the outflow of funds.

Balanced drilling program — In oil and gas tax shelters, a type of investment arrangement that combines exploratory drilling (high risk) and developmental drilling (low risk) for diversity.

Balanced mutual fund — A mutual fund whose investment objective is to minimize risk by investing in a variety of investments that typically include bonds, preferred stock, and common stock.

Balance of payments — The accounting for the monetary value of a country's exchanges (in total) between itself and other nations (foreign payments versus foreign receipts) usually for a period of one year. It uses the double-entry system of accounting and is much broader in scope than the balance of trade. See "Balance of trade."

Balance of trade — The difference between the amount a country imports from and exports to other countries. It only deals with merchandise. If imports exceed exports, then a trade deficit results, and if exports exceed imports, a trade surplus results.

Balance sheet — A formal financial statement showing the financial position of an economic entity at a certain point in time. It summarizes all assets owned by an entity as well as the manner in which the summarized assets are owned (through both debt and owner's equity). Total assets must equal total liabilities and owner's equity. Also see "Personal balance sheet."

Balloon mortgage — See "Balloon note."

Balloon note — A type of promissory note that usually calls for periodic payments, which are insufficient to amortize the principal before maturity, and a final lump-sum payment (known as a balloon payment) that is equal to the principal plus any accrued interest at maturity.

Bank — A financial institution whose principal business is to receive and hold money (deposits), make loans, cash negotiable instruments, discount commercial paper, perform trust functions, and other banking services. Commercial banks fall into two classifications: federally chartered (national banks) and state chartered banks.

Bank account — Any deposit on account with a bank (such as a savings or checking account).

Bank-by-phone account — A special account which allows bank customers to conduct certain transactions by using a pushbutton telephone.

Bank draft — An order of payment (such as a check) drawn by an appropriate official of the bank on its own cash account.

Banker's acceptance (BA)[3] — A draft or bill of exchange accepted by a bank or trust company. The accepting institution guarantees payment of the bill. It is generally used to finance foreign trade between a seller and a buyer, who is unknown to the seller. Because of their negotiability, in many instances banker's acceptances are traded freely in the money market before their maturity dates.

Bank holding company — Generally, a large bank that holds enough voting stock in one or more smaller banks for the purpose of controlling them.

Bank note — A promissory note drawn by an appropriate official of a bank, made payable to bearer, and intended to be circulated as money.

Bank reconciliation — A summary of one's banking activities that brings the bank statement balance and checkbook balance into agreement. The general formula is to add any outstanding deposits to and subtract any outstanding checks from the bank statement balance. To the checkbook balance add any unrecorded deposits made to the account; subtract checks that have not cleared and any charges assessed by the bank. Adjustments for errors must also be made. Only deposits and checks that are dated on or before the date of the bank statement are used in the reconciliation.

Bank reserve — The amount of cash that a bank must have on hand to meet the demands of depositors.

Bankruptcy — A condition whereby an entity is unable to pay its debts when due. It may apply to an individual, partnership, association, corporation, or other entity. Straight bankruptcy is a type of liquidation that involves collection and distribution to the creditors by the trustee of all nonexempt property in order to satisfy claims. Chapters 11 and 13 of the Bankruptcy Code are rehabilitation provisions which provide relief for the debtor in the form of reorganization, rather than liquidation, allowing the creditors to look toward future earnings rather than liquidated amounts, which are usually less than the debt. Bankruptcy can be either voluntary or involuntary. Also see entries "Chapter 11" and "Chapter 13."

Bargain sale — A sale of property for an amount less than fair market value.

Barron's Confidence Index[4] — A weekly market index prepared by *Barron's*. The index is a ratio of the average yield on best grade corporate bonds to the intermediate grade corporate bonds. The ratio is high when investors are confidently buying bonds below top grade and low when investors take refuge in high-grade bond issues.

Barron's 50-Stock Average[4] — A weighted stock price average of 50 stocks, using the same dollar investment in each component company; it is calculated using the closing composite prices as of Thursday each week.

Barter — The exchange of goods or services without money.

Basic form (HO-1) — See "Homeowners' insurance policy."

Basis — An amount used to compute gain or loss from sale or exchange of property. Generally, the basis of an item is its cost; if it was inherited, then the basis, generally, would be its fair market value on the date of death (or date of receipt or alternative valuation date, whichever applies); if it was received via a gift, then the basis, generally, is the donor's basis plus any gift tax paid that is attributable to the item's appreciation (for gifts in 1977 and beyond). Basis can be adjusted, however, for capitalized expenditures, depreciation, casualty losses, and other transactions. Also see "Adjusted basis."

Basis for depreciation — The amount of an asset's basis used for depreciation purposes.

Bearer — One who possesses a negotiable instrument that is indorsed in blank or payable to bearer or payable to cash (i.e., transferable without indorsement).

Bearer bond — A bond whose ownership depends upon actual possession. Interest is usually received by coupons that are clipped off and redeemed at an authorized bank.

Bear market — (1) The selling of securities, which in turn brings prices down; (2) a general consensus that prices, usually security prices, will fall.

Bear spread — An option strategy, using puts or calls or both, that will become profitable if the underlying security declines in price.

Belly up — A term generally used to describe a business that is unable to continue.

Beneficial enjoyment — Generally, the enjoyment of property for a

[4]*The Dow Jones Averages, A Nonprofessional's Guide* (New York: Dow Jones, 1981).

person's own personal benefit, and not merely a holder of property such as a trustee or other fiduciary.

Beneficial estate — Generally, the postponed right of a beneficiary to possession of certain property; the expected estate is beneficial in the sense that a beneficiary takes such property solely for his or her own benefit and not for another (i.e., not as a trustee). Beneficial estate commonly refers to the passage of real estate.

Beneficial interest — (1) A benefit resulting from an indirect involvement in property or business, as opposed to actual personal ownership or direct control; (2) pertaining to a future interest in property, a recipient is to have complete ownership for his or her own personal use and enjoyment. Also see "Beneficial estate."

Beneficial owner — A person entitled to ownership of property, but does not possess legal title. An example is an investor who owns stock, but leaves the certificates with a brokerage firm.

Beneficiary — One who benefits or will benefit from a specified condition or an act of another. The beneficiary usually is a person or other entity designated to receive something, such as life insurance proceeds, trust distributions, annuity distributions, or a testamentary gift from a deceased's estate. Also see "Incidental beneficiary," "Primary beneficiary," and "Secondary beneficiary." Compare "Heir."

Benefit — For insurance purposes, payment to be made by an insurance company according to the terms of an insurance contract.

Benefit period — A specified period in which insurance (commonly health and disability) benefits apply.

Benevolent corporation — A not-for-profit corporation, usually created for charitable purposes.

Bequeath — To transfer personal property in accordance with a will. Also see "Bequest."

Bequest — The transfer of personal property, as opposed to real property, pursuant to a will; a legacy. Such inheritance is not included in a beneficiary's gross income for income tax purposes. The basis of such property is the fair market value on either the date of the testator's death, date of receipt, or alternate valuation date, whichever is chosen by the estate's administrator. Compare "Devise."

Best's Flitcraft Compend — A primary source of detailed life insurance policy data concerning specific premium rates, policy dividends, and other policy-related elements for a majority of life insurance companies in the United States.

Best's Insurance Reports: Life/Health — A reference showing the financial stability of a majority of U.S. life insurance companies, including financial statements, summary of operations, history, management, and Best's ratings.

Best's Insurance Reports: Property/Liability — A reference showing the financial stability of property and casualty insurance companies, including financial statements, summary of operations, underwriting policies, history, management, and Best's ratings.

Best's Key Rating Guide: Property/Liability — A quick reference guide providing summarized information on property and casualty insurance business in the United States. Some 2,000 companies are listed.

Best's Settlement Options — A source of insurance data comparing different settlement options offered by many life insurance policies of the various companies. Included in the reference are settlement options, such as cash surrender value, monthly life income benefits, and periodic interest income.

Beta — A measure of risk showing how a stock or a portfolio is expected to perform in relation to the market as a whole. A beta of 1 signifies that changes in a stock's value are likely to correspond to changes in the market in the same proportion. A beta of 1.3 means that a stock's value is likely to rise or fall 30 percent greater than the market. On the other hand, a beta of .85 means that a stock's value is likely to move by only 85 percent of the market. Thus, if the market moves up 10 percent, then a stock with a beta of .85 would probably move up only 8.5 percent.

Betterment — (1) An improvement made to an asset by replacing an existing portion of the asset with a superior portion. A betterment may or may not prolong useful life or increase value, but it is a capitalized expenditure; (2) for purposes of local taxes, a tax assessed on property because of an additional value received as a consequence of public improvements (e.g., a sidewalk on one's property).

Bid — (1) An offer to purchase, as in an auction; (2) an offer to perform subcontracting services.

Bid and asked — The manner of quoting over-the-counter securities, where "bid" designates the highest price the market is willing to purchase and "asked" denotes price is the lowest price a seller is willing to sell.

Bid bonds — An indemnity bond required in public construction contracts guaranteeing the performance of the bidder. It must be filed at the time of bid and is used to protect a public agency from breach of contract.

Bilateral contract — A contract in which both contracting parties give promises (i.e., a promise for a promise); a reciprocal agreement (e.g., if you promise to deliver, I promise to pay).

Bill broker — A person who negotiates the sale or purchase of commercial paper; a money market middleman.

Bill of exchange — A draft; a negotiable instrument where three parties are involved: one party draws an order on the second party to pay a sum certain to a third party at a stated future time. A check is a bill of exchange payable on demand: one party writes a check directing a bank (second party) to pay the payee (third party) sum certain on demand.

Bill of lading — Documentary evidence issued by a carrier in exchange for the receipt of goods for the purpose of shipping them. It describes the goods for identification, states the name and address of the shipper, contains the terms of shipping, point of destination, and person to whom the goods are to be delivered. It also serves as evidence of title to the shipped goods. A bill of lading may either be negotiable or nonnegotiable, although household goods shipped by an individual on a common carrier are generally documented in a nonnegotiable bill of lading.

Bill of sale — A legal instrument transferring title from the seller to the buyer. It is commonly used in sales of personal property.

Binder — (1) A receipt for money deposited to secure the right to purchase property, normally a residence, in accordance with terms previously agreed upon between buyer and seller; (2) A document issued by a title insurance company reporting the condition of title as of a certain date and stating certain qualifications that must be met before a policy of title insurance can be issued.

Binding receipt — A receipt given to a prospective insured for initial premium payment in the application process of life insurance. It gives limited protection to the applicant; permanent protection depends upon acceptance by the insurance company. If the company issues a policy, then it becomes effective as of the date of the binding receipt. If the application is not approved, then the binding effect ceases immediately.

Blackout period — Refers to a period where survivors are ineligible to receive Social Security benefits (usually ages 16 through 60).

Blanket contract — (1) A contract covering a group of people, products, etc., over a stated period of time; (2) A type of health insurance coverage affording protection for members of a certain class or group who are not individually identified.

Blanket fidelity bond — A fidelity bond providing broad coverage on all of an employer's workers, such as a bank's or brokerage firm's employees, to protect against dishonest and other specified inequitable acts which could be committed against customers, clients, or other parties. Also see "Fidelity bond."

Blanket medical expense — A provision in a health insurance contract entitling the insured to collect a maximum-dollar benefit, without regard to any limitations on types of individual medical costs.

Blanket mortgage — A mortgage covering two or more assets, typically real estate. In some instances, it covers all real property, both present and future, of a mortgager (also known as "general mortgage").

Blanket policy — An insurance policy covering many different items or properties in one location or many different locations of the same item or property. A common example would be a policy covering a building and all contents, or a policy only covering the contents of five similar buildings in different locations.

Blank indorsement — An indorsement of a negotiable instrument by simply signing one's own name (by the indorser) without specifying to whom the draft or note is to be paid and without restricting future negotiability. A blank indorsement produces an instrument payable to bearer, rather than to the order of a certain payee.

Blended-rate loan — A refinancing plan generally for real estate that mixes the interest rate on an existing mortgage with current rates.

Blind pool[1] — A limited partnership arrangement where capital contributed by the limited partners is not committed to a specific property, project, investment, or other expenditure. Instead, the general partner is authorized to invest the contributed capital in accordance with the partnership agreement.

Blind selling — A manner of selling goods without allowing the purchaser an opportunity to inspect them before executing a purchase.

Block[2] — The purchase or sale of a large number of shares of stock or dollar value of bonds that are sold as a unit. Although the term is relative, 10,000 or more shares, or any quantity worth over $200,000, is generally considered a block. The use of a block for bond purchases and sales varies with the user and normal market round-lot practices.

Blue chip stock — A high quality stock of a well-known company whose financial position is generally of the highest caliber, and whose stock is widely held. Such companies are sometimes thought of in terms of holding the dominant position in a particular industry in a manner not subject to wide cyclical swings. The holding of "blue chip investments" is a common requirement of trust agreements.

Blue Cross, Blue Shield — A nonprofit, independent, health insurance corporation generally organized on the local level to provide protection for its members against hospital costs (Blue Cross) and medical, surgical and other costs of medical care (Blue Shield).

Blue list — A daily publication by Standard & Poor's generally listing municipal bond offerings, including coupon rates, yields to maturity, and the issuer.

Blue skying[2] — A general term used for the qualification of securities for sale in any of the United States under their own securities law. Also used for the registration of broker-dealers or their agents. The expression "blue skying" means lacking substance (e.g., right out of the blue—having no worth). These state laws provide that new securities issuers qualify by providing information about the issue and the issuer so that buyers may judge the issue's value.

Blue sky laws — State laws pertaining to the offerings and sales of securities in order to protect investors from fraudulent schemes.

Board of directors — In a corporation, a governing body of persons who are elected by stockholders; top management. Their main functions are to set company policy, appoint a president and the vice-presidents, declare dividends, and generally oversee the administration of company policy. They typically consist of officers of the corporation along with non-company members.

Board of examiners — A state regulatory agency whose principal function is to examine applicants for practicing in a licensed, professional field.

Board of Governers — A seven-member board appointed by the President of the United States to govern the 12 Federal Reserve banks. Each member of the board has a 14-year term. Their main functions are to control credit policies on a nationwide basis, issue currency, issue government securities, and act as fiscal agent for the U.S. government.

Board of trade — Generally for investment purposes, a commodity exchange. Also see "Chicago Board of Trade."

Bodily injury — Generally means injury to the human body, or sickness or disease sustained by an individual during period of coverage. It includes shock-related illnesses, and in some cases mental or non-physical injuries.

Bodily injury liability insurance — Coverage against claims made against the insured arising from legal liabilities for damages from bodily injury sustained by any other person (except other insureds under the same policy).

Bogus check — A check written by a person who does not intend for it to be honored; a sham.

Boilerplating — Using verbatim the sentences, paragraphs, etc., which have a definite meaning in other documents in the process of preparing a similar document.

Bona fide — In good faith; without dishonesty; sincere; with integrity.

Bona fide purchaser (BFP) — A buyer of property who pays valuable consideration, has no notice of defects in the property's title or outstanding claims of others, and acts in good faith.

Bond — (1) A type of debt, usually long-term, issued in certificate form by a corporation, municipality, or other issuer, which typically promises to pay a specified rate of interest over a certain period of time. On the expiration date (date of maturity) the entire face amount is paid. Bond prices are directly influenced by prevailing market rates and are set according to the present value of annuity and lump-sum (interest and face amount) payments of the bond. The holder of a bond is a creditor and as such is not able to vote on the board of directors (also see "Bearer bond," "Bond discount," "Bond premium," "Callable bond," "Convertible securities," "Coupon bond," "Debenture," "Industrial development bond," "Municipal bond," "Registered bond," "Revenue bonds," "Serial bond," "Treasury bond," and "U.S. savings bond" and "Zero coupon bonds"); (2) a contractual arrangement that guarantees the performance of the person bonded (also see "Bail bond" and "Surety bond"); (3) a contractual arrangement that provides protection against dishonest acts of employees (also see "Fidelity bonds"); (4) any pledge of future performance.

Bond discount — The difference between a bond's face amount (usually $1,000) and its purchase price, which is lower. Bond discount arises because a bond's stated rate of interest is less than the market rate at the time of sale. Also see "Amortization of discount."

Bonded warehouse — Generally, a warehouse licensed by the federal government to insure against loss of customs duties, where goods subject to customs duties are stored.

Bond fund — A mutual fund (regulated investment company) dealing primarily in bonds. Some funds invest exclusively in municipal bonds or high-grade corporate bonds. The portfolio is so arranged to provide predictability of return and in the case of municipal bond funds a tax-free return.

Bond premium — The difference between a bond's purchase price, which is higher, and its face amount (usually $1,000). Because the bond's stated rate or coupon rate is higher than the prevailing market rate, it is more valuable and therefore sells for a price above its face. Also see "Amortization of bond premium."

Bond rating — A grade of bond resulting from an extensive, professional financial analysis. The highest rating is Aaa or AAA; the two largest and most respected rating agencies are Standard & Poor's and Moody's.

Quality	Moody's	S&P	Description*
High-grade	Aaa	AAA	Bonds that are judged to be of the best quality. They carry the smallest degree of investment risk and are generally referred to as "gilt-edged." Interest payments are protected by a large or exceptionally stable margin, and principal is secure.
	Aa	AA	Bonds that are judged to be of high quality by all standards. Together with the first group, they make up what are generally known as high-grade bonds. They are rated lower than the best bonds because margins of protection may not be as large.
Medium-grade	A	A	Bonds that possess many favorable investment attributes and are to be considered as upper medium-grade obligations. Factors giving security to principal and interest are considered adequate.
	Baa	BBB	Bonds that are considered as medium-grade obligations, i.e., they are neither highly protected nor poorly secured.
Speculative	Ba	BB	Bonds that are judged to have speculative elements; their future cannot be considered as well assured.

Quality	Moody's	S&P	Description*
Speculative *(continued)*			Often the protection of interest and principal payments may be very moderate.
	B	B	Bonds that generally lack characteristics of the desirable investment. Assurance of interest and principal payments or of maintenance of other terms of the contract over any long period of time may be small.
Default	Caa	CCC	Bonds that are of poor standing. Such issues may be in default, or there may be elements of danger present with respect to principal or interest.
	Ca	CC	Bonds that represent obligations which are speculative to a high degree. Such issues are often in default or have other marked shortcomings.
	C		The lowest rated class in Moody's designation. These bonds can be regarded as having extremely poor prospects of attaining any real investment standing.
		C	Rating given to income bonds on which interest is not currently being paid.
		D	Issues in default with arrears in interest or principal or both payments.

*Sources: *Fundamentals of Investment Management and Strategy,* by Geoffrey Hirt and Stanley Block (Homewood, Ill.: Richard D. Irwin, 1983), *Moody's Bond Record* (Moody's Investor's Service), and *Bond Guide* (Standard & Poor's).

Bondsman — A person who guarantees the performance of another person pursuant to a bond; a surety (e.g., a bail bondsman).

Bonus stock — (1) Stock issued with another security as an inducement to boost the latter's sales; (2) watered stock.

Bookkeeping — The process of keeping financial transactions in an orderly fashion, usually in a prescribed format, and the preparation of condensed summaries.

Book value — (1) The accounting value of a company, found by subtracting total liabilities from total assets; also known as owner's equity. Book value is not the same as fair market value; (2) an accounting value of a particular asset, found by subtracting depreciation, a reserve, or allowance account from the asset's cost. This is also known as net book value.

Book value per share — A measurement alluding to the value of a share of stock with regard to owner's equity. It is sometimes used in comparison to a stock price in price-value analysis. However, because owner's equity is used in the computation (which is historical cost rather than fair market value), it is not the same as the fair market value of a stock in terms of its current selling price. The formula is as follows:

$$\text{Book value per share} = \frac{\text{Owner's equity}}{\text{Number of shares outstanding}}$$

Boot[1] — For income tax purposes, the receipt of unlike property, usually cash, pursuant to a like-kind exchange. Qualified like-kind exchanges are not subject to tax liability, unless boot is received (in which case the unlike property may cause a partial or an entire amount of gain realized from the exchange to be taxed, or any gain from the boot—the difference between the boot's adjusted basis and fair market value—may be taxed). Also see "Tax-free exchange."

Bracket creep — The upward movement of taxpayers' taxable incomes into higher tax brackets because of cost-of-living-adjusted salaries due to inflation. The result is less spendable income than before in terms of stable dollars.

Branch banking — A banking system governed by state statutes, allowing parent institutions to operate branches throughout a state. In some states interstate branch banking is permitted. Also see "Bank holding company."

Breach of contract — Failure to perform, without legal excuse, in accordance with a contractual arrangement. Such failure can cause partial or whole breach of contract.

Breach of trust — A violation of the fiduciary duty of a trustee pursuant to a trust arrangement. It can be any action which is contrary to the terms of the trust, a wrongful omission, excessive use of a trustee's authority, or a wrongful misappropriation of trust assets.

Breach of warranty — The failure of a promise, the falsehood of a statement, or failure to perform an executory agreement (i.e., certain actions will be taken or status quo will be maintained). In real estate, failure on the seller's part to pass title to the buyer via the conveyancing document.

Break-even analysis — An analysis concerning selling price, fixed cost, varible cost, profit, and volume. It is also called cost-volume-profit analysis (CVP). At the break-even point, total sales revenue exactly equals total costs (i.e., zero profit or loss). The general formula is as follows:

$$
\begin{gather}
\text{Selling price per unit} \times \text{Number of units} = \\
\text{Variable cost per unit} \times \text{Number of units} + \text{Total fixed costs} \\
+ \text{Profits (if any)}
\end{gather}
$$

Bridge financing — A loan made during an interim period (e.g., between a short-term and long-term loan); a loan made to allow the borrower time before obtaining a more favorable long-term lending arrangement. It is commonly used in financing the purchase of large assets, such as real estate, especially when interest rates are expected to decline.

Broad form — An insurance endorsement that provides more comprehensive coverage; common in insuring buildings, comprehensive general liability, and marine insurance.

Broad form (HO-2) — See "Homeowners' insurance policy."

Broker — Generally, a person licensed to sell a certain asset for commission without owning title to the property; a person who brings together a buyer and seller; a negotiator of sales or purchases for himself or others. For example, a stockbroker buys and sells stock for the account of others. An insurance broker sells insurance from two or more companies (as opposed to an insurance agent who represents only one company). A real estate broker is licensed to be in the business of selling to third parties, managing, and negotiating loans on real estate for others.

Brokerage — The commissions or other compensation of a broker.

Broker-dealer — A securities brokerage firm licensed by the Securities and Exchange Commission and the appropriate state authorities to conduct the business of buying and selling stocks, bonds, and other securities.

Budget — (1) A financial plan over a short period (usually one year or less) apportioning various expenditures by specified amounts pursuant to the expected or allocated amount of revenue; (2) to economize.

Budget mortgage — See "PITI."

Building and loan association — A financial institution whose primary purpose is to accumulate and maintain a fund for the purpose of assisting its members in the purchase or building of homes for themselves.

Building code — A set of local laws enacted to control the construction of buildings, such as design, materials, and remodeling.

Bulk — In total; unbroken; merchandise that is not weighed, not measured, or not counted; property sold by sample that fairly represents a whole quantity.

Bulk mortgage — A nonpossessory lien on property in bulk.

Bulk sale — A relatively large sale not a part of the ordinary course of business and involves a major portion of inventory, supplies, or other assets. Sometimes refers to a complete liquidation.

Bullion — Gold or silver of a high quality of purity.

Bull market — In securities trading, the upswing of prices.

Bull spread — In the trading of options, such as puts and calls, any position that shows a gain if the underlying asset increases in value.

Burnout — A description of a tax shelter that begins to lose its tax savings attributes. Typically, burnout refers to a real estate tax shelter that begins to experience phantom income. Also see "Phantom income."

Business — Any commercial activity, profession, or trade engaged in for the purpose of earning a livelihood or profit.

Business agent — Generally, a person hired in an agency capacity to conduct the day-to-day affairs of a union, not-for-profit or commercial activity.

Business bad debt — See "Bad debt."

Business broker — An individual in the business of arranging the sale of small businesses in a manner similar to that of a real estate broker selling real estate.

Business cycle — An economic cycle consisting of prosperity, decline, then prosperity. The cycle normally covers a period of approximately two to eight years on a rotating basis.

Business expenses[1] — Deductible expenses which are incurred primarily for the furtherance of a profession, trade, or business. They must be reasonable in amount, as well as ordinary and necessary in nature.

Business insurance — A broad term generally referring to any type of protection against loss in a business setting.

Business interruption insurance — Special coverage for loss of earnings in the event an insured's business is disrupted by fire or other specified peril.

Business organization — (1) Any entity or group of persons engaged in a commercial activity for profit. It includes individuals acting alone as sole proprietors, together as partners in a partnership, an incorporated entity (corporation), and an association; (2) the internal structure of a business, which consists of the board of directors at the top, president, vice-presidents, then something similar to assistant vice-presidents, district supervisors, district managers, managers, foremen, and workers.

Business purpose — See "Profitable intent" and "Hobby loss rule."

Butterfly spread[2] — An option strategy where an investor sells two calls, then buys two calls, one with a strike price higher and one with a strike price lower than the short calls. The investor is partially hedged in either direction and hopes to profit from the call premium received and restricted movement of the underlying stock.

Buy-down financing — A type of financing arrangement, usually associated with consumer home purchases, where the seller subsidizes part of the loan by paying a portion of the interest charges and thereby reducing the buyer's initial monthly payments.

Buyer's market — A description of any market where prices have fallen in favor of the buyer. Generally, it is caused by a surplus of goods or services without an appropriate increase in demand or simply a decrease in demand without a corresponding increase in goods or services.

Buying on margin — Buying securities by using money borrowed from a broker for a portion of the purchase price. Also see "Margin."

Buy limit order — An investor's instruction to a broker or specialist to purchase a certain stock at a price no higher than a specified amount. Limit orders can be good for one day or good until canceled.

Buy-sell agreement — A contract between two or more parties, who together have related interests in certain assets, where a remaining party agrees to purchase the interest of a withdrawing party. It provides for an organized disposition of a business or investment interest and is commonly used to set the value of such interest for income and estate tax planning purposes. In many buy-sell agreements, life insurance is used to provide necessary capital to execute the transaction in case of a death of a party to the contract.

Buy stop order — An investor's instruction to a broker or specialist to purchase a certain stock, but only if its price reaches or exceeds a specified level. When the stock's price reaches or exceeds the specified value, a stop order automatically turns into a market order which signifies an immediate purchase at the best available price. Stop orders can be good for one day or good until canceled.

C

Cafeteria benefit plans — An arrangement provided by employers that allows employees to choose fringe benefits up to a specified amount. After the Tax Reform Act of 1984, only benefits which are otherwise excludable under the Internal Revenue Code can generally be offered in a qualified cafeteria benefit plan.

Calendar spread — See "Horizontal spread."

Calendar-year taxpayer — Any taxpayer whose tax year begins on January 1st.

Call — An option to purchase 100 shares of stock at a certain price for a stipulated period of time.

Callable — A security that can be purchased by its issuer (e.g., callable bond and callable preferred stock).

Callable bond — A bond that can be redeemed at the option of its issuer for a stated price (redemption price).

Call loan — In securities trading, a loan made by a broker to an investor purchasing stock on margin. It is generally secured by collateral on deposit and is callable by either the broker or investor at any time.

Call option — See "Call."

Call premium — An amount paid over face value upon redemption of securities by an issuer.

Call price — The total price paid for redeemed securities.

Canceled check — A check that has cleared a drawee bank and has no subsequent value except to serve as evidence of payment.

Cancellation — (1) A complete termination of a contract; nullification; (2) in insurance, the termination of a policy prior to expiration.

Cancellation clause — A clause in a contract, such as a lease, which allows either party to cancel or terminate the agreement according to its terms.

Capacity — For insurance purposes, the maximum amount of insurance a company will accept on one particular risk.

Capital — (1) A very broad term usually meaning assets employed to create wealth or earnings (e.g., investment capital); (2) money available or earmarked for investment; (3) in general, money, funds, or cash; (4) owner's equity; (5) total assets of a business; (6) one of the factors of production, such as machinery, factory buildings, etc.

Capital account — (1) In financial accounting, an account representing the contribution(s) of a company's owner(s) which is generally available to creditors in case of liquidation; (2) owner's equity.

Capital appreciation — An increase in value of an investment, such as a rise in a stock's price. A mere increase in value is not a taxable event.

Capital asset — For income tax purposes, almost all assets other than inventory, depreciable business assets, trade receivables, land used in a trade or business, certain artistic works created by its owner or a copyright thereto, letters, memorandums and other similar properties made by or to the taxpayer, and public documents purchased or otherwise received for an amount less than fair market value. It includes personal belongings such as jewelry, home, auto, boat, appliances, clothes, investments in stocks, bonds, real estate, most inheritances, and other personal assets not mentioned above.

Capital asset transactions — When capital assets are held for a period required for long-term status (longer than six months for tax years before 1988) and are subsequently sold for a gain, such gain qualifies for preferential long-term capital gain treatment if it is not offset by any capital losses. When capital assets are held for a period of exactly six months or less (short-term) and are sold for a gain, the entire gain is included in gross income (i.e., the gain is ordinary income), if it is not offset by any capital losses.

Capital budget — A long-range financial plan directed toward the accumulation of funds for fixed assets such as land, buildings, and equipment.

Capital contribution — Generally, assets or services provided by investors in a partnership, corporation, or other venture for profit, which includes cash, property, and in some cases actual services rendered.

Capital cost recovery system — A complex depreciation system developed to provide investment incentives and to incorporate the effects of inflation and differing rates of economic depreciation.

Capital expenditure — An expenditure that is not fully deducted or expensed in the year a transaction occurs, but instead becomes an asset or an addition to an existing asset. Thus, the purchase of any asset is a capital expenditure. The cost of improvements, betterments, or additions, which prolong life or add value to existing assets, are also capital expenditures. For income tax purposes, improvements, betterments, or additions are added to an asset's basis, which will generally increase any allowable future depreciation deductions. Assets that are acquired and expected to last longer than one year are generally capitalized in the year of acquisition.

Capital gain — For income tax purposes, gains realized from the sale of capital assets. Also see "Capital asset transactions."

Capitalization ratio — The percentages of equities that make up a company's financial structure (e.g., short-term debt 10 percent, long-term debt 20 percent, preferred stock 10 percent, and common stock 60 percent). Also see "Debt-to-equity ratio."

Capitalized — See "Capital expenditure."

Capital loss — For income tax purposes, losses realized from the sale of capital assets (i.e., the adjusted basis was greater than selling price).

Capital market — Generally refers to the buying and selling of long-term debt, such as bonds, mortgages, common stocks, and preferred stocks in well-organized exchanges (e.g., New York Stock Exchange). Also see "Money market."

Capital stock — A share of a corporation which represents ownership. It includes all classes of common and preferred stock.

Capital structure — The arrangement of a company's equities: debt (both short-term and long-term) and owner's equity (such as preferred stock and common stock).

Capricious value — An appraised value derived from a whimsical and impulsive notion; it does not reflect fair market value.

Carried interest[1] — A sharing interest found in oil and gas tax shelters where the general partner is relieved from some initial operating costs in the early stages of operation by the limited partners in exchange for more initial revenue (for the investors). After the limited partners recoup their costs, their revenues will decrease and the general partner's revenue will increase.

Carrier — (1) An insurance company accepting the risk (or carrying the insurance); (2) a person or company in the business of transporting goods or passengers.

Carryback — A provision in the Internal Revenue Code (Section 172(b)) allowing taxpayers to use a net operating loss against income taxes paid in each of the three taxable years preceding the net operating loss (and a carryforward over the following 15 years).

Carrying charges — (1) Any additional charges, other than interest, assessed by a creditor for providing installment credit (e.g., service charges or handling fees); (2) for investments, expenses incurred for holding investment property (such as interest, rent, taxes, and handling costs).

Carrying value — For an investor in bonds, an amount which is adjusted according to the amount of interest received versus interest accrued. The difference between the two types of interests will either increase or decrease the carrying value, depending upon whether the bond was purchased for a discount or premium. The starting point for carrying value is the price of the bonds. For an example of discounted bonds, say 10 bonds are purchased for $9,400 ($10,000 face value) which are to pay 10 percent per year semiannually, but are to yield 11 percent (the current market rate). Upon receipt of the first interest payment of $500 (5 percent × $10,000) and the computation of accrued interest $517 (5.5 percent × $9,400), the $17 difference is added to the purchase price to equal a carrying value of $9,417. After all interest payments have been made (maturity date), the carrying value will equal face value. The carrying value is a similar concept to the balance of principal in other debt obligations. Also see "Amortization of bond discount" and "Amortization of bond premium."

Cash advance — (1) A loan made in cash from using a credit card at a participating bank; (2) any advance payment for future services to be rendered or goods to be received.

Cash basis of accounting — A method of accounting for income and expenses that recognizes revenue only when cash is received and recognizes expenses only when cash is paid. Also see "Accrual method of accounting."

Cash basis taxpayer — One who uses cash basis accounting.

Cash discount — A reduction in billing price allowed by a seller if payment is made within a certain period of time (e.g., 3/10/n30 means a 3 percent discount is allowed if paid within 10 days or the entire amount is due in 30 days).

Cash dividend — A corporate distribution made in cash from a company's earnings and profits to its shareholders. Cash dividends are paid after a formal dividend declaration (date of declaration) by the board of directors to all stockholders of record as of a certain date (date of record). Generally for income tax purposes, the first $100 ($200 for married filing jointly) is excluded from taxation. Also see "Return of capital dividend," "Stock dividend," "Tax preference items."

Cash equivalent doctrine — Generally, all taxpayers must include in their gross incomes amounts that are earned or profits. Cash basis taxpayers are to include such amounts when actually or constructively received, even if property is received rather than cash. Thus, in a taxable event the amount of such property is included in gross income (usually at fair market value).

Cash flow — (1) Total cash receipts minus cash outflows; (2) the net inflow of cash from earnings, rents, dividends, interest, royalties, annuity payments, trust payments, or other income less cash expenses attributed to such income (e.g., carrying charges).

Cash flow per share — The total amount of cash inflow per share of common stock:

$$\text{Cash flow per share} = \frac{\text{Total cash flow}}{\text{Average number of shares outstanding}}$$

Cash flow statement — An informal financial statement showing all inflows and outflows of cash. Such statement is usually prepared monthly.

Cash generated from operations — In the investment analysis of a corporation's earnings, a figure that portrays the net cash flow derived from the sale of its services or inventory less cash expenses. It is sometimes used in judging the quality of net income (accounting net income versus cash generated from operations), such as whether credit sales are excessive or not. Or, cash generated from operations can serve as an indicator of future performance when compared with other factors because of its recurring nature. For example, assume Z Company, M Company, and A Company each have a net income of $1 million and are in well-established businesses. Z Company uses credit sales and has an accounts receivable balance at year-end of $250,000 resulting from such sales. M Company sold some equipment and other non-inventory assets for $300,000 and A Company has practically no accounts receivable balance nor any non-inventory sales. The quality of earnings (cash receipts from operations) is definitely in favor of A Company because there are no significant accounts to collect, and its earnings are considered to be recurring in nature rather than from the sale of fixed assets.

Cashier's check — A check drawn by a bank on its own account for a customer in exchange for valuable consideration (e.g., cash) and is made payable to a party named by the customer.

Cash-liquidating value[1] — A liquidity feature offered by tax shelter partnerships where the general partner agrees to purchase an appraised value of a limited partner's interest upon exercise of the agreement.

Cash management — The process of controlling cash and other liquid assets in order to benefit from an expanded holding period or timing of disbursements. For example, receipts are accelerated and disbursements are held until the due date in order to obtain maximum benefits from interest earned.

Cash method of accounting — See "Accounting methods."

Cash or deferred arrangement — If qualified, a profit-sharing or stock bonus plan that allows employees to receive cash immediately or to accrue deferred benefits without inclusion in gross income until receipt (401(k) plan).

Cash position — Typically, this refers to cash and near-cash items (such as marketable securities); liquid-asset position.

Cash refund annuity — An annuity that allows a lump-sum refund to a beneficiary in case the annuitant dies before receiving the amount of original cost.

Cash reserves — For a life insurance company, an amount that must be available to guarantee future obligations in accordance with state law.

Cash surrender value — In life insurance policies and annuity contracts, an amount of cash available to a policyholder upon canceling or surrendering the contract before death (or in the case of an endowment contract, before maturity). It equals cash reserves less any withdrawals, unpaid loans, unpaid interest on loans, and cancellation charges.

Cash value — (1) Cash surrender value of a life insurance policy; (2) fair market value of an item; (3) the price of property if sold for cash immediately (i.e., without holding such property a reasonable amount of time until a buyer appears); liquidity value.

Cash value option — An option available to the policyholder of a life insurance contract at the time of surrender (i.e., when premiums are not paid) to receive the cash surrender value. Other options include extended term insurance and paid-up insurance. Also see "Nonforfeiture."

Casual employment — Employment that is characteristically irregular, occasional, uncertain, or temporary in nature. Usually such employment is without fringe benefits and in some states may not be subject to worker's compensation (at the employer's election).

Casualty insurance — Insurance that is usually concerned with the legal liability imposed upon an insured for losses caused by injuring others or damaging the property of others. Each state defines the kinds of insurance that a casualty insurer is permitted to write.

Casualty loss — For income tax purposes, deductible losses arising from the destruction of property because of an identifiable event that is sudden, unexpected, and unusual in nature. Damages from willful acts or willful negligence are not deductible casualty losses. Qualified casualties normally include damages from storms, floods, tornados, hurricanes, automobile accidents, sonic booms, fires, and vandalism.

Catastrophe — A severely damaging event, such as a hurricane, in which insurance companies collectively pay $5 million or more in benefits; any loss that can financially destroy the stability of an insurance company (catastrophic loss).

Cattle-breeding arrangements[1] — A syndicated tax-sheltering investment in the production of cattle. It consists of two different kinds: seed-stock and commercial-breeding. Seed-stock arrangements are primarily concerned with upgrading cattle and generally require more expertise. Commercial-breeding shelters typically produce calves for sale, but occasionally retain them for further breeding. Less risk is normally associated with commercial-breeding activities, although most cattle-breeding arrangements are considered to be extremely risky investments.

Cattle-feeding arrangements — A syndicated tax-sheltering arrangement involving the purchasing of steers, fattening them over a short period, and selling them for a higher price. Due to the many changes in tax law, however, limited partnership arrangements have been hurt in this area.

Caveat — A warning; let the person beware.

Caveat emptor — Let the buyer beware. This usually applies to non-consumer sales such as auctions where the buyer must inspect all purchases carefully because he or she must take the risk regarding condition or quality, unless a warranty or misrepresentation exists.

Caveat venditor — Let the seller beware.

Cede — To grant, yield, assign, give up.

Certificate — (1) A written official representation stating that a certain formality has occurred, a specific condition exists, a stipulated act has or has not been performed, or a particular obligation or right exists; (2) in insurance, a document issued to individuals covered under a group policy stating the general provisions of their coverage.

Certificate of deposit (CD) — A negotiable instrument issued by a bank, evidencing a time deposit. Upon maturity, the depositor or other appropriate holder will receive the deposit plus stated interest, which is usually at or near the prevailing market rate for short-term government securities. Thus, interest on CDs are higher than ordinary passbook accounts if held to maturity, but withdrawal privileges are not available without a substantial interest penalty.

Certificate of eligibility — As applied to veterans, a document obtained from the Veterans Adminstration stating that the named veteran is eligible for a VA loan.

Certificate of incorporation — A document filed with the appropriate state officials (usually the Secretary of State) evidencing the existence of a corporation. Also see "Articles of incorporation."

Certificate of stock — A document exhibiting ownership in a corporation. The corporation, class of stock, number of shares, par or stated value, and the owner's name is generally presented on the face of the certificate.

Certificate of title — In real estate, an opinion written by an attorney, who has examined abstracts or chains of title, stating the condition of title to a certain parcel of land. It is sometimes furnished by a title insurance company, but the company is only liable for the professional performance (or lack thereof) of its examiner.

Certified check — A check written by a bank's customer that is guaranteed by the bank. Such check will have the words "accepted" or "certified" written on its face along with the date and signature of a proper bank official. A certified check becomes the bank's obligation to pay when presented by the appropriate party. Thus, it is the obligation of a bank to hold necessary funds in order to pay a check written by one of its customers from a his or her own personal account. A bank is under no obligation to certify a check, unless a previous agreement is made. Also see "Cashier's check."

Certified copy — A copy of a document that is attested to be an exact duplicate by an officer holding the original.

Certified Financial Planner (CFP) — An individual who has met the requirements to hold the CFP designation as set by the College for Financial Planning in Denver, Colorado. CFPs must exhibit general knowledge in investments, insurance, tax planning, retirement planning, and estate planning.

Certified Public Accountant (CPA) — An individual licensed by a state regulatory board to attest audited financial statements, to represent clients before the Internal Revenue Service, and to hold one's self out as an expert in public accounting.

Certiorari — A review by a higher court of the findings of a lower court. In modern times, it is usually associated with the United States Supreme Court, which judiciously uses the writ of certiorari to choose its cases.

Chain of title — The consecutively arranged order of successive conveyences pertaining to a certain parcel of realty. It commences with the original owner (typically the government) and ends with the present holder.

Chairman of the board — Generally, the highest ranking board member of a corporation. He is elected by the board of directors and in some cases is the chief executive officer (CEO) of the corporation.

Chapter II (reorganization) — A reorganization under court supervision because a business (debtor) is unable to pay its debts as they become due or because the likelihood of insolvency is high. The action may be initiated either voluntarily or involuntarily. Generally, the business is allowed to continue as the debtor submits a plan of reorganization, which is to be approved or modified by the creditors. If an agreement cannot be finalized, the corporation will be liquidated under court supervision.

Chapter 13 (wage earners) — A voluntary plan developed and proposed by a debtor who has regular income (as wage earner) to a bankruptcy court. The plan provides additional time (usually three to five years subject to court approval) to pay off debts. Generally, the plan must allow future income to be supervised by a court-appointed trustee until all specified debts are satisfied. Only the court can approve or deny such plan, not the creditors. Filing under Chapter 13 provides relief by stopping all collection and bankruptcy proceedings against the debtor.

Charge account — An accounting device used to keep the balance of credit purchases, carrying charges, and interest, as well as payments made; an arrangement for purchases on credit. Also see "Accounts payable."

Charge-off — In accounting, an adjustment of an asset account by writing-off, amortizing, or eliminating (such as write-off of an account receivable).

Charitable contribution deduction — A donation to a qualified charitable organization allowing the donor an income tax deduction. Cash or property, not services, is allowed up to a maximum limit of 50 percent adjusted gross income among other limitations (such as type of property, type of organization, order of deductibility, and carryover provisions). Also see "Charitable organization."

Charitable lead trust — Generally, a trust to which a grantor transfers income-producing property, from which contributions are made to various qualified charitable organizations, with a remainder interest vested in a chosen individual (e.g., a family member). In effect, this gives the grantor an income tax deduction each year for income that would have been earned by him or her, a gift and estate tax deduction for qualifying trusts, as well as retain the property in the family.

Charitable organization — An organization engaged in benevolent acts for the good of the public; for tax purposes, any organization operated exclusively for religious, charitable, scientific, testing for public safety, literary, educational, fostering amateur sports, or preventing cruelty to children or animals that is qualified by the Internal Revenue Service. Practically all churches, nonprofit schools and hospitals, and other benevolent organizations, such as the United Way, Salvation Army, Goodwill, Girl Scouts, and U.S. political subdivisions qualify.

Charitable remainder trust — A trust formed to pay income to a noncharitable beneficiary and to pay the entire remainder interest to a qualified charitable organization or purpose. Charitable deductions are allowed for qualified contributions of a remainder interest in trust for income, gift, and estate taxes. Such trusts must either be a charitable remainder annuity trust or a charitable remainder unitrust.

Charitable trust — Any trust created to support religion, education, relief of poverty, health, a governmental or municipal purpose, or other cause that is qualified by the Internal Revenue Service. Generally, the purpose of a charitable trust is to benefit a sufficiently large and indefinite class of people in such manner that the community would be responsive to the benevolent purposes of its enforcement.

Chartered Financial Analyst (CFA) — A securities analyst or portfolio manager who has met the experience and testing requirements for receiving the designation. Generally, a CFA must exhibit general knowledge in accounting, securities analysis, ethics, portfolio management, and other business-related fields.

Chartered Financial Consultant (ChFC) — An individual who has met the requirements for the designation as set by the American College in Bryn Mawr, Pennsylvania. Generally, a ChFC must exhibit general knowledge of insurance, investments, retirement planning, estate planning, and income tax planning.

Chartered Life Underwriter (CLU) — An individual who has met the requirements for the designation as set by the American College in Bryn Mawr, Pennsylvania. Generally, a CLU must pass 10 examinations, on life and health insurance as well as other broadly related business subjects.

Chartered Property and Casualty Underwriter (CPCU) — An individual who has met the requirements for the designation as set by the American Institute for Property and Liability Underwriters in Malvern, Pennsylvania. Generally, a CPCU must pass 10 examinations, on general insurance and other broadly related business subjects.

Chartist — An investment analyst whose principal technique consists of interpreting charts which plot price movements of a security and charts showing market changes in order to perceive developing patterns and trends; technical analyst. Compare "Fundamental analysis."

Chattel — Personal property.

Chattel mortgage — A security interest in or lien on personal property.

Check — A three-party negotiable instrument, where one party writes it (the drawer) payable to another party (the payee) on demand at or on a bank (the drawee); a type of draft. The magic words of negotiability must appear on its face: "payable to order" or "payable to bearer."

Check register — An expanded checkbook showing the accounts where payments were made; a cash disbursements journal.

Chicago Board of Trade (CBT) — The largest commodity exchange. It trades in both commodity futures, financial futures, and futures options on Treasury bonds. The Chicago Board of Trade is the parent company of the Chicago Board Options Exchange.

Chicago Board Options Exchange (CBOE) — An exchange trading security options.

Chicago Mercantile Exchange (CME) — A large commodity exchange primarily known for trading in international currencies, livestock, meat, and lumber. It is the parent company of the International Monetary Market.

Child care credit — An income tax credit available for qualified individuals who are employed and incur expenses for household and dependent care services that are necessary to maintain gainful employment (Form 2441).

Child support — A payment made in accordance with a divorce decree or separation agreement subsidizing the rearing of one's children. Child support payments are not included in the recipient's income for income tax purposes, and they are not deductible by the payer.

Chilling a sale — A conspiracy among buyers or bidders at a sale or auction to lower prices by suppressing competition.

Chose in action — A right to an action to procure money (recover debt) or to possess property held by another. Chose in action is the right of action for possession rather than actual possession.

Chose in possession — Items in possession (rather than a right to possession).

C.I.F. — See "Cost, insurance, and freight."

Circa — Approximately or around a certain date.

Civil action — An equitable or legal action brought to enforce or protect private rights; generally, any legal action other than criminal action.

Civil law — Law chiefly concerned with private rights and remedies, rather than criminal. Laws which are established by a nation or political subdivision peculiarly for itself.

Claim — (1) A demand for property as one's own; (2) an assertion of some right; (3) in insurance, a demand by an insured for payment from an insurance company because of the occurrence of an insured event (e.g., death, disability, medical bills, hospitalization, damage or destruction of property, defects or challenges to the title to real estate, surety loss, and acts of negligence).

Claim adjustment process — The procedures of checking an insured's coverage, inspecting damages, investigating the occurrence which caused damage or loss, attempting to reach agreement concerning settlement, and filing all necessary reports and forms.

Claim of right doctrine[1] — Taxpayers must include in gross income amounts that are actually or constructively received and are unrestricted.

Claims Court (U.S.) — A federal court of original jurisdiction that hears tax cases and other matters.

Class action suit — A legal action brought on by one or more persons of a group, who have similar claims, without having to join all members. It has become an increasingly popular way for consumers to combat unfair pricing when only one isolated instance would probably have an insignificant effect.

Classification of risks — In insurance, the rating of a particular risk according to the nature of items to be insured or occupation of proposed insured, location and situation involved, present condition of the items or health of the individual, and other relevant factors.

Classified property tax[1] — A system of taxing property according to its classification. Certain classes are taxed at rates much higher than others, and special classes are exempt altogether.

Classified stock — In a corporation, common or preferred stock that is authorized, according to the articles of incorporation, to have different classes which carry different characteristics as to rights and privileges. For example, assume Class A common stock has dividend and voting privileges, but restricted transferability; Class B common has dividend rights, but no voting privileges and restricted transferability; Class C common has dividend rights, no voting privileges, and unrestricted transferability.

Class life — Under the accelerated cost recovery system (ACRS), the number of years an asset's cost is to be expensed: light duty trucks and automobiles have a 3-year class life, most all other equipment and machinery have a 5-year class life, and buildings (other than low-income housing) have an 18-year class life).

Class-year vesting — For profit-sharing employee benefit plans, a type of vesting where each contribution made by an employer becomes a 100 percent nonforfeitable right after a certain period of time has elapsed. That is, each year's contribution vests separately, which is generally no later than the end of the fifth year following the particular contribution.

Clayton Act — A federal law enacted in 1914 to supplement the Sherman Antitrust Act. It prohibits mergers that might hinder competition or create a monopoly, exclusive dealing arrangements, price discrimination, tying arrangements, and interlocking directorates.

Clearinghouse — A place where banks and other financial institutions exchange checks and settle other claims to reconcile their balances. Practically all clearinghouse functions are now performed automatically on computers.

Clear title — A title to property which is free and clear from any liens, burdens, obstructions, or other limitations; marketable title.

Client's privilege — The right to privacy between a client and a doctor, clergy, or attorney; the right to keep secret the communications between an attorney and his or her client.

Clifford trust — A reversionary trust generally used by high-income taxpayers to shift income to others. It usually entails the transfer of passive, income-producing investments to a trust for a period of time (usually 10 years), after which ownership of trust assets revert back to original transferor. One of the following characteristics must be met: (1) the trust arrangement is established for a period of more than 10 years, or (2) the trust arrangement is based on the life of the beneficiary (regardless of life expectancy), or (3) the trust arrangement is based on the life expectancy of a third party (life expectancy must be greater than 10 years). It is commonly used to spread income to family members. Sometimes called a short-term reversionary trust.

Close corporation — A corporation whose voting shares of stock are held by either one or few shareholders. Generally, if a few shareholders own such stock, they are a group joined together through some common interest or family relationship. Close corporation stock is not publicly held, and its shareholders usually benefit personally from controlling corporate policy. In most cases, transferability of a close corporation's voting stock is restricted.

Closed-end investment company — A publicly held investment company investing in stocks of other corporations and having a fixed number of outstanding shares, which are traded on a stock exchange. Unlike mutual funds, closed-end funds do not redeem their shares for net asset value (NAV); instead, the shares are bought and sold at a prevailing market price just like other stocks of publicly traded corporations. Because market factors directly influence a closed-end company's price per share, the fundamental concern for this type of investment is a selling price below the net asset value (discount), which sometimes creates a buying opportunity for investors. They are also known as closed-end investment trusts (CEITs) and publicly traded funds. Compare "Mutual fund."

Closed-end investment trust (CEIT) — See "Closed-end investment company."

Closed-end lease — A long-term rental agreement allowing the lessee to "walk away" after the end of its term. Compare "Open-end lease."

Closed-end mortgage — A mortgage having no provisions for additional loans. Most all consumer home loans are closed-end. Also used in mortgage bonds as a provision that prohibits the issuer from using the same collateral without obtaining permission from the holders of the first mortgage.

Closed insurance policy — An insurance policy that does not allow changing its terms or rates.

Closed stock — In consumer sales, merchandise that must be sold in entire sets, rather than in individual pieces. Common in sales of silverware and china, it is generally without guarantees for replacing lost or damaged pieces.

Closely held corporation — See "Close corporation."

Closing — (1) in real property transactions, the final steps in completing a sale: money or other assets are delivered, mortgage is secured, and all necessary documents are recorded or executed in accordance with the Real Estate Settlement Procedures Act. Such documents may include deed, survey, abstract of title, mortgage, promissory note, insurance policies, and receipts for taxes and utilities; (2) in general sales, the point at which a sales presentation begins to directly bring a prospective purchaser into agreement in order to finalize the sale.

Closing costs — Incidental amounts paid in finalizing a real estate transaction. Generally, these costs include fees for various legal and financing services such as title examination, property appraisals, surveys, title insurance, deed preparation, credit reports, notarizing documents, settlement statement, escrows for certain subsequent obligations, discount points, and loan origination fees.

Closing statement — In real estate transactions, a written statement disclosing financial settlement between buyer and seller. It lists in detail the purchase price less expenses plus any other amounts due the seller to arrive at net selling price.

Cloud on title — An invalid claim or encumbrance on real property, which, if valid, would affect the owner's rights (e.g., a deed is erroneously drawn up to specify a different tract of land from the one orginally agreed to—this is an invalid claim which creates a cloud on the different tract of land).

Club account — A special savings account established for a particular purpose (e.g., Christmas Club account).

COBOL — Common Business Oriented Language; a computer language that was developed for accounting or other business purposes.

COD — See "Collect on delivery."

Code — For income taxes, the Internal Revenue Code.

Codicil — An explanation, addition or alteration to an existing will. If a testator dies leaving a will and one or more codicils, then the last will constitutes all such documents taken together. Thus, codicils are merely used to change a will rather than to implement an entirely new one or to completely revoke an old one.

Codification — The process of gathering and systematically organizing the laws of a particular subject, such as codifying the tax laws into the Internal Revenue Code of 1954.

Coinsurance — (1) In general, an arrangement which calls for sharing an insured risk; (2) in property insurance, a provision in a policy requiring the policyholder to maintain a certain amount of insurance equal to a stipulated percentage of its fair market value. All losses will be fully paid, up to the policy's face amount, if the amount of insurance carried is at least equal to the specified percentage; (3) in health insurance contracts, a clause stating that the company is liable for a certain percentage (usually 80 percent) for covered expenses in excess of the deductible and the insured is liable for the residual (usually 20 percent); (4) a reinsurance arrangement between insurance companies.

Coinsurer — An individual or company who shares a loss covered by an insurance policy. Coinsurer typically applies to an insured owner of damaged property who did not maintain enough insurance to comply with the policy's coinsurance provision and consequently must suffer a portion of the loss.

COLA — Cost-of-living adjustment; it is sometimes used to measure the amount of increased wages or benefits to be paid due to inflation.

Collateral — (1) Generally, property used as security to cover the principal amount of a debt or other obligation in case of default. Also see "Collateral security"; (2) something parallel to, addition to, complementary to, or attached to another object in a contingent or subordinate manner.

Collateral ancestors — Usually, ancestors who are not in direct line, such as uncles, aunts, and cousins.

Collateral security — A pledge given to guarantee the validity of a direct security, in that if the direct security fails, a creditor may use the collateral security for satisfying the debt.

Collateral trust bond — A bond issued by one company and secured by the holding of marketable securites, usually, of other corporations. Such holdings are placed in a trust. A collateral trust bond is also known as a "collateral trust certificate."

Collectibles — (1) Generally, items that are gathered and held because of desirable effects—beauty, possible value-appreciation, age, and scarcity; (2) for tax purposes, assets which are prohibited as investments for individual retirement accounts, such as art, rugs, alcoholic beverages, antiques, gems, coins, gold, silver, stamps and other similar items; (3) any obligation held by one in which payment may be called for by legal means and is relatively certain, such as promissory notes, accounts receivable, and bonds.

Collect on delivery (COD) — A method of purchasing items whereby the carrier is instructed to collect for the cost of goods before delivery or the goods will be returned to the seller.

College for Financial Planning — A nonprofit organization that develops courses of study and tests worthy candidates for the Certified Financial Planner (CFP) designation.

Collision insurance — Insurance covering damages caused by collision with any object, which is either moving or stationary, to an insured object (e.g., an automobile or a truck). It reimburses an insured for such damages after an adjustment for the amount of an appropriate deductible. One important aspect of collision insurance is that coverage still applies while any person, who reasonably believes he or she has the right to use an insured vehicle, is operating it. Collision insurance only provides protection against loss sustained to an insured vehicle, not bodily injury or liability caused by a collision.

Color of title — Pertains to the appearance of good title, but in fact, contains some defect.

Co-maker — A person who signs a promissory note with one or more persons, and each is equally responsible for payment; a type of surety.

Combination personal-lines package policy — One policy providing coverage for consumers in more than one area of insurance, such as basic casualty, basic property, and forms of life-health protection. It usually provides the insured with a discount when compared to purchasing individual policies in each area of insurance coverage.

Combination policy — Any insurance policy combining coverages customarily reserved for two or more policies (e.g., a combined home and auto policy).

Comex^2 — A commodity exchange in New York City. Formed by merger of four prior exchanges, Comex trades futures in metals, petroleum, coffee, sugar, and financial instruments.

Commerce — Generally refers to trading, buying, and selling of goods and services on a large scale between relatively large entities, such as corporations, states, and nations.

Commercial bank — A financial institution whose principal functions are to receive demand deposits and time deposits, make short-term loans, engage in trust activities, accept and pay checks, issue safe-deposit boxes, and various other financially related services. Because banks lend money, accept deposits, and retain only a small portion thereof (called reserves), they have the ability to "create" money.

Commercial broker — A person who negotiates the sale of items without holding title or possession.

Commercial insurance — (1) In general, virtually any type of insurance that is issued by a for-profit company and is voluntary in nature. It is life, health, disability, casualty, property, liability, fire, marine, surety, fidelity, aviation, title, malpractice, and other insurances. Commercial insurance generally refers to the insurance industry or insurance business, as opposed to compulsory governmental or social insurance (e.g., Social Security), cooperative insurance (e.g., Blue Cross/Blue Shield), or voluntary governmental insurance (e.g., Federal Crop Insurance Corporation); (2) any type of business insurance, rather than personal insurance; (3) sometimes refers to a specific type of surety arrangement where one party to a contract is guaranteed against loss because of breach of contract by the other party (e.g., construction contract bonds).

Commercial paper — (1) Broadly defined, negotiable instruments used to pay debts normally occurring in the course of business. It includes drafts, bills of exchange, promissory notes, etc.; (2) in the money market, a short-term promissory note issued by large corporations and sold at discount. They have a maturity period of 270 days or less and are not required to be registered with the Securities and Exchange Commission.

Commission — Compensation paid for the selling of goods and services. It is determined by taking a percentage of the total dollar amount sold, a fixed amount per item, or any other method that varies according to volume. This type of compensation tends to provide incentives for salespersons to prospect, make presentations, and close sales. Insurance agents and brokers, real estate agents and brokers, stockbrokers, financial planners, loan originators, travel agents, automobile salespersons, commercial carrier representatives, auctioneers, and other salespersons are customarily compensated in this manner. Compensation by salary is unlike commissions in that payment is made regardless of output. Many compensation packages, however, combine commissions and salary.

Commission agent — See "Commission merchant."

Commissioner of insurance — A state official in charge of enforcing state insurance laws. Also known as superintendent of insurance or director of insurance.

Commission merchant — A person who receives goods on consignment and sells such goods for commission in his or her own name. Also known as commission agent or factor.

Commitment fee — An amount paid by a borrower to a lender for the latter's commitment in making a loan. It is very common in real estate mortgages.

Commodities exchange — An organized facility where commodity futures, and to a lesser extent commodities, are bought and sold. A few exchanges, such as the Minneapolis Grain Exchange, however, do concentrate on nonfutures trading. It originates and supervises the trading of contracts and is regulated by the Commodity Futures Trading Commission (CFTC).

Commodity — (1) Anything that is valuable, useful, or serviceable and can be sold. Goods bought and sold during the course of commercial trade; merchandise; (2) a staple or other item (such as wheat) bought and sold in a commodity exchange. Also see "Commodity futures."

Commodity fund — Generally, a regulated investment company specializing in commodities. Some deal exclusively with agricultural commodities, metals, financial futures, or any combination thereof. They must be registered with both the Securities and Exchange Commission (SEC) and the Commodity Futures Trading Commission. An event that is peculiar to such funds occurs when the net asset value falls below a specified level of beginning assets (such as 60 percent) in that all positions are immediately closed.

Commodity futures — Contracts for the future delivery of commodities. They are traded on regulated commodity exchanges and represent the future delivery of such commodities during a specified month (typically March, May, July, September, December). Some of the more common commodities traded in this fashion are corn, rice, soybeans, wheat, cotton, soybean oil, potatoes, pork bellies, coffee, sugar, cocoa, lumber, plywood, gold, oats, silver, platinum, live cattle, and live hogs. Also see "Forward contract" and "Futures contract."

Commodity Futures Trading Commission (CFTC)[2] — The Federal regulator of commodities exchanges and all futures trading, headquartered in Washington, D.C.

Commodity price index — Generally, any price index pertaining to commodities, such as a spot price index, consumer price index, futures price index, wholesale price index, etc. The Dow Jones Spot Index (prices for immediate delivery) and Dow Jones Future Index (prices for future delivery) are two examples of indexes measuring current prices of commodities.

Common disaster clause — A clause in a will or life insurance policy providing an alternate (secondary) beneficiary when the insured and primary beneficiary die simultaneously.

Common law — Any law that is not enacted by legislation (e.g., case law).

Common law liability — Any responsibility placed upon a party, because of injury or damage to others, by laws that derive their authority from custom, usage, or prior court decisions.

Common stock — A certificate representing ownership in a corporation, which generally entitles the owner to receive a portion of company's earnings (dividend), the right to vote in the election of members of the board of directors, and to receive any remaining assets (in the order of priority) in case of liquidation. Common stock is listed as part of contributed capital in the owner's equity section of a balance sheet. Also see "Classified stock" and "Preferred (pfd) stock."

Common trust fund — A trust fund that is composed of many different individual trust funds, which are commingled to reduce administrative costs and to diversify investments. Banks, trust companies, and pension funds often use this type of fund management, which is regulated by statutes.

Community property — Property that is deemed to be owned jointly by husband and wife. Property that was not acquired from separate funds or other sources as separate property is community property in community property states (i.e., not property owned prior to marriage or received by gift or inheritance). The community property states are Arizona, California, Idaho, Louisiana, Nevada, New Mexico, Texas, and Washington.

Commutation of taxes — An exemption or settlement from taxes (such as an ad valorem tax) because of prepayment.

Comparative sales method — In real estate, a method of estimating a certain property's fair market value by comparing recent prices of similar properties in the same area.

Compensating balance — A minimum amount of money that a

bank's customer is required to keep on deposit for the purpose of securing a loan, avoiding bank service charges, or obtaining a future line of credit.

Compensatory damages — Damages awarded an injured party only for injury in an effort to make good, replace, or compensate for such loss. Generally, compensatory damages received for personal injury are nontaxable, even if they represent loss of income. Such damages received for loss of business income, however, are usually taxable.

Complex trust — (1) Any trust not classified as a simple trust. Generally, a trust allowing the trustee control over distribution of trust income, at least one of the beneficiaries is a qualifying charitable organization, or a distribution of corpus is made; (2) A trust having detailed provisions outlining the functions of the trustee (or other matters) in comparison with a simple trust. Compare "Simple trust."

Compound interest — Any account or fund that allows interest to be earned on both principal and accrued interest. Compound interest results when interest earned during one period becomes an amount on which future interest is computed. In other words, compound interest is the principal plus any accrued interest multiplied times the rate of interest. This method will expand the principal much faster than without compounding.

Comprehensive automobile insurance — Automobile insurance that provides coverage for all perils except collision. Also see "Automobile insurance."

Comprehensive coverage — Generally in insurance, a term designating coverage of a variety of losses; broad protection.

Comprehensive form (HO-5) — See "Homeowner's insurance policy."

Comprehensive major medical — A type of health insurance policy designed to provide blanket medical expense protection offered by both a basic medical plan (which covers hospital room and board, doctor's and nurses services, surgery, prescription drugs, medicines, anesthesia, blood, oxygen, X-rays, and other items and services) and catastrophic medical protection (high maximum limits). It usually carries a low deductible ($50–$250), coinsurance (typically 20 percent–80 percent, which means the insured pays 20 percent for all medical expenses incurred in excess of the deductible), and in some policies a stop-loss amount (the insurer pays all losses in full above a certain amount, say $5,000). Also see "Group major medical expense insurance."

Comprehensive personal liability insurance — A type of liability insurance which provides protection against loss arising out of legal liability against an insured for injuring or causing damage to others. It does not include business or automobile liabilities.

Comprehensive policy — A general term which usually means an insurance policy providing broad coverage.

Comptroller — The person in charge of an accounting department. The chief management accounting executive who is reponsible for compiling, reporting, and interpreting financial and tax accounting information. In most companies, the comptroller reports directly to the chief financial officer.

Compulsory insurance — Any type of insurance that is required by law (such as Social Security and automobile liability insurance).

Compulsory sale — An involuntary sale of property because of eminent domain, failure to pay taxes, or similar circumstances.

Conciliation — A friendly settlement of a dispute or bargaining process.

Concurrent estates — The simultaneous ownership or possession of property by two or more persons (e.g., tenancy in common).

Condemnation — The taking of private property without owner's consent under the right of eminent domain for the purpose of public use. According to the U.S. Constitution, just compensation must be paid to the owner.

Condition — As used in law and business, something contingent upon the occurrence of a specified event.

Conditional indorsement — An indorsement of a negotiable instrument which fixes a condition to the indorser's contingent liability, other than the ability of other parties to pay. All subsequent transferees must either comply with such condition or be sure it was done (e.g., pay Jones if XYZ work is done, signed Smith). A special indorsement that includes a condition. Also see "Restrictive indorsement" or "Qualified indorsement."

Conditional sales contract — A sales contract where the seller holds title to property until the buyer fulfills a specific condition, at which time title passes to the buyer. Typically, such condition is settlement of full payment.

Condition precedent — An arrangement whereby a certain occurrence must take place before an agreement becomes effective. One party must act before the other is obligated; failure to perform by the first party relieves the obligation of the second party. According to most insurance agreements, insureds must provide the insurance company with timely notice and proper proof before a claim becomes payable. An inheritance or distribution from a trust may be a condition precedent in that the beneficiary must perform a certain task before any transfer can be made.

Condition subsequent — An arrangement whereby a certain occurrence must take place after an agreement. Failure to perform may relieve the second party or defeat the continuance of an estate. For example, in an insurance proceeding failure of an insured to cooperate in defending a claim may relieve the insurer's obligation to pay. For an example applying to distributions of a trust or estate, a certain condition must be maintained or fulfilled in order to continue such payments.

Condo conversion — The process of selling individual units in an apartment house (i.e., turning rental units into condominiums).

Condominium — A residential building with two or more separate units that are individually owned (interior space). The rest of the property (common area), such as land, recreational facilities, and grounds, is proportionately owned.

Condominium unit-owners' form (HO-6) — See "Homeowner's insurance policy."

Conduit principle — An accounting technique for income tax purposes enabling particular forms of business organizations to "pass through" certain tax benefits, such as tax deductions and tax credits, directly to its owners (e.g., partnerships and S corporations).

Confession of judgment — A voluntary submission to a court by a debtor stating that debt is owed to a creditor for a specified amount.

Confidence game — A system of wrongful presentations, trickery, deceit, false representations, and device in order to gain the confidence of prospective contributors in an effort to take their assets.

Confidential communication — Communications intended to be received only by the person to whom it is addressed; privileged communication between two parties. Confidential communication is generally determined by the circumstances in which the parties interact (i.e., without the presence of an accompanying third party who is not necessary for the communication). Also see "Privileged communications."

Confidential dealings — Business or other dealings performed in secrecy (e.g., private communications between two persons).

Confidential relationship — A fiduciary relationship between two parties, such as client–attorney, patient–doctor, and husband–wife.

Confirmation — A written memorandum or verbal statement showing that a certain occurrence did take place or an amount is accurate; an affirmation, verification, or approval (e.g., a credit confirmation).

Confirmation of sale — The approval of a court-ordered sale and its terms, conditions, or price.

Confirming bank — A bank which will honor a letter of credit that was previously issued by another bank.

Confiscation — The taking of private property without compensation because of illegality of the confiscated property (such as narcotics) or other circumstances contrary to law.

Conflict of interest — An unethical situation where a person serving as a fiduciary gains personal monetary benefit because of direct or indirect use of his position (e.g., a public official only contracts public business with his construction company even when such company's bids are not competitive). Any misuse of a fiduciary relationship for personal gain.

Conformed copy — An exact duplicate of a document with written explanations, such as a note replacing the copied signature stating that such signature is valid.

Confusion of debts — A circumstance that terminates a debt by the happening of a mutually offsetting event which satisfies such debt. For example, a creditor, who is a named beneficiary of a debtor's life insurance policy, receives enough proceeds to satisfy the debt.

Conglomerate — A corporation comprising smaller companies representing different industries. Such diversification is typically obtained in order to avoid cyclical swings in profitability. Textron Inc. is generally considered to be the first conglomerate.

Conjugal rights — The rights of married persons.

Consanguinity — A blood relationship between two or more persons as opposed to a relationship by marriage (affinity); a lineal consanguinity is a descendant or ascendant, such as a father and son, whereas a collateral consanguinity is a blood relationship only through a common ancestor, such as an uncle and niece.

Consent dividend[1] — An arrangement where stockholders agree to be taxed on a "dividend" even though no dividend is actually paid by the corporation. A consent dividend is used to circumvent the accumulated earnings tax and, perhaps, the personal holding company tax.

Consent judgment — An agreement between two parties that a judgment is binding and the dispute is settled.

Consequential loss — A loss sustained because of an indirect influence from an accident or other event causing damages or decline in value. For example, a homeowner suffers a consequential loss in that his property's value declined when a zoning law is changed to allow a shopping center to be built next door. In insurance, consequential losses, such as loss of profits on inventory destroyed, must be specifically stated in an insurance policy (e.g., business interuption insurance) before coverage applies. For example, a manufacturor may have insurance to replace a production facility and all its contents, but to lose revenue for eight months may be disastrous. In this case lost revenue is a consequential loss.

Consideration — One of the essential elements of a contract; it is the inducement or compelling influence that causes a party to enter an agreement (i.e., a coveted right, property, money, promise, act, forbearance, or some other benefit). All parties to a legally enforceable contract must intend to suffer a legal detriment, which does not necessarily have to be economic in that a promise to give up gambling or drinking is good consideration. Past consideration and preexisting duties, however, are generally not valid consideration for a legally binding contract.

Consignment — The process of entrusting goods to another, without relinquishing title, for the purpose of selling, storing, or transporting. Typically, consignment refers to a method of marketing goods where the owner turns items over to a seller, who does not hold title and only acts as a selling agent for the owner. Title passes to the final buyer upon sale. In turn, the seller is generally compensated by a sales commission. Also see "Commission merchant."

Consolidated balance sheet — A balance sheet showing the combined effects of a parent company's balance sheet and its subsidiaries. Such combination must be made when the parent owns more than 50 percent of the outstanding voting stock of each subsidiary and the companies are in the same general industry.

Consolidated bonds — Bonds issued to combine existing debt by replacing outstanding bonds that were previously issued at different times.

Consolidation — In accounting, the combination of two or more companies into one new company.

Consolidation loan — A loan that replaces two or more existing loans, thus consolidating debt payments into one payment which is sometimes more manageable.

Constant dollar method — An investment strategy that calls for maintaining a portfolio according to a certain dollar amount of stocks and a certain dollar amount of bonds. At periodic intervals buying or selling activities are used to keep the relative amounts constant as values fluctuate. Also see "Formula plan."

Constant ratio method — A technique of calculating an annual percentage rate on a loan that uses an add-on method of figuring interest.

Constant ratio plan — An investment strategy that calls for maintaining a portfolio according to a certain constant ratio of stocks and bonds; a formula plan. Also see "Formula plan."

Construction contract bond — See "Contract bond."

Constructive eviction — (1) For leased rental property, any act by a landlord that substantially interferes with a tenant's possession, use, or enjoyment in such a manner as to render the property entirely or partially unfit, but is not actual eviction. An example is when a landlord fails to supply hot water to a tenant's apartment and the tenant leaves; (2) in real estate sales, the inability of a purchaser to gain possession because of a superior title held by a third party. It is a breach of covenants of warranty and quiet enjoyment on the part of the seller.

Constructive notice — Legal notification of involved parties without personally contacting them, such as publishing in a newspaper or appropriately making a recording in public records.

Constructive ownership — For tax purposes, a doctrine which allocates a higher percentage of ownership to a shareholder of a corporation than the actual percentage of ownership, because a related party owns similar shares. It is used in special circumstances pertaining to tax law. In essence, constructive ownership combines all percentages of related parties. For example, Jones owns 35 percent of XXX Corporation, his brother owns 25 percent, and his father owns the remaining 40 percent. In this case, all parties are deemed to constructively own 100 percent of the corporation.

Constructive receipt — As applied to taxable income, money or other property that is received, could have been received, or spent at the option of the taxpayer, and is not subject to significant restrictions.

Such amounts are includable in taxable income—even if they were not actually received or spent by the taxpayer. For example, an individual directs his bank to credit interest on a savings account in the following year instead of during the present year, when interest would customarily be applied. Even though the interest is not actually received, all amounts pertaining to the present year are deemed to be constructively received and are therefore taxable in the present year (because the taxpayer was entitled to interest payments and actually controlled the timing of their receipt).

Constructive trust — A trust devised by operation of law to remedy an inequitable situation. For example, when a person fraudulently acquires title to property, he holds it in trust for its rightful owners.

Consumer credit — Generally, any loan made to individuals for personal use, rather than business use, such as to purchase an automobile or boat, and the use of credit cards. Also see "Truth-in-Lending Act."

Consumer Credit Protection Act — See "Truth-in-Lending Act."

Consumer Price Index (CPI) — A measure of general price level for consumer items. It consists of about 400 goods and services sold in cities across the United States that are selected and weighed in the computation according to their relative importance to consumers. Specifically, there are two different indexes, one pertaining to urban consumers (CPI-U) and the one pertaining to urban wage earners (CPI-W). The consumer price index reflects changing prices in individual products, purchasing power of the dollar, and the cost of living in general. It is commonly used as a basis for applying cost-of-living increases for various compensation and retirement arrangements.

Consumer Product Safety Act (CPSA) — Federal legislation establishing safety standards for manufactoring and transporting consumer products.

Contents broad form (HO-4) — See "Homeowner's insurance policy."

Contemplation of death — An expectation of death because of threatening circumstances portending its arrival, such as an impending danger or the existence of a terminal illness. Contemplation of death, as applied to property transfers and estate taxes, generally refers to the underlying cause of a certain transfer and was deemed to occur for all transfers made within three years of a decedent's death. All gifts made in contemplation of death are excluded from a decedent's gross estate for estate tax purposes unless the transferor retains a life estate in such property, transfer takes effect only upon transferor's death, transfer is revocable, transfer creates a power of appointment, or proceeds of a life insurance policy are transferred to the executor or beneficiaries.

Contest of will — Any kind of attempt through legal means to contest the probate of a will or property distribution therefrom.

Contingency — A condition upon a stated event; generally, an agreement will be binding if a specified event occurs.

Contingent annuity option — An option for persons under a certain type of retirement, annuity, or life insurance plan to choose an annuity to be paid after his or her death to a contingent annuitant for life.

Contingent beneficiary — In life insurance contracts, a person in line to receive life insurance proceeds if the primary beneficiary is not living.

Contingent fees — A manner of compensation that must be paid only upon the happening of a specified future event. For example, the commission of a real estate broker is paid only if the property is sold.

Contingent interest — An interest subject to an uncertain future event.

Contingent liability — A liability not presently owed, but may become payable upon the occurrence of a certain event. For example, Smith indorses a check drawn by White. Smith's liability is contingent upon the failure of White to pay.

Contingent life insurance policy — A life insurance contract that provides protection for two or more insureds, whereby the face value is payable upon death of one insured with automatic continuance of insurance for all covered survivors.

Continued bond — A bond allowing the holder to choose between redeeming it or continuing to hold it at the same, or in some cases a different, interest rate.

Contract — A legally binding agreement made between two or more parties. To be enforceable, all contracts must contain the following elements: offer and acceptance, legal capacity to contract, consideration, and subject matter must not violate public policy. All parties must voluntarily be mutually obligated to perform or not to perform, as well as be competent.

Contract bond — Generally, a type of surety bond for contractors in construction, supply, and maintenance activities. Contract bonds can be used to guarantee the faithful performance of contractors in completing a project on schedule (performance bond), to guarantee credit from lending institutions, or to guarantee the payment for all labor and materials (payment bond).

Contract for deed — See "Installment land contract."

Contract of sale — An agreement between a seller and a buyer under which the seller agrees to convey title of property when payment is made by the buyer in accordance with its terms.

Contract premium — The gross premium of a life insurance contract.

Contractual lien — A voluntary claim, encumbrance, or security in property, such as a mortgage.

Contractual plan — A method of purchasing mutual fund shares by agreeing to periodically buy a certain dollar amount of shares over an extended period (e.g., $600 a month for 10 years). Such plans generally call for sales commissions to be deducted from payments made in the first few years, and some plans offer decreasing term insurance. A contractual plan tends to provide a method of forced savings, sometimes with added benefits.

Contrarian investment strategy — An investment philosophy primarily based on planning investment moves in an opposite direction of the masses: sell when most are buying and buy when most are selling.

Contribution — (1) In insurance, an insurer's obligation to pay a portion or entire amount of loss; (2) the right of one who pays a liability common to others to recover his or her portion. For example, Davis pays a debt in full that was proportionally owed by Green and Davis. Davis may recover her portion of debt from Green; (3) in employee benefits, an amount paid into a retirement plan or other employee fringe benefit plan. They may be made by the employer or employee or both, depending upon the type of plan and the qualifications involved; (4) for income tax purposes, see "Charitable contribution deduction."

Contributory insurance plan — A type of group-term life insurance that is funded by employee contributions or employer contributions for a limited amount of coverage with an option for more insurance to be purchased by employees.

Contributory retirement plan — An employee retirement plan that calls for employees or possibly their dependents to contribute to a portion of the cost of retirement benefits. It is also called a "Thrift plan."

Contrivance — A clever plan or devise designed to deceive.

Conventional loan — In real estate, any loan that is not backed by a government-insured program (e.g., non-VA or non-FHA mortgage). It can amount up to 95 percent of the appraised value of real estate over a 30-year amortization.

Conversion — (1) A privilege granted to holders of convertible bonds or preferred stocks to exchange them for common stock; a similar choice given to holders of stocks in a mutual fund to exchange for other stocks in a different fund; (2) an unauthorized involuntary taking or other alteration of another person's property; (3) changing an apartment complex into condominiums.

Convertible security — A bond, preferred stock, or mutual fund share that can be exchanged for a different stock or other security in the same company at the option of the holder.

Convertible term insurance — A type of term life insurance that can be exchanged for permanent (whole life) insurance without evidence of insurability at the option of the policyholder.

Conveyance — Generally, the transfer of title to real estate by deed. It also includes the transfer of some other interest in land by instrument, such as a mortgage or an assignable lease.

Conveyance tax — See "Transfer tax."

Co-obligor — A party jointly bound with others to an obligation.

Cooperative apartment — An apartment complex that is owned by a corporation whose stock is held by all tenants. The right to occupy an apartment is obtained by buying stock in the corporation. Each tenant, though, does not individually own his own dwelling unit. Compare "Condominium."

Coordination of benefits (COB) — For health insurance claims, a method of coordinating all benefits payable from two or more health insurance policies so that the entire amount of benefits do not exceed the full cost of allowable medical expenses. It is primarily used to avoid overinsurance.

Copyright — An intangible right to publish and sell literary or other artistic works for a statutory period of time.

Corner — An arrangement where a group of investors in combined effort attempt to buy up and hold a commodity or security until demand far outruns supply and prices experience an abnormal rise.

Corn-hog cycle — An overly simplified hypothetical illustration of the regulatory effects of competitive influences upon changing prices. For example, when prices of hogs are high, the price of corn will also be high because farmers will customarily want to raise more hogs; this will cause an increase in demand for corn, which generally means higher corn prices. But to simultaneously cut costs and to profit from higher hog prices, farmers will naturally sell some of their stock before they mature. This move will increase the supply of hogs, which will generally decrease hog prices, and eventually depress the price of corn since there are less hogs to feed and because farmers raised a large amount of corn in an effort to profit from higher corn prices. Because of lower hog prices, farmers will then reduce their hog production and, in a short period corn prices will drop even further because of the compound effect of a decline in demand and oversupply. Inexpensive corn prices means producing hogs will become cost-effective again, and hogs will be kept for breeding instead being sold. Withholding hogs from the market decreases supply and the price of hogs will usually rise: The whole cycle begins anew.

Corporation — A legal entity, separate from its owners, formed to carry on a mission or business as stated in its corporate charter. It is an intangible and artificial being created by law and may operate for profit or not for profit. A corporation is given many rights and privileges possessed by natural persons, such as the right to own property, to sue and be sued, to incur debts, to enter into contracts in its own name, and to hire agents to carry on its mission or business. The major characteristics of a corporation as opposed to other forms of business organizations are limited liability, perpetual existence, ease of transferring ownership, centralized management, and separate authority (i.e., stockholders do not have the power to bind the corporation to contracts unless they are authorized agents of the corporation). When associated with a business purpose, a corporation must generally be incorporated under state law.

Corpus — For a trust, the main principal or capital (body of assets) of a trust as opposed to the income earned from it during a taxable year.

Correspondent bank — A bank that conducts business for another bank in the capacity of an agent.

Corridor deductible — A type of supplemental health insurance plan designed to coordinate benefits by using a deductible (the "corridor" of uncovered expenses) to bridge two health insurance plans together.

Cosigner — One who signs an obligation (e.g., a promissory note) or other instrument along with another, generally to provide credit support, and thereby assumes equal responsibility as all other cosigners. Also see "Co-maker."

Cost and freight (CAF) — A sales price that includes the cost of goods plus freight, but no other charges.

Cost basis accounting — Historical cost accounting; assets are recorded at cost on a balance sheet rather than at fair market value.

Cost basis accounting is in conformity with generally accepted accounting principles (GAAP).

Cost-benefit analysis — A budgeting technique that analyzes future purchases by comparing desires and needs with the price to be paid. That is, if a benefit to be bought is perceived to be less than its purchase price, then the item or service in question will not be acquired and vice versa.

Cost depletion[1] — For income tax purposes, a method of expensing the cost of a natural resource. It is figured by dividing the cost of a natural resource by the total estimated number of units to be produced, then multiplied times the actual units sold during the taxable year. It is similar to the units-of-production method of depreciation. The cost depletion method, alone, cannot yield depletion expenses beyond the cost of the natural resource. Compare "Percentage depletion."

Cost, insurance, and freight (CIF) — A sales price that includes the cost of goods plus insurance plus freight charges.

Cost-of-living raise — An increase in compensation for employees because of rapidly rising prices. It is usually based on a consumer price index.

Cost-plus contract — A construction or production contract that calls for a total purchase price, typically, to be made up of material plus labor cost added to a stated percentage thereon. Cost-plus contracts are commonly used when production costs or other variables cannot be reasonably estimated.

Cost recovery method — (1) Generally, any depreciation, amortization, or depletion method that systematically expenses the cost of an asset over a period of time; (2) a statutory method of depreciation of qualified assets for income tax purposes. Also see "Accelerated cost recovery system."

Cost recovery property — Depreciable property that qualifies for the accelerated cost recovery system.

Cost-volume-profit analysis — See "Break-even analysis."

Countercycle investment — Any investment that performs in a manner that is opposite to general economic and market conditions. Generally thought of as investments that provide relatively stable income, such as high-grade bonds and certain preferred stock of financially sound companies.

Counter offer — In negotiating terms of a contract, an offer made by an offeree. It terminates the original offer and becomes a proposal to the originator of the first offer. An inquiry or request for different terms is not a counter offer and has no effect on the original offer. In certain sales contracts, however, additional terms are mere proposals for different terms and will not have the effect of rejecting the original offer.

County records — Public records kept by county clerk (usually in a county courthouse) that give notice of changes in titles, liens, and easements in real estate and other matters as required by law.

Coupon bond — A corporate or municipal bond which has small detachable coupons that are to be presented for payment of interest at a bank on or shortly after the interest payment date. Generally, coupon bonds are unregistered and the detachable coupons become bearer paper on the date such interest becomes payable. Also see "Bearer bond."

Course of business — Procedures, techniques, or other actions normally done in a certain trade or business.

Court of Appeals (U.S.)[1] — A federal court that hears appeals made from courts of original jurisdiction, which are the U.S. Tax Court, U.S. District Court, and the U.S. Court of Claims.

Court of Claims (U.S.) — See "Claims Court (U.S.)."

Covenant — Virtually any written contract; more specifically, an agreement in writing between at least two parties where one pledges to the other(s) that something has been done, will be done, or will not be done (e.g., covenant not to compete, convenant not to sue, covenant against encumbrances, covenant for quiet enjoyment, covenants for title, covenant of warranty, covenant running with title, covenant running with land, and covenant to convey). They may be expressed (covenants "in deed") or implied by certain words in a deed, though not expressly stated (covenants "in law").

Cover — (1) Any act intending to reduce the risk of loss; (2) to protect against loss, as with an insurance policy; (3) to hedge an investment position, such as a short sale against the box (the short sale is covered); (3) to actually deliver stock in closing a short sale; (4) after breach of seller, a right given to a buyer to purchase like goods in good faith without unreasonable postponement and to recover certain damages from the seller.

Coverage — The amount of insurance or protection provided by an insurer.

Covered option — An option is said to be "covered" when the underlying asset, usually a security, is owned by the option writer. For example, Barnes writes a call option on ZZZ stock. If Barnes owns at least 100 shares of this stock, then he has a covered option; if he does not own 100 shares of ZZZ, then he has a "naked option." Also see "Naked option."

Cover note — In insurance, a written document issued by an agent stating that coverage is in effect. Also see "Binder."

Credible — One entitled to obtain credit; a person worthy of trust; reliable.

Credit — (1) The ability of a person to obtain a loan; the financial worthiness of a person or business to borrow money as demonstrated by the history of such borrower to meet prior financial obligations, available collateral to secure an obligation, and capacity to repay the amount borrowed with interest; (2) in taxation, an amount subtracted directly from a tax liability, as compared to a deduction which merely reduces taxable income; (3) in accounting, the right-hand side of an account: credits increase revenue, liabilities, and owners'equity accounts, and they decrease expense and asset accounts.

Credit accident and health insurance — Accident and health insurance typically sold through banks and other financial institutions in connection with an installment loan. Generally, it is a type of group insurance issued to borrowers to cover loan payments during periods of disability caused by accident or sickness.

Credit bureau — An organization that gathers financial information about individuals and businesses. More specifically, the credit history, character, and reputation of borrowers are collected and furnished to subscribers (merchants and financial institutions) upon request. Credit bureaus are organized at the local level, but are regulated by federal laws.

Credit card — Generally, a plastic card issued by a business or financial institution for the purpose of charging purchases or obtaining money on credit. Compare "Debit card."

Credit discount — A reduction of a debt, usually for making a payment during a specified period.

Credit for child and dependent care expenses — See "Child care credit."

Credit insurance — Any type of insurance that provides coverage on a borrower in the event, which is specified in the policy, he or she is unable to pay.

Credit life insurance — A life insurance policy issued on the life of a borrower to cover the balance of a loan payment in case of death. It is usually a type of decreasing term insurance.

Credit line — An available amount of credit extended by a bank or other creditor.

Credit memorandum — A statement provided by a bank informing a customer that his or her checking or savings account has increased. However, when issued by a credit card company, department store, or other creditor, it means that a customer's charge account is reduced. In general, credit memorandums serve notice that an account is being adjusted (in a favorable direction) because of errors, purchase returns, or allowances, etc.

Creditor — A person or business to whom a debt is owed.

Credit rating — An appraisal of a borrower's history of paying prior debts. It is kept by a credit bureau and used by prospective creditors in deciding whether to extend credit or grant a loan.

Credit report — A confidential statement issued by a credit bureau (or an individual independent of the company asking for the report) who has made an investigation into a person's or business' reputation, financial standing, credit rating, character, etc. Credit reports are used by banks, insurance companies, merchants, and others to assess a credit risk.

Credit scoring summary — A method of evaluating credit risk by taking into consideration certain data which are given weighted points. Some of the data includes home phone, years on the job, other credit, years at present address, credit bureau report, age of automobile, and whether or not one is a present or past customer.

Credit slip — Generally, a written memorandum issued by a store for a purchase return or allowance. In most instances it can either be cashed or used to purchase other merchandise in the same store.

Credit standard — Criteria used to evaluate a credit risk. A traditional method uses character, collateral, and capacity to pay.

Credit terms — All essential factors comprising a loan, such as amount borrowed, interest rate, amount of payment, payment period, discounts for rapid repayment, and other considerations.

Credit union — A financial institution formed to grant loans to and receive savings from its members. Members of a credit union are usually associated with some common interest, such as employees of the same employer.

Cross hedge — In investment strategies, a hedging position consisting of two different forms of a security. It is positioned as such because of differences in maturity dates or quality characteristics between the two securities.

Crossover point[1] — The point reached in leveraged tax shelters where taxable income exceeds current tax deductions because of accelerated depreciation taken in the early years and decreasing amounts of interest payments.

Cross-purchase agreement — An insurance arrangement typically for partnerships and closely-held corporations where each partner or shareholder maintains enough life insurance on each other to fund the purchase of a deceased's equity in the business. It is a way of facilitating the transfer of equity upon the death of one of the owners.

Crown trust — An interest-free demand note or trust fund. This arrangement has been restricted by the Tax Reform Act of 1984.

"Crummey" trust — A trust having special powers, one of which permits the beneficiary to withdraw limited amounts of trust income or corpus or both, generally, up to the amount excludable from gift tax ($10,000).

Cum dividend — With dividend; generally applies when a share of stock is sold after a dividend is declared but before the date of record. That is, the buyer is to receive the dividend. Compare "Ex-dividend."

Cumulative dividend — Dividend on preferred stock that will be in arrears if not declared and paid. Also see "Cumulative preferred stock."

Cumulative preferred stock — A type of preferred stock that entitles its holder to receive dividends for a stated amount each year. If a dividend is not declared or is not sufficient to meet the stated amount due, then cumulative preferred dividends will be in arrears until declared and paid in future years. Unpaid cumulative preferred dividends must be paid before dividends are paid on common stock.

Cumulative voting — A type of voting arrangement for shareholders of a corporation in electing the board of directors. Each shareholder may vote by using the total number of shares owned multiplied by the number of directors to be elected. All such votes can be cast for one or more directors, which generally allow minority interests to be represented on the board. For example, Baker owns 200 shares of stock and seven directors are to be elected. Baker has 1400 votes which can all be placed on one candidate.

Currency — In banking, paper money as opposed to coins and checks; dollar bills.

Current account — An account that is open (between a debtor and creditor) which may or may not have a balance.

Current asset — Assets that are expected to be used up or converted into cash by a business within one year or within its operating cycle, whichever is longer. Current assets normally include cash, marketable securities, accounts receivable, notes receivable, and prepaid expenses. They are short-term assets listed on a classified balance sheet in order of liquidity.

Current income fund — A mutual fund whose primary objective is to pay high income from dividends or interest or both to its shareholders.

Current liability — A short-term liability; a liability that is to be paid within one year or within the operating cycle of a business, whichever is longer; a liability that normally requires the payment or use of a current asset. Current liabilities include accounts payable, short-term notes payable, accrued expenses payable, and deferred revenues.

Current ratio — A ratio used in financial statement analysis that attempts to measure the short-term debt-paying ability of a company. It shows a firm's strength in working capital position by exhibiting the company's ability to pay its current liabilities with current assets. Thus, the current ratio is a liquidity ratio and is also known as the working capital ratio. Short-term creditors are usually interested in it for credit-evaluating purposes. The ratio is as follows:

$$\text{Current ratio} = \frac{\text{Current assets}}{\text{Current liabilities}}$$

Current yield — The present rate of return on an investment, taking into consideration its current selling price and income receipts or increased value or both. For income producing securities, it is computed by dividing the security's payments for the past 12 months—dividends or interest—by its current selling price. For appreciated investments, see "Internal rate of return." The current yield is normally used, however, to compare alternatives between different income-producing investments which are presently available. It is also known as "current return." For mutual funds, the current yield is sometimes based on an average purchase price over a certain period.

Curtesy[1] — Under state law the husband's right to his wife's property after her death.

Cushion bond — A callable bond where a peculiar situation arises when the bond's selling price is tainted (suppressed) because of the callable feature. When interest rates decline, bond prices rise; the price of callable bonds, however, may not rise much, if any, above the call price because the market fears the bond will be called. Such bond is a cushion bond. It does offer, however, considerable protection in a market of falling bond prices.

Custodial account — Any account where cash or other property is entrusted to an agent for safekeeping for another.

Custodian bank — Generally, a large bank holding money for another bank.

Customs duty — A federal tax on imported goods.

Cyclical stock — A common stock that experiences price swings in a manner directly related to and correlated with the conditions of the market or economy. It generally applies to stocks of capital-intensive companies who serve a big-ticket durable goods market, such as automobile and large appliance manufacturers. Also see "Blue chip stock," "Countercycle investment," "Growth stock," and "Income stock."

D

Damages — See "Compensatory damages" and "Punitive damages."

Date of declaration — The date that the board of directors of a corporation declares a dividend. Also see "Date of payment and "Date of record."

Date-of-deposit-to-date-of-withdrawal method — See "Actual balance method."

Date of exercise — As used for incentive stock options, the date an option is used to purchase underlying stock.

Date of grant — As used for incentive stock options, the date such options become available to an individual.

Date of maturity — The date an obligation is to be paid in full.

Date of payment — The date a dividend is actually paid to the shareholders of a given company. Also see "Date of declaration" and "Date of record."

Date of record — The date on which all stockholders who hold stock in a dividend-declaring corporation are eligible to receive a dividend on the date of payment. It usually falls between the date of declaration and date of payment. Also see "Date of declaration" and "Date of payment."

Day order — An order to buy or sell a certain security or commodity before the end of a trading day. It is automatically canceled when executed or expired at the end of the day.

D.B.A. — (1) Doing business as; (2) Doctor of Business Administration.

Dealer — A person or business who purchases goods with intent to resell them to others, and not to keep or consume such items for his or her own account. Generally, a dealer holds title to goods; a broker does not. The most distinguishing characteristic of a dealer is that he or she holds items of inventory (i.e., all items are generally held out for sale), whereas an investor holds the same items until profitable circumstances appear (not ordinarily held out for sale) and a consumer purchases goods for consumption. For income tax purposes, dealer status may be placed on individuals when the frequency of buying and selling certain otherwise investment properties (such as real property) is relatively high. Dealers are not allowed the preferred long-term capital gain treatment on such items, unless careful attention is given to assure a valid intent to hold an investment, rather than just another part of inventory. Also see "Broker," "Investor," and "Trader."

Death benefit — An amount to be paid to a beneficiary upon the death of a covered individual. A death benefit may include the face value of a life insurance policy (with any adjustments), the residual of an annuity, or an amount paid by an employer of a deceased employee.

Debasement — The reduction of intrinsic value in coins by decreasing the amount of precious metal contained in them.

Debenture — An unsecured bond that is only backed by the general credit standing of the issuing corporation. Companies that are financially sound are usually the only ones able to conveniently issue debentures.

Debit — The left-hand side of an account; used in accounting to increase expense and asset accounts and to decrease revenue, liability, and owner's equity accounts.

Debit card — A bank card that, when used, automatically transfers money from the cardholder's cash account. It is different from a credit card in that no credit is extended. Compare "Credit card."

Debit memorandum — A statement issued by a bank to a customer indicating that his or her checking or savings account has been decreased. However, when issued by a credit card company, department store or other creditor, it means that a customer's charge account balance has increased. In general, debit memorandums serve notice that an account has been adjusted (usually unfavorably) because of errors, service charges, or some other reason.

Debt — An obligation to pay money or other asset to or render services for a creditor. Loans, financial bonds, credit cards balances, account payables, promissory notes, and other liabilities and obligations are considered debt.

Debt financing — For corporations, the issuance of bonds and notes rather than stock; borrowing money.

Debtor — A person or business that is obligated to pay a debt.

Debt service — (1) The extinguishment of a debt over a period of time through periodic payments. It includes principal, interest, and all other charges; (2) the total amount of a loan payment currently due or applying to one year.

Debt-to-equity ratio — A financial ratio used by investors and creditors to determine the overall solvency of a company. It can be figured one of two ways: total liabilities divided by total stockholders' equity, or long-term debt plus preferred stock (at par value) divided by total stockholders' equity. The resulting figure will be stated similar to "1 to 3," which would mean the company's financial structure is made up of one part liabilities to three parts stockholders' equity.

Debt-to-total-capitalization ratio — A financial ratio used by investors and creditors to determine the overall solvency of a company. It is a type of debt-to-equity ratio that is found by taking total liabilities and dividing it by total liabilities plus stockholders' equity. The resulting figure here will be a percentage, such as 33 percent—the company has a financial structure made up of 33 percent debt, 67 percent stockholders' equity.

Deceased — A dead person.

Decedent — Commonly, a deceased person who died recently.

Decedent's estate — All property owned by a deceased person at the time of death.

Declaration — In insurance, a statement by a person or business applying for insurance that is normally used in the underwriting process for determining a premium. In most instances, it becomes part of the policy.

Declaration date — The date on which a dividend is declared by a corporation's board of directors.

Declaration of estimated tax by individuals — A procedure of periodically paying federal income taxes that is applicable to self-employed persons and certain employees who have an additional taxable income not subject to income tax withholding (Form 1040-ES).

Declining balance method of depreciation — An accelerated method of expensing the cost of an asset by computing decreasing amounts of depreciation over its expected useful life.

Decreasing term insurance — A type of term insurance where the face value of the policy declines over a period of time. It is commonly used to coincide with mortgage loans because of its declining balance.

Deductible — In an insurance policy, a stated amount which the policyholder must pay for each claim or covered accident before receiving any insurance recovery. Deductibles range from $50 to $25,000, depending upon the type of insurance coverage (e.g., automobile insurance or health insurance). As a general rule, the higher the deductible, the lower the premium.

Deductible clause — In an insurance policy, a clause specifying the amount of deductible for each loss. It is commonly used in policies where many small losses are to be expected, such as dents in an automobile or office visits to a doctor.

Deductions[1] — For income tax purposes, amounts subtracted from gross income to arrive at taxable income. The two significant categories are deductions for adjusted gross income (business expenses, investment losses, moving expenses, IRA and Keogh contributions, alimony payments, employee business expenses, deduction for married couple, etc.) and deductions from adjusted gross income (itemized deductions). Also see "Itemized deductions."

Deed — Generally, a written instrument conveying title to real property.

Deed of trust — A written instrument used in some states as a security arrangement for a loan. It is used in place of a mortgage in that title is held by a third-party trustee until the loan is paid in full.

Deep-discount bond — A bond having a coupon rate below the market rate for similar investments and, therefore, must sell for a price well below face value.

Deep in the money — As used in option trading, a strike price is well below the market price (for calls), or a strike price is well above the market price (for puts). It generally means that the current position of either the option writer or holder is very favorable in contrast to the other position.

Deep shelter[1] — A tax-shelter investment that generates enough tax losses to provide investors with significant deductions and credits in the early years of its existence.

Default — As used in business, the failure to pay interest or principal or both by a corporation, government agency, or individual as required by a debt instrument.

Defeasance clause — A clause in a mortgage which defeats such mortgage when the accompanying debt is satisfied.

Defeasible — That which can be revoked, annulled, or terminated.

Defeasible title — A title that is not presently annulled, but could be made void in the future; not absolute title.

Defective title — Not good title; title to a negotiable instrument or real property transferred through illegal means (e.g., fraud, illegal consideration, and breach of faith) or otherwise lacks all essential elements to transfer good title.

Defensive investment — Generally, any investment made primarily to protect against loss from a decline in market prices (i.e., a countercyclical investment, such as a public utility stock or high quality preferred stock).

Deferral — (1) A postponement; (2) a financial strategy that postpones income, and the income taxes thereon, in the current period. The delayed income will be taxed in future periods, generally as it is received. The primary benefit of a deferral strategy is the present use of money which would have been paid in taxes had such a strategy not been implemented.

Deferred annuity — An annuity where periodic payments to be received by the annuitant are delayed until a specified future date, such as the annuitant's 65th birthday. Also see "Annuity."

Deferred bonds — Bonds which are allowed to delay interest payments for a specified period of time.

Deferred compensation — Current earnings that are not paid until a later date. The basic strategy is to reduce current taxable income, which in effect yields less income tax, by delaying payment until the recipient is in a lower marginal tax bracket. The postponed benefit is allowed to accrue additional earnings (e.g., interest and dividends) without tax consequences when the arrangement satisfies the requirements of a qualified plan. Ordinarily, the period of receipt for periodic payments begins at retirement, but a lump-sum distribution may be available.

Deferred expense — A prepaid expense; any expense that is paid in advance but has not been incurred, such as prepaid rent or prepaid insurance.

Deferred group annuity — Generally, a type of pension funding for employees where an employer purchases a deferred annuity from an insurance company for each person per year of participation. The insurance company in turn guarantees payment for the amount of an annuity purchased for each participant. Deposit administration contracts, however, have become more popular in recent years, and thus, deferred group annuity contracts are rarely issued at the present time.

Deferred income — Income received before a sale is made or services are rendered. It applies particularly to accrual basis accounting. For cash basis taxpayers, deferred income is generally taxable upon receipt.

Deferred-premium life insurance — A type of life insurance where a small initial premium is paid by an insured and further premium payments are delayed over an extended period by the use of a promissory note. After such period expires, premium and note payments become due. It is generally marketed to college students who typically do not have money for life insurance premiums until they become employed in later years.

Deficiency — (1) Money owed to the Internal Revenue Service; (2) that portion of a debt not satisfied by sale of mortgaged property.

Deficit — (1) Net loss for an accounting period in that expenses exceed revenues; (2) generally, an accumulation of net losses plus dividend payments in excess of net income over the life of a corporation; used instead of "retained earnings."

Deficit spending — A period when cash outflows exceed cash inflows.

Defined-benefit plan — A pension plan that has predetermined benefits for the participants, and contributions are actuarially determined to fund these benefits. In other words, the benefit for each employee is planned and contributions are adjusted to meet the expected pension liability. Benefits may be paid over a period of time (usually over the life of the retiree) or in one lump sum.

Defined-contribution plan[1] — A retirement plan that provides a separate account for each individual participant whose benefits only accrue through contributions and earnings. The balance of the account is either systematically paid out over a period of time (usually over the life of the retiree) or paid in one lump sum. In other words, the contribution for each employee is planned, and whatever is available during the period of distribution is paid out.

Deflation — Generally, an across-the-board decrease in prices, which leads to an increase in the purchasing power of the dollar (or other currency). It can occur for a number of reasons, but primarily due to a decrease in overall spending (a decline in demand) or a significant increase in the supply of goods and services or some combination thereof.

Delinquent account — A debt where payment is past due.

Delinquent tax[1] — An unpaid amount of tax for which the due date has passed. Penalties and interest are usually assessed.

Delisting — The removal of a stock from an exchange.

Demand deposit — Any type of cash account in a bank or other financial institution where a depositor can demand a withdrawal by writing a check or shared draft on his or her account. Compare "Time deposit."

Demand note — A promissory note that is payable upon demand by holder. Also see "Crown trust."

Demographics — Statistics on population, such as size, growth, income, and density, for a certain geographic region.

Dental insurance — A specialized group health insurance plan used as a fringe benefit for employees. Group dental coverages are typically designed to provide preventive care and protection against unusually high dental expenses for all participants. Most plans cover ordinary and reasonable fees for regular cleaning, fluoride treatments, and oral exams, but a deductible and coinsurance participation is customary for most other dental work. The deductible generally ranges from $25 to $100 and coinsurance participation by the insured ranges from 20 percent to 50 percent, depending upon the plan. For other dental work, such as fillings, X-rays, surgery, and extractions, 80 percent of the cost is covered by the insurance company; for more involved work such as crowns, bridges, and orthodontic procedures, 50 percent is typically covered. Most all dental plans are limited to a specified annual amount per person, which normally ranges from $750 to $2,000.

Dependent — For income tax purposes, an individual who has met all requirements for a dependency exemption on another taxpayer's return. The requirements are (1) dependent's gross income must not exceed $1,000 a year, unless he or she is a child under 19 or a full-time student; (2) more than one half of support is provided by claimant; dependent is (3) resident of claimant's home or is a specified relative, (4) is a U.S. citizen or resides in a country contiguous to the U.S., and (5) does not file a joint return, unless to merely claim a refund without being required to file jointly.

Depletion — For income tax purposes, an expense resulting from the extraction of a natural resource ("wasting asset") and incurred upon its subsequent sale. The two different methods of computing a depletion allowance, for certain taxpayers, is cost depletion and percentage depletion. Under cost depletion, the price allocated to the natural resource is divided by the total estimated number of units to be extracted, which yields the amount of depletion expense per unit sold. Strictly using the cost method will not provide depletion allowances beyond the cost of the natural resource. Under percentage depletion, a statutory percentage is used to figure the amount of depletion. Expensing under the latter method will provide deductions beyond the wasting asset's cost. In many cases, taxpayers are allowed to choose either method each year.

Deposit administration group annuity — Generally, a type of group retirement plan where an employer's contributions are first made to a deposit fund, then as participants retire an annuity is purchased with assets out of the fund.

Deposit insurance — Insurance for depositors of a member bank, savings and loan, or other financial institution. Also see "Federal Deposit Insurance Corporation" and "Federal Savings and Loan Insurance Corporation."

Depository trust company[2] — A central securities certificate depository, and member of the Federal Reserve System, through which members may arrange deliveries of securities between each other through computerized accounting entries without physical delivery of the certificates.

Depreciation — (1) For income taxes, a statutory method of expensing the cost of an asset over its class life or depreciation range, depending upon when it was placed in service; (2) in financial accounting, a rational and systematic method of expensing the cost of an asset over its estimated useful life. Also see "Accelerated cost recovery system," "Declining balance method of depreciation," "Straight-line depreciation," "Sum-of-the-years' digits method of depreciation" and "units of production method of depreciation"; (3) a decline in value.

Depression — A prolonged period of sluggish economic activity that is characterized by little productivity, little or no amounts of new capital investment, large number of business failures, extensive unemployment, deflation, and a very low income level among workers.

Descend — To transfer property by succession, commonly through the terms of a will. Also see "Succession."

Descendant — (1) a blood relative in direct line from an ancestor, such as a daughter, granddaughter, great-granddaughter; it sometimes includes adopted children; (2) a person who is to receive the proceeds of an estate.

Descent — (1) A blood relative, also see "Lineal heir"; (2) generally, the receipt of ownership of property by inheritance.

Determination letter[1] — A letter written by a district director of the Internal Revenue Service clarifying the status of a certain tax-related matter. It is usually an opinion on either the qualification of a retirement plan or tax-exempt status of an organization.

Devaluation — Generally, an intentional reduction in the value of a nation's currency with respect to gold or other currencies in order for its exports to be more competitively priced.

Development drilling — A type of drilling program found in many publicly held oil and gas tax shelters where proven reserves are extracted. Usually a development drilling program is not considered as risky as an exploratory program because oil deposits have already been discovered.

Devise — The transfer of real estate by a will.

Devisee — One to whom land is transferred by the terms of a will.

Devolution — The transfer of property, rights, office, etc., to a successor.

Directors — Generally, persons elected by a corporation's stockholders to oversee, replace, and direct the management of a corporation.

Disability — Generally, the inability of a person to continuously perform normally required duties pertaining to one's present occupation as a result of an injury or sickness. For some disability policies any one of the following characteristics must be present: a person must be unable to work at any gainful occupation (total disability), be under the regular care of a physician, be confined to a home or hospital (continuously within doors), or experience an unusually long waiting period before benefits begin. As a general rule, the less restrictive a disability provision is, the more expensive such coverage will be. Each disability clause or plan will specify its own details as to what constitutes a disability and the requirements for receiving disability benefits. Also see "Health insurance" and "Permanent disability."

Disability benefit feature — An option in some life insurance and annuity contracts to waive any premiums or to pay a monthly income if the insured becomes totally or permanently disabled.

Disability income insurance — Generally, a type of health insurance that provides replacement income to disabled insureds who are unable to maintain gainful employment as a result of an accident or illness.

Disbursements — Payments made.

Disclaimer — (1) A statement limiting one's liability in case certain published information is inaccurate; (2) refusing to accept an estate or gift; (3) refusing to accept a claim, right, or obligation.

Disclosure — For consumer financing arrangements, the publishing of all significant terms of credit, such as the annual percentage rate, all finance charges, and the number and amount of payments.

Discount — A reduction of a total sum, such as a sales discount.

Discount bond — A bond selling for a price below its face value. Generally, this occurs because the market interest rate is higher than the bond's coupon rate, or the bond pays no interest, such as a zero coupon bond.

Discount broker — A securities broker who, typically, only executes buy and sell orders for his or her customers, with reduced commissions. The major difference between a full-service and discount broker is that the former provides opinions, guidance, and other investment-related services while the latter usually does not.

Discounted cash flow — A technique of analyzing a series of future payments or receipts or both by using present value analysis.

Discounted note — A promissory note sold for an amount less than its purchase price or face value.

Discount loan — A type of lending arrangement where finance charges are first deducted and the remaining amount is then lent to the borrower.

Discount points — Additional charges for government-backed home loans, such as VA and FHA loans, to make the lender's yield comparable to conventional loans. Each point is one percentage point of the amount of a loan and is borne by either the seller or the buyer. Also see "Points."

Discount rate — The interest rate charged by the Federal Reserve for loans to member banks. Because it is set every two weeks, the discount rate acts as an indicator of monetary policy of the Federal Reserve System. An increase in the rate may show that credit is tightening, which will cause business activity to slow down; a decrease may provide a future decline in the cost of borrowing money, which will normally enhance business activity.

Discount yield — A measurement of the annual yield for discounted securities computed as follows:

$$\text{Yield} = \frac{\text{Discount}}{\text{Face value}} \times \frac{360}{\text{Days to maturity}}$$

Discovery period — In certain insurance policies and bonding arrangements, a specified period of time (after the cancellation of a contract) during which the insured is allowed to discover a recoverable loss, which is one that occurred during the period of coverage, and to file a claim.

Discrepancies — Differences or inconsistencies between two objects which should ordinarily be identical.

Discretion — The privilege or right of acting within the constraints of one's own judgment or conscience. The ability to choose a course of action with unrestricted authority which should be reasonable in light of the circumstances.

Discretionary account — As used in brokerage houses, a customer's account where a stockbroker buys and sells securities or commodities at the broker's own discretion. Usually, carte blanche is given to the broker in that his professional judgment is the sole basis of selecting purchases and timing sales for the benefit of his or her customer.

Discretionary authority — Authority given to a person in a fiduciary capacity to use his or her judgment when acting on behalf of another.

It is generally subject to the "prudent man rule." Also see "Prudent man rule."

Discretionary beneficiaries — Beneficiaries of a discretionary trust or other discretionary arrangement.

Discretionary income — (1) For individuals, income that is left after all payments have been made for debt-service, taxes, and life-essential items. It is usually computed for a period of one year and is generally associated with income available for investment or pleasure or both. Compare "Disposable personal income"; (2) income distributed from a discretionary trust or similar discretionary arrangement.

Discretionary trust — Any trust where the trustee has the right to accumulate income for future distribution or trust income is to be paid at the discretion of the trustee.

Discrimination — Unfair treatment arising from an unreasonable distinction between two persons or objects.

Discrimination of employees — For employee benefit plans, disproportional benefits favoring one group of employees over another. Benefit plans that are qualified for tax purposes must not favor highly compensated employees, stockholders, or officers.

Dishonor — The refusal to pay a negotiable instrument when properly presented for payment.

Dismemberment benefits — In certain health insurance plans, generally, a provision for a lump-sum payment for loss of sight or limbs resulting from an accident.

Disposable personal income — For individuals, income left after all taxes and other government collections (e.g., fines, tags, and licenses) have been paid. That is, spendable income that is available for consumer purchases and investment; it is much broader in scope than discretionary income. Also see "Discretionary income."

Disposition — For federal tax purposes, any transfer or loss of ownership of property, such as abandonment, exchange, sale, gift, donation, or contribution.

Dispossess proceedings — The eviction process of a tenant from rental property by a landlord because of a breach of rental contract.

Dissaving — Spending more than present income by using savings or borrowings or both.

Dissolution — (1) The termination of a business organization, such as a partnership; (2) the cancellation of a contract.

Distrain — The seizure or holding of personal property as security for payment of rent or other obligations (e.g., services to be performed, payment of taxes, or appearance in court).

Distress sale — The sale of property where prices are typically well below fair market value because the seller is unduly compelled to act (e.g., liquidation sale of a foreclosure).

Distributable net income (DNI) — Generally, the taxable income of a trust with certain adjustments (i.e., adding back deductions for distributions, personal exemption, dividend exclusion, net tax-exempt income, long-term capital gains deduction for gains allocated to corpus, net capital losses, and subtracting net long-term capital gains allocated to corpus). If distributed, it serves as the maximum amount that the beneficiaries can be taxed and the maximum amount that the trust can deduct. The character of DNI (such as long-term capital gains or tax-exempt income) carries over to the beneficiaries upon distribution.

Distribution — (1) The marketing of consumer goods or services; (2) the payment of money or other assets (e.g., corporate distributions to shareholders, trust or estate distributions to beneficiaries, and retirement plan distributions to employees or other beneficiaries); (3) the sale of a large block of stock.

Distribution channel — The process of delivering goods or services from a manufacturer to consumers through warehouses, distribution centers, middlemen, wholesalers, retailers, company salesmen, etc.

Distribution in kind — (1) For federal income tax purposes, a corporation in a complete liquidation will not be subject to income taxes upon distribution of its property with certain exceptions; (2) any type of distribution consisting of property "as is."

Distribution period — A period in which payments are made to a recipient, such as annuity payments to an annuitant.

Distributive clause — A provision in a trust agreement that governs the distributions of trust income and corpus.

Distributive share — The portion of an estate available to an heir in accordance with statutes dealing with intestate estates; the amount of partnership assets available from the liquidation of a partnership.

District Court (U.S.)[1] — A federal court of original jurisdiction that litigates tax cases, among other topics. The distinguishing characteristic of this particular court, as compared to other courts dealing in tax matters, is that a jury will hear the case.

Diversification — An investment strategy to reduce risk by selecting securities in different companies or industries. The general thought is that if changes in market prices or the economy adversely affect one type of company or industry, then it should enhance another type, thereby reducing an investor's exposure to volatile market-price fluctuations.

Divert — When applied to money, the unauthorized use of cash.

Divided interest — Different interests in real or personal property, such as an owner and tenant.

Dividend — A distribution by a corporation from earnings and profits (past or present) to its shareholders in accordance with the declaration of the board of directors.

Dividend deposit — For permanent life insurance policies, the amount of dividends and interest accumulated by the company for a policyholder.

Dividend exclusion[1] — The amount of dividends received from U.S. corporations that is excluded from federal income taxes. (In 1985, married individuals were allowed a $200 exclusion for dividends when filing jointly; $100 for all other individuals.)

Dividend option — Certain alternatives, provided to a policyholder of permanent life insurance, for methods of applying or receiving dividends. Generally, the dividends may be paid in cash, applied to future premiums, left in an interest-bearing account (dividend deposit), applied to one-year term insurance, or used to buy paid-up additional life insurance. Also see "Dividends (on life insurance)."

Dividend payout ratio — A percentage indicating the rate a company pays a dividend with regard to its earnings. It is used for investment purposes in comparing two or more companies that are somewhat similar (e.g., in the same industry and approximately the same size).

$$\text{Dividend payout ratio} = \frac{\text{Common-stock dividend per year}}{\text{Earnings available for common stock}}$$

Dividend reinvestment plan — A method of acquiring stock through dividends. Certain companies and brokerage houses allow shareholders to obtain stock of the same company through the reinvestment of dividends. The acquisition is usually made at a discount or without brokerage fees.

Dividends (on life insurance) — Earnings distributable to policyholders of participating life insurance policies. Such amounts are not taxable to the recipient if the dividends are less than the amount of premiums paid. Also see "Dividend option."

Dividend yield — The rate of return for dividends paid during the year on a share of stock for a given company in regard to the stock's current selling price. It is quite useful for comparing similar investments, such as income stocks. The dividend yield is stated in a percentage:

$$\text{Dividend yield} = \frac{\text{Dividends paid (last 12 months)}}{\text{Stock's current price}}$$

Divorce — The legal termination of a marriage, which may result in certain consequences such as property settlements, child support payments, and alimony. Also see "Annulment."

Document of title — Any instrument indicating that possessor of such document is entitled to hold or deliver (or both) the goods to which it refers. Examples include a bill of lading and a warehouse receipt. Unless it specifically states otherwise, a document of title is negotiable.

Doing business as (d/b/a) — Used for entities carrying on a trade or business under a different name, such as James Barnes d/b/a Westwood Grocery.

Dollar bond — A bond quoted by its selling price rather than its yield to maturity, such as certain foreign and municipal bonds.

Dollar-cost averaging — A method of systematically purchasing the same company's stock over a period of time. A fixed amount is used to purchase stock at certain points in time, usually at regular invervals such as $300 a month for 24 months. This process tends to reduce risk by averaging the cost per share of all shares purchased and will yield a profit if the selling price exceeds the average price paid.

Domain — The ownership of land; an immediate, absolute, and complete ownership of real estate. Also see "Eminent domain."

Domestic corporation — (1) A corporation, organized in a state where it does business, is a domestic corporation in that particular state. For example, a corporation organized in California is a domestic corporation in California, but a foreign corporation in any other state; (2) For federal tax purposes any corporation organized in the United States.

Domicile — The residence of an individual where, if absent, he or she intends to return.

Dominion — Complete ownership of property, usually holding title and possession.

Donative intent — For purposes of a charitable contribution, a gift made to a charitable organization without intending to receive any economic benefit in return.

Donative trust — A trust created for the benefit of another by the acquisition of property on behalf of a beneficiary and without any payment required by the beneficiary.

Donee — One who receives a gift from a donor; the recipient of a bequest.

Donor — One who provides a gift to a donee. Also, a creator of a trust.

Double assessment — A tax assessed twice on the same property.

Double-declining-balance method — An accelerated method of depreciation in which the initial rate of depreciation expense is twice that of the straight-line method.

Double indemnity — Generally, a rider attached to a life insurance policy providing that in case the insured should die in a certain manner, usually by accident, then the beneficiary will receive a benefit equal to twice the policy's face amount.

Double taxation — The taxing of the same income or other items twice. For example, a corporation pays income taxes on its earnings, distributes a dividend from those earnings, and the shareholder is subsequently taxed on dividend income.

Dower — Generally, a widow's right to claim ownership in real estate belonging to her deceased husband. It has been amended or replaced in most jurisdictions.

Dow Jones Bond Averages — An average portraying general price movements in bonds. There are two different averages: one consists only of industrial bonds and the other is made up of public utility bonds.

Dow Jones Futures Index — A measure of general price movements of commodity futures.

Dow Jones Industrial Average (DJIA) — An average representing price movements of stocks on the New York Stock Exchange. It is the most commonly accepted indicator of average stock price movements in judging the performance of the stock market as a whole. The DJIA consists of 30 stocks, which are Allied Corporation, Aluminum Company of America, American Brands, American Can Company, American Express, American Telephone and Telegraph, Bethlehem Steel, Chevron, Du pont, Eastman Kodak, Exxon, General Electric, General Foods, General Motors, Goodyear, Inco Ltd., International Business Machines, International Harvester, International Paper, Merck and Company, Minnesota Mining & Manufacturing, Owens-Illinois, Procter & Gamble, Sears, Texaco, Union Carbide, United Technologies, United States Steel, Westinghouse Electric, and Woolworth.

Dow Jones Spot Index — An indicator of changes in commodity spot prices.

Dow Jones Transportation Average — An average of certain transportation stocks indicating the price trend of transportation stocks in general.

Dow Jones Utilities Average — An average showing general price movements of public utility stocks.

Down payment — The initial payment for the purchase of a home or other item that is encumbered by an obligation to pay the balance of the purchase price. The down payment is usually made at the time of purchase and ranges from 5 percent to 35 percent of the total price.

Downside risk — The probability that an investment, such as a convertible bond, will fall in value because of external market influences or fundamental factors.

Down tick — In securities trading, the lower price of a security than that of the previous transaction.

Dowry — The assets a woman brings to her husband upon marriage.

Dow theory — An investment theory based upon the premise that the price movements of a certain group of stocks, chiefly the Dow Jones Industrial and Transportation Averages, can predict future price movements of the stock market. It was originally developed by Charles Dow in the 1880s and is still widely accepted today.

Draft — A three-party negotiable instrument where one party (drawer) instructs another party (drawee) to pay a third party (payee) on demand or at a definite time; a bill of exchange. A check and a trade acceptance are types of drafts. Also see "Check" and "Bill of exchange."

Drawee — A bank or other entity to whom a check or other draft is directed. Also see "Draft."

Drawer — The person who writes a check or other draft and is conditionally liable to pay the amount indicated on the instrument to the holder if the drawee does not pay. Also see "Draft."

Dread disease insurance — A specialized type of health insurance designed to provide coverage only for treatment of a stipulated disease, such as cancer insurance.

Drop shipment — Delivery of goods directly from a manufacturer, rather than through wholesalers or retailers, although a wholesaler usually earns revenue from the sale. The term applies to consumers or retailers, and it implies that the middleman is not eliminated, but such an arrangement may save on shipping expenses.

Dry goods — An old-fashioned name for cloth sold by the yard.

Dry hole — A nonproductive oil or gas well.

Dry trust — A trust where the trustee's only duty is to distribute trust assets to the beneficiaries. Also see "Passive trust."

Dual fund — A specialized investment company which pays to one class of shareholders all dividends (income shares) and to another class of shareholders (capital shares) the gains from the sale of income shares. A dual fund normally carries a fixed expiration date.

Due and proper care — The amount of care necessary to prevent the occurrence of an accident. It usually implies that a person's actions are without negligence.

Due and reasonable care — The amount of care reasonably expected of a prudent person under the same or similar circumstances; ordinary care.

Due consideration — Sufficient consideration to a contract. Also see "Contract" and "Consideration."

Due date — For income tax purposes, the date on which one's income tax return is due. For calendar-year individuals, the due date is April 15th, with optional extensions.

Due notice — Proper notice; notice that is reasonably intended to reach a certain person or the general public.

Due-on-sale clause — For home mortgages, a provision in a lending agreement that allows a lender to demand full payment of a loan's balance upon the subsequent sale of an encumbered house. It has the effect of preventing a buyer from assuming the loan.

Dummy corporation — A corporation formed without an intention to carry on a business; existing in form only; a shell (e.g., a corporation primarily formed to avoid income taxes or personal liability).

Durable goods — Generally, consumer goods that are reasonably expected to last longer than three years, such as automobiles, refrigerators, washing machines, books, and furniture.

Dutch auction — A method of selling property where the initial public offering price is stated above its value and is subsequently reduced until sold.

Duty — (1) An obligation to obey the laws or to perform in a reasonable manner; (2) a tax levied upon imported goods or exported goods.

Dwelling — A residence.

E

Earned income — Income received by an individual as a result of his or her personal efforts (wages, salaries, bonuses, commissions, fees, etc.), rather than income received from passive sources (dividends, interest, rents, capital gains, etc.).

Earned income credit — A refundable income tax credit for a low income individual (or married couple filing jointly), who maintains a household for himself or herself and a child (who may or may not be a dependent). To qualify, a taxpayer must not have earned income or adjusted gross income in excess of a certain level ($11,000 in 1985).

Earned premium — A portion of an insurance premium that is properly allocated to an insurance company for a period of coverage provided prior to expiration or cancellation of an insurance policy.

Earned surplus — A relatively obsolete term for retained earnings. Also see "Retained earnings."

Earnest money — Generally, an amount of money paid when entering a contract by a purchaser as a pledge to carry out the terms of the agreement. In most cases it is part of the purchase price (e.g., a deposit).

Earning capacity — As applied to disability insurance, the ability of a disabled worker to receive reasonable compensation for employment (after impairment as opposed to before impairment).

Earnings — Broadly defined, income from all sources. Also see "Accrual method of accounting," "Cash basis of accounting," and "Retained earnings."

Earnings per share (EPS) — A measure of the earnings of a company attributable to one share of common stock. It is sometimes used as a benchmark for determining profitability of a company with regard to the number of shares of common stock (and common stock equivalents) outstanding, and it is used for comparison purposes. Essentially, earnings per share is net income available to common shareholders divided by the number of common shares outstanding. Primary EPS uses common stock and common stock equivalents (i.e., most items having conversion privileges, such as options, warrants, and sometimes convertible securities) in its computation, whereas fully diluted EPS indicates the occurrence of converting all potentially dilutive convertible issues in its computation.

Easement — A right to use land belonging to another. It can be for the benefit of another parcel of land, such as the right to cross another's property to get to one's own property (appurtenant) or for the personal benefit of the individual (in gross). Some easements cannot be separated from the land to which it is attached (even when transferred, which is a covenant running with land) and others have a certain or contingent duration. Easements are typically used with properties over which a public utility crosses with its lines or pipes, or a railroad crosses with its tracks, or an individual, who owns adjacent land without access to roads, passes across.

Economic loss — For insurance purposes, the total estimated loss (both covered and uninsured losses) suffered by an insured for accidents and other mishaps over a given period. It includes legal costs, administrative costs, property damages, hospital expenses, funeral expenses, etc.

Economic Recovery Tax Act (ERTA) — Major tax legislation passed in 1981 that had, as one of its principal purposes, incentives for capital spending by manufacturers, small businesses, and investors. One of its most controversial provisions is the accelerated cost recovery system (ACRS), which provided taxpayers with a more beneficial system of depreciation.

Economics — (1) The study of using limited resources for maximum satisfaction. Some of the more important factors incorporated in the subject of economics include human behavior on an aggregate basis (wants or desires of the masses), geography (including weather), natural resources, capital and entrepreneurship, capability of labor, flow of money, political climate and regulatory practices, state of technology and transportation, availability of goods and services, and changes in world affairs; (2) virtually anything pertaining to a business entity's or country's economy.

Economize — To conserve money by purchasing less or at lower prices or both; to be frugal; to use thrift.

Economy — (1) The management of resources; (2) a complex system of consumers', businesses' and governments' interactions taken as a whole. Also see "Economics."

Educational assistance program — A written, nondiscriminatory plan available to all qualifying employees who take courses that are paid for by the employer.

Educational expenses — For income tax purposes, an employee is allowed a deduction (itemized miscellaneous deduction) for certain educational expenses paid by him or her. Generally, such amounts are deductible if the education is required by the employer for maintaining salary status or job, or improves existing skills required for an individual's present occupation. No amounts incurred, for educational expenses leading to a change in profession, occupation, or trade are deductible, however.

Effective date — The date an insurance binder goes into effect and coverage begins.

Effective interest rate — (1) An annual rate of interest computed by dividing total interest received by total amount invested in one year; (2) the minimum rate of interest investors are willing to accept for a given interest-bearing investment, when the present value of both interest payments and principal (lump-sum payment) are taken into consideration. It is the same as the effective yield or market rate of interest.

Effective-interest-rate method — A method of calculating periodic revenue from a bond by multiplying the carrying value of a bond (initially, its cost) by the market rate on the date of issuance. For income tax purposes, it is used for original issue discounts (OID) for bonds issued after July 1, 1982. Also see "Amortization of bond discount," "Amortization of bond premium," "Bond discount" and "Bond premium."

Effectiveness — The degree to which an objective is reached without, necessarily, taking into consideration its cost. Also see "Efficiency."

Effective rate of return — See "Internal rate of return."

Effective tax rate — The percentage of taxes paid from total income as calculated as follows:

$$\text{Effective tax rate} = \frac{\text{Taxes paid}}{\text{Total income received}}$$

Efficiency — Receiving the maximum output from a project with minimum input; cost-effectiveness; economy.

Efficient market hypothesis — Essentially, a stock market where investors prefer the highest yields with the lowest risk and where the current market price of common stock accurately reflects its value. All currently available information has already been taken into account by the market, and present prices cannot be used to project future prices.

E.g. — Exempli gratia; for example (literally for the sake of an example).

Elective benefits — In accordance with certain life insurance policies, one benefit chosen over another (e.g., lump-sum benefit may be substituted for weekly indemnity). Elective benefits are also used in employee benefit plans where employees are able to tailor their benefit packages.

Electronic funds transfer (EFT) — A computerized system of immediate processing of transactions made with a debit card, credit card, or other media. It virtually eliminates the use of cash or checks in that all accounts are automatically adjusted.

Eligibility requirements — For retirement plans, conditions that must be satisfied before an employee can participate in an employer's retirement program (e.g., an eligibility waiting period of 1 to 36 months or attaining a certain age, such as 25). Eligibility requirements also refer to qualifications that must be attained before retirement benefits become distributable as such (e.g., the completion of 15 years of company service and reaching the age of 62).

Elimination period — A stipulated period of time which must elapse before insurance coverage begins (e.g., 30 days).

Embezzlement — The taking of property belonging to another and using it for one's own benefit, through otherwise lawful possession. Embezzlement occurs where a person in a position of trust, such as a fiduciary, is in control or possession of the assets and fraudulently converts them to his or her own use. Money received through acts of embezzlement is taxable.

Eminent domain — The right of a government to acquire private property for public purposes in exchange for just compensation to the owner.

Emolument — Profit, compensation, fees, or perquisites derived from holding an office or arising from employment.

Employee[1] — A person who works for and is under the will and control of another in return for compensation. Partners and sole proprietors cannot employ themselves and cannot be considered as employees of their businesses. Employee status is important for withholding requirements and qualified nontaxable benefits available for employees. Also see "Independent contractor."

Employee annuity — A special exclusion of retirement benefits is allowed to an employee who contributes after-tax dollars to any portion of his or her employer's qualified retirement plan. The employee must receive the total amount contributed within three years, through periodic receipts upon retirement. Such amounts are received tax-free up to the total amount contributed in after-tax dollars by the employee, and all further receipts become fully taxable (IRC Section

72(d)). For example, Dawson paid $20,000 in after-tax earnings into her employer's qualified retirement plan. After retiring, she is to receive $12,000 per year. All retirement payments will be received tax-free in year one ($12,000). Then in year two, she will receive $8,000 tax-free and $4,000 will be taxable. All subsequent amounts received will be fully includable in her gross income.

Employee assistance programs (EAP) — As a component of human resources management, employer-sponsored programs set up to help employees with personal problems that affect job performance and productivity, such as alcohol abuse, drug abuse, emotional problems, financial problems, and family problems.

Employee benefits — Benefits offered by an employer for employees, such as medical insurance, life insurance, pension plans, profit-sharing plans, employee assistance programs, educational assistance programs, group-legal services, financial planning services, disability insurance, dental insurance, property and liability insurance, 401(k) plans (cash or deferred compensation), and voluntary employee benefit associations (VEBAs).

Employee death benefit — A payment made by an employer of a deceased employee to a widow or other beneficiary, as an act of affection or charity. It is excluded from the recipient's gross income for an amount up to $5,000 (IRC Section 101(b)).

Employee Retirement Income Security Act (ERISA) — A 1974 federal law regulating the funding, administration, vesting, and distributions of retirement plans. Essentially, it protects an employee's interest in retirement benefits.

Employees' trust[1] — A trust established and maintained for the benefit of employees (e.g., a pension trust). Qualified contributions made to an employee's trust are deductible for an employer and tax-deferred for an employee.

Employer Stock Ownership Plan (ESOP) — A specialized form of stock bonus plan which provides employees with retirement benefits consisting of the employer's stock (or cash if elected) in return for favorable financing and tax benefits for the corporation.

Employment agency — (1) A firm in the business of finding employment for individuals; (2) a state-operated agency for the benefit of both employment seekers and employers.

Employment letter — A letter from a present or past employer of an individual stating that the latter is or was an employee, the length of employment, and compensation paid.

Employment tax — See "Payroll tax."

Encumbrance — Virtually anything having an adverse legal effect on the ownership of property by diminishing the interest of the owner. Especially something that decreases the property's value or impedes its transfer, such as a mortgage, claim, easement, mechanic's lien, or unpaid taxes. Encumbered property is generally used to mean that such property has a liability attached to it.

Endorsee — One to whom a negotiable instrument is assigned by indorsement (same as indorsee).

Endorsement — (1) The transfer of a negotiable instrument by signature or stamp of the payee, accommodation indorser, or drawee (e.g., indorsement of a check), causing the latter to become contingently liable (same as indorsement); (2) for an insurance policy, an attachment that amends, alters, extends, or otherwise changes the terms of coverage provided in the standard form. Also see "Rider."

Endorser — One who signs his or her name on the back of a negotiable instrument in order to transfer to another (same as indorser). Also see "Endorsement."

Endowment contract — A life insurance policy that provides coverage from the beginning of the contract to maturity (the endowment period) and guarantees payment of a specified sum (with necessary adjustments) to the insured, even if still living at the end of the endowment period. The face value of the policy (adjusted for items such as loans or dividends) will be paid to beneficiaries upon the death of the insured. The endowment period typically has a duration of 10 to 20 years or the attainment of a specified age.

Energy tax credit[1] — Before 1986, an allowable income tax credit for qualified taxpayers purchasing and installing specified energy-related property. The two broad classifications are residential energy credits and business energy credits. For residential energy credits, there are two different types of expenditures: energy conservation (e.g., insulation and caulking) and renewable energy source (e.g., solar power).

Enhancement — Something done to increase the value of a business or property.

Enrolled actuary — A person enrolled with the Federal Joint Board for the Enrollment of Actuaries who performs actuarial functions in designing insurance or retirement premiums and benefits for a company or trust.

Enrolled agent — A person eligible to practice before the Internal

Revenue Service (IRS) after passing an examination administered by the IRS.

Entailment — For property transferred by inheritance, a different course of descent than that of the customary rules of sequential devolution.

Enterprise — A business venture.

Entertainment expenses — For purposes of an income tax deduction, ordinary, necessary, and reasonable expenses incurred for a qualified activity, which is one that is directly attributable to the furtherance of one's trade or business, or an employer's trade or business. All such expenditures must be appropriately recorded, including the persons entertained, business relationship, amount, and where the activity took place. An expense that is considered indirectly related to ("associated with") business activity, which is one where the atmosphere is not conducive to a quiet business discussion such as a night club or football game, must directly precede or follow a directly related activity, such as a business discussion or quiet business meal.

Enticement — (1) A type of marketing method used to lure consumers to purchase a product or service; (2) the wrongful persuasion to commit an unlawful sexual act.

Entity — A person, separate and distinct unit, or organization that conducts business or legal affairs on its own (e.g., proprietorship, corporation, trust, or estate). Also see "Legal entity."

Entrepreneur — Generally, a person who undertakes risks to develop and initially manage a business venture for the purpose of making a profit. Sometimes "entrepreneur" refers to a businessman, proprietor, innovator, capitalist, or investor in a business venture, as opposed to a salaried worker, such as a manager.

Entrust — To give property over to a person in a fiduciary arrangement.

Envelope system — A simple budgeting system designed to control expenditures by keeping separate envelopes of budgeted amounts of cash. Each envelope is labeled by its representative account. When cash is needed for an expenditure, it is simply taken out of the appropriate envelope (budget), so that any remaining cash (balance of a budget) can be observed, and cash payments can thereby be controlled.

EOM — End of month; it usually specifies terms of sale on invoices or purchase orders in that "net EOM" generally means that payment in full is due by the end of the month following a sale. Thus, goods purchased on May 12 with an invoice marked "net EOM" would mean full payment is due May 30.

EPA mileage rating — A miles-per-gallon rating devised by the Environmental Protection Agency to be used for comparison purposes of new cars.

Equal Credit Opportunity Act — Federal legislation designed to prevent creditors from discriminating against potential and existing borrowers on the basis of race, religion, sex, national origin, or marital status.

Equal division — A provision in a will that specifies equal distribution of an decedent's estate; "share and share alike."

Equal Employment Opportunity Commission — A federal agency in charge of ending discrimination of hiring, firing, promoting, training, and all other conditions of employment, because of race, religion, sex, national origin, or marital status.

Equipment leasing arrangements — A carefully structured tax sheltering arrangement for high-income taxpayers, who have substantial net worth. It is usually in the form of a limited partnership. In a typical equipment leasing limited partnership, the general partner invests in equipment, such as railroad cars, computers, airplanes, ships, cargo containers, automobiles, trucks, etc., for the purpose of leasing them to third parties. The economic benefit other than tax savings is cash flow from rentals and in some cases profits from the sale of leased property.

Equipment trust — A specialized financing device where equipment is purchased by a trustee with both his or her funds and the lessee's funds. In turn, the trustee then leases it to the lessee for a fee.

Equipment trust bonds — Bonds secured by certain equipment. Also see "Equipment trust."

Equitable — That which is impartial, just, and fair.

Equitable mortgage — A legally enforceable lien, which is not perfected, against real estate, such as the transfer of property as collateral without formalizing an agreement; a constructive mortgage.

Equitable owner — A named beneficiary of property held in trust.

Equitable title — An ownership interest without holding legal title, such as buyer under a land contract where the buyer has use of the property, but the seller holds legal title until the obligation is satisfied.

Equity — (1) As used in business and real estate, the residual of total assets less total liabilities; the equity in a parcel of real estate is its fair market value less all liabilities associated with it; net worth, net assets, stockholders' equity, or capital equity; also see "Equity security"; (2) something impartial, just, and fair.

Equity buildup — As used in real estate, an increase in an owner's claim, as opposed to a creditor's claim, on property through reduction of debt (principal) on a mortgage, increasing property values, or making appropriate improvements. For businesses, equity buildup is provided by inflation, owner contributions, and revenues.

Equity ratio — A ratio showing the percentage of claim the owners (stockholders) have to the assets of a given corporation, as opposed to the creditor's claim (which can be found by subtracting the equity ratio from one).

$$\text{Equity ratio} = \frac{\text{Total stockholders' equity}}{\text{Total assets}}$$

Equity security — Stock; a certificate showing ownership in a corporation. If there is no preference as to dividend payments, it is common stock. If there is a preference as to dividend payments, it is preferred stock.

Equity-sharing mortgage — A financing arrangement for home buyers where an investor contributes a portion or all of the down payment or contributes a portion of monthly mortgage payments in return for a percentage of profit when the home is sold. In this way, first-time home buyers and others are able to afford the purchase of a new home.

Equivalent bond yield — An annualized yield computed on a short-term, non-interest-bearing security for the purpose of comparing it with the quoted yields of interest-bearing securities.

Equivalent taxable yield — The yield a tax-free municipal bond investor would expect from investing in a taxable bond that is otherwise similar. For example, a taxpayer in a 35 percent marginal tax bracket is currently receiving 10 percent yield in municipal bonds. The equivalent taxable yield from taxable bonds is 15.4 percent and is calculated by using the following formula:

$$\text{Equivalent taxable yield} = \frac{\text{Tax-free interest rate}}{1 - \text{Marginal tax bracket}}$$

Errors — Mistakes in judgment, by negligence, or from accidents and without intending to mislead or deceive.

Errors and omissions — As used in liability insurance, applies to protection from liabilities arising from errors and omissions in the performance of professional activities other than medicine. Errors and omissions typically applies to professional services such as accounting, banking, insurance, legal, and financial planning.

Escalation clause — A provision in a written agreement providing for certain adjustments in future payments (usually rent, wages, or total contract price of the construction of a building) in accordance with a specified event (e.g., property tax increase or overruns of estimated cost) or changes in a standard-of-living measurement (e.g., a cost-of-living index, such as the Consumer Price Index).

Escape clause — A provision in a written agreement providing the parties with an option to void the contract, in whole or in part. The escape clause specifies how each party can avoid liability or performance by strictly complying with its terms.

Escheat — The reversion of property to the state upon death of the owner because the deceased left no will or no apparent legal heirs. Any reversion of assets because a rightful owner cannot be found, however, may be subject to a subsequent lawful claim by such owner.

Escrow — The deposit of certain assets with a third party for the sole purpose of holding such assets until the occurrence of a specified event, usually when all conditions of a contract are fulfilled. For example, Cook sells land through an installment note to Davis and deposits the deed in escrow. Upon receipt of the last installment payment, the deed will be delivered to Davis. It has the effect of ensuring that Davis will receive the deed after Cook receives the money, and Cook will receive the money before the deed is given to Davis.

Escrow agent — A person acting in a fiduciary capacity who is instructed to deliver certain assets in accordance with an escrow arrangement. In this manner an escrow agent acts as an agent for both the provider and recipient of assets held in escrow. Also see "Escrow."

Essence of the contract — A mutually agreeable condition of a contract, which is accepted by the parties to be of vital consideration in that sufficient performance can only be attained by exact compliance with such terms. Also see "Consideration."

Estate — (1) The interest or right one has in real and personal property; all property owned by a person at death; (2) the house and grounds of substantial proportion belonging to a wealthy individual.

Estate by the entirety — The co-ownership of property by a husband and wife. If one dies, the other takes the entire property under original conveyance (right of survivorship).

Estate for life — See "Life estate."

Estate for years — Any interest in property for a given period of time, such as a lease.

Estate in fee simple — See "Fee simple estate."

Estate of inheritance — All property available to descend to heirs (e.g., a life estate is not part of an estate of inheritance).

Estate planning — Organizing a person's estate, in accordance with prevailing tax laws and other legal as well as personal constraints, in such manner as to gain maximum benefit toward the desires of the individual in the event of his or her death. Also see "Personal estate planning."

Estate tax — A tax levied on the right of an individual to transfer property at death. It is based on the fair market value of the decedent's estate at the time of death or the alternate valuation date. The general formula is as follows:

> Gross estate
> − Allowable deductions
> = Taxable estate
> + Adjusted taxable gifts
> × Tax rate
> = Tentative tax
> − Qualifying gift taxes paid
> − Allowable unified transfer tax credit
> − State death taxes paid
> − Other credits
> = Net estate tax

Estimated tax payment — A quarterly tax deposit for income taxes, not otherwise subject to withholding, made before filing an income tax return (Form 1040ES). Also see "Declaration of estimated tax by individuals."

Estoppel — The restraint of a person from claiming a contradictory position, as indicated by his or her previous acts or assertions. Estoppel generally arises when someone relies on the acts or assertions of another, to the detriment of the former. For example, Morris promises to pay all expenses of building a school, if the community will build it. When the community in good faith builds the school with reasonable intent to rely on Morris's promise, an enforceable promise has been made (promissory estoppel): Morris cannot take a contradictory position because of his prior assertion.

Et al. — Et alii; "and others."

Etc. — Et cetera; "and other unspecified things" or "and so on."

Ethics — Principles of appropriate professional standards of conduct.

Eurobond — A bond issued in Europe, typically denominated in dollars, by an international corporation or government outside the boundary of the issuer's home country. By issuing such bonds, the borrower is sometimes able to raise money very quickly and at lower interest rates.

Eurocurrency — The circulation of currencies outside the boundary of the home country.

Eurodollar — U.S. currency held outside the United States, usually as a deposit in a foreign branch of a U.S bank or in a foreign bank (typically in Europe).

Evasion — Generally, avoiding legal consequences or other matters through the use of deception.

Eviction — The removal of a tenant from rental property, usually by process of law.

Evidence of insurability — As required by an insurance company, statements made by a potential insured or other evidence, such as a physical examination and prior medical records, indicating his or her degree of acceptability for insurance.

Evidence of title — A document verifying ownership in property; a deed.

Ex cathedra — Something having authoritative weight.

Exceptional circumstances — Conditions that are normally infrequent and highly unusual in nature.

Exceptions — Specific exclusions from the operation of a contract. For insurance policies, specifically expressed circumstances that are not covered by a policy.

Excess clause — For some insurance policies, a provision stating that a particular insurer's liability is to begin only after all other insurance has been exhausted.

Excess insurance — An insurance policy or bond protecting the insured against specified perils by applying only to losses in excess of a stated amount. The risk of loss not covered by excess insurance may be carried by the insured or another insurance company (primary insurance). This arrangement is typically used in liability insurance.

Excess interest — For participating life insurance policies and annuities, the amount of interest paid in excess of interest guaranteed.

Excess itemized deductions[1] — The amount of itemized deductions actually subtracted from adjusted gross income. Itemized deductions must exceed the appropriate zero bracket amount in order to decrease taxable income. This is necessary because the zero bracket amounts are already incorporated into the tax tables and tax-rate schedules. Also see "Zero bracket amount" and "Itemized deductions."

Excess-of-loss insurance contracts — A basic type of reinsurance between insurance companies designed to protect against large losses.

Exchange — (1) A swap of property or services for property or services. Also see "Like-kind exchange" and "Tax-free exchange"; (2) a place where securities, commodities, or other investments are purchased and sold.

Exchange broker — One who makes trades in money, such as foreign currencies, for others.

Exchange listing — A company's stock listed on a stock exchange, as opposed to being traded over-the-counter.

Exchange members — Investment houses and individuals who have met securities exchange membership requirements (e.g., New York Stock Exchange) enabling them to execute transactions on the floor of that exchange. Such membership is commonly referred to as having a seat on the exchange.

Exchange privilege — A provision in many mutual fund arrangements where a shareholder can trade from one fund to another fund, which is operated by the same fund management, with little or no cost.

Exchange rate — The price of foreign country's money in terms of another country's currency.

Excise tax — A tax levied on services (such as the tax on performance of an act or privilege) and on goods (such as manufacturing taxes). It usually includes all taxes or licenses other than those imposed on income.

Exclusion ratio — See "Annuity ratio."

Exclusions — For tax purposes, specified amounts not included in gross income or in the gross estate. For insurance purposes, hazards, perils, damages, property, or other specified circumstances not covered by the policy.

Exclusive agency — Generally, allowing an agent the right to sell property but the owner reserves the right to personally sell the property without paying a commission.

Exclusive contract — An agreement where one is bound to only purchase or to only sell another's goods or services. These contracts are generally found to be a restraint of trade and therefore illegal.

Exclusive listing — In selling real estate, a written agreement where the owner agrees to pay to the broker a commission or fee if the property is sold during a specified period, even if the broker is not directly responsible for the sale. Usually, however, the broker agrees to put forth a "best effort" to make a sale.

Exclusive ownership — See "Fee simple estate."

Exculpatory clause — A clause in a contract providing that upon default a named party shall be held harmless.

Ex-dividend — Without dividend; the buyer of stock does not receive a dividend on recently purchased stock because he or she is not the stockholder of record. Stock which is purchased after the date of record but before the date of payment. Also see "Date of record" and "Date of payment."

Executed sale — In securities transactions, the sale of securities on the floor of a stock exchange.

Executive-job-loss insurance — A highly specialized type of insurance for executives who are involuntarily terminated from their jobs.

Executor — A person designated by an individual in a will to carry out the administration of the latter's estate upon his or her death. Also see "Administration of an estate."

Executory contract — An unfinished performance or execution in regard to a contract.

Executory sale — An unfinished sale.

Executory trust — A trust that requires further settlement or conveyance to be made by either the trust's creator or the trustee.

Executory warranties — In insurance, warranties made by an insured as to the performance of certain acts (e.g., the insured will put in a fire alarm) or continue to maintain existing conditions. Also see "Warranty."

Executrix — A female executor.

Exemplary damages — Damages awarded to a plaintiff in excess of financial loss to punish or to make an example of the defendant. Such damages are usually awarded because of outrageous conduct on the part of the defendant (such as wicked, malicious, violent, or oppressive behavior) in order to console the plaintiff for mental anguish or degradation. They are also known as "punitive damages." Exemplary damages may be received tax-free by the plaintiff, when associated with personal damages.

Exempt income — See "Tax-exempt income."

Exemptions[1] — A deduction from adjusted gross income in accordance with personal or dependency qualifications. For income tax withholding purposes, amounts claimed as qualified reductions in an employee's earnings that are withheld by an employer. Also see "Dependent" and "Personal exemptions."

Exempt property — Property not available to creditors in a bankruptcy proceeding.

Exempt securities — Securities not required to be registered with the Securities and Exchange Commission under the Securities Act of 1933 and exempt from the margin requirements of the Securities Exchange Act of 1934. Examples include securities from government, municipal, nonprofit religious, educational, charitable organizations, commercial paper, and private placements.

Exercise price — The price at which the holder of an option can buy the underlying asset (e.g., call option or incentive stock option) or, in the case of a put option, sell the underlying asset. For stock options, the exercise price is sometimes referred to as the "strike" or "striking" price. The exercise price is also the price at which a right or warrant can be used to purchase stock.

Ex parte divorce — A divorce proceeding where one spouse is not present.

Expectancy of life — According to current mortality tables or medical opinion, the number of years an individual can expect to live.

Expectant heir — Heir apparent; one in line to receive an inheritance.

Expend — To pay out money or other resources.

Expensed — The accounting for an expenditure by deducting it against income on an income statement.

Expenses — (1) The expenditure of money or other resources; (2) items subtracted from revenue, rather than being capitalized (which are generally expensed over their period of usefulness or class life). In strict cash basis accounting, only amounts paid in cash are expensed; in accrual basis accounting, amounts incurred are expensed; (3) for income tax accounting, amounts allowed by the Internal Revenue Code to be deducted from gross income to arrive at taxable income; (4) for financial accounting, (generally accepted accounting principles) outflows or exhaustion of assets that are not required to be capitalized or incurring liabilities (or any combination thereof) for the production of revenue . Also see "Accounting methods," "Accrual method of accounting," and "Capital expenditure."

Experience — For insurance purposes, an insured's or class of coverages' premium and loss record.

Experience rating — The modification of a premium as determined by an insured's loss experience over a period of time.

Expiration — For insurance purposes, the termination of coverage because of a lapse of time through the policy period, rather than from cancellation.

Expiration date — (1) For an insurance policy, the date on which coverage ceases to be in effect; (2) for equity-type options, the date on which it expires (for listed options Saturday after third Friday of the month of contract at 10:59 p.m., Central Standard Time).

Expiry — For insurance purposes, the end of a term insurance policy, which causes termination.

Exploration expenses[1] — Qualified expenses incurred for exploration of a mine or other mineral deposit before the development stage is reached. These expenses are, generally, fully deductible in the tax year in which they are incurred, if they are subsequently recaptured when the mine is producing.

Exploratory drilling[1] — A type of drilling program that searches for new oil and gas reserves. As compared with developmental drilling, exploratory drilling is usually a riskier investment and is generally offered in mixed (balanced) drilling programs.

Ex post facto — Something occurring after the fact.

Exposure — For insurance purposes, the degree to which an object or person is exposed to risk of loss, arising from hazardous conditions or other loss contingencies.

Express trust — A trust created for specified purposes through terms, usually written, by one or more parties intending to create a trust as opposed to a trust inferred by law.

Express warranty — In commercial sales, any affirmation of fact or promise that is not an opinion or merely sales talk, and such affirmation becomes part of the basis for bargaining (including advertisements, samples, models, or descriptions). It is not necessary for the seller to use the words "guarantee" or "warranty" for an express warranty to apply (Uniform Commercial Code Section 2-313). Also see "Warranty."

Ex-rights — Securities sold without rights.

Extended coverage insurance — Additional coverage beyond a basic policy. For property insurance, protection provided beyond a basic fire insurance policy for damages caused by smoke, explosion, civil commotion, hailstorm, windstorm and other specified perils. Additional coverage beyond a basic policy. Also see "Nonforfeiture."

Extended term insurance — In a life insurance policy, a nonforfeiture option for extended coverage in the event premium payments cease, in which case the cash surrender value is used to purchase term life insurance generally for the policy's face amount. The length of coverage for insurance so purchased depends upon the insured's age at the time of lapse and the amount of cash surrender value available. Also see "Nonforfeiture."

Extension[1] — (1) For income tax purposes, an additional period for delaying an income tax payment beyond the due date for reasonable circumstances (Form 4868); (2) for a promissory note, an additional time granted after maturity date in order to pay the principal due and any appropriate interest.

Ex testamento — In accordance with the terms of a will.

Extractive industry[1] — A type of industry that takes natural resources directly from the earth (e.g., oil drilling or mining industry).

Extrahazardous — For insurance purposes, conditions that are unusually and highly dangerous.

Extraordinary gain or loss — For financial accounting purposes, an event that is both unusual in nature and infrequent in occurrence.

F

Face amount — (1) The amount of insurance stated on the face of a life or other insurance policy to be paid to a named individual upon the occurrence of a stipulated event. It does not include additional proceeds due, such as accrued dividends, additional insurance acquired through dividends, or double indemnity through accidental death; (2) the stated principal of a bond, note, or other instrument to be paid at maturity, excluding accrued interest.

Face value — The value of a financial instrument as shown upon its face. Also see "Face amount."

Facility — In lending arrangements, the total amount of credit available to a certain borrower as determined by a particular lender. It is based on all outstanding obligations plus any additional credit allowed.

Facility of payment clause — For insurance and annuity contracts, a provision authorizing an insurance company to pay benefits to someone other than the named beneficiary, insured, or annuitant.

Factoring — The process of purchasing accounts receivable at a discount from a company and collecting money from such accounts.

Fair cash value — See "Fair market value."

Fair Credit Billing Act — Federal legislation (1975) providing legal guidelines for settling disputes between consumers and creditors in billing errors and in the quality of merchandise bought by users of credit cards.

Fair Credit Reporting Act — Federal legislation (1971) regulating the credit reporting industry, such as credit bureaus, credit investigations, collection agencies, and computerized information systems. Two important elements of the act are that consumers are allowed access to their own credit files, and consumers have the right to correct errors therein.

Fair Debt Collection Practices Act — Federal legislation (1978) regulating debt-collecting activities.

Fair Labor Standards Act — Federal legislation (1938) providing a minimum wage standard (adjusted by later legislation), specifying a maximum 40 hours a week for industries in interstate commerce, prohibiting employment of children (under 16) with few exceptions, and prohibiting employment of persons under 18 in dangerous jobs.

Fair market value[1] — Generally, an assumed value agreed upon (hypothetically) between a willing buyer and willing seller, both parties having relevant knowledge and neither being unduly compelled to act.

FAIR plan — A government and insurance industry cooperative plan designed to provide property insurance, such as fire, riot, beach and windstorm coverage, for persons otherwise unable to obtain such insurance (Fair Access to Insurance Requirements).

Fair return on investment — A return on investments that is comparable (i.e., somewhat equal) with regard to similar investments in the same geographic area.

False advertising — The misrepresentation of property or services generally through the media.

Family allowance — Distributions of assets, usually money, from an estate to the deceased's family for support during estate administration.

Family automobile doctrine — In some states, the owner of a vehicle may be liable for the negligence of a family member having authority to use it.

Family auto policy (FAP) — A type of personal automobile insurance covering an entire family that is generally similar to (and commonly replaced by) a personal auto policy (PAP). Major aspects of a FAP as compared to a PAP are: no liability coverage for nonowned vehicles, medical expenses are covered only up to one year after an accident, personal effects are covered for loss from fire or lightning, and permission must be granted to persons (other than relatives) in possession of the vehicle. Also see "Personal auto policy (PAP)."

Family expense policy — A broad term generally referring to a type of life insurance policy which covers both the policyholder and immediate dependents (e.g., spouse and children). It is usually designed to cover family expenses for a certain period of time (e.g., four years) if the breadwinner dies, or funeral and other expenses if a dependent dies.

Family income policy — Specialized life insurance for an entire family generally consisting of both whole life (or other form of permanent insurance) and decreasing term insurance on the breadwinner, with the spouse and children covered for lesser amounts (usually with term insurance). In case of the breadwinner's death, the program is designed to provide a specified monthly income to the named beneficiaries (up to a certain date). The period of periodic receipts is called family income period, after which the entire face amount of the whole life portion becomes payable in full. The income benefit portion of a family income policy is funded with the decreasing term insurance element of the plan. Thus, the program is designed to provide income to the family over a period of time that continually diminishes as the breadwinner continues to live. Should the breadwinner live beyond the family income period, then only the face amount of the whole life portion is available upon his or her death. In addition, some policies have early income-termination events, such as when the last child turns 21, the monthly income stops and the face amount is due. For example, West purchases a family income policy to provide insurance for herself and family. The family income period ends on January 1, 1997. Assume West dies on January 1, 1990, then income will be received by the family for the next 7 years, after which the face value of the whole life portion is payable. Assume instead that she dies in 1999, then only the face amount is due.

Family income rider — A type of family income life insurance plan whereby the full face amount of a whole life policy is paid upon the death of the breadwinner, rather than at the end of the family income period, and income is paid to the family according to a decreasing term life insurance schedule. Also see "Family income policy."

Family income splitting — Generally, any of various techniques used to divide income between family members in order to avoid income taxes, in that younger members of a family are typically in a much lower tax bracket.

Family maintenance policy — Specialized life insurance providing coverage for an entire family, consisting of both whole life (or other form of permanent insurance) and level term insurance on the breadwinner, along with less coverage on dependents (usually term insurance). This program is designed to provide the beneficiaries of the breadwinner's policy a fixed monthly income period after the death of the breadwinner, if he or she dies within the period of coverage provided by the term insurance portion. It differs from a family income policy in that the income period of a family maintenance policy does not diminish but remains fixed. Also see "Family income policy." If the breadwinner happens to live beyond the term insurance coverage, then only the face amount of the whole life policy is payable. For example, Brooks purchases a family maintenance policy on himself and his family. The term coverage is for 25 years and the family income period is 20 years. If Brooks dies within 25 years after coverage begins, then the family will automatically receive income for the next 20 years; afterward, the face amount of the whole life portion is payable. Should he die after 25 years, then only the face amount of the whole life is due.

Family of funds — A group of mutual funds managed by the same company.

Family policy — A broad term generally referring to one of many types of life insurance coverages for an entire family in one policy. Typically, whole life (or some other form of permanent life insurance) coverage on the husband with lesser amounts of insurance on the lives of dependents (usually term insurance). Normally, premiums are based on the life of the husband, and the number of dependent children have no effect as to the amount of premium due.

Family purpose rule — In a few states, parents may be liable for negligent acts of their children. Also see "Family automobile doctrine."

Family trust interest — Generally, a testamentary trust set up for beneficiaries other than the surviving spouse, designed to take full advantage of the unified transfer tax credit for property transferred to it upon the settlor's death.

Fannie Mae — See "Federal National Mortgage Association."

Fare — The price to travel on passenger transportation.

F.A.S. — Free alongside ship. Seller incurs all transportation charges to destination's dock ("alongside ship"), where the buyer is then responsible for loading onto a carrier or other means of transportation. It is mainly used in export or import shipments.

Federal crime insurance — Insurance coverage for robbery, burglary, and larceny written directly by the Federal Insurance Administration where there is a critical shortage of crime insurance offered at affordable rates; is available for both businesses and residences.

Federal Deposit Insurance Corporation (FDIC) — A corporation of the federal government established to insure bank deposits up to a statutory limit (for 1985, $100,000). Deposits in all national banks and participating state banks are covered.

Federal funds market — The borrowing of money between banks on an "overnight" basis.

Federal funds rate — A negotiated rate between banks for lending of excess reserves from one to another. The federal funds rate is one of the earliest indicators of monetary conditions in the funds market.

Federal Garnishment Law — A federal law (1970) limiting the amount of wages that are subject to garnishment.

Federal Home Loan Banks (FHLB) — Federal institutions (12) that loan to savings and loans, savings banks, cooperative banks, and others making long-term mortgage loans. They also regulate these lending institutions in a manner similar to the Federal Reserve banks' arrangements with commercial banks.

Federal Home Loan Mortgage Corporation (FHLMC) — A corporation of the federal government established to purchase conventional and government-backed home mortgages from members—institutions who have their deposits insured by a federal agency—for the purpose of reselling them to the public as mortgage-backed, pass-through securities, such as bonds and discount notes. The FHLMC is also known as "Freddie Mac."

Federal Housing Administration (FHA) — A federal agency under the Department of Housing and Urban Development (HUD) established for the purpose of insuring FHA-approved mortgage loans on residences.

Federal Insurance Contributions Act (FICA) — A federal law that imposes social security taxes on employers, employees, and self-employed individuals. Also see "Social security."

Federal Land Banks (FLB) — Regional banks (12) administered by the Farm Credit Administration for the purpose of granting long-term loans to farmers via a land bank association. Land bank associations are owned by farmers borrowing from them in that all borrowers must purchase stock in the association.

Federal National Mortgage Association (FNMA) — A privately owned, government-regulated corporation whose function is to buy conventional and government-backed mortgages when mortgage money is in short supply and to sell them when demand for mortgages declines. It buys mortgages with money raised through sales of short-term notes and debentures. The FNMA is also known as "Fannie Mae."

Federal Open Market Committee (FOMC) — The Federal Reserve System's operating arm consisting of 19 members: 7 Federal Reserve Board governors and the 12 regional Federal Reserve bank presidents (of which only 5 can vote—the president of the New York Fed and 4 others are on a rotating basis); considered to be one of the most influential, and powerful committees in America in that they establish Fed policy for regulating the money supply, which tends to dictate the level of future economic growth.

Federal Reserve (Fed) — A general term for the Federal Reserve System.

Federal Reserve Board — A 7-member board of governors regulating the activities of the 12 Federal Reserve banks.

Federal Reserve System — A national system of monetary control exercised by the Federal Reserve Board essentially through its influence on credit.

Federal Savings and Loan Insurance Corporation (FSLIC) — A corporation of the federal government established to insure deposits in thrifts, savings and loans, and similar financial institutions.

Fee simple defeasible — See "Defeasible title."

Fee simple estate — Complete and unrestricted ownership. Fee simple estate entitles the owner to sell or otherwise dispose of property, even through inheritance or gift, without conditions or limitations as to such transfer. Also known as "fee simple" or "fee simple absolute."

FHA mortgage insurance — Insurance for mortgage lenders on loans made with small down payments.

FICA — See "Federal Insurance Contributions Act."

Fidelity bond — A contract where a surety company agrees to reimburse an employer for the dishonest acts of employees. Also see "Surety."

Fiduciary — A person in a position of trust where he or she acts for another's benefit (e.g., a trustee or an executor of an estate). A fiduciary must act as a "prudent" person would under the circumstances. Also see "Prudent man rule."

Fiduciary bond — A type of surety bond required by law for persons acting as a fiduciary, such as trustees, administrators, and executors of an estate, guardians, custodians, receivers, and liquidators, to guarantee that they will properly fulfill their duties.

Field audit — An Internal Revenue Audit conducted on the taxpayer's premises.

FIFO — First-in, first-out; a method of accounting for inventory in that the first items received in inventory are the ones used to figure cost of goods sold (regardless of the actual units sold). When prices are declining, FIFO will yield a higher cost of goods sold than other methods of computing inventory. Compare "LIFO."

Finance — (1) The management of money and investments; (2) to borrow or otherwise raise money for purchases; (3) anything pertaining to money.

Finance charge — (1) the cost of deferring payment of purchases or borrowings; (2) the cost of borrowing money.

Finance charges (consumers) — The cost of borrowing money for purchases made by using either a charge account or credit card. The fundamental formula for computing monthly finance charges is as follows:

Monthly
finance   =   Monthly finance rate × Account balance
charge

Various retail stores and credit card companies compute finance charges differently on their customers' accounts. Four basic computations are: the adjusted balance method, average daily balance method, past due balance method, and previous balance method. The main difference between each method is that the balance varies according to the type of method used by the lender. The adjusted balance method uses the account balance at the end of the billing period to find the monthly finance charge. The average daily balance method uses a weighted average of the account balance throughout the current billing period. The past due balance method allows the borrower to pay off any outstanding balance without a finance charge. (This is commonly used by bank credit cards.) Any outstanding balance left over, however, will be assessed a finance charge by one of the other methods (usually average daily balance); the previous balance method uses the balance at the end of the previous billing period. All consumer lending arrangements must reveal a reasonably accurate annual percentage rate and explain the method used in figuring such charges. Also see "Adjusted balance method," "Average daily balance method," "Previous balance method," and "Truth-in-Lending Act."

Finance company — A general term for companies specializing in making relatively small, short-term loans to individuals and small businesses. Typically, finance companies charge higher interest rates than most banks and credit unions.

Financial accounting — Generally, the method of accounting used by publicly held companies for their financial reports to stockholders; generally accepted accounting principles.

Financial Accounting Standards Board (FASB) — An independent board that establishes generally accepted accounting principles.

Financial future — A futures contract in interest-related securities, such as Treasury bills, Treasury bonds, and certificates of deposits. Also see "Futures contract."

Financial loss — A requirement of an insurable interest, which must indicate that an insured may suffer a financial hardship as a result of a certain peril(s).

Financial planning — A systematic organization of an individual's financial and personal condition toward achieving his or her specific economic goals. It generally entails writing down all financial objectives, designing a plausible plan, setting up detailed budgets, implementing the plan, and periodically reviewing and evaluating the system as a whole.

Financial position — Total assets and the corresponding manner in which they are owned as shown by a balance sheet.

Financial responsibility laws — State laws requiring the owners of automobiles to obtain liability insurance or show proof of financial capability as a condition for obtaining a license or registration.

Financial statement — Any report summarizing the financial activities of an individual or business for a given date or period. A balance sheet, income statement, statement of changes in financial position, and statement of retained earnings are customarily referred to as the financial statements of a publicly held company.

Financing cost[1] — The cost of borrowing money (interest, closing costs, and other related charges).

Finder's fee — A payment for bringing together two individuals for a transaction (e.g., borrower and lender, issuer of securities and underwriter, or buyer and seller).

Fire insurance — Insurance for direct losses in specified properties resulting from fire and lightning. A basic fire insurance contract generally indemnifies an insured for actual cash value (i.e., replacement cost new less amounts attributable to economic obsolescence, decline in market value, and wear and tear of physical property from ordinary use).

Firm bid — An unconditional offer that is to remain open until acceptance or refusal.

Firm order — An order to buy or sell given to a broker-dealer where the order can be executed within a given period without confirmation from the customer.

First mortgage — A mortgage with a priority right to payment before all subordinate encumbrances in case of default.

First mortgage bond — A bond secured by a first mortgage on property.

First right-of-refusal — A right, generally given to a person in an adverse position if certain property is sold or otherwise disposed, to purchase such property before any other buyer. For example, James, a tenant of a leased building, is given first right-of-refusal in her lease agreement to purchase it if the building is ever up for sale. In some closely held corporations, the corporation is given a first right-of-refusal to purchase stock of a shareholder who wishes to sell, in order to keep outstanding shares with existing stockholders.

First-year commission — In insurance, any commission payable to a salesman from the receipt by the company of first-year premiums, as opposed to residuals in the latter years.

First-year premiums — In insurance, all premiums due within the first year that the policy is in effect.

Fiscal policy — A comprehensive national policy designed by government to direct its expenditures and receipts toward desirable economic goals.

Fiscal year — Any 12-month period other than January 1 through December 31.

Fixed annuity — A contract specifying that an annuitant will receive a fixed amount of income over a certain period or for life.

Fixed asset — Tangible, long-term property used in the operations of a business. It is not expected to be turned into cash within 12 months (or the operating cycle, if longer than 12 months). Examples include land, buildings, machinery, and equipment. Fixed assets are listed as a major category of a classified balance sheet.

Fixed capital — (1) Stockholder's equity (i.e., permanent investment in a business); (2) money invested by a business in fixed assets, such as property, plant, and equipment.

Fixed income — Consistent amounts of income rather than variable income. Fixed income usually refers to amounts received by a retiree from a fixed annuity, fixed pension, or other form of retirement benefit, but it also includes interest received from bonds or preferred stocks. The significance of fixed income is that it does not increase during periods of inflation, thereby leaving its recipient with less spending power.

Fixed-income investment trust — A unit investment trust that typically invests in a certain type of security, such as municipal, government, or corporate bonds, for the purpose of providing fixed income to its holders. Its units are usually sold through brokerage houses.

Fixed-period option — A clause in a life insurance policy providing the beneficiary with an option to receive the proceeds in installments over a fixed period of time, such as 5 or 10 years.

Fixed-price contract — An agreement between buyer and seller where the buyer agrees to purchase goods or services for a certain price.

Fixed-rate mortgage — A traditional mortgage for buyers of real property where a loan's interest rate and mortgage payments are fixed. Compare "Adjustable rate mortgage."

Fixed trust — A unit investment trust consisting of an unmanaged fixed portfolio of securities, normally interest-bearing bonds. Also see "Fixed-income investment trust," "Participating trust," and "Unit investment trust."

Fixture — Items of personal property attached to realty in such a manner that they become part of the real property. Fixtures generally convey to a buyer of real property, unless they are trade fixtures or are specifically excepted.

Flat — (1) In insurance, a policy not having a coinsurance clause; (2) in investments, a security sold without accrued income, such as without accrued interest or dividends (also see "Flat bond"); (3) for real property, an apartment or a floor of a building used as a dwelling unit.

Flat bond — A bond trading without accrued interest.

Flat cancellation — In insurance, the termination of a policy before coverage takes effect. Full refund of paid premium is usually required of the company.

Flat-dollar-deductible clause — In insurance contracts, a provision specifying a certain amount of money to be subtracted from a loss before the loss-benefits are received.

Flat price — A quoted sales price that has no other adjustments; total price, including handling, processing, taxes, and all other charges.

Flat tax — A tax assessed by one tax rate.

Fleet policy — A single insurance contract covering a number of automobiles owned by one insured. Coverage may apply to each automobile as designated in a policy, or a policy may provide automatic coverage for all automobiles.

Flexible expenditures — See "Discretionary income."

Flexible rate mortgage — See "Adjustable rate mortgage."

Float — (1) A time lag between when a check is written and when it is deducted from the balance of a checking account by the institution; (2) for investments, the number of shares held by the public.

Floater policy — An insurance policy covering movable personal articles (i.e., having no permanent location), such as jewelry, baggage, sporting equipment, and furs. Three major types of floater policies are personal property floater, personal effects floater, and personal articles floater. The personal property floater covers practically all personal property (except autos, boats, airplanes, etc.) both inside a home and outside. (The broad coverage attributable to homeowner policies has practically replaced this coverage.) The personal effects floater is basically traveler's coverage in that it insures against losses occurring away from home. The personal articles floater provides all-risk, additional coverage on personal property and is normally attached to a homeowner's policy.

Floating debt — A general term referring to short-term obligations that are either due within 12 months or payable on demand, as opposed to long-term debt.

Floating lien — See "Add-on clause."

Flood insurance — Generally, coverage provided by the federal government (through the Federal Insurance Administration via private insurance agents) for losses because of flooding, although some policies are privately written through special and allied fire coverage. Most homeowner's policies, however, exclude flood damage coverage because such risk was evaluated to be "economically uninsurable" without charging unreasonable premiums.

Floor broker — As a member of an exchange, one who executes trades for brokerage firms that experience an excessive volume in trading. As an employee of a member firm, one who executes trades for customers of the member firm.

Floor plan financing — A type of lending arrangement for retailers (typically automobile dealers) where similar items can be purchased and included in inventory without taking out separate loans.

Floor trader — A member of a securities or commodity exchange who trades for his or her own account without having to use a broker.

Flower bonds — Generally, U.S. government bonds used to pay a deceased owner's estate taxes. They are typically bought at substantial discount, and subsequently used at face value to pay the tax. For estate tax purposes, however, they are valued at face value for inclusion in gross estate, rather than at fair market value. The U.S. Treasury has not been authorized to issue these bonds since March 3, 1971.

FOB — "Free on board." Generally, FOB shipping point or FOB destination signifies the location where title to shipped goods will pass. For example, assume Nash, who lives in Los Angeles, purchased goods in New Orleans, FOB Los Angeles. Title to such goods will pass in LA, therefore seller is responsible for shipping and insurance charges; the invoice price or total price should include such amounts.

Forbearance — Restraint; not acting; postponement of enforcing a right, usually associated with creditors or would-be plaintiffs.

Forced loan — A loan made by necessity rather than for profit, such as when a promissory note becomes due and payable and the debtor cannot pay without an extension of the original loan.

Forced sale — Any involuntary or necessary sale to satisfy an obligation or to make an inventory adjustment. Such sales usually result in prices that are lower than those normally received in ordinary retailing circumstances. A liquidation sale, overstocked inventory sale, or discontinued items sale are examples.

For collection — A restrictive indorsement of a negotiable instrument not intending to transfer title, but rather to allow the transferee to collect it.

For deposit only — A restrictive indorsement of a check that restricts further transfer unless the indorsement is completed.

Foreclosure — The termination of all rights, interest, and title to property held by a mortgagor for the purpose of selling such property to satisfy a claim held by the mortgagee.

Foreign bill of exchange — A type of negotiable instrument drawn in one country (or state) and payable in another.

Foreign-earned income — Generally for income tax purposes, an individual's earned income from sources within a foreign country directly attributable to services performed (IRC Section 911(b)(1)(A)).

Foreign exchange — A market trading foreign currencies.

Foreign exchange rate — The price of one country's currency stated in the currency of another.

Foreign-income exclusion[1] — Qualified income earned while working abroad that is excluded from the gross income of U.S. citizens. Up to $80,000 ($85,000 in 1988, $90,000 in 1989, and $95,000 in 1990 and thereafter) of earnings may be excluded by either bona fide residents of foreign countries or U.S. residents living abroad for 330 days out of any 12 consecutive months during 1986 and 1987 (IRC Section 911).

Foreign trust — Any trust created in a foreign country and applicable under its laws. Foreign trusts were widely used as a tax shelter to avoid U.S. income taxes, but their use has since been curtailed.

Foresight — Reasonable anticipation for future events.

Forfeiture — Something surrendered, typically as penalty, for not acting in accordance with an agreement.

Forgery — The fraudulent alteration, execution, or transfer of any writing purported to be that of someone else (e.g., fraudulently signing another's check and cashing it).

Formal contract — A written agreement, as opposed to an oral one. Also see "Contract."

Forms of business organization — The manner in which an owner or owners of a business possess and control it. There are three basic types (with variations): proprietorship, partnership, and corporation. A proprietorship has only one owner, who individually owns all assets and has absolute control; a partnership has two or more owners of business assets and divided control; a corporation is a separate legal entity that owns all its assets and is controlled by agents, which are hired by the board of directors (who are voted in by stockholders). Also see "Corporation," "Partnership," and "Sole proprietorship."

Formula plan — Any systematic or mechanical method of investing in securities for the purpose of taking advantage of cyclical price swings in the market. A formula plan essentially relies on the common assumption that security prices will always fluctuate, and it minimizes emotional prejudices by establishing certain rules, which must be strictly followed in order for the system to work. Also see "Constant dollar method," "Constant ratio plan," "Dollar-cost averaging," and "Variable ratio plan."

Fortuitous event — Any event occurring by accident or chance.

Forward buying — The purchasing at current prices of a contract for delivery of goods in the future.

Forward contract[1] — A special (e.g., nonstandardized and nontransferable) contract between a buyer and seller for the future sale of an item under agreed-upon terms. Forward contracts are not traded publicly on a regulated commodity exchange.

Forwarding agent — A company or individual who receives and ships cargo for others. Typically, a forwarding agent receives many small loads and ships in bulk for lower rates.

Forward market — A market consisting of participants trading commodities or securities at an agreed-upon price for delivery on a future date.

Foundation — A public or private charitable institution that receives endowments for the purpose of providing for others.

401(k) plans — See "Cash or deferred arrangement."

403(b) annuity — A tax-deferred annuity only available to employees of a tax-exempt organization.

Fractional share — Less than whole share of stock, such as ¼ share.

Franchise — A license privately granted to an individual or business to manufacture, distribute, market, store, or otherwise conduct business in such manner as provided by the franchisor under its name.

Franchise deductible — In insurance contracts, the amount of a deductible that a loss must equal or exceed before the entire amount of loss is paid. A straight deductible is always deducted from a loss; in a franchise deductible, the deductible amount is a threshold at which point the entire loss is indemnified if damages equal or exceed it.

Franchise insurance — A type of life insurance that resembles group life in that each participant's insurance is determined by a formula, and it is usually offered by an employer. Unlike group life insurance, however, each participant receives an individual policy. The employee or employer or both may pay the premiums on the policy. If an employee pays any portion of a premium, the employer collects and remits it to the insurance company. Often such premium is at or near regular group life rates. Franchise insurance is typically used where regular group life insurance is not available because of insufficient number of group participants. Generally, there is no medical examination, but the insurer may reject any prospective participant because of failing to meet standards of insurability as determined from answers to questions in the application. Such policies are ordinarily yearly renewable term. Small professional societies and similar organizations offer franchise insurance to their members as a benefit of membership. Franchise insurance is also called "wholesale insurance."

Fraternal benefit society — A not-for-profit organization which provides insurance benefits (e.g., life, health, disability, and hospitalization) to its members. Insureds under such system usually participate in the earnings of the society, but are also levied assessments when future benefits are deemed inadequate or insufficient.

Fraternal companies — A specialized insurer providing life or health benefits to a restricted group with a common interest (e.g., a church group). They have no stockholders and the insureds participate in the company's experience. Typically, a fraternal company is a nonprofit organization operating for the benefit of its insureds and beneficiaries. Also see "Fraternal benefit society."

Fraud — Deliberate deception created by an individual with intentional reliance thereon by another, for the purpose of unlawful or unfair gain. In tax cases, the IRS has the burden of proving fraud.

Freddie Mac — See "Federal Home Loan Mortgage Corporation (FHLMC)."

Free alongside ship — See "F.A.S.."

Free and clear — A deed to real property without liens.

Freehold — An estate in real property for an indefinite duration (e.g., a right of title in real property for a lifetime).

Free on board — See "FOB."

Fringe benefit[1] — A benefit received by an employee in addition to compensation, which may or may not qualify to be excluded from an employee's taxable income, but is usually tax-deductible for the employer.

Frivolous tax return — A tax return composed of unquestionably inappropriate or insignificant information filed with the Internal Revenue Service. The filing of a frivolous tax return carries a penalty; at one time such returns were frequently filed by tax protestors.

Front-end load — In a mutual fund savings plan where an investor agrees to periodically purchase mutual fund shares, and total commissions are assessed for all planned purchases during the early years of the program. Thus, an investor's account under a front-end load arrangement is not fully credited with share purchases until all load charges have been satisfied.

Frozen asset — (1) Generally, an asset that cannot be sold, such as an asset used as security for a loan; (2) an asset not easily convertible into cash without substantial loss.

Full coverage — (1) The amount of insurance covering the full amount of loss and without any deductible (hence, small losses are covered in full); (2) an "all risks" form of insurance providing coverage for all insurable perils.

Full disclosure — (1) A legal requirement for certain individuals (e.g., sellers of consumer goods, real estate brokers selling homes, lenders of consumer credit, and candidates for political office) to reveal pertinent facts about specified transactions, data, or other significant information; (2) in accounting, a principle stating that all events that could have a significant impact on a user's decision must be revealed.

Full-service broker — A securities broker that provides customers with services other than merely executing buy/sell orders, such as giving investment advice, providing sophisticated current investment analyses, issuing checking or other highly liquid accounts with money market interest and with credit or debit cards, or issuing individual retirement accounts, among other various services.

Full-service bank — A commercial bank providing all of the traditional banking services, such as maintaining checking and savings accounts, cashing checks, lending money, issuing or cashing traveler's and cashier's checks, and maintaining lock boxes.

Full-replacement coverage — A provision in property insurance contracts providing indemnity without any reduction for depreciation.

Full settlement — An agreement reached between two parties that renders a mutual release of all previous obligations between them.

Functional — Something that performs its intended use or purpose.

Functional obsolescence — Generally refers to assets that have become outdated or inefficient due to technological advances or discoveries.

Fundamental analysis — A type of investment analysis that takes a quantitative, in-depth look into the financial and other business affairs of a particular company. The essential principle of fundamental analysis is that the price of a company's stock is greatly influenced by the company's performance. The expectation of future performance is determined by current and expected overall economic conditions as well as the financial strengths and weaknesses of a company. By using the income statement, balance sheet, and statement of changes in financial position, the strengths and weaknesses can be demonstrated by using ratios and other related formulas. Compare "Technical analysis."

Funded debt — Long-term liabilities, generally pertaining to bonds or other long-term obligations (as opposed to short-term borrowing).

Funded insurance trust — A trust, consisting of life insurance policies and income-producing assets, of which the income from the latter pays all premiums of the former.

Funded retirement plan — A retirement plan where funds are set aside to earn income and to pay future benefits.

Funding — The capitalization or financing of an organization or project.

Funds — In general, money.

Fungibles — Each unit of a particular commodity, good, or security which is identical or equivalent to other individual units, such as a bushel of corn or 100 shares of ABC Corporation common stock.

Further advance — A loan subsequent to an earlier loan, usually on the same collateral.

Future-acquired property clause — In a mortgage arrangement, a provision stating that property acquired after a loan or certain other event will be subject to a lien. Also see "Add-on clause."

Future advance clause — A provision in a lending arrangement allowing the borrower the privilege to borrow additional money on the same collateral.

Future interest — The delayed privilege of possession or enjoyment in land or other property. Such privilege of possession or enjoyment will arise upon the occurrence of a future event. Examples include a remainder interest, reversionary interest, or contingent interest.

Future performance — An act that is to occur subsequent to a specified event, such as a promise to act after a contract is signed.

Futures contract — An agreement to either accept delivery of a certain item at a future date (a purchase) or deliver a certain item at a future date (a sale). The price in either case is determined at the current market price of the object, not the item's price in the future. Hence, a buyer wanting huge amounts of oats is able to make an agreement to accept the commodity in the future at the currently available price, and thus be shielded from future price increases in oats. A speculator, on the other hand, would offer such a contract to deliver oats (though rarely would oats actually be delivered by a speculator because the contract is nearly always settled before delivery date), in hopes the price of oats will decrease, thereby making the contract more valuable (short position). Another speculator, who hopes for future price increases, would want to make a contract at the currently available price for the future acceptance of oats (long position). Also see "Futures market."

Future service benefits — As used in employee benefit programs, accrued benefits pertaining to service after the plan's effective date.

Futures market — A market which trades in futures contracts. Generally, such trading is done in organized exchanges (e.g., Chicago Board of Trade and Chicago Mercantile Exchange); futures contracts are typically traded for commodities, raw materials, or financial instruments. Commodities and raw materials commonly traded include corn, oats, soybeans, soybean meal, soybean oil, wheat, barley, flaxseed, rapeseed, rye, cattle, hogs, pork bellies, cocoa, coffee, cotton, orange juice, sugar, copper, aluminum, gold, platimum, palladium, silver, NY gasoline, heating oil, crude oil, and lumber. Financial futures include British pounds, Canadian dollars, Japanese yen, Swiss francs, German marks, Eurodollars, sterling, long gilt, Ginnie Maes, Treasury bonds, Treasury notes, Treasury bills, bank CDs, S&P 500 Futures Index, major market index, NYSE Composite Futures, and KC Value Line futures. Also see "Futures contract."

G

GAAP — See "Generally accepted accounting principles."

Gain — For income tax purposes, the excess of the amount realized over the adjusted basis of property subject to a sale, exchange, or other taxable disposition. Also see "Gain realized" and "Gain recognized."

Gain realized[1] — (1) In a nontaxable exchange, the excess of fair market value of all items received over the adjusted basis of all items given. If no boot is received or appreciated property given, then none of the gain realized will be gain recognized (taxable); (2) the maximum amount of gain that can become taxable gain. Also see "Gain recognized."

Gain recognized[1] — Generally, the amount of taxable gain resulting from a sale or exchange. In a sale, the amount of gain recognized is the fair market value of amounts received (typically cash) in excess of the adjusted basis of the item sold. Whether this gain qualifies for long-term capital gain treatment, recapture of depreciation, or recapture of investment tax credit (all of which have a direct impact on gain recognized) depends on the type of asset sold and, perhaps, the required holding period. In a like-kind exchange, the amount of gain recognized is the lesser of gain realized or boot received. Also see "Gain realized."

Gambling — (1) Participating in any wagering activity, which consists of paying for a chance of receiving more than originally paid in; (2) for investors, an investment in a highly speculative venture where the odds of loss greatly outweigh the odds of receiving a return.

Game of chance — Any activity where success or failure depends entirely on probabilities, rather than on the expertise and skill of each participant, such as a lottery.

Garnishment[1] — As a result from a legal proceeding, the withholding of money (usually earnings) of a debtor for payment of a debt.

Gasoline tax — An excise tax assessed by both state and federal governments on the purchase of gasoline. Gasoline taxes are not deductible as an itemized deduction by individual consumers.

Genealogy — The study of a family's ancestry and history.

General benefits — As used in a condemnation, direct or indirect benefits resulting from a condemnation, on any properties not taken. For example, a farmer loses a portion of farmland for the construction of an interstate highway. One pasture not taken is located at a proposed busy entrance-exit, making it extremely valuable. This is a general benefit, which cannot reduce due compensation.

General bequest — As directed by a testator, a bequest to be paid out of the general assets of an estate, rather than a specific bequest of a particular object. For example, Tyler bequeaths 500 shares of IBM stock to Smith; the estate is solvent, but has no IBM stock. If this is interpreted as a specific bequest, then ademption applies. If this is interpreted as a general bequest, then funds from the general assets of the estate will be used to purchase 500 shares of IBM. Also see "Bequest."

General contractor — An individual or company who contracts to complete an entire project, rather than a specific portion. By doing so, reponsibility to complete such project is assumed by the general contractor, who ordinarily hires subcontractors to work on specific parts of the project.

General executor — An executor who has broad powers to administer a whole estate to final settlement.

General legacies — A testamentary gift of money from the general assets of an estate. Also see "General bequest."

General liability insurance — A form of insurance which protects the insured against claims arising out of a legal liability to pay for losses or damages because of a personal, professional, or business involvement. Basically, general liability insurance is all types of liability coverages other than automobile liability and employer's liability insurance, such as the keeping of pets, participation in sporting activities, and professional malpractice, as well as owners', landlords', tenants', and businesses' exposure to visitors, delivery persons, children, trespassers, salespersons, and so forth.

General lien — (1) A lien that attaches to all property owned by the debtor, instead of to a specific property; (2) the right of a creditor, in accordance with a prior agreement, to hold collateral security, which pertains to a different lien, until all accounts are settled in full.

Generally accepted accounting principles (GAAP) — The fundamental body of conventions, rules, and procedures that defines the practice of accounting for the financial activities of all publicly held corporations for the primary purpose of comparability. GAAP is largely developed through established accounting procedures derived from the general practice of accounting and from pronouncements from the Financial Accounting Standards Board.

General obligation bond — A municipal bond that is secured only through the faith, credit, and general revenue raising powers of the issuing government agency.

General partner[1] — As opposed to a limited partner, a managing partner in a partnership who has authority to manage the day-to-day affairs, to control all partnership assets, and to bind the partnership in business-related transactions. Usually, in a tax-shelter investment the general partner is the originator, developer, and promoter of the activity. A general partner has unlimited personal liability to satisfy all partnership debts in case of partnership default. Compare "Limited partner."

General partnership — A partnership consisting of only general partners. Compare "Limited partnership." Also see "General partner."

General power of appointment — A right given to an individual to transfer the ownership of property, which is currently held by another party such as a trust or estate, in a manner that permits such person to select himself or herself. For example, Peterson creates a trust whereby Jackson is given the power to select any person she wishes to have the trust's property. Because Jackson is able to choose herself, she is said to hold a general power of appointment.

Generation — (1) A group of people having a common, contemporaneous culture or social attitude; (2) A single stage of descent from at least one common parent; (3) for generation-skipping transfers made to non-family members, 12½ to 37½ years younger than the grantor is generation one, and every 25 years thereafter is another generation.

Generation-skipping tax — Generally, a tax imposed on a generation-skipping transfer of a property, right, or virtually any ability to receive property as a result of such transfer. A generation-skipping transfer is a transfer which splits a beneficial interest between two generations, where one generation is at least two generations younger than that of the transferor. For example, Larkins creates a trust for the purpose of paying all income to his son, and upon his son's death, Larkins's grandson is to receive all trust property. In this case, Larkins's son becomes the deemed transferor. The first $250,000 of transfers per child of the creator of a generation-skipping trust or equivalent is excluded.

Generation-skipping trust — A trust which transfers a beneficial interest between two generations, where one generation is two or more generations subsequent to that of the creator. A generation-skipping trust may or may not be subject to the generation-skipping tax, depending upon the amount and other circumstances involved. Also see "Generation-skipping tax."

Gentlemen's agreement — A verbal agreement between two parties which is not reduced to writing and may not be enforceable.

Gerontology — The study of aging.

Gift — A voluntary, gratuitous transfer of property without receiving any economically significant consideration in return. A gift must have all such requisites: capacity and intent of the donor to make a gift, and delivery and acceptance by or for the donee.

Gift causa mortis — Generally, a gift made because of an expectation of the donor's death with specific conditions: death must appear certain due to a physical disorder and eventually results (because of the disorder), and the gift is to only take place in the event of such death, which in fact occurs.

Gift in contemplation of death — See "Contemplation of death."

Gift inter vivos — A gift made by a donor while living, as opposed to a gift made after death, which is a testamentary gift.

Gift splitting — Generally for gifts made by married individuals (or any two or more individuals who have ownership), a method of avoiding the status of a taxable gift by donating $10,000 or less per donor-donee each year. For example, a man wants to give each son $20,000 each year. If his wife consents, the gift splitting provision will allow both husband and wife to observe the $10,000 limit per donor-donee and make the $20,000 nontaxable gift to each son.

Gift tax — Generally, an excise tax imposed on tranfers made for no (or inadequate) consideration while the transferor is living. Gifts of $10,000 or less between a donor and donee during a taxable year are tax-free. Gifts in excess of $10,000 during a taxable year are taxable gifts to the extent such gift exceeds $10,000. Under current law, in 1986 accumulated taxable gifts of $500,000 and in 1987 accumulated taxable gifts of $600,000 can be transferred without actually paying a gift tax because of the unified transfer tax credit. All accumulated taxable gifts, however, will be added to the donor's gross estate at death. Also see "Estate tax."

Gift-tax marital deduction — Qualified gifts from one spouse to the other without incurring a gift tax. All outright gifts qualify for the deduction.

Gift to Minors Act — See "Uniform Gift to Minors Act (UGMA)."

GI loan — See "Veterans Administration (VA) loans."

Gilt-edged security — A high-quality security known for an established record of dividend or interest payments. It typically refers more to bonds than stocks.

Ginnie Mae — See "Government National Mortgage Association."

Ginnie Mae pass-through[2] — A security that represents a proportional interest in a pool of mortgages. The security is called a pass-through because homeowners send monthly mortgage payments to a bank, which passes through the security holder's share of the payment after deducting a service charge. Timely payment of interest and principal is guaranteed by the Government National Mortgage Association (GNMA or Ginnie Mae). Original principal amount is stated on the security certificate, but remaining principal's balance is reduced monthly. The technical name for these securities is GNMA Modified Pass-Through because the coupon rate or production rate on the certificates is modified by the deduction of $1/2$ percent from the loan rate of the mortgage pool. This deduction pays for the sponsoring bank's services. The principal is passed through without deduction. Also see "Government National Mortgage Association."

Glut — An oversupply of a commodity or service, which generally leads to a decline in its price.

Give notice — Generally, to communicate the termination of a relationship which is to occur at a future date, such as an employee "gives notice" to his or her present employer that the resignation of such person is to take place in two weeks.

GNMA — See "Government National Mortgage Association."

GNP — See "Gross national product."

GNP deflator — A revised computation of gross national product incorporating the effects of inflation and which is stated in terms of a stable-value dollar.

Go-go fund — An agressive-growth mutual fund that has as its major objective the rapid growth of capital, rather than the payment of dividends or interest. These funds typically buy speculative and growth stocks; in riskier funds, they may even execute short sales, speculatively purchase puts and calls, and use leverage to achieve such growth.

Going price — See "Fair market value."

Going public — Generally used to mean that a privately held corporation is issuing its first shares for sale to the public.

Golden handshake — An inducement for an employee's early retirement which may be made in the form of a lump-sum payment (e.g., the present value of "lost earnings" because of retirement) or monthly income (e.g., the amount of lost retirement benefits because of early retirement).

Golden parachute — A large bonus or other form of compensation that becomes payable to an executive of a corporation when it is taken over by another company, which terminates the executive's employment.

Good faith — Something done with good, honest intentions and without knowledge of wrongful circumstances which would ordinarily provide reasons for further inquiry.

Good faith deposit — In securities transactions, a deposit required by brokerage firms when a first-time customer enters into a transaction (usually 25 percent of the transaction).

Good faith purchaser — One who buys in good faith in that a prudent purchaser has no knowledge which would require an inquiry as to the seller's title or any other discrepancy.

Good-till-canceled order (GTC) — In securities transactions, an order to execute a buy or sell transaction, typically at a stop price, that continues in effect until it is either executed or canceled by the customer. A good-till-canceled order is also known as an "open order."

Goodwill — As used in accounting, an intangible asset resulting from the excess paid for a company over the fair market value of its assets. A purchaser is willing to pay such excess amount because of a well-established business, good public relations, well-respected reputation, existing marketing contacts, high employee morale, good management, location, etc.

Government National Mortgage Association (GNMA) — A wholly government-owned corporation (under the Department of Housing and Urban Development) that assists in financing home mortgages by purchasing mortgages from private lending institutions and guaranteeing securities backed by government-insured loans. Also see "Ginnie Mae pass-through."

Government property and liability insurance — A government insurance system covering a wide range of losses for exposures such as flood damage, credit losses on exports, property value declines because of war, savings and checking account losses, crop insurance disasters, and crime or riot damage.

Government securities — Generally, bonds or other securities issued or backed by a local, state, or federal government.

Grace period — A period of time after a scheduled due date in which payment can be made without being delinquent, such as an insurance policy (usually 30 days), mortgage, monthly rent, and other installment payments.

Graduated lease[1] — A leasing agreement calling for varying amounts of rent (usually increasing) in accordance with stipulated terms (periodic appraisal, consumer price index, increases of tenant's income, etc.)

Graduated payment mortgage — A type of home mortgage loan in which monthly payments begin at a lower amount than conventional loans for an initial period (e.g., three years) and then rise to either a level amount or incremental amounts for the duration of the mortgage. Usually, the annual payment increase reduces the loan's principal, rather than being applied as interest.

Graduated tax rates — Tax rates that increase (up to a certain percentage) as taxable income increases (up to a maximum amount).

Grandfather clause — A provision in a new regulation that allows all those who are under the existing system to be exempt from the fulfillment of further qualifications.

Grant — The conveyance, gift, compensation, allowance, funding, or permission given by one who has ownership or authority to another. Three examples include a grant of money given by the government or private organization to fund scientific research, a transfer of land by the government without adequate consideration, and the transfer of ownership of real property by deed or other document.

Grant date — See "Date of grant."

Grantee — The recipient of a grant; the person named in a deed who acquires ownership of real property.

Grantor — The transferor of a grant. The creator of a trust is considered the grantor of such property. Also see "Option writer." The transferor of real property.

Grantor trust[1] — A type of trust in which the grantor retains control over the trust's assets or income (or both) and is taxed on income generated by the trust.

Gratuitous — Something given or performed without economic or legal consideration.

Gray area[1] — An area in law not easily defined, evident, perceived, etc.

Grievance procedures — The system of filing a complaint by an employee or employer regarding a work-related situation.

Gross — In financial planning, in toto, whole, aggregate, or without reductions.

Gross estate — All assets that are required to be included by the Internal Revenue Code in a decedent's estate for estate tax purposes. All such assets are generally valued at fair market value on the date of death or alternate valuation date, whichever is chosen by an estate administrator.

Gross income[1] — Income received in the form of money, property, or services that is not specifically excluded from taxation by law. A flow of wealth must occur (earnings, wages, sale or exchange of property, etc.,), there must be actual or constructive receipt, income must be realized (a transaction must occur to produce income), and income must be recognized in accordance with the Internal Revenue Code.

Gross margin — See "Gross profit."

Gross national product (GNP) — Generally, a measure of the total amount of a nation's output for a period of one year. The GNP is stated in terms of the prevailing value of a dollar for that year. Compare "GNP deflator."

Gross premium — The amount of premium payable to an insurance company without any reductions (e.g., for dividends).

Gross profit — Total revenues less cost of goods sold. Gross profit does not include other operating and nonoperating expenses.

Gross profit ratio — A ratio generally used to analyze the trends of inventory costs of a particular enterprise by comparing the ratio over a number of years in the same company and by comparing the current year's gross profit ratio between companies within the same industry:

$$\text{Gross profit ratio} \ = \ \frac{\text{Gross profit}}{\text{Net sales}}$$

Gross revenues — Revenues that are not reduced by returns, allowances, or expenses.

Gross sales — Total sales, that is, without any reductions such as sales discounts and sales returns and allowances.

Ground rent — Rent paid only for the use of land, not for the use of buildings or other property.

Group accidental death and dismemberment insurance — A type of group health insurance designed primarily to replace lost income by providing a specified payment for the loss of life, eyesight, or limb because of an external accident. It is generally offered as an employee fringe benefit, but can be purchased through professional and other nonprofit organizations. Also see "Group health insurance."

Group annuities — Under a pension plan, annuities set up for employees by an employer for purposes of providing retirement benefits. If an insurance or pension company is used, the employer is given a master plan and all participants are given individual membership certificates that outline all benefits. A group annuity may take the form of either a refund annuity or straight-life annuity. There are two basic plans: defined benefit and defined contribution. Under a defined benefit (fixed benefit) plan, the benefits to be received are determined in advance and all contributions are set to fund it. In a defined contribution (money purchase) plan, the cost is fixed and whatever annuity credits are bought will determine the benefit.

Group credit health insurance — Insurance specifically designed to pay a disabled debtor's payments until recovered or until the balance of a certain debt is paid.

Group creditor life insurance — A type of group life insurance plan where a lending institution is provided a policy to insure the lives of debtors who plan to pay off a loan on the installment basis. It serves to guarantee all covered loans in the event a borrower does not live to complete the payments.

Group dental insurance — A specialized class of group health insurance that covers most dental services. See "Dental insurance."

Group disability income insurance — An income plan that is usually provided as a form of group health plan (from an employer or professional organization) and is primarily designed to relieve participants from financial distress caused by disability. Group disability coverage generally provides protection against losses from nonoccupational accidental injuries and nonoccupational sickness. Most policies establish a maximum duration of benefits, such as for two years or up to age 65, while others are payable for life. When group disability income benefits are received by a disabled employee, they are usually taxable income. Also see "Group health insurance."

Group health insurance — Generally, any one of several types of group insurance that indemnifies an insured because of a health-related off-the-job accident or sickness. (Worker's compensation normally covers on-the-job injuries or sickness.) Two broad categories of group health insurance are medical expense reimbursement and income reimbursement. Medical expense reimbursement pays for the cost (or portion) of most forms of medical costs; income reimbursement pays for loss of income because of disability, dismemberment, or accidental death. The general types of such coverage are group hospital expense insurance, group surgical expense insurance, group regular medical expense insurance, group major medical expense insurance, group dental insurance, group vision care insurance, group disability income insurance, group accidental death and dismemberment insurance, and health maintenance organizations (HMOs). Group health plans are typically provided to employees on either a noncontributory or contributory basis and through professional associations or other organizations on a contributory basis. Also see "Group insurance."

Group hospital expense insurance — A form of group health insurance designed to provide coverage (reimbursement) for in-hospital room and board and medical expenses to insureds, usually employees who suffer from a nonoccupational injury or sickness. Such plans are generally limited by a per day amount for room and board and hospital medical-care expenses, while other plans have only a "reasonable and customary" limitation on in-hospital medical charges. Most all group hospital expense plans include coverage for surgical and nonsurgical charges, though such benefits and corresponding limitations must be clearly stated in the group contract. Also see "Group health insurance."

Group hospital-medical-surgical expense insurance — See "Group hospital expense insurance."

Group insurance — Any one of several types of insurance that is offered through a group of individuals having a common interest, usually an employer and employees, and requiring group underwriting techniques. One contract is issued to the employer or group representative and each participant or family is issued an individual certificate. The two broadest categories of group coverage are life and health insurance. An employer is willing to provide group insurance to employees as a fringe benefit because it enhances employee morale, attracts and retains employees, fulfills a social obligation toward an employee and family, and helps maintain productivity. Two important aspects peculiar to group insurance, however, are that benefits may only be available during an employee's working years, and the coverages are often not enough to meet the entire cost of medical expenses and needs arising from disability or death.

Group legal insurance — A prepaid legal-expense plan generally offered to employees as a fringe benefit. Such coverage protects insureds against legal bills up to a specified limit and usually with qualifications. Some plans are of a "closed panel" variety, only offering services from a certain list or panel of attorneys, while other plans permit an open choice, allowing the insured the option of choosing any attorney.

Group life insurance — Any of several forms of life insurance offered only to members and their dependents of a certain group. The major categories of group life insurance are group-term, group permanent, and group creditor coverage. Employers customarily obtain group-term and group permanent life insurance for their employees, and financial institutions maintain creditor life insurance for their borrowers. Many trade, labor, professional, fraternal, and other similar organizations offer group life insurance to their members and dependents. Also see "Fraternal benefit society," "Group creditor life insurance," "Group insurance," "Group permanent life insurance," "Group-term life insurance." Compare "Franchise insurance."

Group major medical expense insurance — A very popular type of group health insurance primarily designed to provide blanket medical-expense-reimbursement coverage for virtually all types of medical expenses, including hospital room and board, medical care and surgery, services of doctors, nurses, other medical-care professionals, prescribed drugs and medicines, X-rays, oxygen, anesthesia, therapeutic equipment, surgical dressings, blood, plasma, and artificial limbs. Deductibles and limits vary according to the stipulations in each plan. Deductibles may range from $50 to $250 and maximum limits may range from $100,000 up. Coinsurance is applied to amounts beyond the deductible, usually on a 80–20 plan. There are two primary types of group major medical plans: supplemental and comprehensive. Supplemental plans are designed for individuals and families with existing group medical insurance, and its benefits are coordinated with such coverage. Comprehensive major medical plans are designed for individuals and families without any other medical expense protection, and it provides blanket coverage. Also see "Group health insurance."

Group permanent life insurance — A type of employee benefit plan whereby an employer or employee or both essentially purchase permanent life insurance over the employee's period of employment. The two basic types of group permanent insurance are group term with paid-up plans and level premium group permanent plans. The overall strategy for such arrangement is to provide the employee with the right of conversion or cash value upon termination or paid-up life insurance at retirement. Premiums paid by an employer are generally not received tax-free by an employee.

Group property and liability insurance — A type of mass merchandising plan sold to groups with a common interest (such as automobile clubs and employers), but with individual selection, rating, and contracts (i.e., not technically group insurance). Automobile insurance is the largest coverage provided by group property and liability insurance.

Group term life insurance — The most popular form of group insurance, which is generally provided by an employer. Other organizations, such as professional and fraternal societies, offer group term life insurance to their members at group rates. Most group term life insurance plans are yearly renewable term. Also see "Group insurance" and "Group life insurance."

Group vision care — A type of group health insurance primarily designed as an employee fringe benefit for the preventive and corrective aspects of maintaining good vision. Most plans cover expenses for examinations, frames, lenses, and fitting up to a maximum benefit limit. It is similar to dental insurance in that it is a prepayment of a regular medical expense for coverage of a particular group. Also see "Group insurance."

Growth funds — A type of investment company that primarily invests in growth-oriented stocks, rather than income-producing assets.

Growth industry — For investment purposes, an industry that grows at a faster rate than the gross national product, relatively few companies dominate the industry, obsolescence does not appear to be significant for the industry as a whole, and earnings are expected to double every six years.

Growth stock — A stock characterized by little or no dividend payout, above-average increases in market value, good prospects for continued rapid company growth and net earnings, and sometimes marked by a high price–earnings ratio.

Guarantee — (1) A person or organization to whom a guaranty is made; (2) a guaranty.

Guarantee clause — A clause in a contract or other instrument that provides security to such document in that the guarantor promises to pay the guarantee under specified conditions.

Guaranteed acceptance life insurance — A special type of nonmedical life insurance policy primarily designed for older individuals (ages 40–80) and others who have a problem obtaining life insurance.

Medical and health questions may or may not be eliminated in the application, but applicants are rarely turned down. The amount of protection is quite limited and decreases automatically with age (ranging from $1,000 to $50,000). The premium level in most such plans is fixed throughout the period of coverage. Deaths resulting from natural causes during the first several years, however, may not provide the beneficiary with a benefit equal to the policy's face value, but will only provide all premiums plus interest.

Guaranteed annual wage — A plan of employment where an employer agrees to maintain a certain number of employees over a specified period. It generally applies to seasonal or cyclical industries.

Guaranteed income contract — An obligation, generally assumed by insurance companies, that provides income to recipients over a specified period or for life. Also see "Guaranteed investment contract."

Guaranteed investment contract — For pension and profit sharing plans, an arrangement whereby an insurance company guarantees a rate of return for a limited period, usually 5 to 10 years, to be applied to a large deposit for funding a retirement plan.

Guaranteed purchase option — A rider attached to an ordinary or endowment life insurance policy (not term) guaranteeing the policyholder the option to purchase additional life insurance at standard rates at certain points in time without a medical examination.

Guaranteed refund life annuities — An annuity feature guaranteeing the payment of all the original cost of the contract or certain number of payments after the annuitant's death. Three basic types of guaranteed refund life annuities are installment refund life annuity, cash refund life annuity, and annuity certain. The installment refund life annuity will continue payments to a designated beneficiary until all payments equal the total purchase price. The cash refund life annuity pays the balance of the cost in lump-sum. The annuity certain provides a certain number of guaranteed payments, such as 25 years, which will continue to a designated beneficiary even after the annuitant's death until such period has expired.

Guaranteed renewable policy — Generally, a type of health insurance policy where the insured has the right to continue the policy throughout an average working lifetime (usually age 60 to 65) by making timely premium payments. The insurance company reserves the right, however, to change premium rates.

Guaranteed sale — In real estate, a guarantee provided in a listing agreement by a real estate broker that if the listed property does not sell within a specified period of time, then the broker will purchase it according to the terms of the agreement (usually at a substantial discount). Some employer's relocation packages provide a guaranteed sale benefit, customarily called a home-buying service, under similar conditions.

Guaranteed security — A bond or stock which has its payments (i.e., interest or dividends) guaranteed by another company. Such guarantee is sometimes developed as a result of a leasing agreement between the issuing company and a lessee. As part of the agreement, the leasing company would guarantee the lessor's interest, principal, or dividend payment.

Guarantor — The provider of a guaranty, that is one who is secondarily liable for payment or the performance of another. Compare "Surety."

Guaranty — (1) A promise by a guarantor assuring the payment of an obligation or the fulfillment of a performance of another person, business, or object; a warranty; compare "Surety"; (2) the holding of something as security for the completion of an obligation or fulfillment of a performance.

Guaranty bond — A bond having attributes of both a surety and fidelity bond to guarantee payment and performance.

Guardian — Generally, a court-appointed adult to manage the affairs of a minor or incompetent individual.

Guild — A social or economic group whose membership consists of individuals with a common vocation, trade, or profession. It serves to organize, promote, and protect their interests.

H

Habendum — In real estate, a clause in a deed defining the extent of a grantee's ownership.

Habitable repair — A term found in leasing agreements where the lessee is to return leased property in reasonable condition.

Hand money — Down payment made in cash; earnest money.

Hard dollars[1] — A term used in tax-sheltering investments for the net amount invested (actual amount of cash or other assets invested less tax savings received).

Hard goods — See "Durable goods."

Hard money — (1) Coins; (2) money in general; cash.

Hard money mortgage — A loan given in return for cash as security. Compare "Purchase money mortgage."

Hardship provision — As used in the transfer from one health plan to another (under the same employer), a participant will be reimbursed regardless of any preexisting condition covered under the old plan or active service requirements under new plan.

Hazards[5] — Various acts or conditions which increase the likelihood or severity of a loss. Ordinarily, many separate hazards are attached to any particular object or person, the sum of which constitutes the perils which cause risk. Hazards may be classified, in general, as either physical or moral.

Head of household — A tax term used to classify the filing status of an unmarried taxpayer (at the end of the year) who maintains his or her principal residence as a home for a child, stepchild, grandchild, or other descendant during a period of more than one half of the taxable year. Such individuals need not qualify as a dependent of the taxpayer. If the child, stepchild, grandchild, or other descendant is married, then he or she must qualify for a dependency exemption. Other individuals, who live in a taxpayer's home for more than one half year, may provide the head of household status to a taxpayer, but only if they qualify for a dependency exemption. See "Dependent." One exception to the "live-in-residence" requirement occurs when a taxpayer maintains another household which constitutes a principal place of abode for a parent, and the taxpayer is entitled to a dependency exemption for such parent. Over one half of the cost of maintaining a household must be maintained by the taxpayer in order to

[5]*General Insurance* (11th ed.), by David L. Bickelhaupt, (Homewood, Ill.: Richard D. Irwin, 1983).

qualify as head of household in all situations (IRC Section 2(b)(1)). Head of Household filing status provides qualified taxpayers with tax tables and rates that are lower than for single taxpayers and married filing separately, but higher than married filing jointly. The zero bracket amount for head of household, however, is the same as for single taxpayers. Compare "Surviving spouse (filing status)."

Health insurance — Any of various forms of insurance primarily designed to alleviate financial burdens suffered by individuals because of illness or injury. Health insurance policies can be grouped in the following manner: (1) medical expense reimbursement (e.g., hospital, surgical, regular medical, or major medical) or loss of income (e.g., total or partial loss that is either covered temporarily or permanently), (2) individual or group underwriting, (3) coverage for accident or sickness or both, (4) occupational or nonoccupational, (5) insured by private company or government agency, (6) first dollar or major medical (catastrophic) coverage, and (7) types of contracts, such as commercial, mail-order, industrial, or special purpose, and cancellable, continued at the option of the insurer, or continued at the option of the insured. Health insurance is sometimes called "accident and health insurance," "accident or sickness insurance," or "medical insurance." Common types of health insurance are hospital expense insurance, surgical expense insurance, physician's care expense insurance, major medical expense insurance, and comprehensive major medical insurance. Disability insurance, group dental insurance, group vision care insurance, group accidental death and dismemberment insurance, and health maintenance organizations (HMOs), worker's compensation, and Medicare and Medicaid also fall under the health insurance classification. Also see "Blue Cross, Blue Shield."

Health maintenance organization (HMO) — An organization developed to control medical care costs (for profit and nonprofit entities) by providing comprehensive health care services to its members for a fixed prepaid fee. Such organizations provide a wide range of health care services through a team of doctors who are salaried employees of the HMO. The incentives of controlling costs is a major objective of a health maintenance organization, which is one reason why preventive medicine is heavily emphasized. Regular reviews of medical care services and second opinions before surgery are other important cost-cutting measures. Virtually all medical and hospital services are covered, and in some cases dental care is available. The two major types of HMOs are individual practice associations and prepaid medical care. Also see "Individual practice association" and "Prepaid medical care."

Heavy market — In securities trading, a market where an unusually vast amount of securities trades hands; an active market with a large number of trades.

Hedge fund — An aggressive growth mutual or closed-end fund which borrows, executes short sales, and trades options in an effort to quickly realize high rates of return.

Hedging — For investments and in gambling, limiting the risk of loss by counterbalancing a present position. For example, Henderson, an investor in stocks, buys 1,000 shares of Overt Company stock and 10 put options. Henderson has hedged because she would not be at risk in case of a decline in Overt's price. Thus, if the stock's price declined, she would exercise the puts or sell the puts for profit. If, on the other hand, Overt's stock price begins to rise, then she would merely allow the puts to expire and sell the stocks for profit. In effect, Henderson is not exposed to the risk of wide fluctuations in Overt Company's stock price.

Hedonism — The practice of pursuing only happiness and pleasure.

Heedless — Careless disregard; inconsideration; without paying close attention.

Heir — (1) Generally, a person who inherits either real or personal property (or both) by will or by law; (2) technically, a person who receives property under the statute of descent and distribution (via intestacy).

Heirlooms — Valued family possessions handed down through generations.

Heirs and assigns — Words commonly found in a deed that provide the grantee a conveyance of fee simple estate.

Hidden asset — As used in investment analysis, an asset carried on a company's books which has a higher fair market value than is currently stated at book value and is not reflected in the market price of its stock; any significant advantage or strength not currently stated in a company's financial statements.

Hidden defect — A faulty portion of an object which cannot be detected through reasonable inspection. If a hidden defect causes harm, then the seller, manufacturer, lessor, or any combination thereof may be held liable.

Hidden inflation — A disguised price increase by providing smaller quantities or lesser quality of goods or services for an unchanged price.

Hidden taxes — Indirect taxes paid by a purchaser without being itemized on a bill of sale, such as customs duty on an imported article purchased at retail in the United States; a tax that is built into a wholesale or retail price.

Highest and best use — In real estate, appraising land at a value which would conceivably bring its highest financial return over a period of time.

High flyer — A stock whose price rises faster than other comparable stocks.

High income fund — A mutual fund whose primary objective is to provide income, in the form of dividends or interest or both.

High liquidity — Any investment that can readily be turned into cash at or near fair market value.

High maximum major medical — See "Major medical expense protection."

High-ratio financing — Generally, the financing of real estate, other than conventional home mortgages, through an unusually large portion of debt. It is likely to occur when a seller needs to sell such property very quickly.

Historical cost — The original cost of an asset which generally must be stated in the financial statements in accordance with generally accepted accounting principles.

Hoarding — The accumulation of any asset in excess of normal needs. Hoarding typically occurs where an individual suspects scarcity of the good or future higher prices or both.

Hobby — An activity not carried on "for profit." Generally, hobbyists conduct such activities for recreation or pleasure and, therefore, all gains and losses are considered personal. If an individual is able to show an intent to profit, then a "for profit" activity, such as a business or investment, will be established. For tax purposes, the general presumption (that showing a profit during any two of the first five consecutive tax years will automatically demonstrate the intent) is not necessarily controlling because the IRS may prove to the contrary: that a "for profit" activity was not actually intended. Other factors must be used in the determination: (1) the manner in which the activity is carried on, such as keeping records in a businesslike manner;

(2) the expertise of the taxpayer or the taxpayer's advisers, (3) the time and effort expended by the taxpayer in carrying on the activity, (4) expectation that assets used in the activity may appreciate in value, (5) the success of the taxpayer in carrying on other similar or dissimilar activities, (6) the taxpayer's income or losses with respect to the activity, (7) the amount of occasional profits, if any, which are earned, (8) the financial status of the taxpayer (i.e., are there substantial amounts of income from other sources?) (9) elements of personal pleasure or recreation (Treasury Regulation Section 1.183(b)). Also see "Hobby loss rule."

Hobby loss rule — Expenses incurred for activities not carried on for profit (i.e., hobbies) can only be deducted up to a maximum amount, which is gross income resulting from the activity. For-profit activities, on the other hand, can create deductible losses against other income. Hobby expenses are only deducted in the following order (up to gross income from the activity):

1. Interest and taxes (or otherwise deductible items—as itemized deductions).
2. Operating expenses other than depreciation (or other basis-reducing expenses such as amortization).
3. Depreciation, amortization, depletion, $100 casualty floor, etc.

HO-8 policy — See "Homeowners' insurance policy."
HO-5 policy — See "Homeowners' insurance policy."
HO-4 policy — See "Homeowners' insurance policy."
Holdback — A portion of a loan kept by the lender until a specified contingency is fulfilled. Holdbacks are commonly found in government-insured loans in order to make necessary repairs and improvements up to certain standards in homes financed with VA or FHA loans.
Holder in due course — A technical term for a person who is entitled to payment of a negotiable instrument (e.g., a check). A holder in due course is a holder who appropriately takes a negotiable instrument for value, in good faith, without any notice of default or dishonorment, and without knowledge of any defense or claim against it. Such person takes a negotiable instrument free from all personal defenses.
Hold harmless agreement — An agreement where one party agrees to pay another party for any specified losses the latter may experience as a consequence of a particular situation or certain circumstances.

Holding company — A dominant company whose primary purpose is owning stock in and supervising management of smaller companies. Normally, a holding company owns the majority interest (more than 50 percent, although this may not always be the case) in order to control.

Holding period — The period of time property is held by a taxpayer. It is usually associated with capital assets: such assets held the required holding period (more than six months for assets sold before 1988), then a long-term gain or loss will occur. Also see "Capital asset transactions," "Settlement date," and "Trade date."

Homeowners' association — A group of people joined together by the ownership of homes in a common section of a town. Homeowners' associations are generally formed to improve or maintain the quality of homes and other structures in a particular neighborhood and surrounding area.

Homeowners' disability policy — A special disability plan which covers mortgage payments when an insured becomes temporarily disabled because of illness or injury. Benefits are normally limited to a few number of years; according to some contracts, however, the loan will be paid in full if the insured dies.

Homeowners' insurance policy — An insurance contract designed exclusively for a homeowner or tenant consisting of a fixed multi-line package of coverages. Depending upon the type of policy, coverages for property losses from fire, lightning, theft, explosion, riot, aircraft, vandalism, and extended coverages, as well as personal liability protection (not automobile accidents or professional liability) are generally included. Perils usually excluded in homeowners' insurance policies include water damage from floods or backed up sewers, war, nuclear hazards, and movements in the earth. An insured may choose the type of policy and increase coverages for his or her dwelling, personal property, liability, and medical payments, but minimum levels are automatically built into the contracts and cannot be separately decreased, except personal property can be reduced to 40 percent of the amount of insurance on the dwelling. For example, the usual amount of coverage for personal property is automatically 50 percent of the amount for the dwelling, but this can be reduced to 40 percent. Deductibles are typically included for property losses and can range from 0 to $2,500 (usually $100). Specified limits of coverage are always stated for individual items, such as money, unscheduled jewelry, furs, stamp collections, guns, and fine arts, as well as personal

| | Policy Section I[5] (property coverage) | | | | Policy Section II (liability coverage) |
	Coverage A	*Coverage B*	*Coverage C*	*Coverage D*	*Coverages E and F*
	Dwelling	Related private structures	Personal property	Loss of use	Comprehensive personal liability and medical payments to others
AMOUNTS	This amount is chosen as the basic contract coverage Minimum $15,000 for forms 1, 2, 8; $20,000 for form 3; and $30,000 for form 5	10% of dwelling amount of insurance	50% of dwelling (worldwide, but only 10% of *contents* amount for property usually situated at secondary residences) Minimum for forms 4 and 6, $6,000	20% of dwelling, or 10% under form 1; and under form 4, 20% of the contents amount; and under form 6, 40% of the contents amount	Basic amounts are: $25,000 (liability) ard $500 (medical payments); Coverage E—liability can be increased up to $500,000 and Coverage F—medical payments up to $5,000, for small added premiums

FORM	
Basic form (No. 1)	Fire and lightning Extended coverage perils (wind, explosion, smoke, and so on) Theft, vandalism
Broad form (No. 2)	All basic form perils as above, plus miscellaneous perils such as falling objects, collapse, water damage, rupture of heating systems, and freezing (essentially these are the broad form fire endorsement perils)
Special form (No. 3)	"All risks of physical loss" except those specifically excluded (such as flood, earthquake, landslide, war, backing up of sewers); broad form on contents
Contents (tenants') broad form (No. 4)	Contents only covered—*not buildings* Covers same named perils as broad form 2 Can be used alone for tenants
Comprehensive form (No. 5)	Covers same all-risks perils as special form 3 but includes both *dwelling and contents*
Condominium unit-owners' form (No. 6)	Covers personal property same as contents broad form 4, but adds: basic limit of $1,000 for additions and alterations to the building, and loss of use up to 40 percent of the contents amount; endorsements permitted for theft when rented to others, and "loss assessments" by the condominium association
Modified coverage form (No. 8)	Covers insureds who own *older homes* with market values much less than replacement values. All losses paid on basis of *actual cash value*, rather than have the replacement cost option apply. (This permits insureds to carry less than 80 percent to value.) The perils included are similar to *basic form 1*, but theft of personal property is limited to $1,000 from the residence premises only.

All forms include the above perils of (1) liability and (2) medical payments. (Additional coverage for "damage to property of others," up to $250, regardless of legal liability, is also a part of each form.)

liability coverage, such as $25,000 per occurrence. Other coverages include damage to trees and shrubs, removal of debris, fire department charges, forgery, credit cards, and counterfeit money. Replacement cost coverage for the dwelling only applies if an appropriate amount of insurance is maintained, which is normally 80 percent or more of the replacement cost. An inflation guard endorsement is available with most plans, which automatically increases the amount of insurance each year. The loss-of-use coverage provides additional living expenses if an insured peril causes a home to be uninhabitable, and it usually carries a limit 20 percent of the amount of insurance on the dwelling. The following is a summary of coverages of homeowners' policies:

Homeowners' multi-line insurance — See "Homeowners' insurance policy."

Homeowners' plus policy — A homeowners' insurance policy that has higher average limits, business property options, slightly higher base deductible, and certain excluded liabilities (negligent entrustment of a car, intrafamily law suits, and written contracts other than those directly related to the home).

Homeowners' '76 program — A stage in the development of modern homeowners' contracts where coverages were both broadened and narrowed as well as made simplified for purposes of readability.

Homeowners' warranty — A new home warranty program offered by a subsidiary of the National Association of Home Builders to primarily protect against major structural defects for 10 years.

Homestead — The residence, including adjoining land, where the head of a family resides; a person's home.

Homestead Act — A federal act allowing a person to acquire federal land.

Homestead exemption — The removal of a homestead from the rights of creditors in accordance with state laws. Also a property tax exemption attributable to the homestead against all or part of state property taxes.

Home warranty insurance — Any of various insurances covering a home buyer against certain defects for a specified period in a newly purchased house, such as faults in heating, wiring, plumbing, electrical system, or other discrepancies.

Honorarium — A gratuitous payment for providing a service, such as making a speech or reviewing a manuscript.

Honorary trust — A purported trust without a charitable purpose and without appropriate beneficiaries, which may not be an enforceable trust depending upon state statutes. Such trusts are usually set up to care for specific animals or to honor a dead person with perpetual care of his or her grave.

Horizontal analysis — A financial statement analysis that indicates percentage changes over a period of time for particular items.

Horizontal spread — In the trading of equity options, the purchase and sale of the same type option for the same number of shares and same striking price, but with a different expiration dates. For example, Hall buys 10 XYZ Apr 50 calls and sells 10 XYZ Jul 50 calls. A horizontal spread is also known as a "time spread" or "calendar spread."

Hospital benefits — Specified benefits provided according to an insurance policy (not necessarily health insurance) for hospital expenses because of illness or injury.

Hospital expense insurance — A common type of health insurance that covers the customary charges for hospital care, such as room and board, X-rays, drugs, laboratory tests, and other similar hospital services. Also see "Health insurance."

Hospital indemnity — A type of health insurance which provides the insured with a specified amount on a daily, weekly, or monthly basis during the period of hospital confinement and without regard to actual hospital expenses.

Hospitalization insurance — See "Hospital expense insurance."

Hospital-medical insurance — A type of health insurance that generally covers all hospital services other than surgery (unless specifically stated in the contract).

HO-6 policy — See "Homeowners' insurance policy."

HO-3 policy — See "Homeowners' insurance policy."

HO-2 policy — See "Homeowners' insurance policy."

House confinement — A stipulation in some disability policies requiring an insured to be confined to a home before benefits are paid.

Household — All persons who reside under the same roof; domestic; family; occupants of the same home.

Housing and Urban Development (HUD) — A federal organization whose primary purpose is to develop and maintain major housing programs.

H.R. 10 plan — See "Keogh plan."

Human life values approach — A method of determining the amount of life insurance needed to cover a breadwinner in case of death so that a family can maintain their present standard of living without a reduction in their present level of income. Basically, the human life values approach figures the estimated future after-tax earnings of the breadwinner and discounts it by present value factors. The required amount of life insurance, then, is the present value of estimated future earnings.

Hush money — A bribe to silence a person.

Hybrid security — (1) A security having characteristics of both debt and equity; (2) a municipal bond combining characteristics of a revenue bond and general obligation bond.

Hypothecate — To pledge as security for a debt without physical transfer.

I

Illiquid — An investment or personal item that cannot be easily or quickly sold for cash at a selling price near its fair market value; not liquid. Any asset, such as raw land in a remote area, that has relatively few or no buyers.

Illusory appointments — Under power of appointment, a transfer of property with certain stipulations; a conditional transfer that is invalid.

Illusory promise — A purported promise that is not binding because the promisor, at his or her own discretion and pleasure, has the option to either perform or not perform.

Illusory trust — A purported trust where a grantor retains a substantial amount of control over property transferred showing that he or she clearly did not intend to relinquish any rights in such property.

Immediate annuity — Generally, a single premium annuity which begins payments to an annuitant at the end of the initial annuity-payment period. An annual annuity normally begins payments one year after purchasing a contract, and a monthly annuity normally begins in one month after purchase, although some contracts may have different annuity-payment schedules. Also see "Annuity."

Immediate family — Close relatives that are next of kin, such as husband, wife, parents, children, brothers, and sisters.

Immediate or cancel order[2] — A customer limit order to buy or sell a security, usually in significant quantity, with this qualification: any portion of the order that is not filled at the limit price is to be canceled.

Imminent peril — A hazard that is very likely to occur; one that is immediate, certain, and impending.

Immovables — Generally, land and and buildings; anything that cannot be removed, transferred, or relocated due to the nature of the object.

Impairment rider — An endorsement attached to a health insurance policy that excludes an existing impaired condition at the time a policy is issued.

Implied agency — A type of actual agency created primarily by prior actions of both a principal and agent causing a third party to reasonably believe an agency relationship exists. See "Agency."

Implied authority — An unexpressed power given by a principal to an agent which is customary, necessary, and proper to execute an expressed authority.

Implied contract — An unexpressed agreement which can be reasonably demonstrated and inferred by the previous conduct of all parties to such contract ("implied by fact"). A contract may also be "implied by law" (actually a quasi contract) where obligations are imposed by law.

Implied trust — A trust created because of implication of law or demands of equity.

Implied warranty — In the ordinary course of commercial and retail sales where a buyer relies on the expertise and judgment of a seller, generally, an unexpressed promise made by a seller of goods and services that such items are reasonably fit for the desired purpose for which they were sold.

Import — A foreign item or service; generally, a good manufactured in a country other than where it was purchased.

Import duty — A tariff on imported goods.

Imprest fund — The maintenance of a certain amount of coins and cash to pay small amounts and change bills; petty cash fund.

Improved land — Land having an increased value because of on-site or off-site additions, such as roads, sewers, electric lines, water, and drainage.

Improvements — Buildings or other additions to real estate.

Impulse buying — An unplanned and usually unessential purchase by a consumer. Candy, ice cream, magazines, and in-store bargains are customarily associated with impulse buying, which is why many grocery, convenient, and drug stores carry such items near the checkout line.

Imputed interest[1] — Interest computed by the Internal Revenue Service on installment contracts which have either no stated interest or unreasonably low stated interest. Imputed interest usually results in more ordinary income, in the form of interest income, to the seller (lender) than would otherwise be attained.

Inactive stock — A stock that has very few buyers and sellers which results in a low volume of trade.

Inadequacy — The obsolescence of an asset directly caused by an individual or business outgrowing its capabilities.

Inalienable — Generally, something that cannot be transferred.

In-and-out trader — A securities investor who speculates for quick profits, usually from price changes occurring only within one trading day.

Incentive contract — A contract between a purchaser and seller where the seller is able to increase profits, without giving up any quality and quantity, simply by keeping costs down.

Incentive stock options[1] — A compensatory arrangement that allows special tax treatment for qualified stock options which are granted to employees. If proper holding requirements are met, an employee will only be taxed when such stock is sold for a gain (long-term capital gain) and not when the option is granted (made available to employees by the employer-corporation) or exercised (used to purchase an employer's stock).

Incentive taxation[1] — A tax policy that promotes investing through the use of tax incentives for the purpose of stimulating business activity.

Inception — The beginning of a contract, will, mortgage, etc.

Inchoate — Something started but not completed; at the beginning stage.

Incidental beneficiary — One who is not a designated beneficiary, but who benefits (directly or indirectly) from the performance of a trust, or other similar occurrence.

Incident of ownership — In estate taxes, an element of ownership attributable to an economic benefit that a decedent has in a life insurance policy that causes the insurance proceeds to be included in a decendent's gross estate, such as right to change beneficiaries, to use the policy as security for a loan, to revoke any assignments, to cancel the policy, or to receive the cash value upon surrender or withdrawal.

Includable income — Income that is included in gross income and thereby subject to income tax.

Income — (1) An amount of money or other assets that are earned over a certain period of time; (2) money or other assets received for products sold, services rendered, or capital invested; (3) any increase in wealth, such as income from earnings as well as assets that have appreciated in value. Also see "Deferred income," "Discretionary income," "Disposable personal income," "Earned income," "Fixed income," "Gross income," "Net income," "Nonoperating income," "Operating income," "Ordinary income," "Passive income," "Personal income," and "Unearned income."

Income approach — See "Income value approach."

Income averaging — A method of computing federal income tax for qualified individuals who experience an unsually large amount of income as compared to the average income of the previous three years.

Eligible individuals must have completed Form 1040 Schedule G and have been a citizen or resident of the United States through the four-year period (three base years and current year) and have provided at least 50 percent or his or her own support during each of the three base period years. The 50 percent support test may be waived if the taxpayer is at least 25 years old and was not a full-time student for at least 4 years after the age of 21, or taxable income received during the computation year is related to work previously performed during 2 or more of the base period years, or files a joint return on which such individual's income is not more than 25 percent of the reported adjusted gross income (IRC Sections 1301–1305).

Income beneficiary — A party entitled to receive income, such as periodic income for life, from the operation of a trust, as an annuity from the proceeds of an insurance policy or other similar arrangement.

Income bond — Generally, a bond that is issued, according to a reorganization by a bankrupt company, in exchange for other outstanding bonds. Income bonds will only pay interest if the appropriate amount is earned or up to the amount earned.

Income disability benefit — For a life insurance policy, generally, an income benefit resulting from a permanent and total disability. For a health insurance policy, generally, an income benefit resulting from a disability, not necessarily permanent, as specified in such contract.

Income from continuing operations — Operating revenues less all operating expenses. Not included in the computation of income from continuing operations are the gains and losses from the cumulative effects of accounting changes, extraordinary items, and discontinued operations. It is sometimes used as a measure of comparison between similar companies in the same industry because income from continuing operations is generally thought of as being recurring in nature.

Income fund — A commonly conservative mutual fund or closed-end fund whose primary objective is to produce income through high-grade investment bonds or high-yielding common and preferred stock or both bonds and stock.

Income in respect of decedent — Income earned by a decedent up to the point of death, but not reported on the final income tax return because of the method of accounting used. This generally occurs where a deceased individual was a cash basis taxpayer, and the estate has not received the income before the final return is filed. Such amounts are included in the decedent's gross estate and will be taxed to the recipients (which may include the estate) with a corresponding tax deduction for any estate tax previously paid. Amounts so received by a beneficiary will keep the same tax-related classification (i.e., long-term capital gain or ordinary income) as would have been reported by the deceased.

Income property — Rental real estate, such as residential, commercial, or industrial property; generally, any asset directly producing income, such as preferred stocks, common stocks with expected dividends, and bonds.

Income reimbursement insurance — Any type of insurance that indemnifies an insured for loss of income. It is generally a type of group health insurance providing payments because of an inability to work due to a covered disability. See "Disability income insurance," and "Group health insurance."

Income securities — Stocks or bonds providing income through dividend or interest payments.

Income splitting — See "Family income splitting."

Income statement — Generally, a financial statement summarizing the operating activities of an economic entity over a certain period of time, usually one year. The income statement shows operating revenues and expenses for the period, as well as nonoperating revenues and expenses, and the resulting net income or net loss. Also see "Accrual method of accounting" and "Cash basis of accounting." An example of the format of an income statement for a merchandising company is as follows:

Net sales	XXXX
Less: Cost of goods sold	(XXX)
Gross profit	XXXX
Less: Operating expenses	(XXX)
Income from continuing operations	XXXX
Add: Nonoperating revenues	XXX
Less: Nonoperating expenses	(XXX)
Net income (or loss)	XXXX

Also see "Personal cash flow statement."

Income stock — A stock that is known for previous dividend payments and an expectation to continue in like manner.

Income tax — A tax computed on profits and income, as determined by the Internal Revenue Code. The tax is levied by the federal government and also by most state governments. Individuals, corporations, estates, and trusts are entities that may be required to pay income taxes. The federal income tax formula for individuals is as follows:

Gross income	XXXX
Less: Deductions for adjusted gross income	(XX)
Adjusted gross income	XXXX
Less: Excess itemized deductions	(XX)
Exemptions	(XX)
Taxable income	XXXX
Tax before credits (from tax tables or rate schedule)	XXX
Less: Income tax credits	(XX)
Taxes payable	XXX

Income tax return — All necessary forms which disclose pertinent tax computations and final income tax liability that must be filed with a taxing authority each year.

Income value approach — A method of appraising the value of rental real property, other income producing asset, or business establishment where the amount of future income is reasonably certain. The income value approach discounts all future receipts by an appropriate present value factor(s) to determine a value at the present time.

Incommunicado — A person who does not intend to reveal his or her true identity, especially when traveling.

Incompetent — (1) A person who is not physically or mentally capable of handling his or her personal financial activities without court-appointed help; (2) a person who is legally qualified to perform a certain act, but is incapable of professionally performing an average or reasonable job; one who is less than mediocre.

Incomplete transfer — A transfer made by a deceased individual during his or her lifetime that must be partially or wholly included in the gross estate (at fair market value) because of the retention of a certain enjoyment or control in the transferred property making the transfer incomplete for estate tax purposes.

In contemplation of death — See "Contemplation of death."

Incontestability clause — A clause in life insurance contracts that provides a time period in which fraud must be discovered by an insurance company in order to avoid liability because of material misstatements made by the insured in the application or at the time such policy was issued. In other words, if an insured dies after a stated period of incontestability (usually two years) and the policy has been kept in force, then the insurance company cannot avoid liability because of fraudulent statements made by an insured in an application for life insurance (except specific exclusions). An incontestability clause may also be found in health insurance contracts where benefits cannot be reduced because of a condition that existed prior to the effective date unless it is specifically excluded by name in the policy.

Incremental cost — An additional cost added to a product or service, such as transportation and handling costs.

Incumbrance — See "Encumbrance."

In delicto — faulty; literally in fault.

Indemnification — (1) The restoration of a person or business who has suffered a loss by replacing, repairing, or making payment for such damage; making one who has suffered a loss whole again; (2) protection against loss, such as a guarantee of reimbursement or the holding of security in case of loss.

Indemnity — (1) Benefits paid for a covered loss; (2) a contract whereby one party agrees to absorb a loss suffered by another (insurance).

Indemnity policy — An insurance policy that only protects against a covered loss that was actually experienced, not for a liability. Compare "Liability insurance."

Indenture — A mortgage or deed of trust that governs the conditions and terms under which a bond or debenture is issued, such as maturity date, rate of interest, and other elements of repayment. An indenture will also name an independent trustee, such as a bank or trust company, to oversee the contractual arrangement.

Independent adjuster — See "Adjuster."

Independent appraisal — A value assessment made by a qualified individual who has absolutely no direct or indirect interest in the outcome of the appraisal; an appraisal made by an expert who is independent.

Independent broker — A member of a stock exchange who generally handles transactions for other brokers.

Independent contractor[1] — An individual whose relationships with clients or customers allow such individual virtually complete control over how to perform a certain task and is only subject to clients' or customers' control when assessing an end product. That is, an independent contractor is directly responsible for the means by which an undertaking is made and is not under the direct control of the desires of an employer as to the actual work or ordinary course of affairs concerning the arrangement. An independent contractor does not have income taxes withheld, social security tax withheld or paid, or workers' compensation provided by the hirer. For example, an accountant is hired to perform tax-planning services for a large corporation. If the entire project is completely under the control of the outside accountant in that only a final report is presented to the company and no other employment relationship exists, then the accountant is considered to be an independent contractor. If, on the other hand, the accountant is hired as a staff accountant of the corporation (required to be in the corporation's office certain number of hours, required to use the corporation's office equipment, required to attend regular meetings, required to report directly to another employee of the corporation on a regular basis, etc.), then the accountant's relationship with the corporation is definitely that of an employee, rather than an independent contractor.

Indestructible trust — A trust which does not allow an invasion of corpus until a specified future time, at which point the trust is terminated. In order for a valid trust to exist, such period must fall within the constraints of the Rule against perpetuities. Also see "Rule against perpetuities."

Index fund — Generally, a mutual fund that is designed to perform in exactly the same manner as a stock index, such as Standard & Poor's Composite Index of 500 stocks.

Indicia of title — A document showing ownership, such as a bill of sale or invoice.

Indigent — One who is in financial need or cannot support himself or herself, or both; impoverished.

Indirect loss — A loss suffered as a consequence of a peril, not considered a direct loss, that is entirely dependent upon subjectivity as to its amount. An example of indirect loss is lost profits from the destruction of inventory or lost income as a result of an accident causing bodily injury and leaving its victim disabled. The direct loss from the destruction of inventory is its cost and the direct loss of an accident causing bodily injury is the cost of all medical services. Indirect losses must be specified in an insurance contract or be written separately as a rider or individual policy before coverage for such loss can apply. Also see "Consequential loss."

Indirect loss insurance — Insurance, such as business interruption insurance and disability income insurance, that protects against specified consequential losses.

Indirect tax — Generally, tax levied upon and paid by an entity other than the ultimate purchaser or user so that the actual tax burden is passed on to someone else (i.e., the consumer). An example would be an excise tax on liquor or gasoline where the tax is automatically added to the selling price.

Individual insurance — Insurance policies issued directly to policyholders, providing personal coverage for him or her (and family, if appropriate), in contrast to group insurance or blanket coverages.

Individual policy pension trust — A type of simplified retirement arrangement normally used by small groups where an authorized trustee purchases individual annuity contracts or permanent life insurance policies for each member. Individual policy pension arrangements sometimes provide both life insurance and retirement income.

Individual practice association (IPA) — A type of health maintenance organization operating within a well-defined geographic area and providing an enrolled population with a full range of health services for a fixed premium. An IPA is normally managed by an insurance company, a foundation sponsored by a local medical society, or a hospital, and is composed of a group of participating physicians. The physicians practice in their own offices and are paid by the organization according to a fixed-fee schedule of payments for services rendered to the organization's members. Under this type of program, the health maintenance organization is susceptible to loss in that premiums paid by members may not always exceed expenditures for medical fees and other operating expenses, which may in turn reduce fees paid to physicians because of a poor overall performance. On the other hand, physicians benefit when operations are profitable. One of the biggest weaknesses of an IPA is that physicians are usually separated, which means interaction between them, as well as the use of specialized equipment, facilities, and technicians, may not always be available.

Individual retirement account (IRA) — A special retirement arrangement for employed individuals who can deduct contributions (up to a maximum per year) and exclude earnings from taxable income. All contributions must be made before the filing date (usually April 15th) and be made in cash; all withdrawals are included in taxable income when made. Prohibited transactions include borrowing from an IRA, selling property to it, using it as collateral, or receiving unreasonable compensation for managing it. Many banks, insurance companies, brokerage houses, credit unions, savings and loans, and other financial institutions are qualified to manage individual retirement accounts.

Indorsee — One to whom a negotiable instrument is assigned by indorsement (same as "endorsee").

Indorsement — The transfer of a negotiable instrument by signature or stamp of the named payee, an accommodation indorser, or the drawee (e.g., the indorsement of a check), causing the indorser to become contingently liable. Same as "endorsement."

Indorser — One who signs his or her name on the back of a negotiable instrument in order to transfer it to another (same as "endorser"). Also see "Indorsement."

Inducement — In a contract, the consideration or benefit to be received by a party to a contract; the reason or purpose for making a contract.

Industrial development bond — A type of municipal bond issued by local authorities to attract industrial corporations for locating plant facilities in the area. The interest paid to bondholders is from a net-lease arrangement with the lessee-corporation. To be tax-exempt, the corporation must allow the facilities to be used for improving civic services or be used for pollution control projects.

Industrial life insurance — Life insurance customarily written in small face amounts, such as less than $1,000, for low income families to help pay last expenses and burial costs. One of the most distinguishing features is that premiums are collected on a weekly or monthly basis by a representative of the insurance company at the policyholder's home. Because of the expense of collecting premiums and handling small claims, industrial insurance carries a much higher premium rate than that of ordinary life insurance.

Industry — (1) In general, the aggregate of a nation's productive output from manufacturing, mining, and processing activities, and excluding agriculture, transportation, and merchandising (e.g., industrial output); (2) a specific area of business in which many companies produce or sell the same type of goods or provide the same type of service, such as the oil industry, airline industry, movie industry, and trucking industry.

Inevitable accident — An accident that, because of the circumstances, cannot be avoided.

Inference — A reasoning process composed of deductions or inductions of existing facts that leads to a logical conclusion.

Inflation — The increase in a nation's overall price level; the effect of rising prices. Inflation is commonly associated with rising wages, higher prices, relatively high money supply, and a decrease in the purchasing power of a country's currency. Generally, it is caused by either (1) an increase in demand (spending) for an existing level of currently available goods and services, or (2) a reduction in the supply of certain goods and services without a change in demand for such items or services, or some combination of (1) and (2). Thus, an increase in the money supply (currency and credit) without a corresponding increase in the production of goods and services will usually cause inflation because consumers and businesses tend to step up their rate of spending under ordinary circumstances. Accordingly, increased government spending without a corresponding and immediate increase in productivity will also cause inflation. An equally important factor is that rising prices in certain goods and services, such as were caused by reduction in oil supplies without a similar decrease in demand, tend to have a pervasive effect upon prices as a whole because such price movements will increase the price of transportation: Any rise in the overall price of transportation will automatically influence the price of virtually all products. Anything that increases the cost of transportation is, therefore, considered inflationary. Once prices are inflated, however, they do not tend to fall in proportion to a drop in the cost of the initiating product.

Inflation guard endorsement — An endorsement to a homeowner's policy that automatically increases the policy amount on all insured properties by a certain amount, typically 1 percent every three months, so that underinsurance is avoided. Also see "Homeowner's insurance" policy.

Infringement — The unauthorized use of or trespass upon another's property or right, such as an infringement of copyright; a violation of a contract or law.

In full — In total; complete amount, such as payment "in full."

Ingress, egress, and regress — The right of a person to enter, pass through, and reenter another's land, such as the right of a tenant on his or her landlord's property.

In gross — An amount that is in total sum without deductions.

Inhabitant — A person who permanently resides in a given home.

Inherent defect — See "Latent defect."

Inherent right — A right of a human being; a right that cannot be given to a person by an outside source.

Inheritance — Technically, property received from an estate of a person who died without leaving a valid will; property received through the law of descent and distribution. Inheritance is popularly used to mean the receipt of any item from a deceased individual's estate, regardless of the existence of a valid will.

Inheritance taxes — Taxes levied upon the right of acquiring property from a deceased individual, as opposed to a tax on the transfer of property, which is an estate tax. Inheritance taxes are generally imposed upon the heirs by state statutes and are sometimes referred to as "succession taxes."

In-hospital indemnity insurance — A type of health insurance that provides an insured with a fixed per diem payment for days spent in a hospital regardless of medical expenses. The payment normally ranges from $20 to $200 per day up to a specified maximum.

Initial margin — In securities trading, a percentage of a purchase price that must be provided by a customer in the acquisition of securities on credit. Presently, a buyer using credit must supply 50 percent of the purchase price as initial margin before a purchase can take place.

Injunction — An equitable order by a court prohibiting one from acting or restraining one from continuing to act. It is generally directed to a defendant who is threatening, attempting, or continuing to perform an injurious act to an innocent party.

In kind — Generally, a payment made to satisfy a claim with similar equivalent property; the same type, category, or class of acceptable payment. For example, Dickerson pays off a loan with "in kind" property, instead of cash, as an acceptable payment for satisfying a debt.

Innocent purchaser for value — See "Bona fide purchaser."

In pari delicto — Equally at fault; literally, in equal fault.

In perpetuity — Without time limitations; forever.

In respect of decedent — See "Income in respect of decedent."

Inside information — Any material information that would influence an investment decision and has not been made available to the general public.

Insider — Generally, any person who is privy to information not available to the general public.

Insolvency — The financial condition of a person not able to pay his or her debts as they fall due or within a reasonable time. Insolvency can occur in any form of organization.

Installment — A partial payment of a debt or other claim, usually subject to an installment sale agreement. Also see "Installment sale."

Installment land contract — An agreement calling for periodic payments to be applied toward the purchase price of land, and upon receipt of last payment, the seller is required to deliver the deed. An installment land contract is also known as "contract for deed," "long-term land contract," or simply, "land contract."

Installment loan — See "Installment purchasing."

Installment method — A method of accounting for a gain recognized from an installment sale. Generally, each payment received will have a pro rata portion of gain and nontaxable return of capital. Also see "Installment sale."

Installment note — A promissory note specifying a loan to be repaid over a certain amount of time, at a stipulated interest rate, and amount of each payment. All consumer installment notes from commercial sales transactions must conform to the provisions of the Truth-in-Lending Act.

Installment payment annuity — A type of deferred annuity that is purchased by annual, semiannual, quarterly, or monthly payments over a period of time. Compare "Single-premium annuity."

Installment premium — A periodic payment for insurance coverage throughout a year, rather than a lump-sum premium payment. Installment premiums are used to make payments become more convenient for the purchaser.

Installment purchasing — Generally, the buying of consumer items, usually expensive ones, by making periodic payments toward the purchase price; a type of credit purchase. Most installment purchase contracts call for a reasonable amount of interest to be paid on the balance of the unpaid purchase price. Also see "Conditional sales contract."

Installment refund annuity — An annuity that remits any unpaid balance (up to the annuity's original cost) to a designated beneficiary in installments upon the death of the annuitant. Also see "Installment refund life annuity."

Installment refund life annuity — An annuity where an annuitant or designated beneficiary is guaranteed to receive an amount equal to the total installment payments previously paid (i.e., the annuity's original cost). Thus, if an annuitant dies before receiving the amount of aggregate payments, then a beneficiary will receive installments for the balance of the paid-in amount, usually without interest. Should an annuitant outlive the total amount paid in, then payments will only continue for the annuitant's life: The beneficiary will not receive anything upon the death of the annuitant. Compare "Life annuity."

Installment sale — Any sale where the total purchase price is not paid within one year. Usually in an installment sale, the buyer makes an initial down payment in the year of purchase and then makes installments in the following years to pay off the balance of the purchase price as well as a reasonable amount of interest. Installment sales are typically arranged between buyers and sellers of real estate and other large assets and are subject to the terms of a promissory note. For income tax purposes, a reasonable amount of interest must be stated in an installment sale contract and paid by the buyer. The seller has the option to account for the total selling price in the year of sale for purposes of determining taxable gain or include a pro rata amount of taxable gain in each installment (depreciable properties may be handled differently). In other words, when the installment sale method is chosen, the seller will have a gross-profit percentage and cost-of-goods-sold percentage that will be applied to each payment received: Only the gross-profit percentage multiplied by all payments received during the year will be included in taxable income.

Institutional investor — Generally, a bank, pension fund, insurance company, mutual fund, large corporate investment account, trust fund, and other similar institutions that buy and sell securities on behalf of a large group of people or normally transact on a relatively large scale, rather than for a single individual. Because of the size and frequency of securities transactions, institutional investors account for approximately 75 percent of the trading on the New York Stock Exchange, and they are able to enjoy competitive commissions and other preferential treatment among most brokerage firms.

Institutional lender — A company that lends money in the ordinary course of business, such as a bank, savings and loan, and insurance company. Individuals and credit unions are generally not considered institutional lenders.

Institutional trading — The buying and selling of securities by institutional investors, such as insurance companies and pension funds.

Insufficient funds — A banking term meaning that a check writer's account balance is not enough to pay the amount of a check which is drawn on his or her account.

Insurability — The degree of acceptability a prospective insured has with an insurance company. Also see "Evidence of insurability."

Insurable interest — A requirement that must be met before an individual can purchase an insurance contract covering the loss of an item, life, or other object. The following makes up the requirement for an insurable interest: the existence of a right or relationship in regard to the object in question must be such that an insured will suffer a financial loss as a result of damage, destruction, or loss of the object. The basis of its use is to prevent gambling, assess the amount of damage, and decrease chances of a potentially dangerous moral hazard.

Insurable value — A value given to property for purposes of determining a loss in the event of an occurrence of a covered peril. It is the stated value of property provided in an insurance contract. It could be cost, fair market value, liquidity value, replacement value, or declared value. In the case of fire insurance, the insurable value of property is any of the aforementioned amounts less indestructible portions, such as land.

Insurance — (1) Generally, any reduction in risk of loss; any protective measure; a hedge; (2) protection against any financial loss that is based upon the happening of a fortuitous event as specified in an insurance contract. More specifically, a contractual relationship between an insurance company and an insured where the former agrees to reimburse the latter for financial loss sustained because of specified contingencies that cause damage, destruction, or loss of subject matter or to pay on behalf of the insured all reasonable amounts for which he or she may be legally liable to pay to third parties, subject to the terms of the contract. Typically, specified contingencies are all events causing damage or loss that are not expressly excluded from coverage. Consideration, which must be received by an insurance company for making a contract of protection against financial loss, is the receipt of at least one premium payment.

Insurance adjuster — See "Adjuster."

Insurance agent — A person authorized by an insurance company to represent it in matters concerning soliciting, paying benefits, collecting premiums, and other related insurance business.

Insurance commissioner — See "Commissioner of insurance."

Insurance company — A corporation or association chartered under local laws that is primarily in the business of writing insurance contracts under either a broad or specific classification, such as life insurance, casualty insurance or surety company. Also see "Mutual companies," and "Stock insurance companies."

Insurance contract — A written agreement between an insurance company and an insured transferring the risk of loss from the latter to the former as specified under the terms of the agreement; an insurance policy.

Insurance dividend — Generally, a partial return of premium paid by an insurance company to an insured. Such dividends are generally not taxable, unless they exceed the total amount of paid-in premiums.

Insurance premium — Consideration paid to an insurance company subject to an insurance contract entitling an insured to receive protection against a covered loss.

Insurance trust — A trust that receives the insurance proceeds upon the death of an insured. A trustee then invests and distributes the proceeds in a manner described in the trust agreement. Although there are many different possible alternatives, some agreements give the trustee absolute discretion to allocate income or principal among beneficiaries as they require money under specified circumstances. Whatever the arrangement, lump-sum proceeds and installments under a "settlement option" are avoided, which allows the principal to remain intact until the occurrence of emergencies or other specified events.

Insured — Generally, one who is covered or protected by an insurance policy as stated on the first page; in most instances an insured is also the owner of such insurance contract. Life, health, and property insurance are commonly carried by an insured and members of his or her family.

Insured mortgage — A mortgage that is insured against the borrower's default: If all foreclosure costs plus any remaining balance are in excess of the proceeds after the mortgaged property is sold, the difference is covered by the insurer. FHA, VA, and independent mortgage insurance companies provide mortgage insurance.

Insurer — An insurance company that has contracted to provide insurance coverage for an insured.

Insuring clause — The provisions of an insurance policy or bond describing the coverage provided by an insurance company to an insured. It generally makes up the bulk of an insurance contract.

Intangible asset — (1) Long-term assets lacking physical substance that are usually acquired for purposes of productive use, such as patents, copyrights, trademarks, franchises, and goodwill. Intangible assets are a listed category of illiquid assets on a classified balance sheet; (2) any asset lacking physical qualities but representing value, such as a life insurance policy, stocks, and bonds. Also see "Intangible personal property."

Intangible drilling costs (IDC)[1] — Certain noncapitalized expenditures that are necessary to prepare oil and gas production and have no salvage value. The costs are generally deductible during the tax year when they were paid or incurred. Examples include repairs, labor, fuel, and utility expenses.

Intangible personal property — For tax purposes, property that has no real value on its own, but represents evidence of value, such as stocks, bonds, commodity futures contracts, and promissory notes.

Integrated deductible — For health insurance, a method of applying the initial deductible of a supplemental major medical expense plan. Generally, the deductible is the greater of a fairly high fixed amount (e.g., $1,000) or benefits paid by a basic plan.

Integration — (1) The process of combining two or more different groups or entities. A horizontal integration combines two or more businesses of the same industry, and a vertical integration combines two or more businesses associated with the same industry, but are in different stages of distribution, such as the merger of a manufacturer, wholesaler, and a retailer of the same product; (2) the coordination of retirement benefits between a pension plan and Social Security by using a specific formula.

Integrity — The quality of honesty, uprightness, and soundness of moral character.

Intent — In law, a state of mind that is usually determined from interpreting one's prior acts.

Interest — (1) Compensation for lending money, such as interest received on bonds; cost of borrowed funds, such as interest paid on a loan. Also see "Accrued interest," "Compound interest," "Conventional loan," "Imputed interest," "Nominal interest rate," "Ordinary interest," "Simple interest"; (2) a legal right, claim, or share of ownership in an asset or business venture, such as an interest in land or a partnership interest.

Interest-adjusted cost method — A method of evaluating the cost of life insurance by taking into account the time value of money. By combining premium payments, dividends, and cash value buildup and present value analysis into an index number, a fairly accurate cost comparison between insurance companies can be attained. The lower the index number, the lower the policy's cost. Also see "Net payment cost comparison index" and "Surrender cost comparison index."

Interest coverage ratio — See "Interest-earned ratio."

Interest-discounted note — A type of promissory note which combines both interest and principal in its face amount. Interest discounted notes are generally written for a short-term period such as a year or less. For example, Lusk writes a promissory note for an amount of $1,100 in exchange for $1,000 cash, and the note is to be paid in one year. The interest of $100 (in effect a 10 percent rate of interest) is already included in the face of the note.

Interest-earned ratio — A ratio used in analyzing the financial condition of a company which indicates the likelihood of interest payments to be made to bondholders and dividends to preferred stockholders. It is also known as "times interest earned":

$$\frac{\text{Number of times earnings}}{\text{cover interest costs}} = \frac{\text{Income before interest and taxes}}{\text{Interest expense}}$$

Interest-extra note — A type of promissory note stating fixed payments to be applied on the balance of principal, plus a declining amount to be paid as interest. As the principal decreases so does the amount of interest. The monthly payment attributable to principal, however, remains fixed throughout the course of the loan. Hence, payments made in accordance with an interest-extra note gradually decrease by the corresponding decline in the amount of interest paid.

Interest-included note — A promissory note stating fixed payments to be applied to both principal and interest. As the principal gradually decreases, so does the amount of interest, and all payments are equal. Thus, at the beginning of a payment schedule, the portion of a loan payment attributable to interest is relatively high, and the portion attributable to principal is low. Toward the end of a payment schedule, just the opposite is true: the portion attributable to interest is relatively low and the portion attributable to principal is high. Also see "Amortization of debt (loan amortization)."

Interest option — In a life insurance policy, an option allowing the beneficiary to receive interest-only payments from the company, leaving the principal intact. All amounts received under such option, however, are taxable interest. An interest option is typically chosen to create a family fund for college expenses, emergencies, a new home, or other future needs.

Interest rate — The percentage of a certain sum of money used to compute an amount to be paid as a cost of borrowing funds.

Interest-rate futures — A contractual commitment to buy or sell a specific financial instrument, such as Government National Mortgage Association Collateralized Depository Receipts (GNMA-CDRs) and Treasury bonds, during a certain month in the future at a price currently established in a market. Interest rate futures are regulated by the Commodity Futures Trading Commission and are mark-to-market at year-end for income tax purposes.

Interest rate risk — The risk of a price decline of fixed-income securities because of an increase in the market rate of interest.

Interim financing[1] — A temporary financing arrangement used during the development or construction stage of a project until permanent financing can be attained.

Interim reports — Financial statements issued by an entity between year-end financial statements, usually quarterly.

Interlocking directorate — A situation occurring where the same directors serve on the boards of several different companies. An interlocking directorate gives the appearance that all such companies are under the same control.

Interlocutory decree — A temporary decree, usually contingent upon the occurrence of some event before a final decree, such as the passage of time.

Intermediary — A broker, adviser, or an organization helping an individual locate or negotiate something, such as an insurance broker. An organization that assists an investor in implementing investment decisions, such as a pension company, mutual fund, or a bank (portfolio intermediaries), or companies which execute orders or provide investment advice (marketing intermediaries).

Intermediary bank — In the banking system of transferring checks and other negotiable instruments for collection, any bank other than the depository bank or payor bank.

Internal control — A system undertaken by an economic entity to protect assets against misappropriations and waste, ensure compliance with management policies and public laws, evaluate the performances of personnel to promote efficiency, and ensure accurate financial data and reliable financial reports.

Internal rate of return (IRR) — As used in evaluating an investment, a rate of return at which the present value of future cash flow equals the initial investment. Internal rate of return is useful in comparing investments when the expected cash flow can be reasonably estimated. For example, assume Edwards plans to invest $10,000 and has two alternative investments with similar risks. Alternative I is to pay him $16,500 in three years and Alternative II is to pay $19,250 in four years. By using IRR, we can evaluate both alternatives with a comparable computation in order to find the one having the highest rate of return: Alternative I has an 18.17 percent rate of return and Alternative II has a 17.79 percent rate of return. Therefore, when only considering their respective internal rates of return, Alternative I is a better choice.

Internal Revenue Agent — An employee of the Internal Revenue Service (Department of Treasury) who is responsible for enforcing federal laws pertaining to the Internal Revenue Code.

Internal Revenue Code (IRC) — The codification of tax laws into one volume, which includes federal income taxes, estate taxes, gift taxes, and excise taxes.

Internal Revenue Service (IRS) — An organization that is part of the U.S. Department of Treasury which is responsible for administering and enforcing the federal tax laws other than taxes on alcohol, tobacco, wagering, firearms, and explosives. Disputes between a taxpayer and the IRS may be heard in either the U.S. Tax Court, U.S. District Court, or the U.S. Claims Court, whichever a taxpayer chooses.

International Monetary Market (IMM) — Part of the Chicago Mercantile Exchange where the trading of futures contracts, which include U.S. Treasury bills, foreign currencies, bank CDs, and U.S. Treasury notes, is done.

International trade — The trading of goods and services between different countries.

Inter se — Between two or more parties; the rights and privileges among two or more parties as opposed to the rights and privileges of outside parties.

Interspousal — Between husband and wife.

Interstate — Between the states, such as the interstate highway system.

Interval ownership — See "Time-sharing."

Inter vivos — Between two or more living persons.

Inter vivos gift — A gift made by a living donor to a living beneficiary.

Inter vivos trust — A trust created and executed during the grantor's life, as opposed to a testamentary trust which takes effect upon the death of the grantor.

Intestate — Without a will. When a person dies without making a will, he or she is said to have died "intestate." It is commonly used to signify the property of a person dying without a will: the intestate's property.

Intestate succession — See "Succession."

In the money — As used in the trading of options, a put or call currently holding a profitable position for the owner of an option. A call is "in the money" when its underlying stock price is above the strike (exercise) price plus the option's cost, and a put is "in the money" when its underlying stock is below its strike price plus cost.

In the red — A business that operates at a loss; net loss.

In toto — The total or whole amount.

Intra — Within; intrastate is within the boundaries of the state.

Intra vires — Within the scope of given powers or authority. An act is said to be "intra vires" when it is made within the rightful power of an individual or corporation.

Intrinsic value — The essential or true value of an item, without regard to special features or aesthetic qualities, generally made up of the value of its separate components. For example, the intrinsic value of a sculpture is only its material worth, not its fair market value; the value of stock as determined by fundamental analysis and not by market (exchange) prices.

Inurement — A benefit or usefulness.

Invasion of corpus — A payment made by a trustee from assets of a trust (i.e., corpus), rather than payments of income.

Inventory — (1) Goods held for sale in the ordinary course of business: raw materials, work in process, and finished goods held by a manufacturing concern for eventual sale or lease to customers (assets classified as inventory are ordinary income properties for income tax purposes as opposed to capital assets); (2) a detailed list of all assets, tangible and intangible, and the value of each item that is required by an insured for property insurance purposes.

Inventory turnover — A ratio used in measuring management's ability to operate effectively in generating enough sales volume to turn inventory over at a rapid pace. The higher the ratio, the faster inventory turns over:

$$\text{Inventory turnover} = \frac{\text{Cost of goods sold}}{\text{Average inventory}}$$

Inverse pyramiding — In commodities trading, a system of expanding a currently held position by buying another contract without depositing more margin by using paper profits (equity) shown in an existing position. The continued use of inverse pyramiding to expand a present position creates a highly leveraged situation that can trigger tremendous margin calls if the corresponding price reverses.

Investment — An expenditure for income-producing or expected appreciated-value property, as opposed to an expenditure for consumption. Virtually any payment made with a reasonable expectation for future revenue or gains.

Investment adviser — Any person or organization engaging in the business of advising others in purchasing or selling investment property. Generally, investment advisers who are compensated and have 15 or more clients, other than banks, brokers, and periodicals, must register with the Securities and Exchange Commission as well as with appropriate state agencies.

Investment banker — A company in the business of underwriting, trading, and marketing new issues, assisting corporations with money management and public relation activities; an underwriter. Investment bankers are middlemen between the investing public and the issuing corporation. Other financial activities include the distribution of large blocks of securities held by an estate or other entity. Compare "Commercial bank."

Investment banking — Generally, underwriting of new security issues. Also see "Investment banker."

Investment bill — A negotiable instrument purchased for investment: acquired at a discount and held until maturity.

Investment companies — Companies that raise money by selling their stock and using their financial resources to purchase securities of other companies. The two main types of investment companies are mutual funds (open-end) and closed-end companies. The capitalization of a mutual fund is not fixed, and the company issues and redeems its own shares according to the underlying net asset value of each share. A closed-end investment company, on the other hand, has a fixed number of shares, and they are traded on an exchange as any other corporation's stock whose price is subject to market influences. Also see "Closed-end investment company," "Money market funds," and "Mutual fund."

Investment Company Act — Federal law passed in 1940 regulating investment companies.

Investment contract — A contract or arrangement where an investor places money or other assets in a business or joint venture in an effort to profit from the performance of others.

Investment property — Property held for income or capital gains or both.

Investment security — See "Security."

Investment tax credit (ITC) — An income tax credit available to taxpayers who purchased qualifying tangible personal property used in a trade or business and placed such property in service during a taxable year in which ITC applies. The amount of investment tax credit ranges from 6 percent to 10 percent, depending upon the types of property involved. Also see "Recapture."

Investment trust — See "Investment companies" or "Real estate investment trust."

Investment yield — The percentage of gain and income received from an investment. Although an investment yield should be annualized—by using the present/future value approach—for purposes of comparison between investments, a simplified formula is as follows:

$$\text{Investment yield} = \frac{\text{Income plus gain from sale}}{\text{Cost of investment}}$$

Investor — One who provides money or other assets for the purpose of purchasing property or other ownership interest with an expectation of making a future profit without providing any significant services.

Invoice — A memorandum provided to a buyer that itemizes the details of merchandise purchased. An invoice generally shows the description, number, type, price, and total dollar amount of each item, as well as the total dollar amount of the entire purchase.

Involuntary conversion — Any theft, casualty, or condemnation which results in a loss or destruction, wholly or partially, of property. Generally, gains realized from an involuntary conversion can be deferred if the owner reinvests the proceeds within a certain period of time into similar property (subject to IRC Section 1033). Losses of personal-use property as a result of a theft or casualty are itemized deductions, but not personal-use property losses from condemnations. Also see "Casualty loss" and "Condemnation."

Involuntary conveyance — Any transfer of real property without the owner's consent, such as through a divorce proceeding, sheriff's sale, tax sale, or condemnation.

Involuntary lien — Any lien that attaches to property without the owner's consent, such as a tax lien or mechanic's lien, as opposed to a lien to which the owner agrees, such as a mortgage.

Involuntary trust — An implied trust created by law to reverse an inequitable situation. It occurs where one party acquires property through fraudulent means and is deemed by law to hold such property in trust for its rightful owners. For example, Jamison, an agent for Aulden, purchases property in his own name and benefit that rightfully should have been purchased for the benefit of his principal, Aulden, and thereby breaches his fiduciary duty. Jamison must hold such property in trust (i.e., an involuntary trust) for Aulden.

IOU — Literally, "I owe you"; a memorandum stating that one party owes another party a specified amount, item, or service. IOUs are not negotiable.

IRC — Internal Revenue Code.

Ironclad contract — An expression used to designate a contract that is considered to be very difficult to break.

Iron-safe clause — A clause in a fire insurance policy requiring the insured to keep certain items, such as books of account, inventory, and other valuable records and articles, in a designated fire-proof area (e.g., fire-proof safe).

Irreconcilable differences — A decision reached by a husband and wife in which they are unable to live together. Irreconcilable differences constitute no-fault grounds for divorce in many states.

Irreparable damages — Damages that result in losses in which a standard of monetary value cannot be determined.

Irrevocable — That which cannot be retracted, reversed, or recalled; not revocable.

Irrevocable designation of beneficiary — A feature of certain life insurance policies where a beneficiary is named without providing the policyholder with a right to change beneficiaries, unless the beneficiary dies or no longer exists (as in the case of a corporation or other entity). Generally, an irrevocable beneficiary has a vested right in the contract.

Irrevocable living trust[1] — A trust created by a living grantor, who cannot cancel or repeal the trust. Transferred property may be taxable to the grantor, trust income is generally taxable to beneficiaries, and transfer of assets may avoid estate taxes.

Irrevocable trust — Any trust that cannot be revoked by its creator.

IRS — Internal Revenue Service.

Issue — (1) An offer of stock or bonds made to prospective investors of a corporation. An "issue" is usually a first-time sale of the particular securities offered; (2) any class of securities.

Issued and outstanding — A phrase used to designate common and preferred stock that has been sold to investors and is not currently held by the issuing corporation; stock held by a person or business other than the issuing company, in contrast to authorized stock, which has not yet been issued, and treasury stock, which is issued but not outstanding. Compare "Authorized issue" and "Treasury stock."

Issuer—In securities trading, an entity that sells its securities to investors.

Itemize — To list each item separately.

Itemized deductions — For income tax purposes, specified expenses, which are typically personal in nature, that are deducted from adjusted gross income. Itemized deductions include allowable medical expenses, charitable contributions, casualty losses, interest paid, state taxes paid, and other miscellaneous expenses. Only the excess of total itemized deductions over the appropriate zero-bracket-amount qualify as a reduction of adjusted gross income.

Itinerant vendor — Generally, a person traveling from place to place selling his or her wares.

J

Jeopardy assessment — An immediate tax assessment levied by the Internal Revenue Service without normal formalities because questionable circumstances regarding the collection of a tax have become known. A jeopardy assessment occurs, for example, when a taxpayer plans to leave this country and the Internal Revenue Service terminates his or her taxable year in order to collect any tax due.

Jerry-built — Something poorly constructed or designed. A structure built with inexpensive materials.

Jobber — A person or business who buys and sells items for others, such as a securities dealer or wholesaler distributor. A middleman between producer and retailer who generally takes titles of goods and resells them.

Job evaluation — An analysis of all positions in an entity with regard to the separate and collective value toward attaining an entity's stated objectives.

Jobs credit[1] — An income tax credit available for employers who hire economically disadvantaged individuals. Also known as the "targeted jobs credit."

Joinder of parties — The uniting of two or more parties toward a common legal objective, either as co-defendants or co-plaintiffs.

Joint — Combined; united; taken together as one; two or more parties joined together as joint venturers, joint tenants, etc. Joint ownership binds all participants jointly so that any legal action must be taken against all of them, not each of them. Compare "Joint and several liability."

Joint account — A savings, checking, or other account in the names of two or more persons, generally providing them with equal rights to it.

Joint adventure — See "Joint venture."

Joint and several liability — A liability allowing a claimant the option to sue all parties jointly or any one (or more) separately if a debt or claim is not settled. A husband and wife filing a joint income tax return provides joint and several liability, which allows the Internal Revenue Service to collect from either or both for up to the full amount of income tax due.

Joint checking account — A checking account with a bank or other financial institution titled in the names of two or more persons who customarily possess equal rights as to ownership and generally the right of survivorship.

Joint enterprise — See "Joint venture."

188

Joint estate — See "Joint tenancy."

Joint life and survivorship annuity — A type of life annuity contract that guarantees payments for the joint duration of two or more lives. The most popular contract provides a fixed amount of income for two persons during their lifetime; upon the death of one recipient, the annuity continues payments without reduction until the death of the last recipient. Some policies that are written for two recipients, however, contain a provision to reduce the survivor's annuity payments upon the initial death of one recipient. Contracts written for more than two persons, on the other hand, generally provide annuity payments without reduction until the death of the last survivor. Also see "Annuity."

Joint life policy — A special type of life insurance policy that provides life insurance coverage on the lives of two or more insureds. The policy's face value will be paid upon the death of any one of the insureds with automatically continued coverage for each survivor. Joint life policies are commonly used by a husband and wife as well as by partners in a business. The types of policies usually written include whole life, endowment, and decreasing term. The major drawback in using a joint life contract is that it typically offers less flexibility for each individual involved, such as conversion features and cash value.

Jointly acquired property — All properties acquired by a husband and wife during marriage.

Joint ownership and survivorship life income option — In a life insurance policy, a type of settlement option for the distribution of life insurance proceeds to a beneficiary, where annuity payments are paid over the duration of two lives without reduction until the death of the surviving beneficiary. Such option can be made by the insured or beneficiary. Also see "Settlement options."

Joint policy — See "Joint life policy."

Joint protection policy — A type of title insurance policy that insures both owner and lender.

Joint return — An income tax return filed jointly by a husband and wife that combines all taxable incomes and qualified deductions of each. Husband and wife are jointly and severally liable to the Internal Revenue Service for payment of any tax due. Because of better income tax rates for married couples filing jointly, it is normally the best filing status.

Joint tenancy — An undivided interest held by two or more persons in property. It is generally attributable to the ownership or other interest in real property, such as life estate and estate for years, although many brokerage accounts are held in joint tenancy by husband and wife (JTWROS). The interests must begin at the same time, accrue under the same conveyance, and share possession equally. The most significant aspect of a joint tenancy is that upon the death of any joint tenant, the entire interest passes to all remaining joint tenants (survivorship) and not to the heirs of the deceased. Also, such interest normally avoids probate. Compare "Tenancy by the entirety" and "Tenancy in common."

Joint tenants — Persons holding a joint tenancy. Also see "Joint tenancy."

Joint tenants with right of survivorship — See "Joint tenancy."

Jointure — Generally, a provision made before marriage giving a life estate to the wife upon the death of her husband. It sometimes takes the place of a dower, although the wife must agree to the arrangement.

Joint venture — A special combination of two or more persons, where a specific venture for profit is jointly sought without any actual partnership or corporation designation. Elements of a joint venture include an express or implied contract showing an intent that a business venture is established, joint control and ownership, contributions of capital or services or both, and the sharing of profits (but not necessarily losses). Joint ventures may or may not be taxed as partnerships, depending upon whether an active trade or business takes place. If a joint venture is actively engaged in a trade or business, then it will be deemed a partnership for income tax purposes.

Journal — (1) In accounting, the book of original entry where day-to-day cash and other financial transactions are recorded, usually in the order in which they occur; (2) a log or diary where events are recorded daily.

Journeyman — The step beyond apprenticeship qualifying a craftsman to work on his or her own.

JTWROS — Joint tenancy with right of survivorship. Also see "Joint tenancy."

Judgment — (1) Opinion or estimate; (2) a decision reached by a court.

Judgment lien — An involuntary lien on properties of a judgment debtor.

Judicial bond — A type of surety arrangement required by a court in judicial proceedings. A fiduciary type of judicial bond is for persons entrusted with property by court decision or procedures, and a litigant type is for defendants or plaintiffs.

Judicial foreclosure — Foreclosure brought about by court action rather than through the terms of a mortgage or lien.

Judicial sale — A sale directed by a court order or decree, such as a sale in a bankruptcy proceeding.

Junior bonds — (1) A misnomer for preferred stock that is enhanced by the provisions of a sinking fund, which obligates its issuer to retire a certain amount of preferred stock on a periodic basis; (2) bonds having a lower priority than senior debt in case of default.

Junior lien — A lien subordinated to a previous lien.

Junior mortgage — An overlying mortgage that is subordinate to a prior mortgage in the order of priority.

Junk bonds — Bonds that carry a low rating (BB or lower) and are considered speculative.

Jurisdiction — The boundaries of authority of a court and its judicial officers, governmental agency, or other entity.

Jurisprudence — The philosophy or science of law.

Just value — In property taxation, the reasonable fair market value of property subject to an ad valorem tax.

K

Kansas City Board of Trade (KCBT) — A commodities exchange specializing in trading agricultural commodities and futures contracts.

Keogh plan — A qualified retirement plan developed exclusively for self-employed individuals and their employees. Generally, Keogh plans must not discriminate in favor of a self-employed person or any employee. Keoghs have tax-deductible contribution limits for both a defined contribution plan and a defined benefit plan. Upon withdrawal, all benefits are taxable. A Keogh plan is also known as a "self-employed retirement plan" or an "H.R. 10 plan." Other restrictions apply so that professional tax advice is required before using this type of retirement plan.

Key employees — As used in qualified pension plans, generally, employees that are officers of the company, owners of more than 5 percent of stock, any one of 10 employees which owns the largest employee interest in the company, or owners having more than 1 percent interest and earning over $150,000.

Key person life insurance — Life insurance written on the life of an individual who is important to a business, such as an officer upon whose life a significant amount of earnings depend. Key positions such as president, vice presidents, and other executive officers are generally provided life insurance for the firm in case of death, for the purpose of replacing lost profits and covering expenses of finding another qualified individual. Should satisfying the requirement of insurable interest become in doubt, an employee can always apply for a policy and name the company as the beneficiary. Key person life insurance is very common in small corporations and for general partners in a partnership.

Kickback — A payment generally made by a seller to a buyer in order to improperly induce present or future purchases. Most kickbacks are contrary to public policy and are therefore not tax deductible as a business expense.

Kicker — An added benefit, bonus, or special feature provided to sweeten a deal, such as a real estate loan or automobile purchase.

Kiting — A wrongful system of misusing funds, which are not owned by the drawer, through the use of two or more separate checking accounts and the time lag between collections (i.e., the float). For example, assume that Smith has checking accounts in two different banks. From his account in the first bank, a check is written (and used by him); but before it is collected by the first bank, a check is written from his account in the second bank and deposited in the first bank to cover the amount of the original check. Before the second check clears, however, a third check, which is written from his account in the first bank, is deposited to cover the second check's amount, and so forth. The system must continue in like fashion until either the drawer obtains the required funds and appropriately deposits them or he is caught. Kiting can usually be detected in companies by auditors who use appropriate auditing techniques.

Krugerrand — A South African gold coin containing one troy ounce of gold.

L

Labor — (1) Human effort, as opposed to materials and overhead; (2) earned income generally derived from working for hourly wages, as opposed to working for salary, commissions, or profit.

Labor union — A group of workers formed primarily for the purpose of bargaining with employers on a collective basis for wages, working conditions, job security, and other group benefits.

Laches — The unreasonable and unexplained delay by a party in attempting to initiate a court action or making a claim, which effectively waives such party's rights. The failure to act within a reasonable amount of time will prevent a party from bringing an action or making a claim. Laches is not the same as the statute of limitations.

Laissez faire — Generally refers to a free enterprise system without government intervention. Literally, "allow (them) to do."

Lame duck session — A legislative session made up of some members who were not reelected, but are voting for the last time. It occurs right after an election and before the new members arrive.

Land — The earth, ground, waters, marsh, pastures, and other natural elements of real estate. Included in land are crops, trees, minerals, and air space indefinitely upward and downward unless specifically excepted or restricted. Land is an essential factor of production for economic growth.

Land bank — See "Federal Land Banks."

Land contract — See "Installment land contract."

Land grant — A donation of public land by the U.S. government to a state or local government, corporation, college, or individual.

Landlord — The owner of rental real estate; a lessor.

Landlord's warrant — A warrant from a landlord to seize and sell at a public auction a tenant's goods for compensation of back rents. It is customarily used to compel payment or other observance of a lease agreement.

Land-poor — Describes a taxpayer who owns unproductive land and does not have enough money to pay property taxes.

Landscape — The natural surroundings of a structure; to change the natural scenery to make it more attractive.

Lapping of accounts receivable — An embezzlement scheme where a bookkeeper is able to collect on a customer's account as well as control bookkeeping entries. By misstating the accounts receivable and eventually writing off one or more accounts receivable as uncollectible, a bookkeeper is able to misappropriate all such amounts without leaving immediate discrepancies in the accounting records. Lapping can usually be detected, however, through the use of generally accepted auditing standards.

Lapse — Generally, the termination of a privilege or right because of a failure to act or the passage of time; an expiration. The termination of an insurance contract because premium payments are in default.

Lapsed legacy — A bequest of personal property where the legatee dies before the legacy is payable. Such bequest either becomes residue or under an anti-lapse statute the legacy passes under the direction of the legatee.

Lapsed option — An expired option, which is therefore worthless.

Lapsed policy — An insurance policy terminated because of nonpayment of premiums.

Lapse ratio — A ratio used by an investor in measuring the quality of business experienced by an insurance company. The lower the lapse ratio, the higher the expected profits.

Larceny — The wrongful taking of another's property with the intent of permanently depriving the owner of it; stealing.

Last-in, first-out (LIFO) — A method of valuing goods (e.g., inventory) that are received in identifiable lots, in that the last lots received are considered to be the first lots sold, regardless of the actual cost of each item sold. The remaining units in inventory are, therefore, valued according to the earliest purchases. For example, assume Jacobson received the following lots of item XYZ:

Date	Quantity	Price	Total
1/2/86	100 @	$11.00 ea.	$1,100
1/10/86	200 @	12.00 ea.	2,400
1/19/86	100 @	14.00 ea.	1,400
1/27/86	200 @	15.00 ea.	3,000
Total			$7,900

Also assume that Jacobson had 310 items of XYZ in inventory. Under LIFO, the last shipments in were considered the first to leave, so that the remaining 310 items are made up of 100 of the $1/2$ shipment, 200 items of the $1/10$ shipment and 10 items of the $1/19$ shipment. Thus, the value of the ending inventory is $3,640 ($1,100 + $2,400 + $140).

Last will and testament — The ultimate designation left by a deceased as to the disposition of his or her property at death.

Late charge — An amount due for failure to make a timely installment payment. Late charges are generally not deductible as interest for income tax purposes.

Latent defect — A hidden discrepancy or defect that could not be discovered through the use of customary and reasonable inspection.

Lawyer — A person licensed by the state to practice law as an attorney.

Layaway plan — A manner of purchasing goods where a retailer holds the items to be purchased upon receipt of partial payment and generally relinquishes the goods when the full purchase price is paid.

Layman — A person not familiar with the esoteric language of a certain profession.

Layoff — An involuntary removal of a worker or group of workers from the payroll because of a decline in business activity, technological changes, or other extraneous source beyond an employee's control. Layoffs can either be temporary or permanent.

Leading indicator — An index that anticipates the movements of the business cycle. It is especially useful in forecasting the general business activity of the nation as a whole.

Lead time — The period of time between the point an item is ordered and when it is actually received.

Lease — An agreement reached between a lessor (owner) and lessee (user) by which the lessor agrees to give possession of property to the lessee for a certain period of time at a specified rate for a certain use.

Leaseback — See "Sale-leaseback."

Leasehold — An estate in real property, usually for a fixed duration in accordance with the terms of a lease.

Leasehold improvements — Capitalized expenditures for improvements made by a lessee to leased property. Leasehold improvements are especially important in condemnation proceedings in deciding a lessee's share of a condemnation award and for depreciation purposes in filing a lessee's income tax return when the lessee makes such improvements.

Leasehold interest — The interest a lessee has in the value of a lease. In a condemnation proceeding the leasehold interest would be computed as the difference between the remaining rents and the rents the lessee would have to pay for similar property. Also see "Leasehold value."

Leasehold value — The value a lessee has in a leasehold interest, which generally applies to long-term leases. For example, Boswell leases a building owned by Holloway. The lease agreement calls for periodic rents of $2,000 to be paid monthly over the next 10 years.

Assume after 5 years, similar available property is renting for $2,500 per month. Boswell has a leasehold value of $500 per month.

Lease with option to purchase — A lease agreement containing an option for the lessee to purchase the leased property. In order for the option to be valid, the price and terms of the purchase must be stated in the option. In many cases each rental payment will include both a lease payment and a portion of a down payment toward the purchase price.

Leave no issue — Without any descendants.

Leave of absence — A temporary absence from work with an intention of returning and which causes no loss of seniority upon return.

Ledger — A book used in an accounting system containing all controlling accounts on separate pages so that the balance of each account can be readily available after postings are made from the journal.

Legacy — A testamentary gift of money or other personal property. In its strictest sense, a legacy is a testamentary gift of money only, and a bequest is a testamentary gift of personal property, although legacy is commonly used to mean both. Also see "Legatee." Compare "Devise."

Legacy tax — See "Inheritance taxes."

Legal — Something within the confines of the law.

Legal age — Commonly, the age of majority, which is typically 18 or 21; it varies among the states and with purposes (e.g., the legal driving age and drinking age are not the same). The age an individual is legally able to make contracts and to transact business.

Legal capital — The par value or stated value of stock that is fixed upon the date of incorporation. Legal capital is an amount that must remain in the firm in order to protect creditors.

Legal description — A geographical identification of land that is acceptable to a court of law as to the description for identifying its exact location. It may consist of a governmental survey, metes and bounds, or lot numbers pertaining to recorded plat.

Legal entity — The existence of an entity, other than a human being, that has separate legal rights, such as the right to make contracts, sue and be sued, own property in its own name, and make decisions through agents as exemplified in the case of a corporation.

Legal heirs — A deceased individual's next of kin; persons in line under the laws of descent and distribution.

Legal investment — Certain investments in which banks or other fiduciaries are eligible to invest.

Legal issue — See "Legal heirs."

Legal notice — An appropriate notice to be given as required by law. Depending upon the circumstances, legal notice may be required to be actual notice, constructive notice, etc.

Legal owner — The owner of property as evidenced by whose name appears on the last executed deed as the owner. A legal owner may have title to property, but could have passed possession on to another party, or title may not hold any rights except that of a lien.

Legal reserve — The amount of liquid assets that are legally required by a financial institution, such as a bank or insurance company, to keep on hand to assure payment to depositors or claimants.

Legal service plans — See "Group legal insurance."

Legal tender — All coins and currency issued by the U.S. government for payment of public and private debts.

Legal title — (1) A title enforceable in a court of law; (2) a title held without ownership rights, such as a title placed with a trustee, as opposed to equitable title, which is with the trust beneficiary.

Legatee — According to the last will and testament, a beneficiary taking money or other personal property, as opposed to real estate, from a decedent's estate. Also see "Legacy."

Lender — A person or institution from which money or other assets are borrowed.

Lessee — One who leases property owned by another (lessor).

Lessor — One who owns leased property and allows another party (lessee) to use such property in accordance with a lease agreement. Also see "Landlord."

Letter of attornment — A letter written to a tenant of leased property stating that the property has been sold and directing him or her to pay rents to the new owner.

Letter of credit — Generally, a letter written by one party directing another to pay money or give credit to a third party on the account of the writer. A standby letter of credit is typically used to "guarantee" against nonpayment by a specified third party.

Letter of intent — A written preliminary understanding of parties who intend to contract in a specified manner. Generally, letters of intent do not create an obligation, but are used as a formal way of stating an intention. They are common in real estate development where parties interested in a project, such as prospective tenants, buyers, sellers, and contractors, will so state in a letter of intent. A letter of intent is also used in mutual fund sales where a fundholder agrees to invest a certain amount into the fund on a periodic basis to qualify for a reduction in sale charges.

Letter ruling — See "Private letter ruling."

Letter security — See "Letter stock."

Letters of administration — A formal letter issued by a probate court appointing an administrator of a deceased individual's estate.

Letter stock — An unregistered stock where the purchaser gives the seller a letter stating that the stock is only an investment and not for immediate resale.

Level premium insurance — An insurance plan for which all premium payments are equal throughout the period of coverage.

Level term insurance policy — A term insurance policy which carries the same face value throughout the contract and usually calls for a rise in premiums over a period of years as long as the policy stays in force. Also see "Term life insurance."

Leverage — The use of borrowed funds to finance an investment which allows an investor to provide a smaller amount of his or her personal funds toward the purchase price. When appropriately used, leverage provides in a higher rate of return on the portion personally invested. For example, Turner invests $10,000 of her own money and borrows $90,000 in order to purchase land valued at $100,000. After one year and not taking into consideration any interest payments, if the value of her land rises by 5 percent, then it will then be worth $105,000. In terms of her portion of investment, the $5,000 increase will be a 50 percent return on the $10,000 she personally contributed. Had she paid for the property entirely from her personal funds, then she would have experienced only a 5 percent return on investment. On the other hand, leverage magnifies a loss just as effectively. Assume that the property value dropped 5 percent and that it is now worth only $95,000. In this case Turner would have lost 50% ($5,000) of her initial investment.

Leveraged investment company — A mutual fund or closed-end investment company that uses borrowed funds to increase the total assets of a portfolio. The essential concept is to increase volatility as well as fund performance especially during a period of rising market prices. The maximum amount of leverage permitted is one third of a fund's total net asset value. Generally, only aggressive investors with high tolerance of risk should invest in investment companies using leverage.

Leveraged lease — A leasing arrangement whereby leased property (e.g., equipment) is purchased with borrowed funds by a lessor and is subsequently leased to a lessee. In most instances, nonrecourse financing is used to purchase the property. Rents paid by a lessee are used to pay off the loan, and the lessor retains the residual value of the property at the end of the contract period.

Leveraged stock — Stock issued by a corporation which has a significant amount of debt in relation to owner's equity.

Levy — In taxation, the assessment and collection of taxes by a government revenue agency, such as the Internal Revenue Service or a state revenue agency.

Liability — (1) Generally, any obligation or debt to be paid; (2) a financial obligation resulting from past transactions which are entered on the balance sheet of an enterprise.

Liability insurance — An insurance contract by which an insurance company agrees to pay for damages that were caused by an insured and suffered by third parties. Generally, before indemnification will be made by the company, the insured must be legally liable to third parties as a consequence of the insured's negligent acts. Bodily injury liability insurance and property damage liability insurance are the two major classifications in the liability insurance field. The three types of contracts written for the broad classifications are policies providing protection against: personal liability perils, business liability perils, and professional liability perils.

Liability limits — The dollar limitation for which an insurance company protects an insured against legal liabilities as specified in an insurance policy. Generally, property damage liability and bodily injury liability covered in general liability policies are subject to a specified limit per occurrence. Automobile liability coverages for bodily injury have two limits: a limit per person subject to an overall limit per accident where two or more persons are harmed. Automobile liability coverages for property damage is written with a limit per accident. For example, automobile liability limits are typically written as follows:

Automobile Liability:

Bodily injury

$100,000 each person
$300,000 each accident

Property damage

$100,000 each accident

Liability risk — The degree of exposure to legal liabilities.

Liable — Responsible for; obligated to; bound by law; accountable for.

Libel — Malicious and injurious publication of false occurrences.

Liberalization clause — A provision in insurance contracts, mostly fire insurance, providing an insured with any benefit arising from an advantageous change that is developed by the insurance company which would broaden existing coverage without additional premium. All extended benefits affected by a liberalization clause automatically accrue to an insured without specific endorsement.

License — Permission granted by an appropriate authority to act in the manner allowed by the granting entity.

Lien — A voluntary or involuntary encumbrance on property for money; the right a creditor has in property as security for a debt.

Lien creditor — A creditor whose claim is secured by a specific property, as opposed to the claim of a general creditor.

Life annuity — An annuity with payments that are entirely contingent upon the life of the annuitant or beneficiary of life insurance proceeds. A life annuity only pays installments while the recipient is living and does not guarantee the return of principal in case the recipient fails to live long enough to receive its total cost. Life annuities are mostly written and marketed as a type of retirement annuity, but may also be obtained as an option of payment of life insurance proceeds. Also see "Annuity."

Life annuity with 10 years certain — A type of life annuity where payments are guaranteed for either the life of the annuitant or 10 years, whichever is longer. Thus, if an annuitant lives 25 years, then the annuity will pay installments over a period of 25 years. Should an annuitant only live 2 years, then the annuity will pay installments to a beneficiary over the remaining 8 years.

Life beneficiary — The recipient of payments or other rights from a trust for the duration of the beneficiary's life.

Life care center — A home for the elderly and permanently disabled.

Life care contract — An agreement to care for and maintain an individual's natural life in exchange for payment of consideration. Life care contracts are executed between elderly persons or disabled individuals and retirement homes.

Life cycle — The stages of a person's life that are classified for the purpose of assessing one's financial needs. Generally, they include young single adult, married without children, family with children, parents living alone, and retirement.

Life estate — (1) An estate in property which only lasts during an individual's lifetime. That is, an estate which is not inheritable as directed by the owner; (2) an arrangement where a beneficiary or life tenant is to receive income from, use of, or other rights of ownership of property for a period limited to his or her life. Upon the death of the beneficiary or life tenant, ownership is terminated and the property will either revert back to the grantor or holder of a remainder interest. Also see "Remainderman."

Life expectancy — The estimated total number of years an individual is expected to live. Age, sex, actuarial tables, and other factors may be used to compute a person's life expectancy.

Life income option — A settlement option of life insurance proceeds providing the beneficiary the right to receive proceeds in the form of a life annuity. Also see "Life annuity."

Life insurance — See "Life insurance policy."

Life insurance policy — A contract between an insurance company and a policyholder by which the company agrees to pay a specified sum to a beneficiary upon the death of the insured during the period such policy is in force. The company must receive consideration (i.e., premium payments) in exchange for the agreement. A policyholder may designate anyone as a beneficiary of his or her own policy, but third parties insuring the life of an individual must have an insurable interest. Also see "Convertible term insurance," "Decreasing term insurance," "Endowment contract," "Extended term insurance," "Family income policy," "Family income rider," "Family maintenance policy," "Group term life insurance," "Industrial insurance," "Joint life policy," "Key person life insurance," "Limited payment life insurance," "Modified life policy," "Mortgage insurance," "Ordinary life insurance," "Paid-up insurance," "Participating policy," "Renewable term insurance," "Single-premium life policy," "Split dollar insurance," "Straight life insurance," "Term life insurance," "Universal life insurance," and "Whole life insurance."

Life insurance proceeds — A sum of money payable to a beneficiary upon the death of an insured. Life insurance proceeds may consist of a policy's total value which accumulates or matures during the period it is in force: face value (plus cash value plus an additional face value if double indemnity) less policy loans and unpaid interest. Basic optional settlement alternatives include lump-sum, specified-amount installments, interest-only payments, life-income payments, and specified-period installments.

Life insurance trust — A trust commonly used in estate planning where all or part of a trust's assets are derived from the proceeds of life insurance.

Life interest — An interest in real or personal property for a period limited to the life of the person having the interest or to the life of another person. A life interest does not amount to complete unrestricted ownership.

Life policy — See "Life insurance policy."

Life tenant — A person who holds an estate in lands for the length of his or her life, or the length of another person's life.

Lifetime disability benefit — Payments intending to replace lost income as a result of total disability so long as the insured lives. Also see "Disability."

LIFO — See "Last-in, first-out."

Like-kind exchange — An exchange of qualified properties that yields no tax consequences on the transfer of the properties. A taxable gain may be recognized from a like-kind exchange if (1) boot is received or (2) boot that has appreciated in value is given. Also see "Tax-free exchange."

Like-kind property — Property held for productive use in a trade or business or investment property (other than stocks, bonds, choses in action, partnership interests, and inventory) that is exchanged for similar property in accordance with a nontaxable (like-kind) exchange (IRC Section 1031). Also see "Tax-free exchange."

Limited collision coverage — A type of collision protection that is only applicable when an insured is not at fault in an accident.

Limited liability — A characteristic of a corporation and limited partnership where an investor is only liable for the debts of the business up to the amount invested (i.e., the investor is not personally liable for business debts).

Limited partner — A partner whose liability to the partnership's creditors is restricted by the amount of the partner's investment in the partnership. An investor who is not personally obligated to pay for the debts of a partnership. Generally, contributions to a partnership by a limited partner must be in cash or other property, but not services, and limited partners must not take part in the management of the partnership's business or they will be deemed general partners.

Limited partnership — An unincorporated form of business organization consisting of at least one general partner and one limited partner formed according to the provisions of state law.

Limited payment life insurance — A whole life contract on which premiums are due for a limited number of years, such as 10, 20, 30, or up to age 65, at which time the policy is fully paid up. If the insured dies before the stipulated premium payment period, however, no further premiums are due and the policy's insurance proceeds will be paid to a beneficiary. Limited payment life insurance and endowment contracts differ in that after the whole life policy is paid up, only the cash value is available to the policyholder, not the face value as is the case with an endowment policy. Thus, the premiums for a limited payment policy are expected to be considerably less than that of an endowment contract.

Limited policy — An insurance policy limited in coverage by excluding certain perils.

Limit of liability — The maximum amount an insurance company will pay in case of a loss, subject to the terms of the policy.

Limit order — In securities trading, an order used by customers directing their broker to buy at a certain price (or lower) or sell at a certain price (or higher).

Limit price — The price set by customer in a limit order: buy or sell at the limit price or better.

Lineal heir — A person who inherits from an ascending or descending relative, as opposed to a collateral heir.

Line of credit — An available amount of money offered by a lender that can be immediately borrowed without a credit check. A line of credit is generally available over a predetermined period and for a maximum amount.

Liquid asset — Cash and any other asset which can be quickly turned into cash at or near its fair market value, such as marketable securities and money market accounts. Compare "Illiquid."

Liquidated damages — A predetermined amount of money that must be paid in order to break a contract. Liquidated damages are generally an estimated amount of the actual damages as a result of a breach of contract and are commonly stated in the agreement.

Liquidating dividend — A dividend paid by a corporation generally in settling its financial affairs. A liquidating dividend represents a return of capital rather than distribution of earnings. Such dividends are received tax-free up to a stockholder's basis and any amounts received in excess of basis are capital gain.

Liquidation — (1) The settlement of an obligation, such as full repayment of a loan; (2) the dissolution and settlement of a business, estate, or other entity; (3) the conversion of an asset into cash, such as the selling of stock or other investments.

Liquidation price — The price of an item sold either to settle a debt or to wind up a business. Because of pressure to sell quickly, a liquidation price is typically below fair market value.

Liquidity — (1) The ability of an asset to be sold or otherwise turned into cash at a price near its fair market value; (2) the relative ease in which an individual or business can meet its obligations without having to sell investment or fixed assets. Also see "Liquidity ratios."

Liquidity ratios — In the analysis and interpretation of financial statements, ratios that are used to indicate a person's or business's debt-paying ability, especially over a short-term period. The liquidity ratios include current ratio, acid-test ratio, accounts receivable turnover, number of day's sales in accounts receivable, inventory turnover, and turnover of total assets.

Listed option — Put and call options traded on an organized option exchange, as opposed to privately traded options or conventional options traded over the counter.

Listed stock — A stock that has met the requirements of a certain organized securities exchange and is traded there.

Listing — In real estate, an agreement made between a broker and owner for the purpose of selling or renting real property. Stated in the agreement are the names of the parties, description of the land, terms of sale (such as price and manner of acceptable payments), terms of broker's compensation, and duration of the listing. Also see "Multiple listing" and "Open listing."

Listing agent — In real estate, an agent representing the broker who obtains a listing on a particular property.

List price — The published price of an item that may subsequently be reduced by negotiation, cash discount, or volume purchase.

Livelihood — The means of support; the manner in which a person earns or passively receives income; one's source of income.

Living trust — See "Inter vivos trust."

Lloyd's of London — An association of independent syndicates located in London who may write any kind of insurance and set their own premiums for their own account. Organized in a manner similar to an exchange, Lloyd's is not an insurer nor does it issue any insurance policies. Proposals for insurance are prepared and presented to members (agents of the syndicates) by brokers, and the syndicates become the actual underwriters of risk. Syndicates are made up of members (referred to as "names") who furnish the necessary capital. Lloyd's principal objectives are to maintain complete records of losses, provide quarters for its members and other support for their transactions or disputes, supervise repairs and salvage throughout the world, help in loss settlements, develop policy forms, investigate all applicants' financial standing, and oversee the solvency of all members. The most remarkable feature of Lloyd's of London is that it provides uncommon types and amounts of coverage that cannot be obtained elsewhere.

Load — Sales fee for the purchase of a "Load fund."

Load fund — A type of mutual fund that carries a sales fee and is customarily purchased from a stockbroker, financial planner, insurance agent, or mutual fund salesman. Compare "No-load mutual fund."

Loan — The lending of money in exchange for repayment of principal and interest.

Loan broker — See "Mortgage broker."

Loan commitment fees — An amount paid to a lender for the purpose of making funds available over a specified period of time at a certain rate of interest. Generally, such fees must be capitalized over the life of the loan for income tax purposes.

Loan constant — In real estate investing, a method of evaluating different types of financing arrangements and is used with other factors of comparison to determine the quality of investment (i.e., net income, debt coverage ratio, and return on equity). It is stated as a percentage of the amount initially borrowed:

$$\text{Loan constant} = \frac{\text{Debt service per year}}{\text{Amount of loan}}$$

Loan origination fees — See "Points."

Loan package — A file consisting of documents compiled by a lender which are necessary for making a determination as to whether to provide a loan. Included in a loan package is the loan application, credit report, letters of employment, financial statement, land appraisal, land survey, and other items.

Loan placement fees — See "Points."

Loan ratio — A ratio used to determine the level of interest rate charged on certain real estate loans. It is expressed as a percentage of the amount borrowed to the selling price; the greater the percentage, the higher the interest rate.

Loan shark — A person who loans money at usurious interest rates and customarily uses or threatens to use violence to force repayment.

Loan value — (1) The maximum amount that can be loaned on property consistent with the lender's policies; (2) a provision in a life insurance policy stating the amount that can be borrowed against the cash value.

Lobbying — Efforts directed toward influencing legislators to enact certain laws or introduce certain bills that favorably affect a particular cause.

Local assessment — A local tax levied on residents and businesses for the cost of improvements, such as sidewalks and sewers. Generally, local assessments are charged to persons who will benefit directly by the improvements; such assessments are not deductible for income tax purposes but instead are added to the affected asset's basis.

Local taxes — Taxes collected by city and/or county governments to finance local public services.

Locative calls — Specific description in a document referring to the identification of land. Also see "Legal description."

Log book — The journal of an aircraft or ship stating every trip taken.

Logrolling — The legislative practice of adding many independent items of special interest to a bill in order to induce enough voters to pass the original bill.

Longevity pay — Additional compensation for extended service in the military.

Long position — The holding of an investment with an expectation of a rise in market value. The holding of stocks, bonds, land, commodity futures, and call options are generally considered to be in the long position. The risk of a long investment is stable or declining market values. Compare "Short position."

Long-term — Depending on the circumstances, the holding of an asset for a period considered to be "long-term," which could be 6 months and a day (e.g., for income tax purposes) or 10 years (e.g., for long-term financing).

Long-term capital gain — The sale of a capital asset for a gain after holding it for the required holding period. Also see "Capital asset transactions."

Long-term capital loss — The sale of a capital asset for a loss after holding it over the period that is required to be long-term. Also see "Capital asset transactions."

Long-term debt — A bond or other debt instrument with 10 or more years to maturity. Compare "Long-term liability."

Long-term financial goals — Generally, attainable financial objectives set for periods varying between 1 and 40 years. Long-term financial goals are typically those which are designed to be accomplished during the working years before retirement.

Long-term financing — Any financing arrangement having 10 or more years to maturity.

Long-term investments — Investments held by a person or business that are not intended to be liquidated within one year.

Long-term land contract — See "Installment land contract."

Long-term lease — Generally, a lease having a duration of 10 or more years.

Long-term liability — In financial accounting, obligations of an enterprise or individual that are due within a period longer than 1 year (or the operating cycle of a business if longer). Examples include mortgages payable, long-term notes payable, and bonds payable.

Loss — (1) In accounting, the excess of costs over income, an unexpected loss from which a future benefit cannot be attained, or the decrease in value of certain property (unrealized loss); (2) in insurance, the amount of damage which may be subject to recovery by an insurance company.

Loss contingency — The outcome of an existing condition which is uncertain, but could ultimately result in a loss.

Loss-control activities — All activities which are primarily designed to prevent the occurrence of a loss or reduce the impact of losses.

Loss leader — In retail marketing, an item advertised and sold for a price below its fair market value for the purpose of attracting customers into a store with the hope that other items will be bought which have not been marked down.

Loss of access — The geographic restraint of an owner of real property to come and go from a public road, which abuts his or her property, usually as a result of a condemnation (e.g., for the building of a limited access highway).

Loss of earning capacity — The degree of damage to one's abilities to perform in his or her trade or business which resulted from an accident. Loss of earning capacity is recoverable as an element of damage in a legal proceeding.

Loss of income benefits — Payments made to an insured because of a covered disability which resulted in an inability to work.

Loss of sight benefit — Generally, a lump-sum or weekly benefit provided by a health insurance policy because of the loss of vision caused by an accident. The amount of benefit typically depends on a schedule of dismemberment and loss of sight benefits that is listed in the policy.

Loss payable clause — A provision in a fire insurance policy listing the priority of claims which authorize benefit payments to persons, other than the owner, who also have an insurable interest in the property, such as a mortgagee or holder of a lien, in the event insured property is destroyed.

Loss payee — A person named in an insurance policy who is to receive insurance proceeds for the loss or destruction of property.

Loss prevention service — A service of design and inspection performed by insurance companies or independent organizations for the purpose of making recommendations toward changes to reduce possible causes of loss.

Loss recognized — A loss resulting from the sale or exchange of an asset that is recognized for income tax purposes.

Lost policy release — A contract signed by the insured releasing an insurance company from all liability under a policy which is missing.

Lost will — A will that was executed prior to a testator's death, but cannot be found.

Lottery — A game of chance for a winning prize in exchange of consideration paid. It is one method used to raise state and local revenues.

Love and affection — Used in conjunction with a gift, but is not considered to be valuable consideration when such is needed.

Lower of cost or market — In financial accounting, a conservative method of valuing inventory and marketable securities where the value of such items are set at the lesser of acquisition cost or fair market value.

Low liquidity — An investment term describing an item that cannot be quickly turned into cash without undue loss.

Lucrative investment — A profitable investment which yields income or gains.

Lump-sum alimony — A settlement of a divorce or separation made in one lump-sum payment, rather than by periodic payments.

Lump-sum death benefit — A one-time payment in full to a beneficiary after the death of an insured.

Lump-sum distribution — The full payment of a vested amount from a qualified or unqualified retirement plan. Generally, such distributions from a qualified plan may be allowed to use both the special 10-year averaging (pertaining to years of service from 1974 and beyond) and long-term capital gain treatment (pertaining to years of service before 1974)—Form 7972, or such distribution may be fully or partially rolled over into an individual retirement account (IRA). In order for an employee to take advantage of the 10-year averaging option, he or she must have been a plan participant for at least 5 years. Lump-sum distributions from an individual retirement account do not qualify for special 10-year averaging.

Lump-sum payment — One payment in full rather than a series of installments, such as a single-premium annuity.

Lump-sum purchase — A purchase in mass where items are not broken up into individual units.

Lump-sum settlement — The payment of life insurance proceeds or retirement benefits in lump-sum rather than by installments.

Luxury tax — An excise tax levied on items not considered to be necessities, such as cigarettes and liquor.

M — 1,000 times a number, such as 50M is 50,000; 50MM is 50,000,000.

M-1 — A measure of the money supply consisting of currency, demand deposits, and interest-bearing checking accounts. Compare "M-2" and "M-3."

M-2 — An economist's expanded definition of the money supply which includes M-1 plus money market mutual funds, savings accounts, Eurodollars issued by Caribbean member banks and held by U.S. residents, and overnight repurchase agreements issued by commercial banks. Also see "M-1."

M-3 — An economist's expanded definition of the money supply which includes M-2 plus large time deposits (CDs) and term repurchase agreements issued by financial institutions. Also see "M-2."

Machine-readable codes — Generally, symbols printed on merchandise that can be interpreted by both people and optical scanners for the purpose of accounting for sales and inventory.

Macroeconomics — The branch of economics which studies a large group of people or products that pertain to a nation's overall economy, such as total unemployment, gross national product, and aggregate spending versus saving tendencies.

Magistrate — A public civil officer, such as a justice of the peace or a police court judge.

Magnetic disk — A storage medium for computers which is useful for direct-access processing.

Magnetic ink characters — The coding imprinted on checks and deposit slips so that special character-reading devices can read it for the purpose of speeding up the clearing process.

Mail order — A method of marketing consumer goods where a buyer chooses items from a catalog or other advertisement and mails or telephones an order to the retailer, who in turn ships the articles to the customer.

Mail order policies — Insurance policies, mainly life or health insurance, sold through advertisements and are typically limited in scope of coverage. One type of mail order policy is the guaranteed acceptance life insurance contract.

Maintenance and repairs — Expenses of keeping equipment in working order. Maintenance is scheduled work that is expected to keep up the condition of equipment (e.g., periodic cleaning and lubricating), and repairs are necessary work to fix a broken machine or part. Generally, the costs of maintenance and repairs are expensed, whereas improvements and betterments are capitalized.

Maintenance call — A notice sent by a broker to a margin account customer stating that more collateral (money or securities) is needed to keep a certain margin account open. If more equity is not deposited within a required period of time, the broker will liquidate a sufficient amount of securities in the account to meet the maintenance requirement.

Maintenance fee — As used in condominiums and other planned developments, generally, a monthly fee charged for maintaining and repairing the common area.

Maintenance requirement — See "Margin maintenance requirement."

Majority — Legal age; an adult according to state statutes (either 18 or 21).

Major medical expense protection — Health insurance designed to prevent catastrophic losses against medical care costs because of illness or injury. The four basic characteristics of major medical expense protection are the deductible, coinsurance, high maximum limits, and blanket medical expense protection. The deductibles primarily range from $100 to $2,000, but only apply during one calendar year to each individual or in some cases per family. The coinsurance feature is a participation provision which states the percentage an insurance company will pay (usually 80 percent) and the insured will pay (usually 20 percent) of all covered costs. Some policies have a high maximum benefit of $50,000, while others have an unlimited amount. A maximum benefit may be specified for each illness or injury, as well as an overall maximum benefit per lifetime. Virtually all types of medical expenses are covered for an illness or injury on a blanket basis.

Make a market — The continual buying and selling of stocks or other marketable investments by floor specialists primarily for the purpose of stabilizing prices. Also, when a dealer quotes bid and offer prices and stands ready to buy and sell at such prices, he is said to be "making a market."

Maker — An individual or business who executes a promissory note; one who signs a promissory note to borrow money. A maker can also be the drawee (signer) of a check.

Malicious act — A wrongful act purposely performed with intent to injure another.

Malpractice insurance — Liability insurance against losses arising from the making of errors or mistakes in the conduct of a profession. Medical doctors, attorneys, architects, accountants, insurance agents and brokers, advertisers, consultants, financial planners, dentists, directors, and real estate agents are included in the professions covered by malpractice insurance. Generally, any professional misconduct, departure from a reasonable and ordinary standard of care, or failure to perform in a reasonably professional manner which causes injury, loss, or damages to others may be deemed "malpractice" and create a liability suit against the professional involved.

Management — The planning, organizing, and controlling of any entity.

Management agreement — In real estate, a contract between the owner of real property and a manager or management company setting forth the terms of duties and manner of compensation.

Management fee[1] — In tax-sheltered limited partnerships, the amount paid to the general partners and others for management services. The fees are usually deductible when paid, or for accrual-basis taxpayers, when accrued.

Manipulation — A system of buying and selling securities, or any other method of creating an appearance of active trading, for the purpose of inducing investors to purchase or sell a particular security or other investment. The ultimate intent of manipulation is to bring about favorable price changes for the one initiating such practice.

Margin — An amount of money or securities deposited with a stockbroker by a customer for the purpose of buying and selling stocks or other investments on credit. The securities so purchased are held by the brokerage firm as collateral against losses to which such leveraged investment may be exposed. In commodities trading, margin is required to ensure the performance of a customer at a future date and is generally required to be maintained on a daily basis. Also see "Margin account," "Margin call," and "Margin maintenance requirement."

Margin account — A brokerage account opened by a customer in order to borrow money from a brokerage firm. A customer may borrow for either purchasing securities on credit or for selling securities short. A specified amount of money or securities must be deposited and maintained in the account. For making a loan, the brokerage firm holds the securities purchased for collateral and charges interest on the balance of amounts advanced. Any dividends or interest attributable to the investment, however, are payable to the customer. The minimum amount necessary to open a margin account is $2,000.

Marginal — As used with real estate investments, a poor cash flow from rents which barely cover expenses.

Marginal land — (1) Land that is not well suited but is adequate for an intended purpose; (2) income from rental property that breaks even, that is, without significant gains or losses.

Marginal tax bracket — An individual's incremental tax rate that will apply to the next dollar of taxable income. For example, if Johnston is in a 35 percent marginal tax bracket, then the next dollar of income will be split between $.35 in taxes and $.65 of disposable personal income.

Margin call — A broker's demand for more money or securities to be deposited because a stock or other investment, which was purchased on margin, has declined in value below the margin maintenance requirement (i.e., the account becomes undermarginated).

Margin maintenance requirement — The minimum amount of equity that must be maintained at all times by customers of a margin account: It is usually 30 percent of stocks so held. Industry rules require a stated percentage which may change with various investments. Compare "Initial margin." Also see "Minimum maintenance."

Marine insurance — Transportation insurance which provides protection against legal liability arising from the loss, damage, or expense from the ownership, operation, construction, maintenance, chartering, or repair of any covered vessel, ship, or craft. The two major divisions are ocean marine insurance and inland marine insurance. Such protection generally includes coverage against liability for personal illness, injury, or death of another and loss or damage to properties belonging to another.

Marital deduction — An unlimited deduction for the entire amount of inter vivos and testamentary gifts made between a husband and wife.

Marital deduction trust — Generally, any trust designed to take advantage of the unlimited marital deduction.

Markdown — Any reduction in selling price.

Market — (1) A public place for purchasing consumer items or services, such as a shopping mall, flea market or farmer's market; (2) a place for buying and selling securities, such as the stock market; (3) the demand for a particular item (such as, an automobile is only worth what the "market" will bear).

Marketability — The ability to sell an item for an amount near its fair market value at a specific place and time.

Marketability risk — The risk of not being able to quickly turn an investment into cash for a price near its fair market value; a risk of illiquidity.

Marketable securities — Stocks and bonds which can be readily turned into cash; highly liquid investment in an intangible instrument.

Marketable title — A valid title to property that can be readily sold to a prudent individual who is made completely aware of any material defects, encumbrances, liens, or contingent litigation; generally, any title which would provide quiet and peaceful enjoyment of such property.

Marketing — Generally, all activities which are concerned with moving goods and services from the producers to the consumers. It includes selling, packaging, distributing, storing, financing, advertising, promoting, transporting, and merchandising.

Market interest rate — The currently available interest rate for a given loan to a specified borrower.

Market order — An order to buy or sell a particular stock, bond, option, or commodity on an exchange at the best available price when the order reaches the floor.

Market price — (1) The actual price at which an item currently trades for in a given market setting; the price an investment last sold for as stated on an exchange; the actual value of a good or service that is currently purchased in the market. Compare "market value."

Market return — An overall average rate of return on the stock market as a whole or large sample thereof, such as Standard & Poor's 500 Stock Composite Index.

Market risk — An uncertainty that stems from changes in general securities trading, and believed to simultaneously influence the value of all securities.

Market share — The percentage share of an established market controlled by one company.

Market value — An estimated price a certain property would command if sold under normal conditions. The highest price at which a willing buyer would purchase such item from a willing seller, both knowing all relevant facts and neither being unduly compelled to act. Same as "fair market value."

Market value approach — In real estate, a method of appraising the value of property by comparing the sales price of similar properties which have recently sold in the area. Two primary factors which must be considered are the degree of similarity between such properties and the conditions under which the previous sales took place. It is also known as "comparative sales method."

Market value clause — A provision used in certain property damage coverages obligating the insurance company to pay for damages up to an amount equal to the established market value with proper adjustments. Also see "Actual cash value."

Mark to market — In the trading of commodity futures, a daily valuation of all open positions, which is made at the end of each trading day, by a clearinghouse of an exchange. Profit may be removed from an account before it is closed, but losses may require more margin or the account will automatically be closed. Mark to market is used for income tax purposes at the close of a trader's taxable year to figure gains and losses of all open positions as of that date.

Markup — (1) An amount added to an item's original cost, which is sometimes stated as a percentage; (2) an amount added to an item's original retail selling price.

Marriage penalty — An additional amount paid in income taxes by a married couple where both spouses work. The amount of marriage penalty is the difference between the tax computed on a joint return and the tax computed on two separate returns where both spouses file as single taxpayers (not, married filing separately).

Massachusetts trust — A form of unincorporated business organization where investors transfer property to trustees who manage the business or investments for the benefit of the holders of trust certificates (or certificates of beneficial interests). The certificates are similar to stock in that they are entitled to income produced by the trust, provide limited liability to its holder, and are transferable. Unlike stock, however, they carry no right to vote on the trustees or other matters. It is authorized by the statutes of the state of Massachusetts to operate in this manner.

Master contract — See "Master policy."

Master deed — The main deed of a condominium complex, which is recorded in public records, granting title of all common areas to the owners of the individual condominiums.

Master policy — (1) For group insurance plans, a policy issued to an employer or trustee that contains all insurance clauses and provisions that define the employee benefits. Each participant is given a certificate representing coverage under the master policy; (2) in property insurance, a policy issued to evidence the coverage of properties located at more than one location. If the property is located in more than one state, then, generally, underlying policies are issued to meet local requirements.

Materiality — The concept that something has influence or effect. That is, if an item is significant or influential to a decision maker, then it is material.

Material fact — A fact which bears significant influence upon reaching an agreement. A fact which, if omitted, would have changed the outcome of a decision. For example, a material fact in an application for insurance is one that would change an insurer's decision either by the amount of premium charged or to decline to provide coverage.

Maternal property — Property descending from one's mother, mother's mother, or other relative from the maternal side of family.

Matured claim — A claim that is currently due.

Maturity — A period of time in which the principal and all interest of a debt or other obligation becomes due.

Maturity date — The date on which a debt or other obligation becomes due and fully payable.

Maturity value — The value of an obligation, which typically includes principal and all remaining interest, on the maturity date.

Maximum daily price range — The price range that a futures contract traded on an exchange can fluctuate.

Maximum foreseeable loss — A method of measuring loss as a result of the occurrence of a certain peril against an insured by estimating the highest amount of damage that could possibly happen and taking into consideration the amount of insurance protection already provided along with any deductibles and coinsurance payments.

Means — (1) Something that causes or aids in causing an end; the manner of achieving an objective; (2) money, capital, property, or resources.

Measures of financial stability — Financial statement analysis ratios that attempt to measure the financial strength and long-term solvency of a company. The measures of financial stability are the debt-to-equity ratio, times interest earned ratio, book value per share, cash flow per share, and owner's equity ratio.

Mechanic's lien — A claim created by local law to provide security of payment for the amount of work performed and materials used in the construction, maintenance, repair, improvement, or refurbishing of property. Generally, when real property is involved, the lien also attaches to the land.

Medicaid — A type of public assistance from state and federal governments providing medical care treatment for individuals whose incomes and total resources are below a certain amount, without regard to age.

Medical expense deduction — The amount of medical expenses used as an itemized deduction for income tax purposes. Virtually all services rendered by a qualified medical practitioner, all prescription drugs (including insulin), health insurance premiums paid, specialized equipment purchased, improvements made to a home solely for medical reasons as directed by a qualified medical practitioner (up to the difference in value before and after the improvement), and travel and transportation (figured per mile when using an automobile, or actual cost incurred when traveling by other means; meals and lodging are qualified and limited per day) are used in the computation of qualified medical expenses. Only the excess of total qualified medical expenditures (less all insurance benefits received or reasonably expected to be received) over 5 percent of adjusted gross income is used as a medical expense deduction in figuring the total amount of itemized deductions.

Medical expense insurance — A general term pertaining to medical coverage against expenses for medical care as a result of illness, injury, or other specified problem. Medical expense insurance includes various forms such as hospital expense, surgical expense, regular medical expense, and major medical expense.

Medical payments coverage — A type of medical expense protection provided in various types of liability policies (e.g., automobile policies) where an insurance company agrees to reimburse an insured and others who suffer as a result of a covered accident. Generally, benefits are paid for medical or funeral expenses which result from specified conditions.

Medicare — A federal hospital insurance and supplementary medical insurance program for the aged created in 1965 as an annexation to Social Security.

Medium of exchange — Money; an item which is used to facilitate the exchange of goods or services and is used as a common standard of measure for purposes of comparison.

Meeting of minds — The process of reaching an agreement between two or more parties after all significant expressions have been presented and considered, resulting in mutual compromise or settlement.

Member bank — A bank that is affiliated with the Federal Reserve System. All nationally chartered banks (i.e., national banks) must join the system, but state banks have the option of whether to join or not. The reserve requirement is that every member bank must place all reserves, except vault cash, in an non-interest-bearing account with a Federal Reserve Bank.

Member firm — As used in securities and commodity trading, a brokerage that is a member of a particular exchange, such as the New York Stock Exchange.

Memorandum check — A check written to a lender for the amount of a short-term loan and which is to be ultimately redeemed by the borrower. A memorandum check is not intended to be presented for payment. The abbreviation "Mem." written on a check serves as evidence of the writer's intention.

Memorandum decision — A decision rendered by a court without providing reasons for making it.

Mercantile — Anything pertaining to the business of buying and selling merchandise.

Merchantability — An implied warranty provided by a merchant that the goods are reasonably fit for the general purpose for which they are intended to be used and will ordinarily pass without objection in the trade.

Merchantable title — Good title generally without defects and litigation that is acceptable to a reasonable buyer having prudence, enabling him or her to hold the item in peace and sell it to another.

Merchant's rule — In interest computations, the use of 360 days per year.

Merger — The acquisition of one company by another. The joining together of two different subjects where one is dominant and controlling over the other. Compare "Consolidation."

Metes and bounds — The boundary lines that are used to describe real property, with terminal points and angles.

Mexican divorce — A divorce from Mexico executed either by mail or by appearance of only one spouse. Such divorce may not be recognized in the United States.

Microeconomics — The study of economic relationships of a certain market, industry, individual, or other entity and is much narrower in scope than macroeconomics.

Middleman — A person or business that brings parties together in order to make a contract. An intermediary who brings together producers and consumers, sellers and buyers, or property owners and lessees for the purpose of transacting business. An agent middleman does not hold title and may act as an agent for both parties. Also see "Broker." A wholesaler, on the other hand, buys direct from the manufacturer and resells for a higher price (usually to retailers), thus a wholesaler holds title and customarily becomes responsible for transporting, storing, and distributing the goods.

Midwest Stock Exchange (MSE) — A national registered stock exchange in Chicago.

Mill — One tenth of a cent, which is used to figure local property taxes.

Mineral interest — An interest in the mineral deposits in designated property, with or without complete ownership of such property.

Mineral lease — A contract between an explorer-developer of mineral property and its owner allowing the former to search and extract minerals in exchange for royalty payments.

Mineral right — The right to extract minerals from land or the right to receive a mineral royalty.

Mineral royalty — Income received from a mineral lease.

Minimum amount policies — A requirement set by an insurance company for the smallest face value that a policy can be written.

Minimum charge — The least amount charged for a service or sale of a package of goods even if the required minimum is not met or bought. For example, some freight carriers have a minimum charge for 100 lbs. of cargo, even if only 45 lbs. (or any amount less than 100 lbs.) is being shipped.

Minimum guaranteed interest rate — For an annuity contract, the lowest interest rate that an insurance company will use during the accumulation period of a deferred annuity in compounding its value. The minimum guaranteed interest rate is virtually always lower than the current market rate.

Minimum investment — In a tax shelter, the least amount of investment that can be contributed by one individual.

Minimum maintenance[2] — The minimum equity, or margin, required either by an exchange or National Association of Securities Dealers (NASD) rules, or by brokerage firm requirements: (1) There is a $2,000 maintenance in all accounts with a debit balance or a short position; (2) the exchanges and the NASD require a 25 percent maintenance on long-margin accounts, and as a general rule, 30 percent on short-margin accounts; (3) many member firms have special maintenance requirements on debt securities, option accounts, or on securities selling below a specified dollar value per share.

Minimum period guaranteed annuity — A type of guaranteed refund life annuity, wherein the annuity payments are guaranteed over a certain number of years. Also see "Guaranteed refund life annuities."

Minimum royalty[1] — In oil and gas tax shelters, an arrangement between the landowner or other lessor and oil driller as to the amount to be paid for mineral rights to the land. Usually, a certain amount of rent or a certain percentage of gross income from the drilling activity is the minimum royalty.

Minimum wage — The least amount of hourly wage that can be paid to qualified individuals in accordance with federal law.

Minor — A person whose age is less than the age of legal competence or age of majority as determined by state law (usually 18 or 21).

Minority interest — An interest in a corporation, usually a subsidiary, where the stockholders collectively own less than 50 percent of the outstanding voting common stock.

Minority shareholder — Any stockholder of a corporation who does not own enough voting shares to control the election of the board of directors.

Misappropriation — A general term meaning the taking of property either for one's own use or for a wrongful purpose.

Miscellaneous expenses — A variety of expenses that when taken separately are not significant enough to merit their own particular classification.

Miscellaneous itemized deductions—Itemized deductions from qualified expenditures for certain items, which include the following: expenses connected with investment activities, career counseling expenses for the same occupation, civil defense volunteer's expenses, college teacher's research expenses, qualified educational expenses, fees to collect interest and dividends, hobby expenses (only up to hobby income), malpractice insurance premiums, office in home, professional dues, professional subscriptions, résumés (pertaining to same occupation), special uniforms and clothes used exclusively for employment (and cleaning expenses thereof), tax counseling and return preparation fees, union dues, and unreimbursed employee expenses (not for an outside salesperson, nor for travel and transportation).

Misfortune — An accident causing personal loss.

Misrepresentation — (1) Any untrue statement which is not in accord with the facts; (2) the failure of a salesperson, broker, dealer, agent, builder, developer of real estate, or other property sold to the general public to disclose all material defects to the buyer; (3) in insurance, an intent to mislead an insurance company with regard to information requested by it in the application process or settlement of a claim.

Misstatement-of-age clause — A clause in a life insurance policy stating that if the insured's age is misstated, then the proceeds payable by the company upon death of the insured will be adjusted to an amount which would have purchased life insurance given the correct age and the premium actually paid. The misstatement of age is not within the scope of the incontestable clause because it is covered by this special provision.

Mistake — An unintentional error not caused by negligence.

Mixed stream of returns — Generally, the annual returns from investments which reveal no particular pattern.

Mixed trust — A trust created for both charitable and private purposes.

Modified coverage form (HO-8) — See "Homeowners' insurance policy."

Modified deductible — A type of insurance deductible that incorporates both straight deductible and franchise deductible features. It is used in some homeowners' policies as a method to discourage exaggerated claims.

Modified life policy — A form of permanent life insurance primarily designed for young families just starting out in that the initial premiums due during the earliest years are lower than comparable ordinary life policies and thereafter the premiums are slightly higher.

Monetarist — A member of the school of conservative economists whose basis for economic thought is primarily focused on changes in the supply of money, in that the government's most important role should be to regulate the growth of the money supply toward maintaining a growth rate of about 5 percent per year. Generally, it is their position that inflation is caused by an overly rapid growth of money supply, and a recession is caused by a decline in the rate of its growth.

Monetary bequest — A pecuniary bequest; a transfer of money by execution of a will.

Monetary policy — A government's overall program for regulating the expansion of money and credit.

Money — Coins, dollars, checks, money orders, traveler's checks, and other items in circulation that can be easily exchanged for payment of debt. Also see "Medium of exchange," "M-1," "M-2," and "M-3."

Money market — A part of the financial market that deals in short-term debt instruments, including Treasury bills, commercial paper, negotiable certificates of deposit, and banker's acceptances. Compare "Capital market."

Money market account (MMA) — A type of checking account offered by financial institutions that carries a competitive interest rate, as experienced by their money market fund, and can be federally insured.

Money market certificate (MMC) — A type of certificate of deposit issued by a bank, savings and loan, or other similar financial institution with a maturity of 6 months or 30 months and an interest rate approximately equal to the average rate of Treasury bills or other government securities. It is also known as a "Money market time deposit."

Money market fund — Generally, a mutual fund that invests in low-risk short-term obligations.

Money market time deposit — See "Money market certificate."

Money order — A type of draft which serves as a check. It is generally issued by a bank, a business, or a government agency to a named payee for a fee that is paid by a remitter; the purpose is to transmit funds. It may be negotiable or nonnegotiable, depending upon the manner in which it is written.

Money-purchase plan — A type of pension plan (and a defined-contribution plan) where an employer contributes a specified amount of money to each participant's account; the benefits are determined by the accumulation of such contributions as well as the plan's investment experience. The employer's contribution is normally based on a fixed percentage of each participant's income, but length of service may also become a factor. The IRS considers a money-purchase plan as providing "definitely determinable benefits" because the benefits are not geared to profits and can reasonably be determined by an actuary.

Money spread — See "Vertical spread."

Money supply — The amount of a nation's money that is available to spend. Also see "M-1," "M-2," and "M-3."

Monopoly — The exclusive control of a particular market that is held by only one seller or a group of sellers acting together through mutual agreement.

Monopsony — The exclusive control of a particular market that is held by only one buyer or a group of buyers acting together through mutual agreement.

Month-to-month lease — A leasing arrangement whereby no written lease obligates the lessee to a fixed term, although appropriate notice of moving or eviction may still apply.

Moonlighting — Working at a second job, either in the same or different line of work or profession.

Moral hazards — For insurance purposes, the hazards which stem from an individual's attitude and other psychological factors that contribute to the assessment of a risk. Included in a check of moral hazards are reputation, character, past history of credit standing and bankruptcy, ethical business practices, and general standard of conduct as perceived by others, such as employers, co-workers, competitors, creditors, and customers.

Moratorium — (1) A legally authorized suspension, postponement, or delay of payment by a debtor; (2) a period of deferment of a legal right or remedy.

Mortality table — A table summarizing the life expectancy of men and women, who are in ordinary health and of a given age. Mortality tables are developed by actuaries from studies of survival rates of a certain group of people and are used by insurance companies in determining the premiums to be charged for life insurance policies and life annuity contracts, as well as other insurance-related purposes. It is also used for measuring the probabilities of life and death.

Mortgage — (1) Generally, a pledge of specified real property as security for payment of a debt or the performance of a duty; a type of lien; (2) a written document representing an interest in land or personal property whereby legal title is conveyed to or held by the mortgagee, but upon payment of a certain debt or performance of a certain duty, such title will become void. According to the provisions of the mortgage, typically, all payments of interest and principal must be made on time, the property must be fully insured and it must be maintained in order to keep up its value. Each state, however, has its own statutes regarding the execution of mortgages. Also see "Deed of trust."

Mortgage banker — Generally, a company engaged in the business of providing short-term mortgage financing by using its own funds rather than bringing together a borrower and lender (see "Mortgage broker"). A mortgage banker may borrow funds, or the company may sell mortgages to investors (large financial institutions such as insurance companies) when permanent, long-term financing is needed.

Mortgage bond — A bond issued by a corporation that is secured by real or personal property. Mortgage bonds will specify the ranking of the mortgages, such as first or second mortgage.

Mortgage broker — A person or company who acts, for a fee, as an intermediary by bringing together a borrower and lender. Generally, a mortgage broker helps in compiling the necessary documents for a loan application. A mortgage broker is also known as a "loan broker."

Mortgage clause — A provision in an individual's life insurance policy making the proceeds payable to a certain mortgagee, in the event of the insured's death, to the extent of any unpaid balance. Also, a provision in a fire insurance policy providing payment to a mortgagee under specified conditions.

Mortgage company — A company authorized to engage in the business of creating mortgages and selling them to investors.

Mortgage discount — See "Points."

Mortgagee — The holder of a mortgage; the bank or savings and loan that takes a mortgage.

Mortgage insurance — Insurance written primarily to protect the lender from loss as a result of a mortgage default, which generally enables the lender to provide a higher percentage of the purchase price.

Mortgage lien — In some states, a lien on property for the security of a debt whereby the mortgagor holds title, and the first mortgagee's claim to the property is generally recognized before all others.

Mortgage life insurance — Life insurance specifically designed to protect the borrower's family from losing their home in case of death or in some cases disability of the breadwinner. Benefits are intended to pay off the balance due on a mortgage or to meet the remaining payments as they fall due. In many instances, mortgage life insurance is decreasing term insurance set up over the period of the loan.

Mortgage loan — Generally, a loan secured by real property.

Mortgage of goods — See "Chattel mortgage."

Mortgagor — Generally, the borrower of money who pledges title to property, or allows a lien, to secure a loan; one who pledges property for a particular purpose.

Mortmain acts — Statutes that place restrictions on the amount of property which a testator may will to charities.

Most suitable use valuation — For purposes of valuing items for estate or gift taxes, the value of such property transferred is made according to its most suitable or best use, which usually provides the highest fair market value. Compare "Special-use valuation."

Movable estate — See "Personal property."

Moving expenses — For income tax purposes, allowable expenses incurred for qualified moves made in connection with employment (either as an employee or self-employed) at a new principal place of work. The deductions are made on Form 3903 and are deductions before adjusted gross income (i.e., not itemized deductions). Two tests must be satisfied: distance and time. The distance requirement provides that a taxpayer's new job location must be 35 miles or farther from the taxpayer's old residence than the old residence was from the previous place of employment. The time requirement provides that an employee must be employed full-time at the new job for at least 39 weeks during the first 12 months after the move, and a self-employed person must remain at the new location (either as an employee or self-employed) for 78 weeks during the first 24 months after the move. Generally, there is no limit on the expense of moving household goods and travel to the new destination; however, house-hunting trips, temporary living expenses; and certain buying and selling expenses of a residence are limited.

Multilateral agreement — An agreement among three or more parties.

Multi-peril policy — An insurance policy providing coverage for two or more perils as specified in a single contract, such as the combination of fire and casualty coverages in a homeowner's policy.

Multiple-line insurance — A description of an insurance package that combines two basic types of coverages: fire and casualty insurance. In some instances, marine and health insurances are included as well. Multiple-line insurance provides more convenient coverage for the consumer.

Multiple listing — A listing of real property, which is for sale, with all members of an association so that another broker can sell the property for a percentage of the original broker's commission.

Multiple-step income statement — An income statement showing revenues and expenses classified in different categories, such as operating revenues, cost of goods sold, gross profit, operating expenses, other revenues and expenses, income tax expense, and extraordinary items.

Multiple support[1] — An agreement between two or more individuals, who jointly furnish more than half of the total support for a dependent, that allows one of the individuals to claim a dependency exemption. Each individual bound by the agreement must furnish more than 10 percent of the dependent's total support.

Municipal bond — A long-term bond issued by a city, county, state, or other public body, other than the federal government, for the purpose of raising money for municipal expenditures. Generally, interest on municipal bonds is not included in taxable income for federal income tax purposes, but may be included in income for state income taxes.

Municipal bond fund — A mutual fund investing in tax-free (for federal income tax purposes) municipal bonds.

Municipal investment trust (MIT) — A type of unit investment trust that invests in municipal bonds in order to give investors tax-free interest (for federal income tax purposes).

Muniments of title — Documents which present evidence of title to property.

Mutual agreement — The reconciliation of two or more parties (meeting of the minds) by reaching a conclusion as to the intent of the parties to perform one or more certain acts or to refrain from performing one or more certain acts.

Mutual benefit association — Generally, a social organization that provides benefits, such as life insurance and health insurance, to its members. Depending upon the group's experience, a mutual benefit association usually must assess all members to meet the claims.

Mutual companies — Insurance companies that operate for the benefit of its policyholders. There is no capital stock, and dividends are typically distributed in proportion to the amount of participating insurance each member purchased from the company.

Mutual fund — A corporation specially designed to invest its money in securities of other companies. A mutual fund raises money by offering its own shares to the public and provides professional portfolio management over its investment activities as well as diversification for an investor. The value of its stock is determined by the value of its portfolio (net asset value, or NAV). There are two different types of mutual funds: load funds and no-load funds. The stock purchased from a load fund is usually through a stockbroker, fund salesman, or insurance agent (the "load" representing a sales fee). No-load mutual funds are purchased directly from the company without sales commission, although there usually is a small transaction cost. Mutual funds are also known as open-end investment companies, which means there is no limit to the number of shareholders and shares that can be redeemed at their net asset value directly from the company. The fund profits by collecting management and transaction fees. One aspect peculiar to mutual funds is that they are allowed to distribute an allocated amount of long-term capital gains and tax-free dividends (if the fund qualifies) which retain these tax characteristics in the recipient's hands.

Mutual savings bank — A thrift institution that does not issue capital stock, but is owned by depositors as evidenced by a certificate of deposit. Mutual savings banks differ from commercial banks in that the former generally participates in long-term loans rather than short-term loans. Most mutual savings banks are located in the Northeast, and they are similar to a mutual savings and loan.

Mutual savings and loan — A type of savings and loan that is legally owned by its depositors, who receive "dividends" paid out of the firm's operating profits, rather than guaranteed interest as a corporate savings and loan or commercial bank pays. The "dividends" paid to depositors are treated as interest for income tax purposes and are rarely reduced by the board of directors.

Mutual wills — Two or more separate wills written for two or more people that contain reciprocal provisions favoring each other.

N

Naked options — Uncovered; call options granted or other options written without simultaneously possessing the underlying asset (or similar property) which is subject to such option. Any option position to which the option writer may have to buy or sell the underlying asset because he or she is not adequately covered.

Named insured — As specifically designated in an insurance policy, an individual, group of individuals, or company who are protected against covered perils.

Named perils — A type of insurance policy that specifies the perils which are covered by its terms, as distinguished from a policy that insures against "all risks."

National Association of Realtors (NAR) — An association formed primarily for the betterment of the real estate industry, as a whole, by promoting favorable legislation, providing education for its members, and setting high ethical standards.

National Association of Securities Dealers (NASD) — A membership association of broker-dealers and underwriters in securities that allows, among other privileges, member firms to execute transactions with one another at reduced rates.

National Association of Securities Dealers Automated Quotations (NASDAQ) — A highly automated system that links securities dealers in order to bring together buyers and sellers of over-the-counter stocks (i.e., stocks not sold in an organized exchange).

National banks — Commercial banks chartered by the federal government; therefore, they are members of the Federal Reserve System and are required to carry federal deposit insurance. National banks must conduct their business under federal and state laws, as opposed to state banks who are authorized to do business under state banking laws.

National debt — Money owed by the federal government.

National Foundation for Consumer Credit — A nonprofit organization headquartered in Washington, D.C., and formed to provide debt-counseling services for individuals having difficulties in paying their bills.

Natural death — Death caused by circumstances other than violence or accident (such as "old age" or sickness).

Natural resources — Any resource that has economic value in its natural condition, such as timber, oil, gas, iron ore, and gold.

Near money — Items that can be quickly turned into cash; liquid assets.

Necessities — Any article or service which is essential in sustaining human life, such as food, shelter, clothing, and medical care.

Needs approach — A method of evaluating the amount of life insurance needed by a family in case the breadwinner dies. Financial burdens to be carried by the survivors, such as mortgage payments, income for the surviving spouse and for raising any dependents, dependent's educational costs, funeral expenses, present debts, and retirement income for the surviving spouse, are taken into consideration.

Negative amortization — A phenomenon occurring in certain adjustable-rate mortgages where the principal expands rather than declines over the payment period. Also see "Adjustable rate mortgage (ARM)."

Negative cash flow — The occurrence of cash expenses exceeding cash receipts over a certain period.

Negligence — An omission or unintentional act which a reasonable man would or would not do in the ordinary course of human affairs; the failure to use a proper amount of care as required by the circumstances.

Negligence liability — Liability arising from negligence where a legal duty to act or not to act exists and was breached (usually unintentionally). Also, such act or failure to act was the proximate cause that resulted in injury or damages to another party.

Negotiable — Capable of being legally transferred by indorsement or mere delivery for payment of debts or to be bought and sold. Negotiable typically refers to checks, promissory notes, bonds, stocks, bills of lading, certificates of deposit, etc.

Negotiable instrument — A document that can be negotiated; an instrument that is in writing and signed by the maker or drawer, contains an unconditional promise to pay a sum certain in cash on demand or at a definite time, and is made payable to bearer or to the order of a named payee. Generally, it must not contain any other promise or obligation.

Negotiable order of withdrawal account — See "NOW account."

Net after taxes — Net amount of income after all taxes have been paid, such as the amount of salary or wages left after withholding for FICA, federal and state income taxes, and other authorized withholdings; the bottom line of a income statement (i.e., net income).

Net assets — The residual of total assets over total liabilities; owner's equity.

Net asset value (NAV) — The value of one share of stock in an investment company as determined by the value of all its assets less total liabilities and dividing this amount by the number of shares outstanding. The NAV is used to designate the price per share of mutual funds (both to buy and sell) and a gauge for assessing the value of closed-end investment companies' stock prices.

Net before taxes — Net income before payment of income taxes. Net before taxes is a figure that includes all expenses (including property and sales taxes) other than income taxes and is usually listed on an income statement.

Net capital gain position — The net long-term or short-term capital gain resulting from netting all capital asset transactions for the year.

Net estate — An amount used in estate planning which is the remaining portion of a gross estate after deducting funeral expenses, claims against the estate, and any unpaid obligations included in the gross estate.

Net ground lease — A lease of unimproved real property where the lessee pays property taxes and other expenses.

Net income — The remaining amount of income after all expenses have been deducted; the bottom line of an income statement.

Net lease — A lease requiring a lessee to pay the expenses of leased property such as taxes, insurance, maintenance, and other carrying charges, in addition to rent.

Net level premium — A payment for insurance coverage that remains the same from year to year.

Net listing — A real estate listing whereby the broker is entitled to receive as commission any amount of the selling price over a given net amount.

Net loss — The residual amount of expenses, which exceed revenues, as shown on an income statement.

Net operating income (NOI) — In real estate investments, the remaining amount after subtracting operating expenses from rental income; a property's income before mortgage payments and taxes.

Net operating loss (NOL)[1] — An allowable deduction derived directly from trade or business activities and casualty losses. An NOL may be either carried back 3 years and then forward 15 years until used up, or only carried forward 15 years.

Net payment cost comparison index — An index used for cost comparisons between different life insurance policies by taking into consideration premium payments to be made, dividends to be received, and the time value of money. The net payment cost comparison index makes shopping for the best value in life insurance much easier. Also see "Interest adjusted cost method" and "Surrender cost comparison index."

Net present value method (NPV) — A technique used to measure prospective investments by discounting future cash flows (by present value factors) and comparing the results with the cost of the investment, which also may be discounted by present value factors if future payments are expected.

Net position — For a securities or commodities investor, the difference between a long position and short position.

Net price — The price of an item or service after all discounts and other reductions have been subtracted; the price that is actually paid by a buyer.

Net proceeds — Gross proceeds less any allowable deductions.

Net profit — Net income. Also see "Net after taxes" and "Net before taxes."

Net profit margin — A measure of profitability indicated by the percentage of net income earned from total revenues:

$$\text{Net profit margin} = \frac{\text{Net income}}{\text{Total revenues}}$$

Net realizable value — The net amount of cash expected from the disposition of an asset.

Net rental — The amount of rents received in excess of expenses paid on rental property.

Net single premium — A lump-sum payment in full for insurance coverage.

Net working capital — A figure portraying the measure of a company's short-term liquidity. Net working capital is the difference between current assets and current liabilities (current assets minus current liabilities).

Net worth — Owner's equity; net assets; the residual of total assets less total liabilities. The amount of claim or equity that an individual has to all assets owned, or in the case of a business, the amount of claim an owner (or owners) has to the assets owned by the business.

Net worth method — A method of reconstructing income by the Internal Revenue Service for a taxpayer who does not maintain an adequate accounting of taxable transactions. It is usually employed in tax fraud cases where an individual conducts an illegal business and does not report a significant amount of its income.

Net yield — The net rate of return on an investment after taking into consideration all commissions, carrying charges, losses, and other expenses.

New York Stock Exchange (NYSE) — The "Big Board"; the oldest, largest, and most widely known stock exchange in the United States. Only the shares of largest companies are allowed to trade on the NYSE (about 1,600 companies), and over 1,300 members (seats) have the privilege to trade such shares directly on the exchange. The price of a share of stock is generally determined by public demand through the execution of orders to buy or sell on the trading floor of the exchange.

90-day letter — A notice of tax deficiency sent by the Internal Revenue Service to taxpayers who either do not respond to a preliminary notice (30-day letter) or who wish to appeal a decision reached at an IRS Appeals Office. Within the 90-day period, a taxpayer may either pay no tax and petition the Tax Court or pay the tax and file claim for refund. If the tax is paid and not refunded by the IRS, then another 30-day letter, appeals procedure, and a statutory notice of claim disallowance is made (if the IRS still refuses to pay a refund). After which time the taxpayer may sue for a refund by carrying the case either to a U.S. District Court or the U.S. Claims Court. Also see "30-day letter."

No arrival, no sale — A provision in a sales contract stating that if the goods do not arrive, then no sale is made and the buyer is not liable for payment.

No-fault insurance — Generally, a form of automobile insurance whereby an insured is compensated for both medical expenses and income losses by his or her own insurance company, regardless of fault. Thus, no-fault insurance is also known as first-party insurance because an insured motorist has the right to collect from his or her own company under certain circumstances. Each state carrying no-fault insurance has its own limitations and restrictions.

No funds — A bank's endorsement on a check stating that the drawer has no funds to cover the check.

No-limit order — An order to buy or sell stock or other securities without specifying a price.

No-load — Without sales commission; many financial products such as life, health, auto, and home insurance, as well as IRAs, mutual funds, and tax shelter partnerships are sold directly from the company offering such items without charging a fee or sales commission. However, in some cases certain companies have been accused of charging hidden fees in alleged no-load products.

No-load mutual fund — A mutual fund whose shares are bought and sold, without charging a sales commission, directly from the investment company that is issuing them.

Nominal consideration — Very small or negligible consideration that is still considered valuable consideration for purposes of making a contract.

Nominal interest rate — The stated rate or coupon rate of interest that a security pays on its face value or par value, as opposed to its market interest rate or yield to maturity which is determined by a security's purchase price, length of time before maturity, and periodic receipts.

Nominal price — The quoted price of a security or commodity that is not actively traded. A nominal price may be based on recent sales prices of similar items, the last selling price quoted, or the economic value of the item.

Nominal trust — A passive trust where the beneficiary has almost complete control.

Nominal yield — See "Nominal interest rate."

Nonacquiescence — A contrary position taken by the Internal Revenue Service as to a result reached by the Tax Court in a regular decision.

Noncallable bond — A bond that cannot be redeemed by the issuer before maturity.

Noncancellable policy — A type of insurance policy that continues in force at the option of the insured, who must make timely premium payments, until a specified age or the occurrence of a specified event.

Noncash expenses[1] — Expenses which are incurred, but do not require the outlay of cash. Depreciation, depletion, and amortization are three major noncash expenses. Bad-debt expense, amortization of a bond premium (taxable bonds), and amortization of organizational costs are other examples. In real estate tax shelters, leverage is used when purchasing rental property in order to increase the depreciable amount to be allocated periodically as depreciation expense to each investor. As a general rule, losses resulting from noncash expenses (e.g., depreciation) make an investment more desirable for tax purposes—especially when the property increases in value.

Nonconforming loan — A loan in which the borrower is behind on his or her payments.

Non-contestable clause — See "Incontestability."

Noncontributory plan — A retirement plan where participants do not contribute.

Nonconvertible — A security that cannot be converted into another type of security.

Noncumulative preferred stock — A class of preferred stock that does not cumulate dividends when they are in arrears. That is, when a dividend is not declared by the board of directors (passed dividend) or the dividend is not enough to meet preferred stock's stated dividend, then it is gone forever and no obligation exists to make up a payment for the lost dividend. Compare "Cumulative preferred stock."

Noncurrent assets — Long-term assets such as equipment, plant, land, and patents. Compare "Current asset."

Nondiscretionary trust — A trust in which a trustee cannot exercise his own judgment as to distributions.

Nondurable goods — Generally, consumer goods that are expected to last three years or less, such as food, clothing, oil, and detergents.

Nonforfeiture — A provision that allows a policyholder of life insurance or a participant in a retirement plan not to forfeit all accrued benefits. For example, the owner of a life insurance policy who does not pay premiums can exercise certain options with regard to the policy's cash values (nonforfeiture benefits) upon surrendering the contract: (1) receive cash values, (2) purchase extended term insurance for the full face amount of the original policy, or (3) purchase paid-up insurance usually for a reduced amount.

Nonforfeiture benefits — Benefits accrued to an individual that are not forfeited and can be controlled by such individual. Also see "Nonforfeiture."

Noninsured pension plans — Generally, a formal or informal pay-as-you-go retirement plan that is funded under no predetermined contributions and calls for payments to retirees out of current earnings. Under such arrangement, there is no valid assurance that retirement funds will be available when an individual retires nor that payments will continue throughout a recipient's life.

Nonliquid assets — An asset that cannot be quickly turned into cash without sacrificing a portion of its fair market value, such as one's residence which has been up for sale for six months.

Nonmarital deduction trust — A trust made up of property not qualifying for the marital deduction.

Nonmember bank — A bank that is not a member of the Federal Reserve System and is primarily regulated by state law.

Nonnegotiable — Not capable of being transferred by indorsement and delivery. A nonnegotiable bill of lading is one that cannot pass title by indorsement and delivery, but may be assigned.

Nonoccupational injury/illness — The occurrence of an injury or illness caused by outside-of-work circumstances.

Nonoperating income — Income that is not earned through the operations of a business. Gains from the sale of capital assets, extraordinary times, and interest revenues are examples.

Nonparticipating policy — An insurance policy that does not entitle its owner to receive dividends.

Nonparticipating preferred stock — Preferred stock that does not share dividends with common stock when declared dividends are in excess of the preferred stock's stated dividend. That is, the maximum amount that a shareholder of nonparticipating preferred stock can possibly receive is the amount of stated dividend.

Nonprobate property — Property which passes to a beneficiary or joint owner that is not subject to a will or intestacy laws, such as life insurance to a named beneficiary or property held as joint tenants.

Nonprofit corporation — A corporation usually chartered for charitable, educational, political, religious, cultural, athletic, civic, professional, or other similar purposes and does not distribute any income to its members; a corporation formed without an intent to produce profits.

Nonqualifying deferred compensation plan (NQDC) — A tax-deferred compensation plan that allows an employee to postpone the recognition of income (because of substantial restrictions) until a future period when such restrictions are lifted.

Nonqualifying stock option — An employee stock option that is subject to taxation. If the stock option does not have a readily ascertainable value, then upon exercise it will be included in an employee's taxable income for an amount equal to the excess of fair market value of the stock (at date of exercise) over the exercise price. If the stock option does have a readily ascertainable value, then it will be included in an employee's taxable income at the date of grant for an amount equal to its fair market value.

Nonreciprocal transfer — A donation; a gift; a contribution without intending to receive anything in return.

Nonrecourse loan — A type of loan where the borrower is not personally liable to repay; generally, the loan is secured by property. Except for real estate, investors are not considered "at risk" for income tax purposes if nonrecourse financing is obtained.

Nonrecurring expense — An expense that is infrequent in nature and typically is not repetitive, such as a casualty loss.

Nonrefund annuity — An annuity in which payments cease upon the death of the annuitant and leaves no benefits for survivors.

Nontaxable exchange — See "Tax-free exchange."

No-par stock — Capital stock issued by a corporation without par value. State laws control the issuance of such stock, which will usually have a stated value. Both stated value and par value represent minimum legal capital.

Normal wear and tear — The gradual deterioration or loss in value caused by normal, ordinary, and reasonable use of property.

Notary public — A public officer who is authorized by a state or the federal government to attest to the authenticity of signatures on a document and to administer oaths.

Note — See "Promissory note."

Notes payable — A liability account used in the accounting of an individual, family, or business to show an obligation in aggregate represented by promissory notes.

Notes receivable — An asset account used in the accounting of an individual, family, or business to show total promissory notes that are owed to such entity.

Notice of action — A notice recorded in public records warning that the title to a certain property is subject to pending litigation. Notice of action is also known as "lis pendens."

Notice of default — A notice filed with the appropriate body to show that a mortgagor is behind in payments.

Notice of dishonor — Notice given to any party (i.e., subsequent indorsers) who may be liable on an instrument that has been dishonored. For example, a bank will give notice to its customer that a deposited check was dishonored.

Notice of loss — Notice given by an insured to his or her insurance company that the occurrence of loss has taken place. Immediate notice is generally necessary according to most casualty insurance policies.

Notice to creditors — A formal notice given to all creditors that a debtor is in bankruptcy proceedings, all claims must be filed by a specified time, and a meeting of creditors is to be held.

Notorious possession — Conspicuous possession of real property that is required in order to obtain title by adverse possession.

Novation — The substitution of a new debt, obligation, or contract for an old one. Novation requires the existence of a previous obligation or contract, a new agreement between the parties, and the extinguishment of the old one.

NOW account — Negotiable order of withdrawal account; an interest-bearing checking account that usually carries some stipulations, such as maintenance of a certain balance in the account.

NSF check — Not sufficient funds check; a check returned to a depositor because the drawer's checking account balance was not enough to cover the check. Also, called an insufficient funds check (IF check).

Numismatics — The buying, holding, and selling of coins as an investment.

Nuncupative will — An oral declaration made shortly before a testator's death and intended by him or her to be the last will. Later, witnesses reduce it to writing. A nuncupative will may or may not be valid, depending upon state statutes.

Nuptial — On behalf of or pertaining to marriage.

O

Oath — Generally, a formal or informal attestation made by a person signifying that he or she is legally and morally bound to perform faithfully and honestly.

Objective — Something that is definite, attainable, and desirable which requires planning and execution of appropriate actions in order to achieve; something worked toward or striven for; the result of a planned course of action; a goal. Obtaining and periodically evaluating an individual's objectives (personal, family, financial, professional, and spiritual) is one of the most important steps in financial planning.

Obligation — A general term for any contract, duty, promise, requirement, or liability that legally or morally confines or coerces one to perform.

Obligee — The one to whom a promise or duty is owed; the promisee.

Obligor — The one who is obligated to perform; the promisor.

Obsolescence — A decrease in value of property because of technological changes and development, or changes in trends and styles, rather than from wear and tear.

Occupancy — (1) In real estate, the taking and using of property; possession; (2) in insurance, the manner in which property is to be used, which is important in determining rates.

Occupational accident — An accident occurring on the job or during the course of one's occupation and generally caused by hazards that are inherent to such activity. Occupational accidents are usually covered by workers' compensation.

Occupational disability — A disability arising from injury or disease resulting from an on-the-job accident or exposure to an excess or ordinary hazard during employment.

Occupational disease — A disease caused by an exposure to hazardous conditions or substances during employment. Occupational diseases are usually covered by worker's compensation.

Occupational hazard — A hazard that is characteristic of a particular occupation.

Occurrence limit — In a liability insurance policy, the maximum amount that will be covered for any one occurrence. For example, in a bodily injury liability contract the occurrence limit is typically stated as $25,000–$50,000, which means for any one occurrence $25,000 is the maximum that will be paid per individual claim with an overall maximum of $50,000 for all claims.

Odd lot — In securities trading, the number of securities bought or sold that is different from the conventional unit of trading. For example, the conventional unit of stocks is 100 shares, so that any amount traded less than 100 shares is an odd lot.

Offer — To hold out for acceptance, counteroffer, or rejection; a proposal to enter into an agreement. The sticker price or asking price of consumer items is generally considered to be an offer to sell.

Offer and acceptance — Two elements, which are required in a contract, that constitute mutual agreement between the contracting parties.

Offering memorandum[1] — A description of a proposed investment provided to prospective investors. It is also referred to as a prospectus.

Office in home[1] — When a portion of a residence is used exclusively and regularly as a place of business or a place to meet with clients, customers, etc., then expenses attributable to such office is deductible for income tax purposes. If an individual is an employee, then the office must only be used "for the convenience of the employer" and not merely for the convenience of the employee.

Officer — In a corporation, positions in top management, such as president, vice-president, secretary, and treasurer, that are authorized by the board of directors to manage and contract for the company; a person in a position of trust who is authorized to act on behalf of a company, government, or other organization.

Off premises — A provision in property insurance providing protection for personal property while it is not on the premises named in the policy.

Offset well[1] — An oil well drilled on property that is adjacent to property which has proven reserves.

Off-site improvements — The development of land adjacent to a particular location that enables such location to become suitable for development, e.g., improvements such as sewers, streetlights, water pipes, sidewalks, streets, and curbs.

Oil and gas lease — A special lease granting the lessee the right to extract oil and gas from a particular location. Generally, the lessee only has an interest in a specific use of the property (i.e., drilling for oil and gas), but not the general use of such property; the lessor is customarily compensated according to the amount of oil and gas extracted.

Old Age, Survivors, Disability, and Health Insurance (OASDHI) — OASDHI is the largest and most widely known social insurance system in the United States, providing social security benefits to retired workers and their dependents, survivors, and disabled workers and their dependents. To be entitled to benefits an individual must be engaged in employment that is subject to social security for a certain number of quarters. There are three benefit schedules of insured status: fully insured, currently insured, and disability insured status. Generally, a worker can become eligible for "fully insured" status (except disability benefits) with 40 quarters of coverage or by having worked at least one covered quarter per calendar year after 1950 (or after age 21, whichever is later) prior to disability, death, or age 62. There are three types of benefits paid if a worker is fully insured: lump-sum death benefit, survivorship income payments, and retirement income payments. The lump-sum death benefit is made to a surviving spouse or child, who is unmarried and less than 18 years of age (unless he or she is in high school, then 18th year is eligible; or unless he or she is disabled, then up to age 22). The survivorship income payments are available to a surviving spouse with at least one dependent child under age 16 (or if the child is disabled then before age 22) and to a surviving spouse at age 65 (or for reduced amounts at age 60, or at age 50 if disabled) and to dependent parents at age 62. Currently insured status is attained by having at least 6 quarters of coverage out of the last 13 quarters. "Currently insured" status only provides eligibility for a lump-sum death payment and survivorship income payments. The lump-sum death payment, which is slightly different than for fully insured status, is made to a surviving spouse or child, who is unmarried and less than 18 years of age (unless he or she is in high school, then 18th year is included, or if disabled, then 22), and the survivorship income payments are made to a surviving spouse with at least one dependent child under age 16 (or if disabled, then 22). To reach "disability insured" status, a worker must have attained fully insured status with an additional 20 quarters of coverage within a 40-quarter period ending with the quarter in which the disability began, although special rules apply to persons under age 31. For this status, disability income payments are generally available to a disabled worker under age 65; to a spouse of a disabled worker at age 62 (or when a child under 16—22 for disabled—is present, or disabled widow at age 50); and to a child of a disabled worker (younger than 18, or if in high school, then 18, or if disabled, before 22).

Oligopoly — An economic condition whereby control over the sales of a particular product is held by a small number of sellers.

Oligopsony — An economic condition existing when sales of a particular product is controlled by a small number of buyers.

Omnibus clause — (1) A provision in an automobile liability policy that extends coverage to individuals other than the policyholder. Generally, persons who have the express or implied permission of the insured are covered under the omnibus clause; (2) a provision in a will or decree of distribution that passes all unspecified property to whomever is named.

On demand — Generally describes a negotiable instrument payable at sight or on presentation.

One-time sale-of-residence exclusion — Taxpayers who are 55 years old and older as of the date of sale are able to exclude a certain amount ($125,000 in 1985) from taxable income if they meet certain qualifications, such as never having used the exclusion before and, generally, owned and lived in the residence at least three out of the past five years.

Onerous gift — A gift subject to a burdensome or unreasonable attachment.

On-site improvements — Structures and other additions permanently erected on a particular location, such as sidewalks, sewers, buildings, streetlights, roads, and fences.

Open account — A type of credit arrangement where a seller extends credit to a buyer without holding any security. An open account is generally based on the credit rating of the customer and can take the form of either open credit, open-end credit, or revolving credit.

Open credit — A line of credit extended by a bank, supplier, or merchant to allow customers the privilege of borrowing or purchasing on credit up to a limited amount without having to obtain approval, without reestablishing one's credit, and without security. The manner of repayment, interest rates, and other terms of credit are usually stated in a credit agreement.

Open-end contract — A contract that permits a customer the privilege of making purchases without a change in the terms of sale over an extended period of time.

Open-end credit — A type of consumer credit generally associated with retail stores where a purchaser is allowed a certain amount of credit purchases on open account. Typically, if the entire amount due is paid in full within 30 days of receiving the bill, then no interest is charged. If the balance is not paid in full, then it may be paid in installments with interest. Also see "Revolving charge account."

Open-end investment company — Mutual fund; a regulated investment company, which is directed by professional managers, that will issue and purchase its own shares at net asset value (NAV) at the initiative of an investor. Generally, there is no limit as to the number shares it can offer. Also see "Mutual fund."

Open-end lease — Generally, a lease where part of each payment is applied to the equity of the item, which allows the lessee to buy it at a reduced amount or participate in the profit or loss from its sale.

Open-end mortgage — A mortgage allowing the mortgagor to borrow additional amounts under specified conditions subject to the same mortgage. Usually, a stated ratio of assets to debts must be maintained.

Open-end transaction — A transaction whereby the parties may adjust or amend the original agreement within expressed or reasonable constraints.

Open listing — A written contract authorizing any real estate agent, who is entitled to participate in the open listing, to receive commissions if such agent closes the sale of real property subject to an open listing.

Open market operations — The trading of government securities by a governmental agency (the Federal Reserve) for the purpose of implementing monetary policy.

Open order — See "Good-till-canceled order (GTC)."

Open price term — In a sales agreement, an undetermined and unsettled amount as to the price of items or services sold. Generally, the parties may still contract if the price is to be determined at a later date.

Operating agreement[1] — In oil and gas activities, an agreement among the leaseholders of oil property indicating who the operator of the lease is and what his or her rights and responsibilities are.

Operating cycle — The average amount of time needed for a business to turn revenue (or capital) into inventory and back to revenue.

Operating expenses — Selling, administrative, and general operating expenses incurred while engaging in a profit-making activity. Non-operating expenses include financing costs, income taxes, and other expenses incurred in producing income that is unrelated to the entity.

Operating income — Income generally earned through the ordinary course of business from operations. It is recurring in nature and does not include revenues or expenses pertaining to extraordinary items, interest, taxes, etc.

Operating lease[1] — A leasing arrangement whereby the lessor does not intend to recover the purchase cost of leased property because of the short duration of the lease agreement.

Operating private foundation[1] — Generally, a private foundation that pays out at least 67 percent of its income for charitable purposes, or whose support generally comes from the general public, or at least 65 percent of whose assets are primarily employed for charitable purposes.

Operating profit — Gross profit (gross revenues less cost of goods sold) less operating expenses.

Operating ratio — A ratio used in the analysis of a company's financial statements that indicates the relative amount of operating expenses incurred in generating sales for a corresponding period:

$$\text{Operating ratio} = \frac{\text{Cost of goods sold} + \text{Operating expenses}}{\text{Net sales}}$$

Operating revenues — Revenues produced from selling goods or providing services.

Opportunity cost — An alternative cost or benefit that is forgone by rejection; an annual rate of return that could have been earned on an alternative investment or the difference between what could have been earned and actual earnings.

Option — An agreement allowing the holder an opportunity to buy or sell a certain asset for a specified price within a given period of time. Also see "Call," "Expiration date," and "Put."

Optionally renewable contract — A health insurance contract that provides the insurer with the right to terminate insurance coverage on any anniversary date or on any premium due date, depending upon the contract, but not between such dates.

Option premium — The price of an option.

Option spread — See "Spread."

Option straddle — See "Straddle."

Option writer — The grantor or maker of the option; the one who allows another the opportunity to buy or sell a certain asset at a specific price; the initial seller of a put or call.

Oral contract — An agreement that is either partially written or not written. Certain contracts must be in writing in order to be enforceable, such as a contract to sell land.

Order — (1) In securities transactions, an instruction from a customer to a broker to purchase or sell a security. Also see "Good-till-canceled order (GTC)," "Limit order," "Market order," and "Stop order"; (2) in the ordinary course of business, a request to buy, sell, or deliver goods or services. Also see "Purchase order"; (3) part of the magic words of negotiability, such as "pay to the order of Jake Smith," that is necessary for a negotiable instrument.

Ordinance — The law or statutes of a municipal corporation or county.

Ordinary course of business — The customary and regular practices of a business in a particular industry, geographic location, profession, etc.

Ordinary income — Income that is only reduced by allowable deductions and taxed accordingly, as opposed to long-term capital gains.

Ordinary interest — Interest computed on principal only (i.e., without any past due interest; not compounded).

Ordinary life insurance — Permanent life insurance typically issued in $1,000 amounts which calls for premium payments over the life of the insured, as opposed to other whole life policies which call for premium payments over a certain period of time or on a single premium basis (e.g., endowment policies). Ordinary life is also known as "straight life insurance."

Ordinary repairs — Recurring expenditures necessary to fix, mend, or otherwise bring broken or worn out items back to working condition.

Organization costs[1] — Expenses incurred in the formation of a corporation or partnership, usually before the entity actively engages in business. For income tax purposes, these costs are amortized over a period of at least 60 months.

Original cost — For income tax purposes, generally, the unadjusted basis of an item; the purchase price plus acquisition costs.

Original issue — The first issue of a particular security.

Original payee — One to whom a check or other negotiable instrument is made payable.

Origination fee — A fee charged by a lender for making a loan. If the fee is for processing purposes in making a personal-use loan, it is not deductible. If the fee, or any part thereof, is a reduction in the rate of interest charged ("points"), then it is deductible when paid by the borrower.

"Or more" clause — A provision in a lending agreement allowing the borrower to make additional payments without penalty.

Out-of-pocket loss — The net amount of loss sustained by one who purchases an investment, personal-use property, or business-use property. For example, Cook purchased 100 shares of Acme Co. Stock for $50 each by paying cash and later sold them for $45 per share. Cook experienced an out-of-pocket loss of $500.

Out-of-the-money — In options trading, a description of an option that if exercised would produce a negative outcome relative to the effect of not exercising it. Thus, an underlying stock selling for less than a call option's strike price or more than a put option's strike price will result in both options being "out-of-the-money."

Outside salesperson[1] — For income tax purposes, a person who solicits business away from his or her employer's premises. Generally, all allowable deductions of an outside salesperson, including entertainment expenses, are taken before adjusted gross income.

Outstanding debt — Unpaid and uncollected debt.

Overage income — As used in a percentage lease, income that is generally tied to the fluctuating levels of business activity and is in excess of the minimum rental or base rental.

Overcharge — To charge more than a reasonable amount or current market value.

Overdraft (OD) — A check drawn on an account that does not contain enough funds to cover it.

Overdraw — To draw on a checking or savings account in excess of the account balance.

Overdue — Past due; not paid upon presentment or on the maturity date.

Overinsurance — The carrying of too much insurance on the same subject.

Overlying mortgage — See "Junior mortgage."

Override — (1) A sales commission collected by a sales manager, real estate broker, or other individual that is determined by the sales commission received by subordinate salespersons; (2) to prevail over another's decision or command.

Overriding royalty[1] — In oil and gas leasing, a royalty interest retained by a lessee upon subleasing the mineral property.

Oversubscribed — A description of a new issue of securities where there are more subscribers than available securities.

Over-the-counter market (OTC) — The trading of securities between securities dealers, who are linked by a communications network, rather than on an exchange; off-board trading.

Owelty of exchange — See "Boot."

Owner's equity — The net residual interest in assets after all liabilities have been subtracted; the portion of total assets represented by the owner's claim.

P

Package mortgage — A mortgage covering both real estate and personal items, such as a home and also a refrigerator, stove, oven, dishwasher, trash compactor, washer, and dryer. In essence, a package mortgage finances the purchase of consumer appliances with, generally, a lower rate of interest (home mortgage rate) than the ordinary consumer borrowing rate.

Package policy — A multi-peril insurance contract provided either as all-risks or comprehensive coverage. All-risks contracts usually cover all perils except the ones specifically excluded in the policy, and comprehensive coverage can either refer to a few stated perils or include many perils. (Generally, the term "comprehensive contract" only refers to a combination form of relatively liberal coverage.)

Padding — The falsification of accounting records by adding items that are nonexistent or did not occur, such as adding names on a payroll of nonexisting individuals or adding fictitious charges in an expense account.

Paid-in capital — The total amount of money and other assets contributed by stockholders of a corporation that is stated in stockholder's equity, as opposed to equity capital generated by the earnings of a company (retained earnings).

Paid-in capital in excess of par — See "Paid-in surplus."

Paid-in surplus — The amount of paid-in capital contributed by stockholders in excess of legal capital; paid-in capital in excess of par; the excess (in toto) of a company's stock issuing prices over its par value.

Paid-up insurance — Insurance coverage for which all premiums have been satisfied. Also see "Nonforfeiture."

PAP — See "Personal auto policy."

Paper — Short-term debt securities.

Paper profit — An investment position showing a gain without the execution of a transaction; an unrealized gain without tax consequences.

Par — Equality.

Parent company — A company that controls one or more subsidiaries.

Parol evidence — Evidence given by word of mouth; extraneous evidence.

Pari-mutuel betting — The betting on racing of horses or dogs whereby the winner shares a small percentage with management.

Partial disability benefits — In some health insurance policies, payments for partial disability may be allowed at a reduced rate. Generally, the test for partial disability rests upon the insured's inability to perform part of his or her work.

Partial limitation — In insurance policies, a provision that sets a specified amount which a loss must exceed before the insurer will indemnify. That is, if a loss exceeds the specified amount, it is completely covered, but if the loss is less than the specified amount, no amount is covered. For example, assume a personal articles floater has a $100 partial limitation provision and a ring valued at $90 along with a bracelet valued at $350 were stolen. The ring would not be covered, but the bracelet would be fully covered.

Participating dividends — Generally, a privilege given to preferred stock to participate in dividends with common stock, after the annual preferred and common stock dividends are paid. Participating dividends occur when dividends are declared by the board of directors and such dividends are more than enough to meet the annual preferred dividend as well as a relative amount for common stock, then the remaining dividends are divided pro rata (in reference to par or stated value) between preferred and common stockholders.

Participating insurance — See "Participating policy."

Participating policy — An insurance policy entitling the policyholder to participate in the earnings or surplus of the insurance company in the form of dividends. Usually, participating policies call for a higher premium than nonparticipating policies, but the difference is normally refunded if the company's experience is favorable. Several dividend options are available for life insurance policies, which typically include cash, reduction of current premium, paid-up additional whole life (increased face amount), accumulated deposit with interest, or additional one-year term amounts.

Participating preferred stock — Preferred stock that may receive dividends in excess of the annual preferred dividend payment when declared dividends exceed a certain amount. Also see "Participating dividends."

Participating trust — A specialized type of unit investment trust that issues ownership interests representing an underlying investment in a mutual fund; a plan company.

Participation — A general provision in insurance policies which states that the insured will share (participate) in each loss by a specified amount or percentage. Coinsurance is a type of participation.

Participation loan — (1) A loan where a lender participates in a project or business venture by receiving a percentage of profits in addition to stated interest in the loan; (2) the combination of two or more banks each loaning a portion of the total amount borrowed.

Participatory annuity — A retirement annuity that is entitled to dividend payments by the issuing company. Generally, such dividend payments are made during the purchase period and may provide the holder with options to receive the dividends in cash, apply them to payments due, or held by the company in an interest-bearing account.

Partner's basis[1] — Generally, the partner's cost of a partnership interest plus partnership earnings and other capital contributions made to the partnership by the partner, less distributions, partnership losses, and nondeductible partnership expenses. A partner's basis will include nonrecourse loans, which are not included in the amount a partner has "at risk."

Partnership[1] — A business arrangement between two or more persons (or other entities) formed for the purpose of actively engaging in a trade or business and to divide the profits therefrom. It is not a separate legal entity, such as a corporation, but similar to two or more proprietors.

Par value — (1) An arbitrarily assigned value of stock as stated in a corporation's charter and printed on a stock certificate; legal capital. Par value has little or no significance as to a stock's market value, but is so designated because of state statutes; (2) the face value of a bond or stock (i.e., the amount printed on the certificate); (3) the balance of a mortgage or trust deed without discount.

Passbook account — A regular savings account offered by commercial banks, savings and loans, and other financial institutions. The account gets its name because the savings institution issues a "passbook" in which the customer's transactions are recorded. Generally, holding money in a passbook savings account is a very safe method of saving cash when insured by federal deposit insurance (FDIC or FSLIC), but the yield is comparatively low: 5½ percent.

Passive income — Income received from passive sources, such as dividends, interest, royalties, rents, and capital gains, rather than income earned by one's labor, such as salary and wages.

Passive trust — A trust where there exist no responsibilities or duties for a trustee to perform.

Patent[1] — The exclusive right to manufacture, sell, or otherwise control an invention, as granted by the U.S. Patent Office. The life of a patent is generally 17 years, depending upon the type of patent granted.

Paternal property — Property descending from one's father, father's father, or other relative from the paternal side of family.

Pawn — A pledge of personal property to secure a loan from a pawnbroker or to secure a debt or engagement with a creditor.

Pawnbroker — A person who lends money on security of personal property, which is held by him or her. If the borrower fails to pay off the loan within a stated period of time (usually 90 days or less) and thereby reclaim the pawned merchandise, it will be sold to satisfy the debt.

Pawnshop — A pawnbroker's place of business where used merchandise is held for sale.

Pay as you go — A system of paying expenses, such as income taxes or a company's retirement plan, out of current earnings when such expenses are incurred.

Payback period — An accounting technique of evaluating the possible acquisition of equipment by estimating the number of years for such equipment to "pay for itself." It is customarily used in conjunction with other measurements in the decision-making process.

Payee — The person in whose favor a negotiable instrument is drawn.

Payer — One who is to make payment.

Payment date — The date on which the holders of record (of a stock) will receive a dividend payment, or in the case of bondholders, an interest payment.

Payoff — The balance due on an existing loan or lien.

Payout ratio — In the analysis of the performance of a for-profit corporation, a ratio indicating the amount of dividends paid to shareholders with regard to earnings per share:

$$\text{Payout ratio} = \frac{\text{Dividends per share}}{\text{Earnings per share}}$$

Payroll deductions — See "Withholding."

Payroll savings plan — A systematic method of savings designed to enforce a plan of accumulating money by automatically deducting a designated sum from one's paycheck and depositing it in any type of savings account. Because money is deducted before a check is made out, a payroll savings plan is a relatively effective way of maintaining a savings program.

Payroll tax — Federal and state taxes based on and deducted from the amount of earnings. Generally, Social Security taxes, employee income tax withholdings, and unemployment taxes are considered payroll taxes.

PE ratio — See "Price/earnings (P/E) ratio."

Peculate — To embezzle.

Pecuniary — Consisting of or relating to money; financial.

Penny stock — Low-priced, highly speculative stocks usually selling for less than $1 per share.

Pension[1] — A retirement plan established and maintained by an employer primarily to provide systematically for the payment of definitely determinable benefits to employees over a period of years, usually for life, after retirement. Retirement benefits generally are measured by and based on such factors as years of service and compensation received by the employees (Treasury Reg. 1.401-1(b)(1)(i)).

Pension Benefit Guaranty Corporation — Federally funded corporation that guarantees payment of employee benefits to qualified individuals upon the termination of a covered retirement program.

Pension funds — Amounts accumulated under a retirement plan that are typically invested in blue-chip securities, real estate, home mortgages, etc.

Pension plan — See "Pension."

Per annum — Annually; each year.

Per capita — By the number of individuals; equal share to each individual.

Percentage depletion — A method of expensing the cost of a natural resource, such as oil, gas, and coal (i.e., "wasting assets"), after extraction and sale. Percentage depletion uses a statutory rate, which is set in the Internal Revenue Code for each type of mineral resource.

Percentage lease — A lease, generally associated with business-use in real property, based upon a percentage of gross receipts or net income of the tenant. Usually, percentage leases consist of a base rental along with a specified percentage of income.

Per diem — Per day; an allowance given in accordance with a number of days.

Performance bond — A bond given to a public authority guaranteeing performance by a contractor in that a construction contract will be completed according to the terms of the agreement.

Performance fund — An aggressively positioned, highly speculative investment company whose primary objective is to yield big returns. Generally, performance funds buy shares of small relatively unknown companies whose stock prices are extremely volatile in that when the market is up these funds show high returns, but when the market is down they typically experience substantial losses; go-go fund.

Performance index — An indicator of investment performace that relates the current price of a group of stocks to a previously established base and uses a weighted average method (relative number of shares outstanding) in its computation.

Peril — An event that may create a loss; hazard; risk.

Periodic — Occurring over fixed intervals of time, such as weekly, quarterly, or yearly.

Perks — See "Perquisites ("perks")."

Permanent disability — Generally, a disability that renders no possible employment for the rest of an individual's life. A presumption made that a person is permanently disabled after an insured has been totally disabled for a continuous period of at least six months, until contrary evidence shows otherwise. Also see "Total disability."

Permanent life insurance — A life insurance policy that covers an individual for life, as opposed to coverage for a temporary period which is commonly associated with term insurance.

Perquisites ("perks")[1] — Compensation or fringe benefits in addition to one's regular salary because of holding a particular position of employment.

Personal-articles floater policy — A property insurance policy that provides all-risks protection on jewelry, golfing equipment, furs, cameras, musical instruments, and other specifically designated personal property. Such items may be insured individually, combined into one personal-articles floater policy, or added to a homeowner's policy.

Personal assets — See "Personal property."

Personal auto policy (PAP) — A simplified, readable and standardized automobile insurance policy for individuals primarily designed to be understandable to consumers and to enhance the comparability between different policies. A personal auto policy generally consists of a declarations page, Part A—Liability, Part B—Medical payments, Part C—Uninsured motorists, Part D—Damage to your auto, Part E—Duties after an accident or loss, and Part F—General provisions. Most of the basic information about the insurer, premiums, policy period, limits of liability for each coverage, description of automobile, parts of coverage (A through D), definitions, etc. are on the declarations page. Part A—Liability shows the policy limits, explanation of coverage and qualifications for other payments, such as defense and supplementary payments. Part B—Medical payments coverage provides the cost of all necessary medical services up to a stated limit for the named insured and anyone else in the insured's car, as specified in the policy. Part C—Uninsured motorists coverage is an option (mandatory in some states) that covers the insured for bodily injury caused by the negligent operator of an uninsured vehicle. Part D—Damage to your own auto covers physical damage for your own automobile, rather than liability for property damage experienced by others. Collision and comprehensive coverage (if elected by the insured) are also included in this section. In Part E—Duties after the accident or loss, duties that must be fulfilled by the insured are explained. Such duties include: prompt notice to be given to the insurance company, cooperation with the insurer in settlement of any claim, no admission of guilt or liability should be made, and no effort to negotiate a settlement should be made by the insured. Part F— General provisions describe such items as extent of liability of the insurance company, geographic limitations of coverage, subrogation, assignment, and cancellation provisions. Also see "Automobile insurance."

Personal balance sheet — A formal financial statement prepared for individuals consisting of assets, liabilities, and net worth. Personal balance sheets customarily report assets at estimated current values rather than historical cost, and liabilities are stated at their estimated current amounts. It is appropriately referred to as a "Statement of Financial Condition." Also see "Balance sheet." The following is an example with footnotes omitted:

RUPERT AND LORI PEARSALL
Statement of Financial Condition
December 31, 1987

Assets

Cash	$	XXXX
Marketable securities		XXXX
Cash value (life insurance policy)		XXX
Real estate investment		XXXXX
Equity interest in EZ Partnership		XXXXX
Automobiles		XXXX
Residence		XXXXX
Household furnishings		XXXX
Personal effects (jewelry, art, etc.)		XXXXX
Vested interest in retirement plan		XXXX
Total assets		$XXXXXX

Liabilities

Credit cards	$	XXXXX
Income tax payable		XXX
Personal installment note payable		XXXX
Mortgage note payable (13% due July 1, 2017)		XXXXX
Total liabilities		XXXXX
Estimated income tax on appreciated assets		XXX
Net worth		XXXXX
Total liabilities, estimated tax, and net worth		$XXXXXX

Personal cash flow statement — A financial statement showing how much revenues were attained and where they were spent:

RUPERT AND LORI PEARSALL
Cash Flow Statement
For the Year Ending December 31, 1987

Sources of cash:

Earnings from employment	$XXXXXX
Dividends and interest	XXX
Miscellaneous	XXX
Total sources of cash	$XXXXXX

Uses of cash:

Groceries	$	XXX
Debt payments		XXXXX
Clothes		XXX
Household furnishings		XXX
Utilities and phone		XXX
Vacation		XXXX
Automobile repair and maintenance		XXX
Medical expenses		XXX
Lawn care		XX
Insurance		XXX
Professional fees		XXX
Entertainment		XXX
Miscellaneous		XXX
Savings		XXX
Total uses of cash		$XXXXXX

Personal catastrophe insurance — See "Umbrella liability insurance."

Personal comprehensive protection — An all-lines insurance policy that combines home-auto property and liability, hospital and disability income, excess liability, and mortgage life insurance into one contract for a reduced premium.

Personal effects floater — Property insurance providing all-risks coverage on personal property that is away from an insured's residence. A personal effects floater customarily includes all items carried by travelers.

Personal estate planning — The process of creating and liquidating an estate, including setting aside information as to where important documents are kept, maintaining an updated will, proper tax planning, and conveying knowledge of all assets and outstanding obligations, so that an individual's goals are achieved. Also see "Estate planning."

Personal exemptions — For income tax purposes, special deductions allowed to all individual taxpayers for oneself, for being blind, and/or being older than 64.

Personal finance company — See "Finance company."

Personal holding company — A corporation usually formed to receive passive income, such as dividends and interest, that is subject to a special tax if such income is not distributed to shareholders.

Personal income — An individual's income from all sources without regard to taxes.

Personal injury protection (PIP) — See "No-fault insurance."

Personal insurance — Any insurance policy providing financial protection against the loss of an individual's life or loss of good health.

Personal liability insurance — Generally, a comprehensive personal insurance covering an insured and members of his or her household for bodily injury and/or property damage to others caused by a covered individual. Personal liability insurance is usually required when one owns a home, keeps a pet, participates in sporting events, and engages in other day-to-day activities where a damaging occurrence is likely to happen.

Personal property — All property that is not land, buildings, or fixtures; personal effects; chattels.

Personal property insurance — See "personal-articles floater policy."

Personal property tax — A tax levied by local government on personal property such as jewelry, automobiles, and household furniture.

Personal risk — Risks that directly affect an individual's physical condition: personal sickness, injury, or death.

Personal savings — The accumulation of the excess of cash inflows over all expenditures.

Personal-service income — Income received because of personal services rendered by the taxpayer: salary, wages, professional fees, commissions, tips, employee pension, etc.

Personalty — See "Personal property."

Per stirpes — In the distribution of estate assets, a method of dividing such assets so that the children of a deceased beneficiary will receive a share of an ancestor's estate, just as their parent would have received if still living.

Petty cash — Currency and coins maintained for the convenience of making small expenditures without writing a check.

Pickup and delivery — The transporting of goods door-to-door whereby such goods are picked up at the shipper's premises and delivered to the customer.

Piecework — A system of compensation by paying for each unit completed.

Piggyback financing — A joint loan made by two or more lenders on the same property under one mortgage or trust deed.

Phantom income — A phenomenon occurring in highly leveraged tax-shelter investments where the deductible interest portion of a mortgage payment declines while the mortgage payment remains the same. The result is a loss of a deduction without a change in cash flow, which leads to a rise in taxable ("phantom") income.

Philately — Collecting stamps as an investment.

Physical damage insurance — Automobile insurance that covers all kinds of physical damage, including collision and comprehensive.

Physical hazards — Generally, conditions which increase the likelihood of loss, such as exposure, location, occupancy, structure, components, operational features.

Physician's expense insurance — See "Regular medical insurance."

PITI — Principal, interest, taxes, and insurance; the elements of a monthly home mortgage payment (i.e., a budget mortgage).

Plaintiff — One who brings an action; the party who seeks remedial relief against a defendant.

Planned community — A real estate development designed to efficiently use land by building family dwellings close together and providing common areas (streets, recreational facilities, etc.). A planned community differs from a condominium development in that the homeowner also owns the land under the house and usually has no direct interest in the common areas.

Planned obsolescence — The designing of goods with high-fashion features so that when styles change, customers will want the latest models. Planned obsolescence is common in the apparel and automobile industry.

Plat — A map showing the division of a parcel of land into lots; a map of subdivisions.

Pledge — A bailment of property to a creditor for security of a debt or other obligation.

Point — Generally, one percent.

Point-and-figure chart — A chart used by technical analysts to track price patterns of a particular stock.

Points — For home mortgages, a fee or charge where one point is equal to one percent of the principal amount of a loan. When "points" are paid by the buyer and are a reduction of interest, then such payment is tax deductible in the year it is made. If points are paid by the seller or are for loan processing fees or other specific services, then it is not deductible by the buyer. Also see "Discount points."

Policy — A contract of insurance.

Policy anniversary date — An annual date specified in a life insurance policy as the date used in figuring premium-payment dates.

Policy dividends — Dividends paid or credited to a policyholder at the end of the year by an insurance company reflecting a reduction of net cost of obtaining insurance.

Policy face — (1) The face amount of insurance as stated in the policy; (2) the initial portion of an insurance contract that contains the essential elements of coverage, such as the name of the insurer, date it takes effect, termination date, consideration paid, and summary of benefit provisions.

Policyholder — The owner of an insurance policy, who may or may not be the insured. Generally, anyone having an insurable interest can become a policyholder.

Policy loan — A loan made to a policyholder of a permanent life insurance contract that has cash values. Generally, very favorable interest rates (5 percent–8 percent) are specified in the policy as well as a table of cash values showing the loan values per year. If the loan is not paid back, then the amount borrowed and any accrued interest is simply deducted from the insurance proceeds. However, if the total indebtedness (amount borrowed plus accrued interest) equals or is greater than the policy's cash value, then the policy may automatically become void.

Policy value — See "Cash value."

Political contributions[1] — Contributions made to a candidate running for a publicly elected office in the United States are qualified for an income tax credit of up to 50 percent on the first $100 contribution ($50). Taxpayer filing jointly can claim a $100 credit on a $200 contribution.

Ponzi scheme — A fradulent investment scheme where "profits" distributed to initial investors are paid from contributions of later investors.

Pool — A group of persons or businesses who combine their financial resources and/or efforts for the purpose of attaining a common objective, such as a mutual fund. Illegal pools include such arrangements that attempt to control prices in a particular industry or to control the price of a particular security or commodity.

Pooled diversification — As used in investing, pooling of funds for the purpose of using professional management in selecting and maintaining a diversified portfolio.

Pooled income fund — A fund defined in the Internal Revenue Code (Section 642(c)(5)) as a trust where donors transfer an irrevocable remainder interest in property to a qualified charitable organization and retain an income interest for the life of a noncharitable beneficiary. If all other criteria are met, contributions made by the donors will qualify for income tax deductions.

Portfolio — (1) All securities held by an individual or an organization; (2) All investments (including real estate and commodities) held by an individual or an organization.

Portfolio management — The theory associated with appropriately balancing risk and return to meet an entity's investment objectives.

Possessory lien — A right given to a creditor to hold property until the debt is satisfied or an obligation is performed.

Postdate — To assign a future date; to write a date on a check or other document that is later than the writing of such document.

Post-nuptial agreement — An agreement made between married persons.

Pour-over — A provision in a trust or will that directs property into another trust or will upon the happening of a specified event.

Poverty — A condition of receiving little or no income; poor; not having material means or comfort.

Power of appointment — Generally, an authority given to a donee, either by will or deed, to dispose of property in a manner that the donor has described.

Power of attorney — Written authority allowing one individual to act on behalf of another either as an attorney or agent.

Power of sale — A provision in a mortgage or deed of trust authorizing the mortgagee or trustee to sell such property upon default.

Pre-authorized payment — An automatic payment system that allows a financial institution or employer to make direct payments from a customer's account or employee's compensation.

Preemptive right — A right given to stockholders to maintain their proportional ownership interest in a corporation by allowing all stockholders the privilege of purchasing the appropriate amount of stock from any new issue.

Preexisting condition — Any mental or physical condition that existed prior to the commencement of an insurance policy.

Preference items — See "Tax preference items."

Preferred creditor — A creditor whose claim has a higher priority of payment than a junior creditor.

Preferred ratings — Quality ratings of preferred stock showing dividend yield and potential price changes.

Preferred risk policies — Insurance contracts offered at reduced premiums because of rigid selection practices by the insurer. For example, a life insurance policy may require a lower premium because the insured is member of a profession whose mortality experience is better than normal.

Preferred (Pfd) stock — Generally, corporate stock that provides a fixed dividend to its holder, when dividends are declared by the board of directors, and a prior claim over common stock to the corporation's assets upon liquidation. Also see "Cumulative preferred stock" and "Participating preferred stock."

Premature distribution[1] — Generally, a payment made from an individual retirement account before a participant reaches age 59½ and not reimbursed within 60 days. A premature distribution will be included in gross income in the year it was made and be subject to a penalty tax.

Premium — (1) In insurance, consideration paid to begin or continue insurance coverage; (2) in bonds trading, an amount paid in excess of par; (3) in options trading, the price of an option; (4) in a short sale, a fee paid by an investor upon delivery of the borrowed shares, which were sold short; (5) for a new issue of securities, the excess of market price over initial selling price.

Premium bond — A bond selling for a price that is greater than par value.

Premium surcharge — An additional premium charged to an insured's insurance coverage because of excessive accidents or traffic violations.

Pre-nuptial agreement — An agreement made between a man and a woman prior to their marriage, typically concerning property rights and other related matters.

Prepaid expense[1] — Payments made in advance of services or goods received. For income tax purposes, these expenditures generally must be capitalized and not deducted if the expense has not been incurred during the tax year. If such expense has been incurred, then the prepaid item can be deducted.

Prepaid interest — Interest paid in advance of the payment date.

Prepaid income — Income received but not yet earned.

Prepaid medical care — A health insurance plan whereby specified health care is provided to members of the plan by participating physicians. Generally, a fixed premium is paid in advance by or for each member for full range of stated health services as specified in the contract. One type of prepaid medical care plan is a health maintenance organization. Also see "Health maintenance organization (HMO)."

Prepayment — Payments made in advance of an incurred expense. Also see "Prepaid expense."

Prepayment clause — A provision in a promissory note, mortgage, or deed of trust allowing the borrower the privilege of providing payment in full before maturity without penalty.

Prepayment penalty — A penalty imposed on a borrower who pays off a loan before maturity.

Prepayment terms — See "Prepayment clause."

Prescriptive easement — An easement granted by a court where no written easement exists (though one is presumed to be given) and use of the land must have been open, notorious, and continuous for a statutory period of time.

Present interest — The immediate use, possession, or enjoyment of property rather than at a future time. Compare "Future interest."

Presentment — For negotiable instruments, the demand for payment or acceptance by the holder.

Present realizable value — See "Present value."

Present value — A financial concept that expresses a certain amount of money to be received in the future in terms of its current value, given that money earns a specified rate of return. For example, assume you can earn 10 percent interest in an alternative investment having equivalent risk, and you are offered $125 in exactly two years if you pay $100 today. Would you take the offer? Yes! Because when you invest $100 at 10 percent interest for two years, you will have only $121. But when you invest $100 for a two-year period and receive $125, the rate of return is 11.8 percent. Thus, $121 to be received in two years at 10 percent has a present value of $100; likewise, $125 to be received in two years at 11.8 percent has a present value of $100. Also see "Present value method."

Present value analysis — See "Present value method."

Present value method — A method of comparing financial alternatives by discounting future cash inflows or outflows by the appropriate factors (present value factors). For example, assume you can earn a 10 percent rate of return on your investments and you have a choice in paying off a debt by: (A) paying $1,000 today; (B) paying $1,350 after four years, or (C) paying $1,650 in six years. Which alternative would you choose? Under the present value method, we must look at the time-value of money in that if you did not pay the full $1,000 immediately (which is its present value), you could invest it in an investment earning a 10 percent rate of return. Therefore, we need to know what is the present value of $1,350 in four years and the present value of $1,650 in six years, and this can easily be done by using a present value table to locate factors that will provide the present value of $1 at a 10 percent rate of return for four and six years. The present value factor of 10 percent in four years is .68301, so $1,350 × .68301 = $922.06 (the present value of $1,350 to be paid in 4 years considering a 10 percent rate of return). The present value factor of 10% in six years is .56447, so $1,650 × .56447 = $931.38 (the present value of $1,650 to be paid in 6 years considering a 10 percent rate of return). By restating the alternatives in terms of present value, which one will you now choose?

(A)	$1,000
(B)	$922
(C)	$931

Obviously, our best alternative is (B) because in terms of present value, it is the least amount to be paid. We can invest $922 at 10 percent for four years and receive $1,350 in four years because of compounding interest and use $78 ($1,000–$922) any way we choose today. The present value method can be employed for any future cash receipt or payment when the amount and rate of return are known. It is especially useful in determining the value of an annuity. Also see "Internal rate of return."

Present value of an annuity — The present worth of an annuity by using the present value method of discounting future cash flows. Also see "Present value method."

Preventive care — Measures prescribed by professionals in the medical and insurance fields to repress or stop illness or injury before they occur.

Preventive maintenance — The keeping of equipment in good working order, such as regularly applying scheduled lubrications and changing oil in an automobile, to prevent costly major repairs.

Previous balance method — A method of computing monthly interest charges on credit cards and charge accounts. The previous balance method applies the monthly interest rate against the beginning balance, ignoring all new charges and payments made during the billing period:

Beginning balance (July 1, 1987)	$2,000
Payments received (July 15, 1987)	(1,500)
Total charges during billing period	+ 750
Ending balance (July 31, 1987)	= 1,250
Finance charges (1½ percent × $2,000)	$ 30

Also see "Adjusted balance method," and "Average daily balance method."

Price — The value of an item in terms of money.

Price discrimination — The illegal sale of identical products or services for two different prices to two different buyers without reasonable justification.

Price/earnings (P/E) ratio — A ratio used in the analysis of a stock's current price showing the multiple of how many times its selling price is greater than its earnings per share:

$$\text{Price/Earnings ratio} = \frac{\text{Price per share}}{\text{Earnings per share}}$$

Price range — A stock's highest selling price and lowest selling price over a specified period of time.

Prima facie — On the face of it; presumed to be true unless proven otherwise.

Primary beneficiary — The person who is to receive the proceeds of a life insurance policy, if alive, upon the death of the insured. If the primary beneficiary is not alive, then the secondary beneficiary will receive the proceeds.

Primary earnings — See "Earnings per share (EPS)."

Primary market — In securities and commodity trading, the initial sale of a securities issue or commodity futures contracts.

Primary offering — A sale of securities where the proceeds go to the issuing company as opposed to another investor. Compare "Secondary offering."

Prime rate — The most favorable rate charged by a commercial bank to its best corporate customers for short-term loans.

Principal — (1) The balance of a debt (excluding interest); (2) the amount of capital invested, as distinguished from profits or interest; (3) a person who has given the power to act as his or her representative to another, who is an agent; (4) the corpus of a trust.

Principal amount — The face amount of a loan or debt security.

Principal of indemnity — An insurance concept that disallows an insured from receiving compensation from an insurance claim for more than the amount of economic loss.

Principles — Basic truths or assumptions; rules.

Priority — The preferential order of importance; the sequence in which claims are to be satisfied upon the sale of property in that priority obligations will be paid before junior obligations, such as bondholders have priority over stockholders in case of liquidation.

Priority clause — A provision in a junior lien stating its subordination to a priority lien.

Private annuity — As used in estate planning, an annuity generally provided to an individual who exchanges income-producing property to another person (typically a family member) in return. The primary purpose of using a private annuity is to pass income property to beneficiaries while simultaneously reducing the annuitant's gross estate.

Private foundation[1] — Generally, a privately funded charitable organization that is restricted from engaging in certain activities and is closely scrutinized by the Internal Revenue Service.

Private insurance annuity — An annuity insured by a private insurance company.

Private letter ruling — A request by a taxpayer for a written statement from the Internal Revenue Service as to how the Service will interpret the tax laws concerning a specific event, which has either occurred or is being contemplated.

Private limited partnership — A limited partnership that is not registered with a state agency and generally has only a few investors.

Private mortgage insurance (PMI) — Mortgage insurance provided by private companies, as opposed to government-sponsored insurance (FHA) or guarantees (VA).

Private offering[1] — An investment proposal that is not required to be filed with the Securities and Exchange Commission. Generally, such offering is made to a limited number of persons who are both well informed as to the affairs of the company, can financially afford making the investment, and are knowledgeable in making investments.

Private property — Any property not owned by a state or the federal government.

Private sector — Economic activities, which are not under government control, carried on by individuals and non-governmental organizations.

Privileged communications — Communications made by a certain individual to another within a protected relationship. The communications cannot be disclosed on the witness stand without the consent of the person making such statements. Depending upon state law, relationships typically considered to be protected are attorney–client, husband–wife, clergyman–penitent, doctor–patient, etc. Thus, a client may communicate with an attorney, and the attorney is not legally compelled to disclose such statements.

Privity — (1) Mutual interest in the same property; (2) entitled to private knowledge because of one's position or relationship.

Probability — The likelihood of occurrence.

Probate — The legal procedure of proving a valid or invalid will. The term "probate" is also used to encompass all matters concerning the administration of an estate or guardianship.

Probate costs — Generally, professional fees incurred in the settlement of a will.

Probate court — A court generally empowered to validate wills and to administer the estate of a deceased, an incompetent, or an underaged person.

Probate sale — A sale of estate property performed under the supervision of the probate court.

Proceeds — The net amount received; total cash received after deducting all expenses. Total amount received from an insurance company arising from a loss, net amount received from the sale of an item, and total amount received from borrowing on a discounted note are examples of proceeds.

Procurement — The acquisition of goods or services.

Producer price index — A price index using a formulated weighted average of certain commodity prices over a given period of time.

Production payment[1] — A certain amount to be received from a portion of oil-producing property.

Product liability — Liability assumed by manufacturers and sellers to compensate purchasers, users, and bystanders who are injured because of a defective product.

Profession — An occupation requiring advanced specialized training and skills well above the level of a layman. Accounting, law, medicine, dentistry, writing, engineering, religion, architecture, teaching, science, social work, insurance, financial planning, and real estate are among the many recognized professions.

Professional executor — An executor having prior knowledge, experience, and usually objectivity and impartiality in dealing with the administration of a person's estate. An example of a professional executor is a bank's trust department.

Professional malpractice insurance — Liability insurance designed to protect a practicing professional, such as a doctor or accountant, if he or she becomes legally liable for malpractice. Also see "Malpractice insurance."

Profit — Generally, gross revenues less costs of obtaining such revenues. Gross profit is equal to net sales less cost of goods sold, while net profit is equal to net sales less all expenses. Profit can also mean gain, benefit, or income received from the sale or use of property.

Profitability ratios — Ratios used in measuring the operating success of an enterprise by analyzing its profits with regard to equity, sales, or assets. Included among the profitability ratios are dividend payout ratio, earnings per share, price/earnings ratio, return on stockholder's equity, net income to sales, and return on operating assets.

Profitable intent — A good-faith attempt to reasonably earn a profit from a business or investment rather than to merely obtain tax-avoidance items or operate a hobby. For income tax purposes, all business and investment undertakings must have a "for profit" intent or such activity will be recharacterized as a hobby. Also see "Hobby."

Profit and loss statement — See "Income statement."

Profit sharing — A specialized type of incentive compensation whereby an employer distributes a portion of the profits to employees in addition to regular pay. Such distributions may be in the form of cash, merchandise, stock, incentive stock options, or some other benefit. In order for a profit sharing plan to qualify for tax benefits as a retirement arrangement, the plan must not discriminate among employees, provide for allocations according to a definite predetermined formula (i.e., generally, in proportion to the compensation of each participant), and include an appropriate number of eligible employees. If an employer experiences little or no profits during a year, then no contribution can be made for that period. Each plan participant has a separate account that is increased for allocated employer contributions, profits, and forfeitures and decreased for expenses and losses. The balance of an individual's account determines the retirement benefit. Funds may be distributed upon the occurrence of a specified event, such as retirement, termination, layoff, disability, or death.

Profit sharing ratio[1] — A mutually agreed-upon ratio by which partners in a partnership share gains. Losses are also shared in this manner, unless a loss sharing ratio exists.

Pro forma[1] — A futuristic financial statement presenting the "what if" effects of a quantifiable variable. For example, a pro forma balance sheet may show the effects of a proposed transaction, such as the purchase of a home and corresponding long-term mortgage. A pro forma cash flow statement showing increased debt-service payments is usually also prepared.

Progressive tax — An income tax system designed to gradually increase the proportion of taxes payable by applying a higher tax rate as the level of taxable income increases.

Promised yield — See "Yield to maturity."

Promisee — One who receives a promise; the person to whom a promise is made, such as a lender.

Promisor — One who gives a promise; the person who makes a promise, such as a borrower.

Promissory note — Generally, an unconditional promise between a maker and a payee whereby the maker agrees to pay a certain sum of money either on demand or on a specific date. Most, but not all, promissory notes are negotiable instruments. Also see "Negotiable instruments."

Promoter — A person who organizes and develops a profit-seeking venture; an entrepreneur.

Promulgate — To publicly and formally announce a statute, ruling, or judiciary decision.

Proof of loss — A formal written document, signed by an insured and submitted to an insurer after the occurrence of a loss, that contains the specifications regarding the property, loss, and insurance. The proof of loss is intended to provide an insurer with an appropriate amount of information in order to determine its liability under contract.

Property and liability insurance — A broad classification of insurance that covers losses arising from the ownership of property, either from losses sustained to an insured's own property or losses sustained to another's property as a result of negligent acts on the part of the insured making him or her legally liable. Traditionally, fire and marine, surety, and casualty insurances fall under this classification.

Property damage liability coverage — Insurance protection against liability for damage or destruction of tangible property belonging to another that is not in the custody or control of the insured. The damage must be caused by an event that occurs during the period the policy is in force and includes loss of use.

Property dividends — Any dividend paid on preferred or common stock that does not include cash, such as merchandise, stocks of other corporations, stock dividends, or other securities of the same corporation (e.g., bonds on common stock, preferred stock on common stock, or common stock on preferred stock).

Property exclusions clause — As used in a fire insurance policy, a provision excluding certain types or portions of property from valuation for purposes of determining the amount of insurance required by a coinsurance clause.

Property insurance — Any of various types of insurance that protects against financial loss arising from the damage or complete loss of property.

Property management — A part of real estate industry that deals with managing rental homes, apartment houses, offices, shopping centers, industrial complexes, etc. Duties may range from merely collecting rents to complete maintenance and leasing or selling services.

Property, plant, and equipment — A balance sheet classification pertaining to an enterprise's long-term assets which are used in maintaining the company's operations.

Property rights — Any type of right one has to real or personal property.

Property settlement — An agreement made as part of a divorce proceeding between two spouses as to how their personal assets will be divided. Generally, property settlements are not taxable events.

Property tax — Any of various taxes levied on real and personal property. In most instances, such taxes are assessed on the property's value. The largest property tax is real estate taxes, which are assessed by state and local governments.

Proportional tax — A tax system that maintains a constant tax rate which is applied against a taxable source regardless of its size. That is, a tax rate which does not change in reference to the size of a tax base. An example of a proportional tax is a flat tax.

Proposition 13 — A property tax limitation measure passed in California in 1978 which reduced property taxes to 1 percent of the value of the property.

Proprietary — Exclusive and private ownership; anything having to do with a proprietor.

Proprietary lease — In a cooperative apartment arrangement, a lease between a tenant-stockholder and the managing corporation.

Proprietorship — A form of business ownership where one individual exclusively owns and controls an entire enterprise. It is commonly referred to as a sole proprietorship.

Pro rata — According to a specified proportion. For example, Nesbit and Jones are partners and they agree to share profits in proportion to their respective capital accounts at the start of their partnership. If Nesbit owns 60 percent and Jones owns 40 percent, then all profit distributions will be made pro rata, 3:2, to both Nesbit and Jones.

Pro rata distribution clause — A fire insurance clause in a blanket policy stating that total coverage is divided by the proportion of value that each location bears to the sum of the values of all insured locations.

Pro rata liability clause — As applied to a policyholder with more than one insurance coverage available, a provision in an insurance contract stating that the insurer is only liable up to a proportion of any loss with regard to its policy limits and all other insurance companies' policy limits.

Pro rate — To divide or adjust proportionally. For example, assume Wiggins is to pay $620 a month rent and moves into an apartment on October 16. If his rent is pro rated, then he will pay $320 ($20 per day × 16 days) rent for his portion of the month of October.

Proration — To divide proportionally.

Prospect — A potential buyer, seller, employee, lessee, etc.

Prospectus — A document given to potential purchasers of initial issuances that provides detailed financial information concerning a company's or proposed investment's operations and objectives along with other material facts of the issuer. For public offerings of non-exempt issues, a prospectus must be filed with the Securities and Exchange Commission.

Prosperity — The most favorable part of a business cycle where, in general, the economy is expanding. Ideally, business activity is rising, unemployment is low, inflation is low, many new companies are being formed, capital investment continues to rise, total credit increases, workers' pay steadily rises, and overall production increases.

Provisions — (1) Qualifications or stipulations in a contract, such as a clause in an agreement; (2) necessary supplies, such as food.

Proximate cause — The direct, dominating, or efficient cause which produces a loss. An unbroken sequence of cause and effect set in motion by the occurrence of a covered peril distinguishes such peril as the proximate cause of damage. For example, fire in a factory is the proximate cause of water damage to machinery when water was used by fire fighters, even though the machinery was not otherwise damaged by the fire.

Proxy — A substitution for a person who is unable to attend a meeting; a written authorization allowing one person to represent and vote the shares of another at a shareholder's meeting.

Proxy statement — A formal statement filed with the Securities and Exchange Commission and subsequently given to stockholders by anyone soliciting stockholder votes.

Prudent man rule — A standard requiring a person in a fiduciary relationship (e.g., a trustee or investment adviser) to perform his or her duties solely in the interest of the beneficiaries, participants, or clients with the care a prudent man would use acting in similar circumstances. Essentially, this means that a person in such position must manage all assets subject to the relationship in accordance with the trust's objectives in a manner that minimizes risk of loss. A fiduciary may become personally liable if the arrangement is not managed in this manner. In some states, certain fiduciaries must only invest in securities designated by the state, called the legal list.

Public accountant — An accountant, not certified by a state examining board, who provides professional accounting services to the public.

Public adjuster — An adjuster who is hired by an insured to act in a representative capacity in negotiating a policyholder's claim with an insurance company.

Public assistance — See "Welfare."

Public corporation — A corporation usually formed for governing purposes to administer public affairs at the local level, such as a city or township.

Public debt — All debts a country has outstanding, which include the debts of both state and national governments.

Public domain — (1) Land owned by the government; (2) publications or documents not protected by copyright.

Public limited partnership — A limited partnership registered with both state and federal authorities and whose ownership interests are typically offered to the public.

Publicly traded issues — Stock that is available for trading by the public and can usually be bought or sold without extended delay.

Public offering — A sale of stock to the public that must abide by state and federal laws, such as Securities and Exchange Commission requirements, as contrasted with a private offering.

Public records — The records of all documents subject to public inspection, which are necessary to give notice. Public records are normally kept in or near the county courthouse.

Public report — A report given by the real estate commission to prospective buyers of a home in a new subdivision stating the general conditions of the neighborhood, such as proximity of schools, shopping centers, and noise level if close to an airport.

Public sale — Generally, an auction open to the public resulting from a foreclosure, unpaid taxes, etc.

Public service commission — A supervisory and regulatory agency created by a state legislature to exercise control over public utilities within the state.

Public utility — A privately owned company which provides such essential public services as electricity, telephone systems, and gas; it is highly regulated by a government agency.

Punitive damages — Damages awarded to a plantiff in excess of bare compensation for loss because of malicious, violent, wicked, fraudulent, or oppressive behavior exhibited by the defendant. Punitive damages are awarded to punish a defendant or to make an example of him or her for performing such acts. Punitive damages for personal injury may not be taxable, but in the case of loss income for business purposes they are taxable.

Purchase agreement — An agreement made between a buyer and seller specifying the terms and price of a sale. A purchase agreement is also a sales agreement or sale.

Purchase-and-sale agreement — See "Buy–sell agreement."

Purchase discount — A reduction in the price of goods purchased because of early payment.

Purchase money mortgage — Upon the sale of real property where the seller finances at least part of the purchase price, a mortgage given by a purchaser to the seller as security for payment. The most significant feature of a purchase money mortgage is that the buyer is deeded title. This financing arrangement is typically done in times of tight money, high interest rates, or when adequate financing is unavailable. Compare "Installment land contract."

Purchase order — A written authorization given to a seller calling for the delivery of goods or services under its terms. Generally, a purchase order is an offer and actual delivery constitutes acceptance.

Purchasing power — The ability to purchase goods and services in reference to a fixed amount of money, changing price levels, and a certain time period.

Purchasing power risk — The risk of changing price levels in the economy, either inflationary or deflationary, that can significantly impact security prices.

Pure life annuity — See "Life annuity."

Put — A stock option allowing its holder to sell 100 shares of stock to the option writer for a specified price before a certain date. Puts can generally be purchased from an option exchange for a duration of three, six, or nine months. Compare "Call."

Pyramiding — An investment strategy that uses more credit, as it becomes available from a certain margin account because of an increase in the value of such stocks, to purchase more stock. Thus, pyramiding is an investment technique which does not require additional cash outlay because of the use of available equity in another investment.

Pyramid sales scheme — A marketing technique of compensating participants with an override for sales made by recruits. Participants are brought into the scheme with visions of financial well-being by enlisting people to sell the product or service, as well as the financial aspects, to others—who in turn sell the idea to more individuals, and so on. The initial participants profit from the sales of their recruits and all others subsequently recruited by them.

Qualified cash or deferred-benefit arrangement[1] — A stock bonus or profit sharing plan that allows employees to either take cash immediately or defer benefits until retirement.

Qualified indorsement — Any indorsement of a negotiable instrument that changes the liability of the indorser in a manner different from what the law ordinarily provides. "Without recourse" is a qualified indorsement limiting the indorser's liability.

Qualified retirement plan[1] — A retirement plan generally funded by employers that meets the criteria set forth in Internal Revenue Code Section 401.

Qualified terminable interest property (Q-TIP)[1] — Qualifying property that is eligible for the marital deduction, even though it is terminable interest property, because the surviving spouse receives the entire income from such property and during the surviving spouse's life the property cannot be appointed to anyone except the surviving spouse.

Quantity discount — A reduced price per item given by a seller to a buyer who purchases a good or service beyond a specified amount.

Quarters of coverage — The calendar quarters in which an individual has contributed to the Social Security System. The quarters of coverage are one of the factors used in determining elgibility for and the amount of benefits.

Quick assets — Cash and other assets which are highly liquid in nature in that they can quickly be turned into cash, such as marketable securities.

Quick ratio — See "Acid-test ratio."

Quiet enjoyment — In real estate, a covenant added to leases and conveyances where the grantor promises that the lessee or new owner shall quietly enjoy possession of the property without disturbances, such as an eviction because of a defective title.

Quiet title — A court action to determine the rightful owner of real property.

Quitclaim deed — A written instrument transferring to the grantee any title, claim, or other interest in real property that the grantor may have. The grantor makes no representation as to having any property to convey and in some states no warranty of valid interest.

Railroad Retirement Act — Federal legislation enacted in 1935 to establish a retirement system for railroad employees and survivor's benefits for their families.

Random walk theory — Hypothesis concerning the movement of stock prices which takes the position that changes in stock prices are purely random and therefore unpredictable.

RAR — Revenue agent's report; a letter mailed to a taxpayer by a revenue agent of the Internal Revenue Service showing any adjustments to his or her income tax return as a result of an audit.

Ratable — That which can be divided or assessed proportionally.

Ratable estate — Real and personal property that can be assessed a tax.

Rated policy — An insurance policy issued by an insurance company at a higher premium rate than a standard policy because of an extra risk taken on by the insurer. In a life insurance policy, for example, an insured's premium may be raised because of poor health or hazardous employment.

Rate of interest — Generally, a percentage rate stating the annual charge of borrowing or lending money. Also see "Prime rate," "Discount rate," and "Yield to maturity."

Rate of return — An annual percentage rate indicating the financial performance of an investment. Rate of return is used in comparing investment and risk alternatives. For example, if you invested $100 today and exactly two years later it was worth $169, then you would have an unrealized rate of return of 30 percent on your investment. Instead, assume you invested $100 and were to receive $25 per year for the next 10 years, after which period you will receive the $100. In this latter case you would realize a 25 percent rate of return on investment. Also see "Internal rate of return."

Rate of return on equity — See "Return on equity."

Ratification — The confirmation or approval of a previous and otherwise avoidable act; the confirmation of a legislative act.

Rating — (1) For financial purposes, the evaluation of an individual's or business's ability to pay off debts; (2) for insurance purposes, an assessment of risk which determines a policyholder's premium.

Ratio analysis — As used in security analysis, the evaluation of information contained in an entity's financial statements by converting account balances into meaningful and comparable relationships. The five major groups of financial ratios are liquidity, profitability, effective asset management, leverage, and per share computations. Some of the more common ratios are current ratio, acid-test ratio, return on equity, return on total assets, return on investment, inventory turnover, accounts receivable turnover, debt-to-equity, earnings per share, price/earnings ratio, dividend yield, and book value per share. Comparison of such data is sometimes useful when made between current and past ratios of the same company, an entity and industry averages, two different companies of the same or different industries, or some other objective criteria in order to assess a company's operating performance and financial condition.

Rationing — A system of allocating goods or services because of scarcity, thus ensuring a more equitable distribution and controlled prices. Rationing is usually implemented in times of emergency, such as war.

Ready, willing, and able — Said of one who is financially capable and is prepared to act, generally, as a buyer.

Real asset — Land and buildings. Also see "Real estate."

Real estate — Land and all permanently attached structures, such as buildings and its fixtures, fences, shrubbery, and the like. Compare "personal property"; the right to own or use real property.

Real estate board — A group composed of members of both the real estate and financial industries whose primary purpose is to further the real estate business in a particular area.

Real estate investment trust (REIT)[1] — An investment vehicle that is required to invest primarily in real estate ventures or mortgages and to distribute 95 percent of its income to at least 100 owners, who are only taxed once upon receipt. Thus, a REIT may be entirely exempt from federal taxation. The trust or corporation must elect such treatment and is further bound by rather strict rules of investment alternatives and distributions.

Real estate license — A license granted by a state agency to sell real property either as a broker or salesman. Generally, education requirements must be satisfied and an examination must be passed in order to obtain the license.

Real income — Income recomputed using constant value dollars which is intended to show the effects of changes in purchasing power.

Realization — Generally, the conversion of an asset into cash.

Realized gain — See "Gain realized."

Realized yield — An expected yield for investors who plan to sell a bond before its maturity date.

Real property — See "Real estate."

Realtor® — A real estate broker who is a member of a local board that is affiliated with the National Association of Real Estate Boards. (Copyrighted and registered by the National Association of Realtors.)

Reassessment — A re-evaluation of property values for tax assessment purposes.

Rebate — The return of a portion of a purchase price representing a discount.

Recapitalization — A rearrangement of a corporation's capital structure, usually as a result of financial troubles. Common stocks, preferred stocks, or bonds are reissued to reflect changes in priority, amount, or type.

Recapture — For income tax purposes, the recognition as ordinary income of certain items previously deducted (such as depreciation) or credits previously taken (such as investment tax credit) in the year property subject to recapture is disposed of.

Receipt — An acknowledgment in writing that cash or other asset has been received or acquired.

Receivable — See "Accounts receivable."

Receiver[1] — A person appointed by a court to oversee property during litigation (such as bankruptcy).

Recession — Generally, a slowdown in the growth of the economy which is less severe than a depression.

Reciprocity — A mutual relationship where a buyer of one party's product is also a seller of a different product to the same party; the business practice of buying from one's customers.

Recision — See "Cancellation."

Reclamation — (1) A banking industry practice of a correcting mistakes in the recording of an amount of a check or other commercial instrument (reclamation is typically done in a clearinghouse); (2) the conditioning of waste land into economically useful property, such as the draining of a swamp.

Recognized gain — See "Gain recognized."

Recognized loss — See "Loss recognized."

Recompense — (1) An award or compensation for services performed; (2) payment for goods lost or damaged.

Reconciliation — The bringing of two different parties or balances to an agreement. Also see "Bank reconciliation."

Reconditioned — The restoration of an item by repairing and/or replacing the defective portion.

Reconveyance — Generally, the transfer of title to real property back to its equitable owner, typically, after a mortgage has been fully satisfied.

Record date — See "Date of record."

Recording — The proper filing of documents, such as deeds, mortgages, and security agreements, in public records to give notice to future buyers, creditors, and other interested parties. Such recordings are governed by the provisions of state statutes.

Recourse — The right of a lender or holder of a negotiable instrument to seek recovery from the personal assets of the borrower or maker. A recourse loan is one where the borrower is personally liable, whereas in a nonrecourse loan only the property subject to such loan is available to satisfy the claim.

Recovery — An upswing in business activity, typically out of a recession or depression.

Recovery property — Accelerated cost-recovery system property; depreciable property.

Redeem — To buy back.

Redeemable bond — See "Callable bond."

Redemption — (1) The purchase of a security by its issuer; (2) any repurchase agreement allowing the seller to buy back an item for a previously agreed-upon price; (3) in real estate, the process of obtaining clear title by canceling a defeasible title when fulfilling a debt, as exemplified by a mortgage foreclosure sale or tax sale.

Redemption period — A period of time in which a mortgage, deed of trust, land contract, etc., is redeemable as provided for by state statute.

Red herring — Upon the issuance of new securities, a statement in red ink on a preliminary prospectus stating that it is not a solicitation, but for information purposes only.

Red ink — Net loss; a losing proposition.

Redlining — An illegal practice of discrimination among financial institutions whereby certain mortgages on properties located in a well-defined area are not considered because of deteriorating conditions.

Redress — Equitable relief from injury or damages.

Red tape — Refers to an excessively bureaucratic system.

Reduced paid-up insurance — One of the nonforfeiture options of a permanent life insurance policy that allows the policyholder to continue a reduced face amount of life insurance in force under the original insurance plan without paying any further premiums. For example, an endowment policy subject to such an election will continue in force for a reduced face amount until the end of the endowment period. Also see "Nonforfeiture."

Reduction health insurance — A provision in a health insurance policy that diminishes a portion of coverage under certain conditions, generally for specific illnesses or other conditions.

Referral — A recommendation given by one person to another for the purpose of engaging in a business transaction with, or obtaining employment from, a particular company. In some cases, a referral fee may be available to compensate the individual making the referral.

Refinance — To pay off a debt with borrowed funds from another debt.

Reformation — The equitable remedy of correcting a contract which, without change, does not express the real agreement or intent of the parties because of a mutual mistake or a unilateral mistake by one party and fraud by the other party.

Refund — A return of money for the purpose of restoring the recipient to an equitable position.

Refund annuity — Any annuity that guarantees part or all of its cost to be returned to the annuitant or his (her) beneficiaries.

Refund claim — A request made to the Internal Revenue Service for refund of taxes overpaid.

Regional stock exchange — Any U.S. stock exchange located outside New York City.

Register — (1) Generally, to record or enroll; (2) a book of public records (e.g., marriages, births, and deaths).

Registered bond — A bond that is registered on the books of the issuer, who pays interest directly to the owner by check. Compare "Bearer bond."

Registered check — A check purchased by an individual and drawn on the funds of a bank, though not certified. A registered check is very similar to a money order.

Registered coupon bond — A bond whose face amount is registered, but not the interest. Thus, the coupons become bearer paper upon the arrival of a certain date.

Registered representative — A person licensed by the Securities and Exchange Commission and an employee of a brokerage firm or other institution authorized to sell securities to the public.

Register of deeds — An officer whose duty is to record instruments pertaining to real estate in public records, such as mortgages and deeds.

Registrar of deeds — See "Register of deeds."

Regressive tax — A tax whose rates are fixed or decrease as the tax base increases, which essentially places a heavier tax burden on the poor.

Regular charge account — A charge account in retail stores which requires full payment to be made within 30 days of the billing date. A regular charge account is a convenience for customers in that small recurring purchases can be paid in one payment each month.

Regular dividend — A corporate distribution of earnings of a certain amount every quarter.

Regular medical insurance — Health insurance where all physicians' services are covered except surgery.

Regulated industry — Any industry that is highly restricted by the government, such as electric light and power companies, the railroad industry, and the telephone industry.

Regulated investment company — An investment company qualifying under the Internal Revenue Code (Section 851) to be taxed only on its undistributed investment income. Investment income is passed through to shareholders as ordinary income, long-term capital gain income, or tax-exempt distributions.

Regulations[1] — Treasury regulations are interpretations of the Internal Revenue Code by the Treasury Department (IRS), as prescribed by the Secretary of the Treasury and authorized by Congress. The regulations are authoritative pronouncements that have the effect of law, unless contradictory to the Internal Revenue Code.

Regulation Z — See "Truth-in-Lending Act."

Rehabilitation expenditures[1] — Certain qualifying expenditures made for the restoration of certified historical structures and commercial nonresidential buildings over 30 years old which qualify for a special investment tax credit. Rehabilitation expenditures made on low-income housing qualify for a special 5-year amortization.

Reinstatement — In insurance, the revival of a policy, which has lapsed or been canceled, to active status. Under reinstatement no new policy or coverage is issued, and only the original insurance is restored at the request of the policyholder. Generally, reinstatement is not available when a policy has been surrendered for cash, but it may be reinstated within a certain period (e.g., 5 years) for nonpayment of premium. All overdue and currently due premiums are usually required to be paid and insurability may have to be evidenced again.

Reinsurance — The assumption of all or part of a risk by a second insurance company (reinsurer) to protect the original insurance company from a risk already assumed; insurance for insurers.

Reinvestment rate — The rate at which a business reinvests its earnings; it is stated as a percentage of equity capital.

REIT — See "Real estate investment trust."

Related parties transactions[1] — Transactions made between two particular taxpayers (because of their relationship) that could be construed as a sham or lacking a valid business purpose. Certain restrictions are placed on gains and losses arising from such transactions. For example, losses arising from a related party transaction are not deductible. Related taxpayers may include partners, corporations controlled by the taxpayer, immediate family and lineal descendants, grandparents, settlor and trust or beneficiaries, etc. Generally, who constitutes a related party depends upon the type of transaction involved since there are separate guidelines for different transactions.

Release — A discharge of debt, as opposed to an extinguishment of debt.

Relevance — In a decision-making process, the degree to which information constitutes significant input.

Reliability — The degree of trustworthiness.

Remainder — A future interest in property which only takes effect either at a certain time or upon the occurrence of a certain event, commonly the death of the life tenant; a future interest that is effective and enjoyable after the termination of another estate. Such interest may be created in anyone other than the grantor. For example, McKee conveys land to Willis for life, remainder to Levitt and her heirs. Compare "Reversion."

Remainderman — Generally, one entitled to the remainder of an estate.

Remaining economic life — The number of estimated years of an item's useful life; the number of years between the year property is appraised and the year such property becomes worthless.

Remedial loan societies — A pawnshop operated by a nonprofit organization that loans money at reasonable rates.

Remise — As used in a quitclaim deed, to give up.

Remittance — The transfer of money, such as through the mail.

Removal bond — A bond posted for the removal of imported items from a warehouse for export purposes to cover possible custom duties had the merchandise remained as domestic inventory.

Remuneration — A reward or compensation.

Renegotiable rate mortgage (RRM) — Generally, a 30-year loan that is periodically renewed at current interest rates.

Renegotiation date — In a leasing arrangement, a date specified in a lease where new terms to an existing contract are to be negotiated.

Renewability — The continuation of an insurance contract. For optionally renewable and conditionally renewable health insurance policies, the insurer has the option to renew; for guaranteed renewable and noncancellable policies, the insured has the option to continue it in force usually up to a certain age.

Renewable term insurance — Term life insurance guaranteeing a policyholder the privilege to continue the policy in force without providing any additional evidence of insurability. A renewable term contract is generally more expensive than a nonrenewable policy, but under both contracts the premium rates will increase for each renewal period.

Renewal — Continuance of an expiring contract, such as an insurance policy or lease agreement. A new contract may be issued.

Renewal option — In a lease, the lessee's option to extend the term of a lease for a specified period.

Renewal premium — For a life insurance policy, any premium due after the initial year.

Rent — Compensation paid for the occupancy or use of property. Rent may take the form of cash, other property, or use of property as an exchange.

Rental agreement — A lease (usually for residential real estate).

Rental property — Any property providing rental income for the owner.

Rental reimbursement insurance — Insurance coverage for property owners that reimburses the loss of rental income in the event of an insured peril.

Rental value — The fair rental value of property for a particular location.

Renter's insurance — An "HO-4 policy"; see "Homeowner's insurance policy."

Repair or replacement cost coverage — For automobile insurance, a personal auto policy (PAP) endorsement for new cars that provides for the full cost of repairing or replacing (less any deductible) without reduction for depreciation and regardless of whether the cost exceeds the automobile's fair market value.

Repairs — The mending of a broken, damaged, or worn-out item. Generally, repairs are expensed rather than capitalized.

Replacement cost — The total cost required to replace an item to the position of its present state; the amount of cash necessary to purchase a similar asset to undertake the same function as the item lost.

Replacement cost insurance — Generally, property insurance, primarily available for buildings, that provides for all necessary expenditures to restore damaged property to its full usefulness, as before the occurrence of an insured event. Replacement cost insurance does not deduct for depreciation.

REPO — See "Repurchase agreement."

Repossession — The recovery of goods by a seller because a purchaser was unable to meet his or her installments.

Repurchase agreement (REPO)[1] — An agreement to buy back a particular item within a specified time at a stated price.

Required return — The rate of return required for a corresponding amount of risk.

Requisition — A written request for materials or supplies.

Rerecording — A second recording of a deed to correct an error. A rerecording is also known as confirmation deed, correction deed, or reformation deed.

Resale — The business of buying and selling goods without any further processing.

Rescind — To nullify or cancel.

Rescission — The termination, annulment, abrogation, or undoing of a contract by placing each party in such position as if no contract was made.

Research and development expenditures[1] — Certain expenditures paid or incurred by a taxpayer in connection with his or her trade or business for research and experimentation which may either be expensed during the taxable year or capitalized and amortized over a 60-month period. In certain cases when research activities are increased, an income tax credit may be available.

Reservation — (1) In a real estate deed or other document of conveyance, a right or interest created by and for the grantor in the property granted. The reservation may be permanent, such as an easement, or temporary, such as a life estate; (2) public lands allotted for a specific purpose, such as an indian reservation.

Reserve — Funds set aside for a specific use, indefinite contingencies, or emergencies.

Reserve requirements — The percentage of deposits that a bank must hold in cash or on account at a Federal Reserve Bank as established by state or federal laws.

Residence — A place where one is settled or lives; a person's home.

Resident alien — A person living in this country without U.S. citizenship.

Residential properties — Real estate consisting of residential housing, such as apartments or other dwelling units, as opposed to nonresidential properties, such as office buildings, warehouses, and shopping centers.

Residuary clause — A clause in a will stating how the remaining assets in an estate (residuary estate) are to be distributed.

Residuary estate — The remaining assets of an estate after all debts, taxes, administration expenses, bequests, and devises have been satisfied.

Residue — See "Residuary estate."

RESPA — Real Estate Settlement Procedures Act. A federal law requiring disclosure of certain settlement costs attributable to the sale of a home that is to be financed by a government-insured lender.

Respondeat superior doctrine — A doctrine stating that a principal will be held liable for the wrongful acts of his or her agent, while the agent is performing within the scope of authority.

Restitution — An indemnification; the restoration of a lost, damaged, or surrendered item or some other injury to a plaintiff.

Restraint of alienation — In real estate, restrictions placed in an instrument of conveyance whereby the grantee is prohibited from making specified transfers of the property. In order to be enforceable, a restraint of alienation must conform to public policy and to the free right of the grantee to sell.

Restricted account — A margin account having an equity level (margin) less than the prevailing margin requirements.

Restricted property[1] — For compensation purposes, property (usually an employer's stock) received by an employee with certain restrictions as to its transfer. Generally, such property is not income to the employee until all restrictions are lifted and there is no longer any substantial risk of forfeiture. In addition, the employer will not receive a deduction until the employee is able to include the property as income.

Restriction — In real estate, a prohibited use of land as stated in a deed. Also see "Restrictive covenant."

Restrictive covenant — (1) A provision in a deed describing prohibited uses of land (such limitations are set forth by previous owners or, for a new subdivision, a developer); (2) a clause in an employment contract or partnership agreement prohibiting one from performing similar work within a certain geographic location and period of time. To be enforceable, the limitations must be reasonable.

Restrictive indorsement — An indorsement of a negotiable instrument which restricts payment in that subsequent holders must either comply with the indorsement or be certain it was done. Two examples of restrictive indorsement are "for deposit only" or "for collection."

Resulting trust — An implied trust that arises by operation of law when there has not been a complete and effective disposition of property. For example, McGee transfers money to a trustee to pay income to Henning for life. After Henning's death, any amount left over remains McGee's by virtue of a resulting trust. Also see "Constructive trust."

Retail — The business practice of selling small quantities to consumers after all markups have been made.

Retail charge account — A credit arrangement with a retail store allowing customers to purchase goods on credit. Also see "Open account" and "Revolving charge account."

Retail installment contract — A written contract for the retail sale of goods between a buyer and seller that permits the buyer to possess the goods or receive services at the time of sale, and allows for payment to be made in installments. Under a retail installment contract, the seller may or may not retain title to the goods, depending upon the contract.

Retail price — Generally, the price of items sold to a consumer in a final sale.

Retained earnings — In the accounting of a corporation, the portion of owner's equity representing past and present net income not distributed as dividends.

Retainer — A fee paid in advance to an attorney for future services.

Retirement annuity — A deferred annuity that is usually purchased with installments by an annuitant during his or her productive years. A retirement annuity begins on a date selected by the annuitant; the amount of retirement benefit depends on the purchase price and date selected. Most contracts are written with optional settlements, such as a cash refund annuity, life annuity, or a life income with guaranteed payments for a certain number of years. Amounts received after the annuity starting date are partially taxable in accordance with an annuity ratio. See "Annuity ratio." For annuity contracts issued after August 13, 1982, amounts received before the annuity starting date are considered income (up to the amount of accrued earnings). For example, assume Singleton purchases an annuity for $30,000 after August 13, 1982, and receives $5,000 before the annuity starting date. Further assume that the annuity is worth $33,000 at the time of that receipt. Of the $5,000 received, $3,000 of accrued earnings ($33,000 − $30,000) is ordinary income and the remaining $2,000 is a tax-free return of capital. For annuity contracts issued before August 14, 1982, just the opposite is true: all amounts received before the annuity starting date are tax-free return capital, up to the amount invested.

Retirement income deficit — A decline in an individual's cash flow created by retirement and computed by finding one's income level immediately before retirement less reduction in expenses, less income from retirement plans, less income from investments, and less Social Security receipts.

Retirement income policy — A life insurance policy that pays monthly income to the policyholder when the policy reaches the end of its term. Compare "Endowment contract."

Return — An expected or required level of earnings from an investment activity.

Return of capital dividend — A dividend paid by a corporation not having sufficient earnings and profits, which is received tax-free by the shareholders (up to their basis in the stock); a return of capital dividend also decreases a stock's basis in a shareholder's hands.

Return of premium policy — In life insurance, a policy or rider that provides for payment of both the face value and total premiums paid (or accumulated cash value) by the insured. In effect, a return of premium policy or rider is permanent life insurance plus increasing term insurance.

Return on assets — A ratio indicating a company's operating effectiveness by showing how much it earns on each dollar invested in the assets of a business (at historical cost) and is computed as follows:

$$\text{Return on assets } = \frac{\text{Operating profit}}{\text{Total assets}}$$

Operating profit is income before taxes and interest.

Return on equity — A profitability ratio measuring the performance of a company by showing its earnings as a percentage of a stockholder's investment:

$$\text{Return on equity } = \frac{\text{Net income}}{\text{Average stockholder's equity}}$$

Return on invested capital (ROIC) — A rate of return for an investor based on the amount of dollars actually invested, not taking into consideration present value:

$$\frac{\text{Return on}}{\text{invested capital}} = \frac{\text{Selling price} - \text{Purchase price}}{\text{Amount invested}}$$

The amount invested is equal to the amount of margin deposit or total "out of pocket" dollars placed into a deal. Return on invested capital is typically used in commodity trading to compute a rate of return on a present position. Compare "Internal rate of return."

Return on investment (ROI) — See "Return on equity."

Return on operating assets — A measure of profitability indicating managerial effectiveness:

$$\text{Return on operating assets } = \frac{\text{Net operating income}}{\text{Operating assets}}$$

Operating assets are all assets presently being used to produce operating revenues, such as factories, machinery, plant, and administration facilities.

Return on total assets — See "Return on assets."

Revaluation clause — A provision in a lease calling for a periodic appraisal of rent and subsequent adjustments.

Revenue — The inflow of assets as a result of the earnings process; total earnings. Also see "Gross revenues."

Revenue agent's report — See "RAR."

Revenue bond — A municipal bond, which is usually unsecured and issued to finance a revenue-producing public project that will provide the necessary financial resources to fund repayment. For example, the building of a municipal airport or sports arena.

Revenue expenditure[1] — An expenditure that is expensed (i.e., deducted against income on an income statement) instead of being capitalized (placed on a balance sheet as an asset).

Revenue procedure (Rev. Proc.)[1] — An administrative pronouncement detailing practice and procedural requirements concerning taxpayers and Internal Revenue Service personnel.

Revenue ruling (Rev. Rul.)[1] — Generally, pronouncements issued by the Internal Revenue Service to indicate the IRS's position on certain specific circumstances relating to a taxable or nontaxable transaction.

Revenue stamps — Upon the sale of real property, state tax stamps affixed or rubber-stamped to an instrument of conveyance (i.e., a deed) to show the amount of tax (formerly a federal tax).

Reverse-annuity mortgage — (1) A way of liquidating part of the equity in a home by selling it and subsequently leasing it back from the new owner. The proceeds upon sale are invested in an annuity, which should provide enough for the monthly rental payment and some added income. Reverse annuity mortgages are typically designed to financially help parents, who sell their home to their children, lease it back, and receive additional income from the annuity; (2) a plan for older citizens to borrow against the equity of their homes and repay the loan upon subsequent sale or out of their estate.

Reverse leverage — As used in investing, the compounding of a loss as a result of a decline in value of a leveraged investment. For example, assume Berry purchases land for $100,000 by paying $10,000 down and borrowing $90,000. Should the land decline in value by a mere $6,000 (6 percent of its total value), then 60 percent ($6,000 / $10,000) of the original investment is showing a loss because of "reverse leverage." Also see "Leverage."

Reverse stock split — The calling in of all shares of a particular class of stock in exchange for a smaller number of shares by the issuing corporation. As a result, stockholder's equity remains the same, but the total number of shares outstanding declines.

Reversion — The right to possession (or any other interest) of the remainder of an estate for a transferor (grantor or testator) commencing upon the expiration or termination of such estate; the right of a transferor of real property to repossess it. For example, Bennington leases a home to Arnold. Arnold's interest in the property is a leasehold and

Bennington's interest is a reversion. Upon expiration or termination of the lease, Bennington has the right to possession (reversion). A reversionary interest also rests in the transferor's heirs. Compare "Remainder."

Reversionary interest — A future right of repossession of property currently held by another.

Reversionary trust — A trust whereby property reverts to the settlor upon termination or expiration of the trust. Also see "Clifford trust."

Revocable beneficiary — In a life insurance contract, the right of a policyholder to change the beneficiary by filing a written request with the insurer.

Revocable trust — A trust that reserves the right of the grantor to reacquire the trust's property. A revocable trust is not exempt from gift taxes or estate taxes upon the grantor's death, but may reduce administrative costs and burdens of ownership that will affect the beneficiary.

Revocation — The cancellation, annulment, withdrawal, or repeal of authority or a contract. The withdrawal of an offer by an offeror or the canceling of a professional license by a state board are two examples of a revocation.

Revolving charge account — A charge account offered by retail stores to customers that automatically provides extended payment terms. Typically, the credit limit and total number of months in which installments are to be made (usually 12 or 24) and interest rate (customarily 18 percent to 24 percent) are agreed to in advance by the store and customer. Purchases are billed in monthly installments with a minimum monthly payment normally required. As old loans are paid off, new loans can be made. For example, assume you have a credit limit of $500 and purchased some items to the extent of your limit on a revolving charge plan. You would likely be required to pay a minimum of $20 to $40 a month, which in turn will allow you to charge again up to the amount of your available credit.

Rider — (1) Generally, an addendum or amendment that is to be incorporated into a larger document without having to draft another document; (2) for insurance policies, any document attached to an insurance policy which modifies its coverage by adding or excluding specified conditions or modifying its benefits.

Right — See "Stock right."

Right of entry — The right of peaceful taking or repossession of land.

Right of first refusal — See "First right-of-refusal."

Right of rescission — (1) The right of an individual consumer to cancel a financing arrangement within three business days where the consumer's principal residence is used as security. A first mortgage, however, is not subject to such right; (2) a right to cancel an agreement.

Right of survivorship — A right of acquiring ownership to property by merely surviving other co-owners. Also see "Joint tenancy."

Right of way — A right to pass over another's land (easement) or a strip of land used as a railway or street.

Rights-off — In securities trading, a situation where a stock and its rights are trading separate and distinct from one another.

Rights-on — In securities transactions, stock that is trading with rights attached.

Right-to-work laws — State laws stating that employees are not required to join a union in order to acquire or retain a job.

Risk — (1) In investing, the probability that an actual rate of return for an investment will be different than its expected rate of return; (2) in insurance, the lack of precise predictability; the degree of hazard, danger, peril, or other exposure to loss of property insured; any moral, economic, or physical uncertainty of economic loss.

Risk assumption — The self-assumption of risk, either by setting aside enough funds to cover a loss or by liquidating other assets; not insured with outside insurance. Also see "Self- insurance."

Risk averse — The tendency of choosing investments with the least amount of risk, but with the highest return possible.

Risk avoidance — In making a decision between alternatives, choosing the alternative with the least amount of uncertainty.

Risk capital — See "Venture capital."

Risk evaluation — The assessment of one's exposure to economic loss, including the probability of loss and the size of potential loss, when making a decision as to what kind and how much insurance to purchase.

Risk inventory — The identification of all exposed risks. Insurable risks include personal risks, property risks, and liability risks. Personal risks can be covered by life insurance, health insurance, and disability insurance; property risks can be covered by homeowner's insurance, automobile insurance, and personal property insurance; liability risks can be protected by homeowner's insurance, automobile insurance, professional malpractice insurance, and comprehensive liability insurance.

Riskless rate of return — The expectation that an investment's rate of return is certain, such as the purchase of a Treasury bill or other federal government security.

Risk management — The execution of planning, organizing, and controlling risk to primarily protect one's assets and income from accidental loss. The three basic elements of risk management are risk inventory, risk evaluation, and selection of method, which includes risk avoidance and loss prevention, self-insurance, and risk transfer.

Risk retention — See "Risk assumption."

Risk-return trade-off — For an investor, the direct relationship between the degree of risk assumed and the expected rate of return that is attributable to taking such risk: for any investment, the higher an investment risk, the higher the expected rate of return, and vice versa.

Risk transfer — The purchase of an appropriate insurance policy for the purpose of financially protecting one's assets, income, or family member in case of an accident or injury.

Rolling stock — As used in the railroad industry, all property that runs on a railroad track, such as locomotives, railroad cars, and wheeled carts.

Rollover — The transfer of funds from one asset or investment to another. For example, the transfer of a lump-sum receipt from a company's retirement plan to an individual retirement account or the sale of a home and subsequent purchase of another within appropriate time limits are tax-free rollovers.

Rollover mortgage — A mortgage that may be exchanged for another.

Round lot — A generally accepted unit in trading securities. On the New York Stock Exchange, a round lot is equal to 100 shares of stock or a bond having $1,000 face value.

Round-trip commission — The commissions charged for both buying and selling an investment.

Royalty — Generally, a portion of profit reserved for the owner of property (or property rights) in allowing another to use such property, including payments made to an author for the privilege of publishing and selling his or her work, compensation to a patent holder for the use of his or her patent, and payments to a landowner for extracting natural resources from his or her land.

Rubber check — A check written without enough funds to cover it; a returned check because of insufficient funds in the drawer's account; worthless or NSF check.

Rule against perpetuities — Principle that a property interest is invalid unless it is created to vest (if at all) within a period prescribed by state statute, which is generally a life in being plus 21 years. The rule against perpetuities is especially influential in drafting instruments relating to trusts and estates.

Rule of 72 — A technique to estimate the number of years a sum of money, which is invested at a certain compound interest rate, will double. The rule of 72 is used by dividing 72 by the rate of interest earned. For example, an investment having a compound interest rate of 10 percent will double a sum of money in approximately 7.2 years (72/10), and an investment having a compound interest rate of 15 percent will double a sum of money in approximately 4.8 years (72/15).

Rule of 78 — As used in consumer loans, a method of apportioning interest throughout the life of the loan so that an appropriate principal balance can be found for any month. The number "78" is the sum-of-the digits from 1 to 12. For an example of how the rule of 78 is used, assume you borrowed $10,000 at 12 percent APR to be paid back in 24 months. Your monthly payment would be $471 and total interest to be paid back is $1,304 [($471 × 24) − $10,000)]. Further assume that you wish to pay the loan off on the 14th payment. The principal balance (not including credit life insurance or other charges) after making the 14th payment is computed as follows:

Total payments made (14 × $471)	$ 6,594
Less: Interest allocated*	− 1,065
Equals: Balance of principal paid	$ 5,529
Total principal	$10,000
Less: Balance paid	− 5,529
Equals: Balance of principal due	$ 4,471

$$* \frac{\text{Sum-of-the digits for 14 periods } (24 + 23 + 22\ldots11)}{\text{Sum-of-the digits for 24 periods}}$$

× Total interest owed [(24 × $471) − $10,000]

= Interest allocated

$$\therefore \frac{245}{300} \times (\$1,304) = \$1,065$$

Running with the land — Generally, a covenant or easement that passes with the land upon transfer in that such covenant or easement cannot be separated from the land.

S

Sabbatical — An extended paid vacation, originally extended to teaching professionals to provide time for travel, research, rest, or intellectual revival.

Safe deposit box — A box used for keeping important and valuable documents or items. A safe deposit box is ordinarily locked with two keys (one kept by the customer and one kept by the institution) as well as locked in the institution's vault.

Safety clause — In real estate sales, a clause in a listing preventing the avoidance of paying a commission upon the sale of real estate within a specified period after the expiration of a listing to a buyer previously provided by a broker.

Salary — The earnings of a person customarily paid periodically each year without regard to the number of hours worked or number of items sold.

Salary-reduction plan — A retirement arrangement for employees where a percentage of their salary is deducted and placed into either an individual retirement account or company sponsored deferred compensation plan. All qualified contributions made by an employee to a salary reduction plan will reduce his or her taxable income and accumulate with tax-free earnings. Thus, only upon receipt will such amounts be taxable.

Sale — A transaction consisting of a transfer of title to property from a seller to a buyer in exchange for payment or promise of payment.

Sale against the box — See "Short sale against the box."

Sale as is — See "As is."

Sale-leaseback — A financing arrangement where the seller of property obtains a lease on such property from the buyer.

Sale on approval — The sale of goods only upon buyer's approval, which may be inferred if goods are kept an unreasonable length of time for approval.

Sales agreement — See "Sales contract."

Sales-assessment ratio — In real estate, a ratio showing the percentage of assessed value to market value.

Sales contract — An agreement to sell goods, such as a contract for the sale of real estate. Also see "Conditional sales contract."

Sales finance company — A company specializing in the purchase of accounts receivable at a discount and subsequent collection.

Salesperson — A seller or agent of the seller of goods or services.

Sales tax — A state, and in some cases local, tax imposed on the sale of goods as an add-on percentage of the total selling price.

Sale with all faults — See "As is."

Salvage — Property that is no longer useful, but has scrap value.

Satisfaction — The fulfillment of an obligation, such as paying off a mortgage or the receipt of a judgment.

Savings — Cash being held, usually in an interest-bearing account, for emergencies or other contingencies, or for a certain objective; earnings not spent.

Savings account — An account in a financial institution that pays interest on money deposited, but such account does not carry check-writing privileges and, generally, no maintenance fees.

Savings and loan association — Any of several federally or state-chartered financial institutions that primarily make home mortgages, but are also allowed to make other loans. Savings and loan associations can obtain deposit insurance from the Federal Savings and Loan Insurance Corporation (FSLIC) or from a state agency. A federally chartered company is known as "Federal Savings and Loan Association," is supervised by the Federal Home Loan Bank Board, and is automatically insured by FSLIC. These financial institutions may provide savings accounts, checking accounts, certificates of deposit, individual retirement accounts, safe deposit boxes, among other services. A state-chartered savings and loan may also be known as a mutual loan association, cooperative bank, homestead-aid benefit association, building society, benefit society, or building and loan association.

Savings bank — A state-chartered financial institution that is primarily designed to make home mortgages and to accept savings, checking, and time deposits paying interest thereon. Mutual savings banks are directed by a self-perpetuating board but are regulated as to the amount of interest that can be paid, how funds are insured, and how funds are to be invested. Also see "Mutual savings bank" and "Stock savings bank."

Savings bank life insurance — A limited amount of life insurance available from a mutual savings bank in the states of New York, Massachusetts, and Connecticut on an over-the-counter basis.

Savings bond — Generally, a nontransferable, risk-free bond issued at a discount by the U.S. Treasury. Also see "Series EE bond," "Series HH bond," and "U.S. savings bonds."

Savings certificate — Generally, any of several certificates evidencing a deposit in a financial institution, such as a commercial bank, savings bank, or savings and loan.

Savings plan — A systematic method of accumulating capital by periodically depositing money into a savings account or mutual fund.

Scheduled payment — Each installment payment that is to be paid in accordance with a credit agreement, which specifies the date and amount due.

Scheduled property — Listed property that is covered by insurance. Scheduled personal property insurance is used to supplement a homeowner's or renter's policy in that certain valuable items, such as a diamond ring, may not be fully covered by a basic policy.

Schedule insurance policy — A list of perils covered in one insurance policy that normally requires separate policies. Only the listed hazards are covered from loss.

Scholarship — Generally, a tax-free grant of money given to a degree-seeking student to help pay for educational costs.

Scope of authority — The authority of an agent to represent his or her principal. An agent may legally represent a principal with actual authority and apparent or implied authority as well. Also see "Agent."

Scrip — (1) Generally, a document entitling the holder to redeem it for money, another asset, or a privilege; (2) temporary money; (3) a distribution by a corporation for a fractional share of stock because of a stock dividend, reorganization, or other management move. Such distribution may be sold or redeemed for a share of stock by remitting the appropriate amount of cash.

Scrip dividend — A corporate distribution that is essentially a promise to pay a cash or stock dividend at a future date; it may be in the form of a promissory note.

Sealed bid — A method of bidding for a contract or for the purchase of an item whereby each bid is submitted in a sealed envelope. All bids are opened at the same time with the most favorable one being accepted.

Seasoned issue — A securities issue that is widely held and trades well in the secondary market.

Seat — In securities trading, a membership on a securities exchange.

SEC — See "Securities and Exchange Commission."

Secondary beneficiary — Generally, a person who is to collect the proceeds of an insurance policy should the primary beneficiary be unable to do so. Both primary and secondary beneficiaries are designated in an insurance policy.

Secondary distributions — In securities trading, a sale of an abnormally large block of stock by a major stockholder.

Secondary financing — Obtaining a loan whose security interest is junior to that of another loan.

Secondary market — The trading of previously issued securities, as in an organized exchange or over-the-counter system. Compare "Primary market."

Secondary mortgage market — The buying and selling of existing mortgages, usually on a package basis, by banks, government agencies, insurance companies, and other lenders for the primary purpose of keeping an adequate supply of money for new loans.

Secondary offering — Generally, any offer to sell previously issued securities. Also see "Secondary distributions."

Secondhand — Used merchandise.

Second mortgage — A mortgage that ranks below a first mortgage (i.e., the second mortgage is junior to the first mortgage) in the order of legal priority. One property may have two or more simultaneous mortgages as liens.

Section 8 housing — A National Housing Act provision that enabled investors to subsidize the construction of low-income housing. In return, these investors received various tax benefits, favorable financing, and government-subsidized rents.

Section 38 property — Tangible trade or business property that qualifies for an investment tax credit. Also see "Investment tax credit."

Section 79 group life insurance plans — Under current tax law, an employer can pay premiums for group term life insurance up to $50,000 of coverage per employee and each employee will receive such fringe benefit tax-free. All amounts of coverage in excess of $50,000, however, will be included in an employee's taxable income at rates established by the Treasury Department.

Section 401(k) plan — See "Cash or deferred arrangement."

Section 403(b) plan — A tax-deferred retirement plan described in the Internal Revenue Code pertaining to employees of nonprofit organizations.

Section 1231 assets — Generally, depreciable business-use assets and land used in a trade or business that are held the required long-term capital gain holding period. Also included as section 1231 assets are certain livestock, timber, coal, and unharvested crops.

Section 1245 property — Depreciable property other than real estate (e.g., automobiles, equipment, trucks, office furniture, machinery, and office equipment) used in a trade or business.

Section 1250 property — Depreciable real estate (buildings and their structual components used in a trade or business).

Secured bonds — Bonds which are backed by identifiable assets pledged as collateral for repayment of principal and interest. Should secured bonds default, then the bondholders would have a priority claim against such assets over unsecured bondholders.

Secured loan — A loan that has property pledged or mortgaged as collateral to secure repayment; e.g., a loan for which a lender holds stocks as collateral.

Secured note — A promissory note that has pledged or mortgaged property to assure repayment.

Secured party — A creditor, seller, employer, etc., who holds a security interest to assure performance.

Securities — Generally, instruments evidencing debt, ownership interests in a business, or the privilege of buying or selling ownership interests. Common stocks, preferred stocks, bonds, convertible instruments, Treasury bills, certificates of deposit, warrants, options, banker's acceptances, investment contracts, voting trust certificates, etc. are among the many different kinds of securities.

Securities Act of 1933 — Federal legislation whose principal purpose is to provide investors with full and fair disclosure of all material information regarding the initial issuance of securities to be sold to the general public. The Securities Act of 1933 requires the filing of a registration statement with the Securities and Exchange Commission before a public sale or offer to sell securities across state lines (or through the mail), requires providing a prospectus to investors, and provides criminal and civil liabilities for failure of proper compliance.

Securities and Exchange Commission (SEC) — A federal agency with broad powers to enforce federal laws regarding the registration, offering, and sale of securities, including securities exchanges, stockbrokers, dealers, and investment advisers.

Securities Exchange Act of 1934 — Federal legislation whose principal purpose is to regulate the trading of subsequently issued securities. Generally, the objectives of the act are to regulate securities exchanges, securities traded in interstate commerce, brokers, dealers, credit used in purchasing securities, and insider's information, and to require the availability of adequate information.

Securities Investor Protection Corporation (SIPC) — A nonprofit corporation created by federal legislation that insures customers' cash and securities of brokers and dealers who are insolvent.

Securities market — The buying and selling of securities either on an exchange or over-the-counter.

Security — (1) Free from risk of loss; (2) pledged or hypothecated property by a borrower to provide additional protection on a loan; (3) a document evidencing ownership, an obligation, or a privilege to buy or sell an ownership interest or obligation. Also see "Securities."

Security agreement — A written agreement between a creditor and debtor which ultimately provides a security interest in collateral property for the benefit of the creditor. A security agreement may be perfected by either taking possession of the collateral or by properly filing the appropriate statements in public records. If a debtor fails to abide by the terms of a security agreement, the property may be sold in order to satisfy the debt for which the security interest was provided.

Security analysis — A rational method of selecting securities by examining material aspects of a prospective investee corporation, such as its financial statements, quality of management, economic forecasts, and projected earnings. Also see "Fundamental analysis."

Security deposit — A deposit made by a tenant or lessee of rental property to secure payment or performance by such tenant or lessee according to the terms of the rental agreement. Security deposits may also cover any damages other than those caused by ordinary wear and tear.

Security interest — The interest of a secured party (i.e., a creditor) in property used as collateral. Also see "Security agreement."

Self-amortizing loan — Any loan requiring payments that consist of both principal and interest.

Self-employed — An individual who is not listed on another's payroll as an employee. Instead, a self-employed individual typically works in his or her own place, with his or her own equipment, and under his or her own schedule. Generally, doctors, dentists, accountants, lawyers, writers, architects, farmers, consultants, and others in similar professions who work alone or in a partnership are considered self-employed. Also see "Independent contractor."

Self-employed retirement plan — See "Keogh plan."

Self-employment tax — Social Security tax levied on self-employed individuals (Schedule 1040 SE).

Self-insurance — The practice of setting aside funds to meet losses instead of obtaining outside insurance coverage.

Self-liquidating — A loan that will pay for itself over time by investing the funds in a profitable undertaking.

Seller's market — An expression meaning that prices are rising and goods are selling at a fairly rapid pace.

Selling agent — In real estate sales, the agent who obtains a buyer, as opposed to a listing agent who obtains the listing. A selling agent and listing agent can be the same individual.

Selling expenses — The expenses incurred in selling an item. Selling expenses for a tax-shelter investment would include the costs of promoting and marketing the investment to prospective buyers. Selling expenses of a home might include commissions paid, advertising costs, transfer and stamp taxes, legal and recording fees, and points. Generally, selling expenses reduce the amount realized from the sale.

Selling short — The selling of securities or other investments that the seller does not own. A typical example would be an investor who borrows stock from a broker to sell in hopes that the price of such stock will decline. If the price does decline, then the investor simply purchases the stock at a lower price and repays the stock to the broker. When such stock was sold, the investor was "short" that particular investment, and when the stock was actually purchased, the short sale was "covered." Also see "Short sale against the box." In commodities trading, a short sale is a promise to deliver a particular commodity by a certain date for a specified price. (Usually, such promises are closed-out before the date of delivery.)

Separate property — Property owned by a married individual in which his or her spouse has no legal ownership interest. Generally, in a community property state, all properties individually owned prior to marriage or received after marriage through gift or inheritance are automatically deemed to be separate property.

Serial bond — Bonds issued simultaneously but are redeemable at different times in the future. A serial bond issue may specify groups of bonds that fall due at different times or the redemption process may select bonds at random in determining which lot will be redeemed at each specified redemption point.

Series E bond — U.S. government savings bond sold at a discount before 1980. The bond, which increases in value, may be redeemed at stated intervals. Interest is deferred until redemption, unless the bond is exchanged for a Series HH bond. The maximum amount of time a Series E bond (issued between May 1, 1941, and April 30, 1952) can be held is 40 years (final maturity date). Bonds issued between May 1, 1952, and November 30, 1965, have a 30-year maturity. Generally, income from these bonds is taxable upon redemption, although a cash basis taxpayer may elect to include in taxable income the annual increment of redemption value.

Series EE bond — U.S. government savings bond issued after 1979 and sold at a discount from face value, which ranges from $50 to $10,000. The bond may be redeemed at stated intervals, that continually increase in value, and interest is deferred until redemption. No interest is actually paid; thus, income from these bonds is taxable upon redemption, although a cash basis taxpayer may elect to include in taxable income the annual increment of redemption value. A Series EE bond is not transferable.

Series HH bond — U.S. government savings bond which pays semiannual interest to its registered owner. The interest receipts are taxable when received. After 1981, a Series HH bond can only be obtained by exchanging a Series EE or Series E bond. Thus, the deferred interest from a previous savings bond can continue to be deferred until redemption of the Series HH bond.

Service charge — An expense charged by a business to a customer for handling, carrying, processing, investigating, fixing, or other similar service generally arising in the ordinary course of business. A bank, for example, levies a service charge on a checking account as a cost of maintaining the service of providing checking privileges to its customer.

Service contract — A written agreement specifying the conditions of repairing or maintaining a product (typically a consumer product) over a limited period of time.

Service industry — All businesses and professions that do not produce goods, such as accounting, transportation, retail trade, law, government, health services, banking, lodging, education, and religion.

Service life — The period of time an item is to be used by a particular person or business. As a general rule, the service life of an item, say an automobile, is less than its useful life. Thus, an individual may intend to use a vehicle only 2 years rather than over its whole useful life, which may be estimated to be 8 years.

Servicemen's Group Life Insurance — Life insurance protection (up to $20,000) via private insurers that is automatically available to each person in the military service.

Service-type benefit — Medical benefits provided by health insurance specifying the maximum benefit in covering the cost of itemized medical services, such as hospital room and board, customary hospital services and supplies, and surgical and nonsurgical procedures, as opposed to direct reimbursement.

Service well — An oil well drilled to increase production in an oil field already having proven reserves.

Servient tenement — In real estate, a parcel burdened by an easement for the benefit of the dominant tenement.

Settlement — An adjustment, termination, or reconciliation between two or more persons in a business proceeding, such as the closing of a sale of a home or a divorce proceeding.

Settlement costs — Incidental fees paid upon the closing of a sale or other settlement. For the purchase of a home, settlement costs commonly include such items as revenue stamps, tax certificate, recording fee, transfer tax, survey fee, platting fee, title examination costs, document preparation costs, miscellaneous settlement fees, title insurance, past due taxes, appraisal fees, cost of credit reports, and notary fees. Such settlement costs paid upon the sale of real property are also known as "closing costs."

Settlement date — In securities transactions, the date payment is made or securities are delivered, which normally occurs five business days after the trade date. The date payment is received for the sale of securities (usually the settlement date) determines when a gain is recognized, but for a securities transaction resulting in a loss, the trade date determines when it is recognized.

Settlement options — In life insurance, optional methods of distributing the proceeds of a life insurance policy to a beneficiary, which typically include lump-sum, specified installments, installments over specified period, interest-only payments, and life annuity.

Settlement statement — In the sale of real estate, a statement prepared by a lender, broker, or escrow agent showing an itemized breakdown of costs pertaining to such sale. A separate settlement statement is prepared for both buyer and seller.

Settlor — A person who creates a trust.

Severance pay — Payment made to an employee upon termination of employment beyond the amount of wages, salary, or commissions actually earned.

Severance tax — A tax levied upon the extraction of natural resources from the ground.

Sham — An transaction or arrangement lacking substance that is disregarded for tax purposes.

Shared-appreciation mortgage (SAM) — A creative financing method for real estate purchases where a mortgage lender shares in the value appreciation of the property upon sale or after a specified period of time. Shared appreciation mortgages are typically used during periods of high interest rates in that the interest rate charged by a lender for these loans is lower than for most other mortgages.

Shared-equity mortgage — A three-party mortgage consisting of the buyer, a co-owner, and the lender, whereby the co-owner (typically a parent to a first-time home buyer) participates in real estate ownership as an investor by receiving value appreciation upon sale, making partial mortgage payments, receiving rent, and enjoying tax benefits, such as depreciation and interest deductions. Generally, costs such as mortgage payments, taxes, and insurance are split between the co-owner-investor and the co-owner-resident, but the co-owner-resident must pay rent to the investor (parent) for use of the latter's half ownership in the property.

Share drafts — Negotiable instruments offered by credit unions to their members to be used in the same manner as checks. A share draft account in a credit union is similar to a checking account in a commercial bank.

Shareholder — Stockholder of a corporation.

Share value — In a money market mutual fund, the constant value of a share of the fund, which is $1.00.

Short — See "Short position."

Short interest — The number of shares sold short at a given time.

Short position — (1) In commodities trading, the selling of a contract to deliver a particular commodity on a certain date at a specified price; (2) in stock trading, the selling of borrowed stock (selling short), which is to be delivered at a later date. Any investor in a short position is anticipating a decline in price.

Short sale — See "Selling short."

Short sale against the box — In securities trading, the engagement of a short sale and the simultaneous holding of underlying securities.

For income tax purposes, the closing of a short sale will result in a long-term capital gain or loss only if the securities subject to the short sale were held for the required long-term holding period prior to the date of executing the short sale. Otherwise, a short-term capital gain or loss will result. Also see "Selling short."

Short-swing profits — Profits obtained by a corporate insider within six months of receipt of stock.

Short term — (1) For income tax purposes, investments held for exactly 6 months or less (prior to 1988); (2) in general, 12 months or less (e.g., short-term debt is due within 12 months). Compare "Long-term."

Short-term capital gain — For income tax purposes, a gain typically resulting from selling an investment held for a period less than that required for long-term capital gain treatment. After all netting procedures have been made and if the net result is a short-term capital gain, then this amount is fully included in taxable income. Also see "Short term."

Short-term capital loss — For income tax purposes, a loss usually resulting from selling investment property, which is held for a period less than that required for long-term capital loss treatment. Also see "Short term."

Short-term disability income coverage — Disability insurance that pays benefits for a disability covered under the plan up to a maximum of two years.

Short-term government securities — Any security issued by the U.S. Treasury due within 12 months (i.e., Treasury bills).

Short-term lease — Generally, a lease covering a period of less than 5 years (10 years in some states).

Short-term living trust — See "Clifford trust."

Shut-in royalty — A royalty paid for the purpose of holding a lease on an oil field having proven reserves of oil or gas, but is not presently in production.

Sick leave — A period of leave granted by an employer to an employee as a result of sickness or injury. Sick leave may or may not be given with pay, but seniority and other benefits are not lost.

Sight draft — A negotiable instrument payable on demand, such as a bill of exchange that is payable at sight.

Signature card — A card signed by a customer and kept on file by a financial institution (e.g., a bank) for the purpose of comparing signatures on checks and other documents.

Signed, sealed, and delivered — Generally indicating that everything necessary has been done to make a settlement, convey property, close a deal, etc.

Silent partner — A partner in a business establishment who shares in profits and losses, but does not take an active part in management of the day-to-day affairs.

Silver certificate — Printed money formerly issued by the U.S. Treasury in exchange for silver coins and circulated as currency. Silver certificates were redeemable in silver, but have since been taken out of circulation and replaced by federal reserve notes.

Simple capital structure — A corporation's stockholder's equity that consists of only common stock and no potentially dilutive securities.

Simple interest — Interest computed on principal only and without compounding. Thus, a simple interest loan does not accrue interest on itself, but only on the amount of principal.

Simple trust — A trust which distributes all income and does not have the authority to make charitable contributions.

Simplified employee pension (SEP) — A qualified pension plan set up by an employer, generally consisting of an individual retirement account for each employee that is modified to permit employer contributions subject to the restrictions of a corporate defined-contribution plan. One unusual feature of a simplified employee pension plan is that all rights to such contributions are immediately 100 percent vested in the employee, which allows the employee to withdraw amounts in the plan at any time (subject to the penalties of early withdrawal in an individual retirement account). A SEP is simplified in that administrative duties and paperwork are reduced when compared to other qualified retirement plans.

Simultaneous death clause — Generally, a provision in a will specifying the disposition of property when there is no sufficient evidence concerning the priority of death of two or more persons.

Sinecure — A job or office requiring no work or duties but with regular compensation.

Single — An unmarried individual; a filing status for income tax purposes.

Single life annuity — An annuity in which payments are contingent only on the life of the annuitant.

Single payment loan — A loan that is to be repaid in one lump sum.

Single-premium annuity — An annuity paid with a one lump-sum payment. Annuity payments may begin after a short period of time or when the annuitant reaches a certain age (e.g., at age 65 when a person is expected to retire).

Single-premium life policy — Generally, a life insurance contract paid for with one lump-sum payment.

Single-step income statement — An income statement that does not classify the different types of revenues and expenses.

Sinking fund — Money that is set aside for the purpose of redeeming bonds, preferred stock (for a corporation), or paying off promissory notes.

Slander — The making of untrue statements, orally, which damage or cause injury to another's reputation, profession, business, employment, etc.

Slant drilling — The drilling for oil and gas in proven reserves from an adjacent property.

Slush fund — Money set aside for illegal purposes.

Small Claims Court — An informal court designed to provide expeditious and inexpensive settlements for cases dealing with amounts up to a statutory limit (such as $2,000). Generally, attorneys are not allowed to practice before the court unless a party to the action.

Smart-money — (1) A wise investment; (2) punitive damages awarded to a plaintiff.

Smoke damage coverage — In fire insurance, an extended coverage endorsement for sudden and accidental damage from smoke, but not from a fireplace.

Social insurance — Insurance that is generally funded, sponsored, or administered by a government agency for the purpose of meeting certain economic standards for a society. Generally, eligibility depends upon contributions to the plan without proving need, but benefits are determined by law. The most widely known examples of social insurance are social security and workers' compensation.

Socialized medicine — Health care paid for by the government and provided to the public.

Social security — Most commonly, Old-Age, Survivors, Disability, and Health Insurance (OASDHI), where employers, employees, and self-employed individuals contribute to a special trust fund for the purpose of providing supplemental income to an individual (or survivors) whose earnings have ceased because of death, disability, or retirement. Reduced benefits may begin at age 62 (if elected), but full benefits may begin at age 65. Also see "Old-Age, Survivors, Disability, and Health Insurance (OASDHI)" and "Quarters of coverage." In general, social security also includes other types of social insurance, such as Supplementary Security Income and Aid to Families with Dependent Children. Social Security was created by federal legislation under the Social Security Act of 1935.

Social security integration — The coordination of social security benefits and other retirement benefits (from private sources).

Social Security tax — A tax on an employee's earnings paid by both employees and employers to fund social security benefits. Self-employed individuals likewise pay the tax. Social security taxes are also known as FICA (Federal Insurance Contribution Act) and are deducted from compensation for employees.

Soft dollars — That portion of amounts invested in a tax shelter which is recouped by tax savings.

Soft market — Generally, a market where prices are declining because of insufficient demand to meet the quantity supplied.

Sole proprietorship — A form of business organization where one person owns all assets and is personally obligated for all liabilities of the business.

Solvency — One's financial ability to pay debts as they become due.

Source and use of funds statement — See "Statement of changes in financial position."

Source document — The original document used in a financial transaction, such as an invoice, bill of lading, or check.

Special assessment — Typically, property tax levied on real property because of direct benefits received on the property, such as sidewalks and curbs built by the city in front of a person's residence.

Special class policy — In life insurance, a rated policy subject to a higher than standard premium because of pilot status or condition of health.

Special executor — An executor whose power is limited to a particular portion of a decedent's estate.

Special form policy (HO-3) — See "Homeowner's insurance policy."

Specialist — (1) In general, anyone who specializes in a certain area of a profession, such as a heart surgeon or brain surgeon in medicine; (2) a member of a stock exchange who specializes in the trading in one or a few stocks.

Special partnership — A partnership formed for the purpose of executing one transaction or a limited number of transactions. See "Joint venture."

Special purpose health insurance — Limited health insurance that either pays a flat sum for accidents causing injury or disability or amount per day while hospitalized because of an accident.

Special purpose life insurance — Limited life insurance coverage designed to provide benefits only for loss of life as a result of a speci fied hazard (e.g., cancer insurance) or other specified occurrence (e.g., while flying on an airline jet).

Specialty fund — A mutual or closed-end fund that concentrates its holdings in one particular industry, group of closely related industries, or geographic location, such as a gold fund or energy fund.

Special-use valuation — An election available to an executor of a decedent's estate for estate tax purposes in valuing real estate at its current-use value rather than its potentially highest fair market value. For example, assume a farmer leaves a large farm which is located near a growing city. For purposes determining the taxable estate, the executor can use the value of the property as a farm, rather than as property available for development, which in the latter case would certainly increase its value.

Specie — Coins made of precious metal, such as gold and silver coins.

Specific bequest — A testamentary gift of a particular item of personal property that is distinguishable from all other items.

Specific performance — The actual performance by a party to a contract as remedy for breach, rather than making payment for damages.

Speculation — The buying or selling of risky investments with the intent of receiving unusually high profits or quick profits as a result of a rise or decline in value.

Speculative investment — Any investment that carries a high risk of loss.

Speculative risk — The degree of uncertainty concerning the outcome of an investment. Treasury bills have virtually no speculative risk compared to an investment in venture capital, which has high speculative risk.

Spendthrift trust — A trust created to provide income to a beneficiary, while protecting the trust's assets from the beneficiary and his or her creditors. The primary effect is to keep a beneficiary from spending all of the money placed in trust for his or her benefit.

Spin-off dividend — A dividend paid by a corporation in shares of stock other than its own.

Split — See "Stock split."

Split-dollar insurance — A manner of purchasing permanent life insurance where a single contract is purchased by an employer or other person (e.g., a parent) on the life of an insured (an employee, son, daughter, etc.). The insured and another party will pay the premiums. The insured agrees to pay the entire first-year premium and all other premiums in subsequent years, which are reduced by policy dividends and contributions made by the purchaser (employer or parent). The amount paid by an employer or parent is equal to the increase in cash value (i.e., it is more like an investment to them). When such policy matures, is discontinued, or otherwise terminated, the policy's cash value is returned to the purchaser (employer or parent); the beneficiary receives the policy's face value upon the death of the insured. Split-dollar life insurance has been approved in most states and is made effective by attaching a special endorsement (split-dollar endorsement) to the policy.

Split financing — A financing technique used by developers to obtain the maximum amount of debt financing in a real estate project. One method of split financing is to split a parcel into separate leasehold and fee interests and finance each separately. An example of this would be where a lender buys land from a developer and leases the land back to the same developer over an extended period of time (e.g., 80 years). The lender also makes a leasehold mortgage loan for the cost of constructing the building. In this manner, the developer-owner is able to deduct, for income tax purposes, all rental payments made for the use of land (rather than the usual interest payments attributable to the financing of land) and depreciation on the building, which is not available for land.

Split-life insurance — A specialized type of life insurance product that basically consists of two components: a deferred annuity contract and a yearly renewable term insurance policy. The distinguishing features of split-life insurance are: (1) it is possible to use the cash value from the annuity portion after a certain period of time without losing life insurance protection, which is not available in a whole life contract without termination or reduction, and (2) the life insurance and annuity components may be written on the lives of two separate individuals. Split-life contracts are not permitted in all states because of some involved legal and tax questions.

Split order — In securities trading, an order directing a broker to buy or sell a particular stock in certain quantities for two or more different prices. For example, sell 500 shares of XYZ Corporation for $25 per share, and sell 400 shares of XYZ for $26 per share.

Spot price — The current cash selling price of a commodity for immediate delivery ("on the spot") at a certain market location.

Spot trading — The cash trading of commodities for immediate delivery, as opposed to trading in futures contracts.

Spouse — A person's husband or wife.

Spousal IRA — A individual retirement account for a nonworking spouse.

Spray trust — See "Sprinkling trust."

Spread — (1) Generally in securities and commodities trading, the difference between the bid and ask price; (2) for bonds, the difference in yields of bonds with different grades; (3) for listed call options, two or more different call options of the same underlying security with different strike prices or maturity dates or both.

Sprinkling trust — A trust providing the trustee a discretionary power to distribute any amount of income to various beneficiaries and to accumulate any undistributed income.

Spudding in — The initial drilling stage for oil and gas.

Square foot cost — A measure of the value of a building or land in terms of one square foot.

Squatter — An individual who settles on another person's land without authority.

Stale check — A check that has been outstanding over an unreasonably long period (usually more than 6 months), whereby the bank is not obligated to pay on it. Generally, however, banks will honor a stale check and adjust a customer's account accordingly.

Standard & Poor's — A widely followed broad-based financial publisher primarily specializing in stocks and bonds of specific companies and industries. Standard & Poor's also publishes well-known and highly regarded stock indexes, such as the S&P 500 Stock Index.

Standard mortgage clause — An endorsement to a fire insurance policy constituting a separate arrangement between the lender and the insurance company, whereby the lender is given legal rights for indemnity in case of the occurrence of a covered peril.

Standard of care — The degree of care that should be exercised by a reasonably prudent individual under similar circumstances.

Standard of living — An economist's concept with regard to possessing those items which are considered essential, given a family's level of income, geographic location, and period of time.

Standby commitment — A loan commitment that provides for the issuance of a short-term loan in the event permanent financing is unavailable. A loan commitment fee is customarily charged by the lender for this service.

Standing loan — An interest-payments-only loan to be paid over the loan's term with principal due in full at maturity.

Standing timber — All uncut trees on a certain piece of property.

Start-up costs — All ordinary and necessary expenditures made before the start of any business activity in a new venture.

State bank — A commercial bank chartered in the state in which it is located rather than being chartered by the federal government. All "national banks" are federally chartered.

State bonds — See "Municipal bond."

Stated interest rate — (1) An interest rate promulgated by a lending institution, which may be slightly different when compounded other than annually, such as interest compounding daily or quarterly; (2) the coupon rate of a bond from which all interest payments are computed. For example, a bond with a face value of $1,000 and a stated interest rate of 12 percent will pay $120 in interest per year. The effective rate or yield to maturity, however, is typically different. Also see "Effective interest rate" and "Yield to maturity."

Stated value — For no-par stock, an arbitrary amount set by the board of directors establishing the legal capital of a corporation. Stated value is not the same as fair market value.

Statement of account — An informal financial document summarizing business activity between a buyer and seller, a customer and bank, or a debtor and creditor, such as (1) a statement sent to a customer of a retail store showing purchases, payments, and balance due, (2) a bank statement summarizing checks that have cleared and deposits received by the bank and the cash balance, or (3) a statement from a credit card company showing similar information.

Statement of changes in financial position — A formal financial statement showing the sources and uses of a corporation's funds.

Statement of changes in stockholder's equity — A formal financial statement showing all changes in stockholder's equity. Basically, the statement will show an increase in stockholder's equity by the amount of net income earned and new stock issued and show a decrease by the amount of dividends declared, net loss experienced, and any other adjustments made in a firm's stockholder's equity accounts.

Statement of financial position — See "Balance sheet."

Statement of retained earnings — A formal financial statement reconciling the balances of retained earnings on the two most recent balance sheets.

Statute of frauds — State law requiring that certain contracts must be in writing to be enforceable. For example, all contracts dealing with the sale of real estate must be written.

Statute of limitations — Law requiring that a certain action must be made within a specified period of time. For federal tax purposes, the statute of limitations limits action, generally, to a three-year period from the date a return was filed. If an inadvertent omission was made by a taxpayer for an amount greater than 25 percent of gross income, then the statute of limitations carries a duration of six years. If a taxpayer intended to file a false return, then there is no time limit.

Statutory law — Public law created by legislative acts rather than by tradition, or judicial or administrative opinions.

Statutory lien — An involuntary lien arising by force of statutory law rather than by contract, such as a tax lien.

Step-out well — In oil and gas drilling, a well drilled on the outskirts of a proven field for the purpose of determining the extent of the reserves.

Step-up lease — A lease agreement calling for increased rents over specified intervals.

Stipend — A salary paid to clergymen or graduate students who are teaching.

Stock — A certificate representing ownership in a corporation.

Stock-bonus plan — An employer's retirement plan established to provide benefits in a manner similar to a profit-sharing plan, except that contributions are not necessarily contingent upon profits, and distributions may be made with the employer's stock.

Stockbroker — A person who is licensed to buy and sell stocks at the request of another; an agent of buyers and sellers of securities. A stockbroker is also known as an "account executive."

Stock cooperative — A corporate ownership arrangement of an apartment where only shareholders of the corporation have the right to occupy a dwelling unit.

Stock dividend — A corporate distribution consisting of the corporation's own stock. If the dividend is only common on common, then no tax consequence will result, but the basis of each share will be reduced proportionally.

Stock exchange — A place where stock and other securities are traded.

Stockholder's equity — The owner's claim in a corporation's total assets.

Stockholder's report — See "Annual report."

Stock insurance company — An insurance company organized for profit and whose shares of stock are publicly held as opposed to a mutual insurance company whose assets are owned by its policyholders. In addition, a stock insurance company pays a dividend to its shareholders; a mutual insurance company pays dividends to its policyholders.

Stock market — In general, the overall trading of stocks in organized exchanges and over-the-counter.

Stock option — Generally, an option to purchase or sell stock for a specified price within a certain period of time. Also see "Call," "Incentive stock options," "Put," and "Stock option plan."

Stock option plan — An employee benefit plan whereby a corporation gives its employees options to purchase its stock for a reduced price within a specified time. Also see "Incentive stock options."

Stock purchase plan — An employee benefit plan whereby employees are allowed to directly purchase their employer's stock.

Stock redemption — The purchase of stock by a corporation pursuant to a complete or partial liquidation of such stock.

Stock right — A privilege to purchase stock from a corporation generally at a price less than the stock's current market value. Stock rights (i.e., subscription rights) are customarily issued by a corporation to its existing shareholders when it wishes to sell additional shares of stock. Such rights have limited duration and may be sold to other investors. Also see "Preemptive right."

Stock savings bank — A savings bank owned by its stockholders, rather than by depositors as in a mutual savings bank. Also see "Savings bank."

Stock split — A method used by a corporation of increasing its number of shares outstanding by exchanging a certain number of new shares for old shares and adjusting the par values or stated values accordingly. Because of a stock split, the market price per share will automatically drop. For example, assume Rogers has 200 shares of ABC stock (selling at $120 per share) and the company executes a 2-for-1 stock split. Rogers now owns 400 shares of the same stock and her basis per share as well as the par value per share have been cut in half. The selling price after the split will usually be above one-half of its former value (e.g., $61\frac{1}{2}$). One primary objective of a stock split is to reduce its price per share to allow it to be more widely traded and thereby result in a higher overall market value.

Stock subscription — An agreement between a prospective stock purchaser and the issuing corporation to purchase a certain number of shares of stock.

Stock warrant — See "Warrant."

Stop-limit order — In securities trading, a stop order to be executed for a price within a specified limit. That is, once the order is activated, such stock cannot be bought for a price above the limit or sold below the limit. Also see "Limit order" and "Stop order."

Stop-loss order — In securities trading, a special order given to a stockbroker to sell a particular stock when its market price reaches or falls below a certain level. Stop-loss orders are a convenient way to protect an investor from a sudden drop in a stock's price.

Stop order — In securities trading, a special buy or sell order given to a stockbroker instructing him or her to trade accordingly once a certain price has been reached for that particular stock. That is, once a specified price is reached, a stop order becomes a market order. For example, Sell 300 XYZ 20 STOP means that if XYZ's price reaches 20 or below, then sell 300 shares of XYZ immediately at the best available price; Buy 400 XYZ 25 STOP means that if XYZ's price reaches 25 or higher, then buy 400 shares immediately at the best available price.

Stop-payment order — An order made by a bank's customer (drawer) instructing the bank (drawee) not to make payment on a certain check.

Straddle — The acquisition of two particular investments which essentially places the holder in a position that is free from the risk of changing prices. For example, assume Moore purchased 1,000 shares of EFG stock five years ago for $10 per share. Further assume that Moore presently purchases 10 put options to sell all his stock any time within the next six months at the current market price of $35 per share. In effect, Moore has engaged in a straddle because he no longer has any economic risk: If EFG's price declines, then he can execute the option to sell at the current market price of $35 per share (resulting in no loss), and if the price moves up, then he can simply allow the puts to expire and enjoy a higher value for his stock. The simultaneous holding of a put and call option on the same stock is a common straddle in options. In commodity positions a straddle may consist of holding a commodity future and sale of another commodity future (same commodity) with different expiration dates. Also see "Tax straddle."

Straight annuities — See "Life annuity."

Straight bankruptcy — See "Chapter 13 (wage earners)."

Straight deductible — In insurance, a stated dollar amount or a percentage of a loss that always reduces the amount of insurance benefits.

Straight lease — An ordinary lease calling for a fixed amount to be paid over the term of the lease.

Straight life annuity — See "Life annuity."

Straight life insurance — See "Ordinary life insurance."

Straight-line depreciation — A method of recovering the cost of an asset by expensing an equal portion of its cost over the life of the property. For example, depreciable property costing $10,000 and having a life of five years will provide $2,000 of depreciation expense per year using straight-line depreciation.

Straight-line method — As used in the amortization of a bond discount or premium, a method ratably amortizing such discount or premium each year.

Straight term mortgage — A mortgage calling for payment of principal in one lump sum at maturity.

Strap — As used for listed options, a position consisting of a call option and a long straddle on the same underlying security.

Straw man — A person who transacts for another party as an agent and takes title to conceal such party's identity in the transaction.

Stream of returns — Reasonably expected amounts of money flowing from an investment, which are either fixed as in an annuity income or bond interest or are mixed as in dividend income or income from a business.

Street name securities — Securities owned by a customer but held in the broker's name.

Strict liability — Generally, a legal concept applied by the courts where certain persons are automatically held liable for damages caused by the manufacture or sale of any defective or hazardous product or cause under special circumstances, such as the keeping of wild animals; liability-regardless-of-fault doctrine.

Strike price — The price at which a call or put option can be exercised.

Strip — As used for listed options, a position consisting of a put option and a long straddle on the same underlying security.

Stripper well — An oil well producing low quantities from an old oil field.

Student Loan Marketing Association (Sallie Mae) — A federally chartered private corporation created for the purpose of providing a secondary market for government student loans.

Subchapter S corporation — A corporation formed under state law and filed with the Internal Revenue Service to be taxed under special provisions, which are very restrictive and are somewhat similar in nature to partnership taxation.

Subcontractor — One who performs under a general contractor or other subcontractor as an independent party, such as a plumber or electrical contractor.

Subdivision — Generally, a residential development resulting from the division of a single tract or parcel of land into smaller lots sold separately and subject to local regulations.

"Subject to" clause — A clause in a deed conveying real property stating that the grantee takes title to such property "subject to" any existing mortgages rather than assuming such mortgages. The original mortgagor remains primarily liable for satisfying the debt.

Sublease — A lease within a lease in that the lessee of the original lease becomes a lessor of the sublease.

Sublet — See "Sublease."

Subordinated debenture — A bond issued on the general credit of the corporation and is subordinated in priority of payment to other debentures, general creditors, and secured bonds.

Subordination agreement — An agreement which states that a priority interest of one party in real estate is higher than that of another party.

Subordination clause — A clause in a junior mortgage stating that an existing mortgage may retain its position of priority upon renewal.

Subrogation clause — In property insurance, a clause allowing the insurer the right to recovery from third parties who are legally liable for loss.

Subscribe — To write at the end of a contract; to sign a document.

Subscription contract — Generally, a contract binding a person to buy, such as a contract to buy securities.

Subscription right — A security giving its holder the privilege of purchasing new securities at a certain price, usually below market value, within a stated period of time.

Subscription service — A publisher of periodically updated financial information on specific companies and industries or taxes.

Subsidiary — A corporation under the control of another corporation.

Subsidy — A grant of money for the purpose of assisting toward a desirable cause.

Subsistence — Support in order to live.

Succession — In real estate, the taking of property by will or inheritance rather than by any other form of acquisition.

Suicide clause — A clause in a life insurance policy which states that in the event of an insured's suicide within a specified period of time (customarily one or two years from the date of issue), then only the amount of premiums received by the insurer will be paid to the beneficiary.

Suitability rule — A rule to be applied to investors in a limited partnership regarding their financial strength in accordance with their earnings and net worth.

Sum-of-the-years' digits method of depreciation — An accelerated method of depreciation that is computed by adding up the number of years in an asset's useful life (e.g., $1 + 2 + 3 + 4 \ldots$) and dividing the sum into the asset's useful life for year one, dividing the sum into the asset's useful life minus 1 for year two, dividing the sum into the asset's useful life minus 2 for year three, etc., and multiplying each year's fraction by the asset's cost. For example, an asset having a useful life of five years and a cost of $9,000 will have a depreciation expense for the first entire year computed as follows:

$$\frac{5}{1+2+3+4+5} \times \$9,000 = 5/15 \times \$9,000 = \$3,000$$

(For year two, the fraction will be 4/15.)

Sunk cost — A cost that cannot be recovered and is considered irrelevant in making a financial decision.

Supplemental major medical plan — Medical insurance coverage acquired in addition to other medical protection for extended hospital, surgical, or medical benefits. Typically, an employee will need supplemental medical insurance to integrate and coordinate his or her group health insurance provided by an employer. Also see "Corridor deductible."

Supplementary contract — A written agreement between an insurance company and a policyholder or beneficiary whereby the company retains the death proceeds and makes payments to the beneficiary according to the settlement option selected.

Supplementary Medical Insurance (SMI) — A voluntary program of Medicare that pays for physican's services, other medical services, and medical supplies not covered under hospitalization insurance (HI).

Supplementary Security Income (SSI) — A program administered by the Social Security Administration for the disabled, blind, and impoverished.

Supply-side economics — Generally, an economic theory based on the principle of increasing productivity in the private sector rather than increasing spending in the public sector in order to stimulate the economy.

Surety — One who agrees to be answerable for the obligation or default of another, thereby providing additional security for another's debt or other obligation, such as a co-maker of a note. A surety differs from a guarantor in that a surety is primarily liable for another's debt, whereas a guarantor is only liable if the principal debtor fails to pay or perform.

Surety bond — An agreement whereby a party (surety) agrees to be responsible for the performance or acts of the principal in expressed obligations with others. Surety bonds include judicial bonds, fiduciary bonds, and contract bonds. Compare "Fidelity bond."

Suretyship — A three-party relationship where one party (surety) agrees to be answerable for the debt, default, or miscarriage of another party (principal), giving a third party (creditor) a secured obligation.

Surgical expense insurance — A health insurance policy that covers either the usual, ordinary, or reasonable cost of a surgical procedure or a fixed-dollar amount per type of operation.

Surgical schedule — A list of surgical procedures that are covered in a surgical expense policy and the maximum amount payable for each.

Surplus — In a budget, the excess between amount appropriated for a particular expenditure and the amount actually spent.

Surrender — To terminate ownership rights by giving back property.

Surrender cost comparison index — An index used for comparing the costs of life insurance policies. The surrender cost comparison index takes into consideration cash values, cost per $1,000 of protection, premium payments, dividends, and the cash value of money. It is most useful if the cash value buildup is an important criteria in making a decision. Also see "Interest-adjusted cost method" and "Net payment cost comparison index."

Surrender value — See "Cash surrender value."

Surtax — An additional tax paid on income or property that was previously taxed.

Surviving annuitant benefit plan — A retirement plan option selected by an annuitant where two or more beneficiaries will receive a designated portion of the survivor's benefit.

Surviving spouse (filing status) — For federal income tax purposes, a surviving spouse may file a joint return for two years following the death of a spouse if the surviving spouse continues to maintain a household for a dependent child.

Survivor benefit — One or more payments to a designated survivor of a deceased individual, such as retirement benefits from a private retirement plan, Social Security benefits, and group health insurance benefits.

Survivorship — The right of one or more persons outliving another to the entire ownership of property previously owned jointly. Survivorship is a manner of receiving an ownership interest in property by living longer than another who had a joint interest.

Survivorship annuity — An annuity that provides payments to a survivor.

Suspense account — An account used to temporarily hold funds for current contingencies.

Sustainable growth — Steady economic growth over a long period of time.

Sweat equity — (1) A method of making a down payment on a house where the purchaser agrees to do work on the property; (2) equity buildup in a home where the owner constructs his or her own improvements.

Sweetener loan — A loan calling for some type of additional incentive to be paid to the lender for either a lower interest rate or higher amount borrowed, such as participation in gross receipts or future value of the property upon sale.

Syndication — A business venture among individuals formed for the purpose of carrying out a particular transaction, investment, or business activity. A syndication obtains investors by engaging in active marketing programs.

Syndication fees — Expenses incurred by a tax-shelter activity for marketing and promoting the sales of its ownership interests. Generally, these expenses are capitalized and not expensed. Examples of syndication fees include accounting fees, attorney fees, brokerage fees, costs of preparing prospectuses, sales material, and other expenses incurred in the marketing effort.

Take-home pay — The net amount of earnings received by an employee after all withholdings have been taken out; the amount of one's paycheck.

Take-out loan — Permanent financing of a real estate project obtained after it is completed.

Tandem plan — A financing program designed to assist selected housing projects in times of tight money and high discount rates by using the combined effort of the Government National Mortgage Association (Ginnie Mae) and the Federal National Mortgage Association (Fannie Mae).

Tangible assets — Assets having physical characteristics which can be seen and touched as well as having corporeal existence, such as real estate, gold, antiques, household furnishings, diamonds, coins, and stamps, as opposed to intangible assets which do not have such characteristics, such as common stock or a contract.

Tangible value — An appraisal of the physical value of real property, such as buildings and land, rather than the value of an intangible item (e.g., a lease agreement with an excellent tenant).

Target benefit plan — A hybrid retirement plan where contributions are set to reach a specified benefit level, but the actual retirement benefit depends solely on the amount of accrued benefit in each participant's individual account. Unlike an ordinary pension plan (i.e., defined benefit plan), an employer is only obligated to make contributions as required by the plan formula, but not to make any other contributions (i.e., for the purpose of reaching the actual benefit targeted).

Targeted jobs credit — See "Jobs credit."

Tax — An amount of money levied upon and paid by individuals, trusts, estates, and corporations for the support of a government.

Taxable estate — In estate taxation, an amount used in the computation of a decedent's federal estate tax. The taxable estate is equal to the gross estate less certain allowable expenses (e.g., funeral expenses, administration expenses, unpaid mortgages, claims against the estate, and other specified expenses), taxes, losses, charitable transfers, and the marital deduction. Also see "Estate tax."

Taxable gift — A gift that is subject to the unified transfer tax (gift tax). Generally, gifts of a present interest that are equal to or less than the annual exclusion ($10,000 per year per donee) and other applicable deductions (e.g., charitable and marital) are not subject to the unified transfer tax; all other gifts, however, are taxable gifts. For example, assume Bensen gives $100,000 to his son during the year. Of the total amount gifted, $90,000 ($100,000 − $10,000 annual exclusion) is considered a taxable gift—although Bensen may not immediately pay taxes on such gift if the unified transfer tax credit is available to offset the amount of tax due.

Taxable income — The net amount of income, after all allowable deductions have been taken, on which an income tax is computed by using either the tax tables (for taxable incomes of less than $50,000) or tax rates (for taxable incomes of $50,000 and more or for income averaging). Also see "Income tax."

Tax audit — A detailed examination of a taxpayer's tax return by the Internal Revenue Service or state revenue agency.

Tax avoidance — A legitimate method of reducing income taxes as opposed to tax evasion, which is illegal. When making an investment, however, tax avoidance must not be the primary purpose—a realistic expectation of receiving economic gains must clearly be the principal objective.

Tax base — The assessed value of real property that is subject to property taxes.

Tax bracket — See "Marginal tax bracket."

Tax Court, U.S. — A federal court that hears cases involving tax matters. The U.S. Tax Court is the only one of three courts of original jurisdiction where a taxpayer, before trial, does not pay an additional assessment as determined by the Internal Revenue Service.

Tax credit — Specified items that are subtracted directly from tax due (before credits) in order to arrive at the final amount of tax liability. Credits are a one-to-one reduction of tax due and, if available, are more effective than an equal amount of deductions in reducing an income tax liability. Also see "Income tax."

Tax credit for the elderly and permanently disabled — A tax credit available for individuals who are 65 and older and receive a very small amount of retirement benefits, or individuals who are under 65, permanently and totally disabled, and receive a very small amount of disability benefits.

Tax deduction — Specified items subtracted from either gross income (i.e., deductions for adjusted gross income) or from adjusted gross income (excess itemized deductions) in computing an individual's income tax liability. Also see "Income tax."

Tax deed — A deed provided to the purchaser of land from a governmental unit at a public sale, which was held because the previous owner did not pay delinquent taxes. The previous owner usually has a certain period of time in which to redeem the property after paying the auction price plus additional costs and interest.

Tax-deferred annuity (TDA) — A nonforfeitable annuity to which employees of qualified nonprofit organizations are able to make tax-deductible contributions. Employers can also make contributions, which qualify as nontaxable compensation for their employees. When an annuity payment is received by an employee, it will be included in gross income.

Tax Equity and Fiscal Responsibility Act (TEFRA) — Major tax legislation passed by the 97th Congress in August 1982 for the purposes of raising revenue because of the size of the federal deficit, promoting fair and equitable taxation, reducing distortions of certain economic transactions, and charging groups who benefit from specific government programs with their costs.

Tax-equivalent yield — The before-tax yield of a taxable bond that produces the same after-tax yield as a tax-exempt security. For example, assume Rollins is in a 42 percent marginal tax bracket and currently holds municipal bonds having a coupon rate of 8 percent. In order to receive the same or better after-tax yield for taxable bonds, Rollins must find such bonds yielding at least 13.79 percent [8 percent / (1 − 42 percent)] because of his marginal tax bracket. The tax-equivalent yield is also known as "equivalent taxable yield."

Tax evasion — The intentional misrepresentation of taxes payable; the fraudulent reporting of income or other taxes, which is illegal. Compare "Tax avoidance."

Tax-exempt income — Income not subject to federal and/or state income taxes, such as gifts, municipal bond income, and scholarships.

Tax exemption — (1) An exemption from paying property taxes granted to certain nonprofit organizations and individuals; (2) for income tax purposes, certain items subtracted from adjusted gross income: personal and dependency exemptions.

Tax-exempt security — See "Municipal bond."

Tax-free exchange — (1) A nontaxable exchange of certain property held for productive use in a trade or business or for investment whereby some or all of the gain realized is not immediately recognized (IRC Section 1031). Instead, such gain is merely deferred. A tax-free exchange must consist of like-kind property, which must be identified as part of the exchange within a reasonable period of time (i.e., 45 days). For example, when Greene exchanges real estate held for investment for other real estate to be held for investment, it is a tax-free exchange. However, intangible property, such as securities, are not qualified for tax-free exchange treatment under Section 1031; (2) a nontaxable transfer of property to a controlled corporation in exchange for its stock (IRC Section 351).

Tax-free money market fund — A money market mutual fund that primarily invests in municipal bonds which are close to maturity and short-term municipal notes. Such municipal bond fund provides income that is free from federal income taxes for its investors.

Tax-free municipal bond — See "Municipal bond."

Tax haven — Any nation that imposes little or no taxes on otherwise taxable transactions making it a preferable location to claim legal residence at or hold assets for the purpose of avoiding or evading U.S. taxes.

Tax lien — (1) An involuntary statutory lien placed by a governmental agency on certain property in which taxes have not been paid; (2) a federal tax lien is a general lien which is placed on all property of one who is liable for unpaid taxes.

Tax loophole — A discrepancy in the tax law or a favorable provision (as intended by Congress) allowing taxpayers to legally reduce their tax liability.

Tax preference items — Specified items that are added back to adjusted gross income in computing the alternative minimum tax: excess depreciation on leased personal property, excess depreciation on real property, amortization of certified pollution-control facilities, dividend exclusion, All-savers excluded interest, mining exploration costs, circulation-of-magazine expenditures, research and experimental expenditures, long-term capital gain deduction, excess intangible drilling costs, excess depletion, and the bargain element of incentive stock options. Also see "Alternative minimum tax."

Tax rate — The ratio of taxes paid to a tax base (such as total income received or valuation of property).

Tax Reform Act of 1984 — Major tax legislation described as the biggest revenue bill and the most comprehensive and complex revision of the Internal Revenue Code ever attempted. The act's primary objective was to raise revenue by targeting tax-abusive transactions.

Tax search — In real estate, that part of a title search that reveals whether there exist any unpaid taxes on the property being searched.

Tax shelter — A generic term meaning any investment providing tax benefits with a reasonable expectation of receiving a future economic return. Tax-sheltered limited partnerships usually provide tax deductions from depreciation and/or intangible drilling costs and/or tax credits in the early stages with possible tax-reduced cash flow during the middle and end of its duration. Qualified retirement plans, such as an individual retirement account, 401(k) plan, or a Keogh plan, are also tax-sheltering investments in that they provide an immediate tax deduction as well as future economic benefits. One of the most important criteria in the design of a tax shelter is whether or not it has economic substance as its primary objective rather than to merely avoid income taxes. Also see "Abusive tax shelter" and "Tax avoidance."

Tax-sheltered annuity (TSA) — See "Tax-deferred annuity."

Tax straddle — Generally, any two offsetting positions with respect to personal property that results in a substantial diminution of a taxpayer's risk of loss. For example, assume Billingsly owns 500 shares of AAA stock, which cost him $5,000, presently sells for $10,000 ($20 per share), and was held for the period required to obtain long-term capital gain status. Further assume that he would like to sell the stock for about $20 a share in the following year without subjecting it to any price fluctuations before such sale. If he purchases 5 put options (the equivalent of 500 shares), which are due to expire next year, to sell the stock at $20 per share, then he will have reduced his risk of loss by simultaneously holding both the stock and the put options. Other common tax straddle combinations include the simultaneous purchase and sale of two commodity futures contracts on the same exchange, but expiring in different months, as well as holding an "in-the-money" call option and a put option for the same underlying security at the current market price.

Teachers Insurance and Annuity Association — See "TIAA-CREF retirement program."

Technical analysis — A study of market trends and relationships for the purpose of predicting price movements, rather than emphasizing the financial data of individual companies. Technical analysts depend largely on the principle that stock prices move with the market, and they rely heavily on their interpretation of statistical charts. Also see "Chartist."

Tenancy by the entirety — Joint tenancy between a husband and wife whereby each owns an equal and undivided interest in the entire property. In the event one spouse dies, the other obtains complete owner-ship without probate. Tenancy by the entirety is different from a joint tenancy, however, in that neither spouse can dispose of his or her interest during the lifetime of the other spouse without consent.

Tenancy for years — See "Estate for years."

Tenancy in common — An undivided ownership interest in real prop-erty between two or more persons. The interest may or may not be equal, each tenant in common may sell his or her interest without consent of the other co-tenants, and in the event one of the co-tenants dies, the decedent's interest passes to his or her heirs or beneficiaries and not to the surviving co-tenants.

Tenant — Most commonly refers to a lessee possessing property under a rental agreement.

Tenant at sufferance — Generally, one who remains in rented prem-ises after his or her right has terminated.

Tenant at will — One holding possession of property with the lessor's permission, but without fixed term. A tenant at will is also known as a "month-to-month" tenancy because a tenant or landlord must gen-erally give the other party 30 days notice prior to termination, de-pending upon state law.

Tenant improvements — Improvements made to rental property, either by the landlord or tenant for the needs of the tenant.

Tenant in severalty — The ownership of real property by only one person.

Tenants Form Policy (HO-4) — See "Homeowners' insurance policy."

Tender — (1) A formal bid to purchase securities; (2) an offer to pay money; (3) unconditional offer to perform in connection with satisfy-ing a claim and the ability to carry out such performance. For exam-ple, Hooker agrees to buy real estate from Hughes. Under the terms of the sales agreement, Hughes must tender an executed deed to Hooker, who in turn must tender the balance of the sales price. If either tender is unjustifiably refused, the refusing party may be held for breach of contract for failure to perform.

Tenements — All things affixed to land, such as buildings and other improvements, and rights which pass with conveyance.

10-K — An annual filing required by the Securities and Exchange Com-mission for virtually all publicly held corporations. The 10-K report contains more detailed information about a company than is required in an annual stockholder's report.

1099 — A federal income tax statement sent by the payor of interest, dividends, non employee compensation, etc., to the recipient (and Internal Revenue Service) for informational purposes.

10-Q — A quarterly filing required by the Securities and Exchange Commission of all corporations whose stock is publicly traded.

Tenure — For employment purposes, a status providing job security given to certain individuals (e.g., college teachers) after a trial period.

Ten-year forward averaging — A federal income tax provision allowing recipients of a lump-sum retirement benefit to greatly reduce their income taxes upon receipt.

Term bond — The most common type of bond: one with a fixed maturity date over a lengthy period.

Terminable interest — An interest in property that will terminate upon the occurrence of a specified event, such as a leasehold.

Term life insurance — Temporary life insurance coverage that only provides death benefits during the period covered (no cash value or loan provisions). Generally, premiums on a term life insurance policy increase during an insured's life when the face value remains fixed. Should the insured live beyond the policy's term (without renewals or extensions), the insurer is relieved of all obligations to pay any benefits. Compare "Whole life insurance."

Terms of sale — All conditions of a sale, other than the price, as specified in a written sales contract, such as manner and timing of payments, delivery, and time of possession.

Testamentary — Transfer of property by will.

Testamentary trust — A trust created by a testator's will and effective upon his or her death.

Testate — Having a valid will and last testament at death.

Testator — A person having a valid will at death.

Testatrix — A woman having a valid will at death.

Testimonium clause — (1) A clause in a document stating the date it was executed and the parties involved; (2) a clause in a conveyancing instrument stating that the appropriate parties are signing it: "In witness whereof, the parties to these presents have hereunto set their hands and seals."

Thinly capitalized corporation — A corporation consisting of a large amount of debt in relation to stockholder's equity. For income tax purposes, a thinly capitalized corporation may not be taxed as a corporation. Stockholders would otherwise prefer this arrangement because interest is deductible and dividends are not.

Thin market — An inactive market characterized by little or no trading and relatively high price fluctuations as compared to heavy trading.

Third market — In securities trading, over-the-counter transactions in securities listed on organized exchanges.

Third party — Generally, a person or entity not a party to an agreement or action.

Third-party beneficiary — A person who is to benefit from an agreement, but is not a party to the contract.

Third-party check — A negotiable check made payable to and originally negotiated by a payee, who is not the present holder; a check held by a third party after it has been negotiated by the payee.

30-day letter — A letter sent by the Internal Revenue Service along with a revenue agent's report (RAR) outlining a taxpayer's appeal procedures before the IRS. If no request is made for such procedures within the alloted time (30 days), then the IRS will issue a "90-day letter." Also see "90-day letter" and "RAR."

Three-cornered exchange — A carefully structured exchange of like-kind properties designed to provide a nontaxable exchange for one of the parties. For example, Jenson wants to acquire Kennedy's land by swapping properties. Kennedy only wants cash or some other property and, therefore, does not wish to swap with Jenson. Boatwright, however, wants Jenson's property. So in order to perfect the deal with Jenson, Boatwright buys Kennedy's land and swaps with Jenson in accordance with the rules of a nontaxable exchange.

Thrift institution — Generally, a savings and loan, savings bank, or credit union.

Thrift plan — An employer's qualified retirement plan that calls for most of the funding (depending on the ratio used) to be made from employee contributions. The employer must also contribute to the plan, but such contribution typically relates to the amount each participant contributes. Usually a thrift plan is used in conjunction with a larger retirement plan to supplement retirement benefits or to provide accumulated savings that may be used by employees before retirement.

TIAA-CREF retirement program — Teachers Insurance and Annuity Association-College Retirement Equity Fund. A comprehensive retirement program for college-level teachers, administrators, and other employees of a nonprofit organization. TIAA represents fixed retirement funds invested in fixed-income securities, and CREF represents investments in equity securities.

Ticker symbol — An abbreviation designating a certain security, which is used to relay trades between buyer and seller as well as other information.

Tight market — A market characterized by active trading and narrow spreads between bid and ask prices.

Tight money — A period in which the availability of borrowed funds (e.g., bank financing) is slim because of high interest rates, lack of institutional funds, or recession.

Time deposit — Generally, an interest-bearing savings account in a commercial bank or other financial institution which may or may not be subject to early withdrawal penalties.

Time draft — A postdated negotiable instrument (e.g., a check) that is commonly used to transfer money from a buyer to a seller. Also see "Postdate."

Time limit — In insurance, a period of time in which proof of loss or notice of claim must be filed.

Time order — In securities trading, an order that will become a market or limit order within a specified period of time.

Time price — The credit price or future payment price of a given item.

Time-price differential — The difference between the cash price (immediate payment in full) and the credit price or future payment price of a given item.

Time-sharing — (1) In real estate, an exclusive right entitling the holder the use of property (usually at a resort hotel or condominium) for a specified time during the year. Time-sharing may take the form of one of the following: (1) A resort operator sells a right to use a suite, room, or cottage during specified times during the year, (2) a single owner of a vacation home rents it out, under an organized reservation system, to others whereby he or she may occupy the home only at designated times during the year, (3) a number of individuals purchase a vacation home as tenants in common and individually use it on a rotating basis.

Time spread — See "Horizontal spread."

Time value of money — The concept that a dollar is worth more today than a dollar received in the future. The reasoning behind the time value of money principle is that interest can be earned over a period of time, so that money received today can earn interest and, therefore, accumulate more value. Also see "Present value" and "Present value method."

Times interest earned — In the analysis of financial statments, a measure of a company's ability to meet its fixed interest obligations:

$$\text{Times interest earned} = \frac{\text{Earnings before interest and taxes}}{\text{Interest expense}}$$

Title — Evidence of ownership.

Title insurance — An indemnity policy in which a title insurance company warrants to cover losses or damages arising from a defect in, liens on, or a challenge to an insured's title in real property. A title insurance company will only agree to cover insurable titles, which are so designated after the company has conducted an extensive investigation.

Title search — In real estate, an investigation primarily focused on recorded documents to determine the present condition of title (i.e., whether there are defects) to a particular piece of property.

Top heavy plan — Qualified retirement plan primarily benefiting key employees.

Tort-feasor — One who is a wrongdoer and guilty of a tort.

Tort liability — A liability arising from a violation of a duty owed to the plaintiff resulting in damages (other than breach of contract), such as an automobile accident where the defendant failed to yield the right of way.

Total asset turnover — In the analysis of financial statements, a measure of how efficiently a company uses its assets in the process of creating revenues:

$$\text{Total asset turnover} = \frac{\text{Net sales}}{\text{Average assets}}$$

Total disability — Generally, an inability to perform the occupation the insured had before such disability began or an inability to perform the activities of any occupation for which an individual can be reasonably retrained. The permanent loss of sight in both eyes, loss of both hands, or of feet are automatically considered total disability.

Totton trust — A revocable trust subject to state laws that is created by an individual with separate funds deposited in a savings account in his or her own name as trustee for another (usually a dependent). After the depositor's death, the money ordinarily becomes the beneficiary's property.

Trade acceptance — A type of draft drawn by the seller of goods and presented for acceptance to the buyer when such goods are purchased. Upon acceptance, a trade acceptance becomes a note receivable for the seller and may subsequently be negotiated in order to raise money before payment is due under the terms of sale. Also see "Bill of exchange."

Trade date — In securities trading, the date on which a transaction occurred, as opposed to a settlement date which is when payment and property are delivered. Generally, trade dates control the holding period of securities for income tax purposes in that upon purchase the trade date is not counted as a day held, but upon sale the trade date is considered to be a day the securities are held. Also see "Settlement date."

Trade discount — A percentage discount from the list price quoted to customers of a certain trade, such as paint sold by a hardware store to commercial painters is usually transacted with a trade discount.

Trademark — A symbol, name, or other distinctive mark used to identify a certain product or company.

Trader — In securities transactions and for income tax purposes, a person who buys and sells securities on a full-time basis for his or her own account and whose primary objective is to obtain short-term gains. A trader is in an excellent position as a taxpayer since he or she is considered to be in a trade or business for deducting all ordinary, necessary, and reasonable expenses, as well as being able to enjoy long-term capital gain treatment upon sale of all securities held the required period.

Trading on the equity — See "Leverage."

Transaction account — See "Demand deposit."

Transfer agent — Generally, a bank or other institution responsible for keeping records up to date on all registered shareholders of a corporation, (e.g., names, addresses, and number of shares held).

Transfer tax — A state tax levied on the passing of title to property that is usually paid by the seller.

Transportation expenses — For income tax purposes, expenses incurred in traveling between the point of origin and the point of destination (e.g., airline tickets). When transportation expenses are incurred for trade or business purposes, they become deductions "for adjusted gross income." Compare "Travel expenses."

Transportation insurance — Generally, marine insurance. See "Automobile insurance," "Aviation insurance," and "Marine insurance."

Travel accident policy — A limited insurance policy (commonly life insurance) covering losses as a result of an accident while traveling, such as on a commercial carrier.

Traveler's check — A special type of check offered by banks and other financial institutions which can be used as cash when signed a second time by the purchaser. Traveler's checks require the purchaser's signature upon acquisition and when subsequently used (must be signed in the presence of the payee). Generally, when such checks are lost or stolen, they may be replaced by the issuing company.

Travel expenses — For income tax purposes, expenses incurred while in and around a destination (away from home), such as meals and lodging. Travel expenses are a "for adjusted gross income" deduction when incurred for trade or business purposes. Compare "Transportation expenses."

Travel insurance — See "Travel accident policy."

Treasure trove — Treasure found; for income tax purposes, a treasure trove is taxable to the finder in the year of discovery.

Treasury bill (T-bill) — A short-term obligation issued at discount to investors by the U.S. government, which ultimately represents a risk-free investment. T-bills are issued in a minimum denomination of $10,000, with additional increments of $5,000 available, at weekly auctions in the form of discounted notes. Such quality securities are highly liquid, mature within 91 days to 12 months, and carry the prevailing short-term market yield for risk-free investments. Because the Treasury bill yield reflects the current market short-term rate, it is sometimes used to periodically set adjustable rate mortgages and other flexible financing terms.

Treasury bond — A long-term U.S. government interest-bearing obligation usually maturing in more than 10 years and issued in denominations of $1,000, $5,000, $10,000, $100,000, and $1,000,000. They are actively traded in the secondary market and are highly liquid.

Treasury certificate — A short-term U.S. government interest-bearing obligation maturing in one year on which interest is paid by coupon.

Treasury note — A U.S. government obligation bearing interest, which is paid by coupon and maturing in one to five years.

Treasury stock — Corporate stock previously outstanding (i.e., issued to stockholders and subsequently redeemed) that is currently held by the issuing corporation. Treasury stock may be reissued or retired, depending upon corporate policy. Unissued or unsubscribed stock is not considered Treasury stock because neither had been previously issued and outstanding.

True rate of return — An annual rate of return on an investment found by dividing its average annual receipts by average annual balance.

Trust — A fiduciary relationship with respect to property where the trust's creator (i.e., the settlor, grantor, or trustor) transfers a property interest, real or personal, to a trustee for the purpose of holding such property in a prescribed manner for the benefit of another (i.e., the beneficiary). Trusts may be actual or constructive and can be created by operation of law or by express agreement. Also see "Clifford trust," "Inter vivos trust," "Irrevocable trust," "Reversionary trust," "Revocable trust," and "Testamentary trust."

Trust agreement — A document specifying the terms of a trust, such as how assets are to be used and invested.

Trust company — An organization primarily formed to professionally administer all trusts that may be lawfully committed to it. The functions of a trust company include acting as executor of an estate, testamentary trustee, transfer agent for a corporation's stock, and custodian for property held in trust.

Trust deed — See "Deed of trust."

Trustee — (1) A person or organization who holds property in trust for the benefit of another in accordance with the trust agreement; (2) a person in a fiduciary relationship holding a position of trust for another (e.g., a banker, an attorney, corporate director, or agent).

Trust fund — Assets (usually cash or securities) transferred to a trustee to be held for the benefit of another.

Trust indenture — In securities trading, the terms and conditions governing the issuance and administration of a corporate bond issue.

Trust officer — An officer of a trust company in charge of a designated portion or all of the assets held in trust.

Trust settlor — The creator of a trust; one who transfers property to a trustee with the intent of creating a trust.

Truth-in-Lending Act — Federal legislation whose main purpose is to provide each consumer with meaningful and uniform information concerning the cost of borrowing money. Such guidelines allow consumers to compare different available alternatives when shopping for credit. Generally, most non-business consumer credit transactions are covered under the Act, including personal property purchases of $25,000 or less, extensions of credit requiring the security of the borrower's principal residence, credit cards, and other borrowings where a finance charge exists or is payable in more than four installments. The finance charge, which includes interest, discount points, loan fees, service fees, time-price differential, and premiums for credit life insurance if made contingent upon granting credit, must be disclosed. In addition, the annual percentage rate, which is the relationship of the total finance charge to the amount borrowed, must likewise be accurately disclosed (within $1/8$ of 1 percent). Under certain conditions, the act allows a borrower to rescind or cancel a credit transaction within three business days (including Saturday) of purchase date or notice of right to rescind, whichever is later. Certain advertisements which exhibit a down payment, an amount of any installment, a finance charge in dollars or that no finance charges are assessed, the period of repayment, or the number of installments are subject to full disclosure.

Turn-key contract — A project that allows a lessee or purchaser of an investment, building, machinery, etc, to begin business or operation by merely "turning the key" to the front door or to start the machinery; a ready-to-occupy or ready-to-operate condition.

U

Umbrella liability insurance — A form of excess liability insurance designed to supplement other liability policies (e.g., homeowner's and automobile insurance). An umbrella policy covers losses in excess of the limits covered by other insurance contracts as well as many situations not already covered.

Unavoidable accident — An accident which could not have been reasonably foreseen or prevented.

Unavoidable cause — A cause not ordinarily and reasonably anticipated or avoidable by a prudent person under similar circumstances (e.g., illness, accident, or death).

Unconscionable contract — A contract that is so one-sided and unfair that it is presumed no reasonable person would agree to its terms on either side: no honest and fair individual would write such a contract on one side and a reasonable person in his or her right mind would never agree to such harsh terms on the other side. A court may void such an agreement or revise its terms to be fair to both sides.

Uncovered option — An option position where the grantor of a call or the holder of a put does not own the underlying stock which is subject to the option; a naked option.

Underinsurance — The precarious position of not maintaining enough insurance coverage with regard to the value of the item(s) insured or less coverage than the risk exposure warrants.

Underlying security — A stock subject to the terms of an option.

Undervalued position — An investment strategy that considers a particular stock in light of known circumstances, such as financial position, industry outlook and trends, and market conditions, which justifies a higher price for the security than what it is trading for currently.

Underwriter — (1) One who insures risks, such as an insurance company or an individual who decides whether applicants are suitable risks for insurance; (2) one who purchases securities directly from the issuer in order to resell them; an investment banker.

Undisclosed principal — A principal for whom an agent is acting, but such principal is unknown by other parties.

Undue influence — Influence imposed upon another to unfairly persuade and ultimately destroy the freedom of one's decision so that it reflects the will of the administrator of such influence rather than the person making the decision.

Unearned income — Passive income primarily received from investments, such as dividends, rent, interest, royalties, and capital gains, rather than from work, such as wages, salaries, or commissions.

Unearned premium — The allocated portion of an insurance premium returned to a policyholder upon cancellation.

Unemployment compensation — State and federal unemployment insurance designed to help workers who are involuntarily unemployed and are looking for work. The aid is in the form of cash so that workers can maintain their standard of living and have time to locate other employment, as well as to promote overall economic stability. Unemployment benefits replace earned income and, as a result, may be subject to state and federal income tax.

Unencumbered — Property that is free of liens or other encumbrances; free and clear.

Unfunded life insurance trusts — A trust which only contains insurance policies on the life of the settlor or other person (e.g., settlor's spouse) as its principal.

Unified credit — See "Unified transfer tax credit."

Unified gift and estate tax — See "Unified transfer tax."

Unified transfer tax — A federal tax on certain gratuitous transfers of property, whether life or death transfers, on a cumulative basis. For the formula of the unified transfer tax at death, see "Estate tax." Also see "Gift tax" and "Unified transfer tax credit."

Unified transfer tax credit — A credit allowed against taxable transfers made during a donor's lifetime (after 1976) and on a decedent's taxable estate. In 1986 the credit is $155,800, which is equal to an exemption equivalent of $500,000, and in 1987 and later the credit is $192,800, which is equal to an exemption equivalent of $600,000.

Uniform Commercial Code (UCC) — A body of law regulating commercial transactions and providing a uniform manner of governing such circumstances throughout the United States (except in Louisiana and with modifications in other states). Commercial transactions such as the sale of goods, investment securities, bulk transfers, commercial paper, bank deposits, letters of credit, collections, bills of lading, secured transactions, and warehouse receipts are included in the UCC.

Uniform Gift to Minors Act (UGMA) — A uniform act adopted by all states allowing a donor to transfer property (typically securities) to a minor without extensive administration or cost. A custodian of legal age must be appointed to act on behalf of the minor, who is taxed on all income from the property. The custodian has the right to collect income from the assets, apply such income toward the minor's support, sell the assets, and otherwise act for the minor without court supervision. The custodianship automatically terminates when the minor reaches legal age.

Unilateral contract — A contract where one party gives a promise in exchange for the performance of an act (i.e., a promise for an act), such as "I promise to pay when you deliver the goods." Compare "Bilateral contract."

Unilateral recission — The refusal of an innocent party to perform contractual duties because the other party did not perform.

Uninsured motorists protection — Additional automobile coverage available for most auto insurance policies where an uninsured motorist or hit-and-run driver causes damage and/or injury to the insured or family members.

Unit investment trust — A specialized type of investment vehicle sponsored by brokerage houses which allows investors to put money into one type of income-producing security by purchasing "units," which usually cost $1,000 each. By collectively investing such amounts, a small investor can participate in relatively large amounts of debt or equity securities (e.g., $100 million or more). Unit investment trusts customarily have a front-end load, and each trust concentrates solely on one type of income security, such as municipal bonds, short-term securities, government securities, preferred stocks, utility stocks, and corporate bonds. When the securities mature, are redeemed, or sold the principal is returned to each investor.

Unitrust — A specialized trust which requires the trustee to pay a certain percentage of the trust's assets to at least one beneficiary, who is not a charity, for life or for a certain number of years, with an irrevocable remainder interest to be paid to a charity. Contributions to a unitrust are allowed a charitable deduction when all qualifications are met.

Units-of-production method of depreciation — A type of depreciation that varies directly with the number of units produced in that if productivity is high, then depreciation expense will be high and vice versa. The units-of-production method is also used in determining the amount of cost depletion and is computed as follows:

$$\text{Amount expensed per year} = \frac{\text{Units sold during the year}}{\text{Estimated total number of units}} \times \text{Cost}$$

Universal life insurance — A permanent life insurance product that gives a policyholder more flexibility than traditional whole life policies in that it allows the owner to change the amount of premiums paid (above a certain minimum), choose the amount of death benefits, and build up cash values (tax-free) at current rates. The balance in cash values is used to fund the life insurance, which is typically priced around the cost of similar term protection.

Unlisted security — Any security not admitted to an organized exchange; an over-the-counter security.

Unmarketable title — A title having defects, which makes the property it represents unsaleable.

Unscheduled personal property insurance — The personal property insurance coverage of a homeowner's policy. Compare "Scheduled property."

Unsecured debt — (1) Generally, any loan that is not backed by collateral; (2) a bond issued only on good faith and the credit rating of the issuer rather than with collateral backing.

Useful life — For accounting purposes, a period of time during which an asset is to be expensed (i.e., period of depreciation).

Use tax — A state ad valorem tax on the use, storage, or consumption of tangible property. A use tax is levied for the purpose of taxing individuals who purchase items in another state without paying sales tax.

U.S. savings bond — A nonnegotiable bond that may only be redeemed by the U.S. Government. Also see "Series E bond," "Series EE bond," and "Series HH bond."

Usury — The charging of an illegal interest rate on a loan.

V

Vacation homes — A residence, usually located in a resort or remote area, used by individuals as a second home but not as a principal residence. In some cases, a vacation home may be rented to others when it is not occupied by its owners, which may provide certain beneficial tax consequences if special rules are properly followed.

Value-added tax — A tax levied on businesses based on the value added to goods during operations of a business, such as manufactured goods as they progress through the manufacturing process.

Valued policies — Policies used to cover special types of property that are difficult to replace or for which the values are difficult to establish. In the event of total loss, the face amount of such policy is to be paid regardless of the property's actual cash value at the time of loss.

Value Line Investment Survey — A subscription service providing summarized financial information on the stocks of a large number of corporations.

Value maximization — The plan of increasing one's net worth by primarily acquiring assets that increase in value (real estate, stocks, etc.), rather than obtaining assets that decrease in value (automobiles, furniture, clothes, etc.).

Variable annuity — Generally, an annuity that accumulates part or all of its income from equity securities, and the annuity payments are dependent upon the income produced or the value attained by such securities. Thus, payments vary with the performance of a securities portfolio. One of the primary reasons for developing a variable annuity is to avoid the harmful effects of a fixed income in that payments are able to adjust in order to keep up with inflation. On the other hand, there may not be a guarantee against loss in the amount of principal by the issuing company.

Variable life insurance policy — A type of life insurance contract that has a variable amount payable upon an insured's death in that the death proceeds are dependent upon the performance of a securities portfolio. Generally, an insurer will guarantee a minimum face value, but the actual death benefit could increase if equity values rise.

Variable premium life insurance — A life insurance contract where only the premiums change with an insurance company's financial experience. Generally, the premium is lower than for comparable whole life policies during an initial period, after which premiums fluctuate up to a maximum amount.

Variable rate mortgage (VRM) — See "Adjustable rate mortgage."

Variable ratio plan — A method of formula investing where an investor holds both a speculative portion and a conservative portion of a portfolio. At predetermined levels, the speculative portion is either increased or decreased in order to more aggressively capture price movements in the market. A predetermined level is set by an investor and is made up of a ratio between the speculative portion and the conservative portion.

Vendee — The purchaser.

Vendor — The seller.

Venture capital — Money available for a new, untried business undertaking which is generally associated with high risk, as well as a high expected return. A venture capitalist customarily requires a substantial portion of a new company's equity as part of his or her compensation so that if the enterprise prospers, the venture capitalist will be well rewarded.

Verbal agreement — An unwritten contract between two parties that may or may not be enforceable.

Vertical spread — In options trading, the buying and selling of two different call options where each has the same expiration date but a different striking price.

Vested benefits — See "Vesting."

Vested remainder — An interest in real or personal property with a future right of possession and enjoyment, usually on a certain date or upon the occurrence of a specified event.

Vesting — Ownership rights; complete ownership status attained by a participant in his or her employer's retirement plan after meeting certain requirements. If an employee leaves the job before retirement, then only the amount of vested benefits can be collected by such employee.

Veterans Administration (VA) loans — Loans, which are guaranteed by the VA, made by savings and loan associations, banks, and other lending institutions to qualifying veterans. A VA loan enables a veteran to buy a home with little or no down payment and, sometimes, at below market interest rates (the interest rate on a VA loan is set by the Veterans Administration Administrator).

Veteran's tax exemption — In some states, a special property tax exemption granted to qualifying veterans or their widows.

Vision care benefits plan — A type of health insurance that is typically offered as a fringe benefit under an employer's group plan for the purpose of covering the cost of an employee's eye examination and glasses.

Voidable contract — A contract that may be voided, but is not void in itself.

Void contract — An unenforceable contract; a contract having no binding effect or legal force.

Volatile — In securities trading, rapidly fluctuating prices.

Voluntary accumulation plan — An unsystematic and informal plan for the holder of a mutual fund to increase his or her shares by purchasing additional amounts at various times and amounts.

Voluntary employee benefit association (VEBA) — A qualified tax-exempt organization funded by an employer or employees (or both) and designed to provide payments to employees and dependents or beneficiaries for life, sick, accident, or other benefits.

Voluntary lien — A lien that is intended to be placed against certain property by its owner, such as a mortgage.

Voucher — (1) A document evidencing the payment or receipt of money (e.g., a canceled check); (2) a system of controlling cash payments by a company.

Voucher check — A check printed with specialized blanks, which are designed to exhibit pertinent information about the payment, such as any discounts received, custom description of the purchase, and invoice number.

W

Wage garnishment — See "Garnishment."

Wages — A general term encompassing any regular payment to an employee based on output or number of hours worked.

Waiting period — For an insurance policy, a period without coverage whereby nothing will be paid in case of an otherwise insurable event.

Waiver — The voluntary relinquishment of a right.

Waiver of premium — A provision in a life insurance contract stating that premium payments will be waived by the company if the insured becomes disabled. The waiver of premium option is usually an endorsement to the policy.

Wall Street Journal, The — The most widely read source of financial news (daily circulation of over 2 million).

Warrant — In securities trading, an option granted by a corporation to purchase its stock for a certain price within a specified period of time. Warrants are actively traded on organized exchanges and generally carry a much longer life than listed options (i.e., puts and calls).

Warrant bond — A bond having at least one warrant attached that allows a bondholder the privilege of buying a share of stock at a specified price within a certain period of time.

Warranty — In general, a legally binding promise, which is given by a seller of goods or services to a buyer, that certain assurances are true and will remain so, subject to specified limitations. Also see "Express warranty" and "Implied warranty."

Warranty deed — A deed conveyed by a grantor to warrant good clear title to real property. It is the best deed a grantee can receive.

Wash sale — In securities trading, a disallowed loss for income tax purposes from the sale of a security as a result of purchasing the same security—or "substantially identical securities"—either 30 days before or 30 days after the sale. For example, assume Darby sold XXX stock for a $500 loss and 25 days later repurchased XXX. The $500 loss is not deductible; instead, it is added to the basis of the newly acquired stock and the holding period of the XXX shares sold are tacked on to the new XXX shares (for purposes of determining long-term capital gain treatment).

Wasting asset — In general, assets having a limited life that are used up, consumed, or worn out because of use or the passage of time. Examples include patents, leaseholds, machinery, natural minerals, equipment, timberlands, copyrights, and buildings. In most cases, land is not considered to be a wasting asset.

339

Watered stock — Stock issued for overvalued consideration, which overstates assets and stockholder's equity.

Water exclusion clause — An exclusion in fire insurance policies disclaiming liability for losses resulting from flood, waves, backed-up sewers, and water below the surface of the ground.

Wealth — The value of all rights and possessions owned by an individual less all obligations which such individual is required to pay.

Wear and tear — For rental property, an expected decline in value because of the normal and reasonable use of property by a lessee.

Welfare — (1) Health and well-being; (2) public assistance.

W-4 Form — A form used by an employee to indicate to the employer the number of exemptions that are to be claimed in withholding for federal income taxes ("Employee's Withholding Allowance Certificate").

When issued — In securities trading, a transaction establishing the contract price with a later settlement date. The settlement date can only be determined when the securities subject to the transaction are issued.

Wherewithal — The means from which a particular payment is to be made; money.

Whipsawing — In securities trading, quick fluctuations in a stock's price.

Whole life insurance — Permanent life insurance policy whereby the face amount is paid upon the death of an insured, whenever death occurs. Whole life insurance is different from term life insurance because under whole life an insured is covered for the rest of his or her life so long as the policy is kept in force, whereas under term insurance coverage terminates after a certain period. Ordinary life and limited-payment life are two major types of whole life policies. Under ordinary life, premiums are payable for as long as the insured lives. Under limited-payment life, premiums are limited for a certain number of years, such as 10 years, 20 years, or to age 65. Cash value buildup, loans against cash value, double indemnity option, waiver of premium option, as well as other features and options are common in whole life insurance contracts.

Wholesale — The selling and distribution to retailers, merchants, or commercial buyers customarily in bulk or in recurring transactions. Wholesale prices are typically lower than retail prices because of quantity purchases and/or no markup for retail profits.

Will — A written declaration of the manner in which an individual wishes to distribute his or her estate after death.

With all faults — See "As is."

Withholding — Deductions from an employee's salary, wages, or commissions for federal and state income taxes, social security (FICA) taxes, and other authorized payments. Such deductions are made by the employer and are to be remitted in the employee's name to the appropriate authorities.

Withholding exemptions — For income tax purposes, qualifying allowances which may be claimed by an employee to reduce the amount of earnings withheld. Withholding exemptions can be claimed for personal exemptions, dependency exemptions, zero bracket amount (if the employee has only one job or, if married, spouse is not employed) and additional allowances (i.e., unusually large itemized deductions, alimony, child care credit, earned income credit, and credit for the elderly).

Without recourse — (1) A qualified indorsement of a negotiable instrument signifying that the indorser declines to assume liability to subsequent holders if payment is refused; (2) a mortgage or deed of trust securing a promissory note without recourse allows the lender to only look to the property for payment in case of default rather than to the borrower's personal assets. Also see "Nonrecourse loan."

Without reserve — As used in auctions, the final bid is the selling price (no price reserved).

With right of survivorship — See "Joint tenancy."

Working capital — The amount of current assets remaining after paying all current liabilities (i.e., current assets minus current liabilities) in which the short-term liquidity of an economic entity is judged.

Workers' compensation — Tax-free benefits paid to employees or their families in case of specific job-related accidents. Compensation laws are state statutes requiring an employer to pay fixed amounts without regard to the matter of negligence or fault and were enacted to prevent a disabled employee from going through the ordeal of a lawsuit and possibly failing to collect any benefits because of some technical defense available to the employer.

Wraparound major medical insurance — See "Supplemental major medical plan."

Wraparound mortgage — A second mortgage on real property, which is provided by a buyer to a seller, that encompasses both a first mortgage plus any equity buildup experienced by the mortgagee (seller) not compensated for by a down payment. While the seller remains obligated to repay the first mortgage, he or she will profit from an interest rate differential in that the interest rate on the wrap-around mortgage (whose payments are used to pay off the original mortgage) is typically higher than the rate on the first mortgage.

W-2 Form — A statement prepared by an employer for an employee showing the amount of earnings withheld for income and social security taxes. A W-2 statement must accompany an employee's income tax return upon filing.

Yearly renewable term — Term insurance covering one-year periods at increasing premium rates with a right to renew at the end of each year. The right to renew is given without having to provide evidence of insurability, and the premium increases at each renewal as the insured's age increases. Yearly renewable term is usually used in group life insurance programs, although some individual policies are also written.

Yield — Generally, an annualized rate of return experienced by an investment.

Yield to maturity — A compound rate of return to be experienced by an investor in bonds who reinvests all cash payments at the same market rate of interest and holds the bonds until maturity.

Zero bracket amount (ZBA) — The maximum amount of taxable income which is in a "zero tax-bracket." The ZBA is built into the tax tables and tax rates as a "standard deduction" for all individual taxpayers. Itemized deductions must exceed the ZBA in order to be beneficial.

Zero coupon bond — A bond issued at a discount without any periodic interest payments. Only at maturity will a cash payment be made. The price of a zero coupon bond is determined by the present value of the face amount, using the prevailing market interest rate for such issue in accordance with its life.

Zoning ordinance — A local law governing the use of land and construction in certain areas.

SUBJECT INDEX

Acknowledgment
Acquired rights
Acting within scope of authority
Actual notice
Adhesion contract
Adjudication
Adverse parties
Adverse use
Affidavit
Affinity
Affirmation
Agency
Agency coupled with an interest
Agent
Age of majority
Agreement
Amalgamation
Apparent authority
Approval
Arbitration
Arbitration clause
Articles of incorporation
Assign
Assignee
Assignment
Assignor
At arm's length
Attachment
Attest
Attestation clause
Attorney-at-law
Attorney-in-fact
Badges of fraud
Bailment
Bankruptcy
Bearer
Bilateral contract
Bill of exchange
Bill of lading
Bill of sale
Binder
Blank indorsement
Bona fide purchaser (BFP)
Breach of contract
Breach of trust
Breach of warranty
Canceled check

Cancellation clause
Cashier's check
Certificate
Certificate of incorporation
Certificate of stock
Chapter 11 (reorganization)
Chapter 12 (wage earners)
Clayton Act
Clear title
Close corporation
Collect on delivery (COD)
Co-maker
Commercial broker
Commercial paper
Commission merchant
Common law
Conciliation
Conditional indorsement
Conditional sales contract
Condition precedent
Condition subsequent
Confidential communication
Confirmation
Confirming bank
Conflict of interest
Confusion of debts
Conglomerate
Consideration
Consignment
Constructive notice
Contingent liability
Contract
Contract of sale
Contractual lien
Co-obligor
Copyright
Corporation
Cosigner
Cost and freight (CAF)
Cost, insurance, and freight (CIF)
Cost-plus contract
Counter offer
Covenant
Cumulative voting
Date of declaration
Declaration date
Defeasible title

Wealth
Wear and tear
Welfare
Wherewithal
Whipsawing
Wholesale
Workman's compensation

REAL ESTATE

Abstract of title
Access
Accretion
Acre
Adverse possession
Aesthetic value
Amenities
Back title letter
Certificate of title
Chain of title
Closing statement
Cloud on title
Color of title
Comparative sales method
Concurrent estates
Condo conversion
Condominium
Constructive eviction
Conveyance
Cooperative apartment
Deed
Dispossess proceedings
Domain
Easement
Eminent domain
Encumbrance
Equitable mortgage
Equitable title
Equity build-up
Escheat
Escrow
Estate by the entirety
Estate for years
Eviction
Exclusive listing

Federal Housing Administration (FHA)
Fee simple estate
FHA mortgage insurance
Fixture
Foreclosure
Free and clear
Freehold
Ground rent
Guaranteed sale
Habendum
Habitual repair
Heirs and assigns
Highest and best use
Homeowners' association
Homeowners' warranty
Homestead
Homestead exemption
Housing and Urban Development (HUD)
Immoveables
Improved land
Improvements
Income value approach
Ingress, egress, and regress
Installment land contract
Internal rate of return (IRR)
Involuntary conveyance
Joint tenancy
Joint tenants
Land
Land grant
Landlord's warrant
Landscape
Lease
Leasehold
Leasehold improvements
Leasehold interest
Leasehold value
Legal description
Life tenant
Listing
Listing agent
Loan constant
Loan ratio
Locative calls
Long-term lease
Loss of access